Contents

Part V
The Place of Literature in the National Struggle

Part VI
Constructive Friend or Destructive Foe: The Debate about Griffith's Relations with Irish Labour

Acknowledgements

This book has had a long gestation. When I first met my future father-in-law, Conn Sheehan, in 1980, he impressed on me his conviction that Arthur Griffith was *the* architect of modern, independent Ireland. As a result of many conversations, I began to study Griffith in the mid-1980s. My father-in-law has given me an enormous amount of help with my research and writing, for which I am eternally in his debt. I only hope that the end product is not a disappointment to him.

I am very much in debt to Mr Diarmaid Hegarty, Director of Griffith College Dublin. Without his practical faith in the project, this book might not have been published for several more years. Truly he is the enlightened overseer.

Seán Ó Lúing was Arthur Griffith's first biographer and his pioneering work remains unsurpassed. Over the years, Seán has given me much help, guidance and encouragement, as he has so generously done to all who have studied or written about Griffith. Happily, Seán is still hale and hearty at fourscore years. Ni bheidh a leithéid ann arís.

I am deeply grateful to the late Mrs Kathy Griffith, widow of Arthur Griffith's only son, Nevin. Kathy was a noble lady who generously made her late husband's wonderful library openly available to me and bore with unlimited tolerance my many intrusions into her home. Ar dheis láimh Dé go raibh a hanam naofa.

Tom Turley's skilled editing greatly improved the quality of expression in the book and Tom made many other valuable suggestions which I have incorporated. My thanks also to Ursula Hannaway for her hard work on the various drafts of the book. And to Fergus Manifold for his sterling work on the design.

I wish to make grateful acknowledgement also of the kindness and courtesy of the staffs of the National Library of Ireland, the National Archives of Ireland, the libraries of University College and Trinity College, Dublin, and of various Dublin Corporation libraries, and Commandant Victor Long of the Military Archives, who furnished me with the photographs used in this book.

Last, but by no means least, I thank my wife, Ann. Her support over the years has been unstinting and without that, this book could never have been written. There are probably few things that put the same strain on family life as researching and writing. Ann, and our children, Elizabeth and Andrew, have endured it all with remarkable equanimity.

For any shortcomings in the book, I am fully responsible.

Foreword

Arthur Griffith gave the Irish nation a coherent and rational philosophy. He put forward his Sinn Féin programme as the inclusive compound of all the Irish traditions, unionist and nationalist. Griffith, whose ancestors came from Ireland's Presbyterian province, aimed to build steel into the Irish character and mould it into habitual acceptance of the solid material virtues of self-development, thrift, civic discipline and the full and fruitful cultivation of Ireland's native resources. Sinn Féin, in its original and true meaning of self-reliance, could never fail, claimed Griffith, and on this concept, through the medium of his journals, and in language of unique persuasion, he based plan upon plan, the primary one being withdrawal of Irish parliamentary representation from London and the setting up in Ireland of a democratically-formed assembly which would command the loyalty of its people. His policy of moral resistance was respected and followed by India.

James Stephens, with the poet's clear eye, saw in Douglas Hyde and Arthur Griffith the chief makers of the new Ireland. Walter Alison Philips, writer of distinguished volumes on European history, paid Griffith, in the first paragraph of his *Revolution in Ireland 1906-1923*, the tribute of an historian, certainly not of an admirer, in accounting him the founder of a remarkable movement which forced Britain to come to what he considered humiliating terms. The testimonial to Griffith of Mahatma Gandhi, greatest of 20th-century leaders, deserves our notice. Our witness is Fenner Brockway, who wrote: 'Thirty years ago I heard Gandhi speak in a tone almost of reverence of the indomitable spirit of the Irish people. He wished from the depths of his being that the resistance had shaped itself in non-violent discipline, but he regarded with wonder its unbreakable resistance. Amidst all the violence he paid tribute to Arthur Griffith, the architect of non-cooperation with the English of Ireland, in his own preparation of India's plan for non-cooperation.'

Civil disobedience, passive resistance, non-cooperation, call it what you will, Arthur Griffith gave the idea a large circulation in the world of his day. India brought it to a successful conclusion. It is a method of protest difficult for an imperial power, professing the rectitude of its ways, to counter. That the maintenance of a non-violent discipline in pursuit of Ireland's aims, in the post-1916 years, was what Griffith hoped for and preferred, is indicated by his advice in a letter from Gloucester Prison dated 23 January 1919: 'Keep the country calm, disciplined and dignified. Let it not be provoked...'

The social policy of Sinn Féin in its pre-1916 phase, when it was dominated by the influence of Griffith, deserves more attention than it has received because in many ways, especially in its proposals for housing the workers of Dublin, it was more progressive and more realistic than that of any other party. Arthur Griffith was well aware of the Dublin slums problem. In the investigative series 'Who owns the slums?' which ran in the *United Irishman* early in 1903 we are told that, in terms of slums, Dublin could only be placed next to the plague-stricken city of Bombay. He was keenly conscious of the housing conditions of Dublin's poor from first-hand experience and denounced them time and again in his journals. In May 1908 his Sinn Féin committee produced a comprehensive housing plan for Dublin which met with no success in Dublin Corporation because, he claimed, political motivation and vested interests in slum property proved too strong. Briefly, his housing policy was: to have houses built for the workers on the new soil acquired by the Corporation at Inchicore, Glasnevin, Baldoyle and other places; to arrange for cheap transit with the railway and tramway companies for those residing in them and, the congestion of the old city being thus relieved, to peremptorily close up or demolish insanitary houses and areas.

Nothing so radical and progressive has to this day been advanced as Griffith's proposal that Ireland should enact a homestead law which would enable every workingman to own his house in full security: 'Whatever the civil offences a workman may commit this I hold to be true, that it is the duty of the wise state to see that the penalty visited upon him shall not go to the extremes of rendering him and his family homeless. I believe in a homestead law which will permit every workingman's family to procure through the State a house at the cost of its building, and to have and to hold that house as its property, free from fear that if poverty and ill ever visit them they will be shelterless in their own country.' Sadly, this civilised measure is, up to the present hour, absent from the statute book.

Robert Lynd gave reasons why Irish socialists ought to support Sinn Féin which, he argued, was trying to create an industrial society in Ireland, the only kind of society in which socialism could flourish. Griffith's friendly association with James Connolly is adequately documented. In the Dublin municipal elections of 1903 Griffith supported the socialists Quaid, Connolly and Lyng. Advertisements in his *United Irishman* include 'Read the *Workers' Republic* (Organ of the Irish

Socialist Republican Party). Every worker should read the series of articles on "Labour in Irish History". Order direct from the offices at 6 Lower Liffey Street, Dublin'. Their views were identical on important issues such as the value of a fair and independent arbitration body for solving industrial disputes.

In the labour troubles of 1913 Griffith praised the responsible policies of Connolly, 'the man in the leadership of the Transport Union with a head on his shoulders'. Griffith was a member of the Irish Neutrality League formed in 1914 with Connolly as its president and they shared, as they were pioneers in, the concept of Irish neutrality.

Griffith never aspired to leadership, preferring to remain in the background as policy counsellor and adviser. The democratic institution of Dáil Éireann was designed out of the thought of many years which he had given to national planning. When he was appointed Chairman of the Treaty negotiation team in 1921 he found himself projected into a primacy which he had never sought, given a task which of its nature was the most difficult ever imposed on an Irishman, which he knew must be controversial, but which he accepted out of a sense of duty. In recommending the Treaty settlement as having 'no more finality than we are the final generation...all nations are going beyond where they are at present', he invoked his profound sense of history. His wisdom has been vindicated.

He was an idealist whose vision was practical. He hoped for his ideal Ireland 'a dominance in Thought, Culture and Development rather than the vulgar dominance of Material Empire'.

Shaw Desmond, a writer of unusual quality who interviewed Griffith many times, has pointed out that he was an advocate of women's rights twenty years before 'votes for women' and women's emancipation became milestones of the 20th century. While he was in favour of women's suffrage, he gave priority to achieving an Irish parliament in the elections to which they could vote. He protested against the batoning of women at suffragette demonstrations in Dublin, just as he denounced the dismissal of Hannah Sheehy Skeffington from her teaching post in Rathmines School of Commerce because of her suffragist convictions.

The classic statement on women's rights came from Griffith himself when, speaking as chairman at the Sinn Féin convention of 1917 on the resolution on female suffrage proposed by Dr Kathleen Lynn, he said: 'I ask the delegates to pass this without any further discussion. From the day we founded Sinn Féin we made no discrimination as to sex for any office in the organisation. Mrs [Wyse] Power was one of the first members of the executive of this association. She and I worked together for years. It must be made clear that women are just as eligible as men for any position in the country.'

With Ireland's adhesion to the European Economic Community the official view was adopted that Griffith's principles of self-reliance had served their day. 'Tá deireadh leis sin go léir anois', as a colleague remarked to me. The positive departure from Griffith's philosophy was actually of earlier date, in the form of the Anglo-Irish Free Trade Agreement and the uncritical acquiescence in it. Read the Oireachtas debates of the time and weep.

A pool of bottomless wealth appeared to exist in Brussels and the continual resort to it resulted in a decline in national morale side by side with an extraordinary improvidence in managing the nation's finances. A national debt of some thirty *billion* pounds does not happen fortuitously. Unemployment soared into the hundreds of thousands. The decline in public morale touched its nadir when a generous subvention of many billions was offered by Europe and received but not with the dignity of gracious acceptance. More was expected in circumstances that offered no possible parallel to the moral plea of Oliver Twist. It was very naturally met with a rebuff. It was an hour of national humiliation, which lacked the withering scorn of an Arthur Griffith.

This was not the sturdy, proud and progressive country that he had worked his heart out for. Happily, to halt the decline, wiser economists bethought themselves of a policy of indigenous industry. Griffith would have applauded. It has produced good results. Never in all this time was his name invoked by public figures who seem to have been too timorous to mention it.

Arthur Griffith would have welcomed our entry into Europe and the opportunities it offered of diversifying our trade outlets. As early as 1904 he wrote on the prospect of opening up Irish-French trade: 'The direct service between Ireland and the Continent, which we have so long advocated, will come into operation on 1st October next....The moral effect of the opening of direct communication between the Continent and Ireland is, however, of more moment to us than even the immediate material advantage. Ireland has been for over a century shut out from Continental intercourse....This isolation of Ireland has had a disastrous effect upon our national character....It was Thomas Davis, we think, who likened the condition of Ireland deprived of direct intercourse with the Continent to Caspar Hauser in his dungeon - to a man shut off from the natural light of the sun and fain to regard his jailer's lantern as the most brilliant of illuminants...'

One of the projects planned by Griffith was a Dictionary of National

Biography and for this he asked the cooperation of his readers. Probably part of what his own contribution might be was his interesting series on Irish Revivalists which appeared in the Dublin *Evening Telegraph*. His *United Irishman* published serially some notable contributions, like 'The Irish Mythological Cycle', a translation from the French by Richard Irvine Best. All but unknown is a second series by Best, 'The Old Irish Bardic Tales', which ran weekly in early 1903. This extensive series, which might well interest poets and scholars, has lain dormant in the pages of the *United Irishman* for almost a century.

W.B. Yeats was a contributor for a while on Irish National Theatre matters; important letters from him appear on 28 January and 4 February 1905. J.B. Yeats wrote regularly for a period. Important chapters on Irish musical history were written by W.H. Grattan Flood. Stephen Gwynn's celebrated 'A Song of Defeat' appeared on 2 May 1903. Was this its first printing? The series on Irish Building Stones ran weekly for a whole year, as did Griffith's own 'Ballad History of Ireland'. His booklet on Berkeley, which was advertised to appear, but has eluded discovery, remains a bibliographical mystery. His *Sinn Féin* weekly carried Tom Kelly's interesting series on the Streets of Dublin. James Stephens was a long-term contributor to *Sinn Féin*.

Griffith was a companionable human being, happy in the society of his friends, a lover of fine books and good music, with a deep pride in his native Dublin. He was the author of the rousing ballad 'Twenty Men from Dublin Town'. He loved the outdoor life and in his earlier years was a keen cyclist. The racecourse knew him not. Griffith was a firm supporter of the Zionist claim for a national homeland. He applauded Canon Hannay for his support of the Irish language and wrote finely himself in its favour. On the contentious question of identity, which occupies the minds of our present writers, he gave his uncompromising views in a leading article in 1913: 'We held, hold, and have taught in this journal [*Sinn Féin*] that the success of the language movement is of infinitely greater importance than the success of any existing political party....Without the Irish language there will never be seen again on this planet an independent Irish nation of any kind. That is our reasoned conviction.' It was an echo from Thomas Davis, from whom his concept of patriotism was basically derived.

Indigenous industry, the equivalent of the self-reliance advocated by Griffith, has proved its value in facing the crisis of the unprecedented unemployment that was part of our European Union experience. With the prospect in view of an expanding Union to include the Eastern nations on its border the challenge to maintain a progressive economy will increase. No longer will funds be easily available from a generous

Europe to help us in difficulties. We cannot seek a magic formula elsewhere. The call must be on our own resources and will to endeavour. The policies that are the heritage to his nation of Arthur Griffith cannot ever be other than a success. Griffith is very much a man of the future.

Seán Ó Lúing, Dublin, June 1997

Introduction[1]

There are several reasons why a fresh assessment of Arthur Griffith is timely. A primary one is that despite his enormous influence on the founders of the Irish State, he is now largely forgotten. W.T. Cosgrave, Michael Collins, Richard Mulcahy and Desmond FitzGerald are among those on the pro-Treaty side who recorded their debt to his teaching.[2] Their testaments are not surprising, but what about the leading anti-Treatyites who were equally fulsome?

'He was the greatest intellectual force stimulating the national revival', wrote Erskine Childers.[3] 'Damn it, hasn't Griffith made us all!' declared Harry Boland to Dr Patrick MacCartan.[4] Sean T. O'Kelly wrote that Griffith's 'political philosophy, so eloquently taught, and his long years of toil and sacrifice, brought the present generation of Irishmen from their knees to their feet, and rekindled in their hearts the almost extinct flame of liberty'.[5]

1971 was the centenary of Griffith's birth and it is revealing to contrast that year with the hundredth anniversary of the birth of Michael Collins (1990) from the point of view of commemorative events. Collins's centenary was marked by the publication of a major biography, by television and radio programmes and newspaper articles, and by a wreath-laying ceremony at his birthplace, a function at which every shade of political opinion in the State was represented. Compare this to the muted manner in which Griffith was remembered nearly twenty years before! A campaign was undertaken by a few private citizens to have a commemorative postage stamp struck in his honour, but Taoiseach Jack Lynch dismissed the idea with the comment that Griffith was 'a Civil War figure'. A thought-provoking piece in the

1 Most of this Introduction first appeared in *Études Irlandaises, XVIII*, December 1993, pp.123-9.

2 W.T. Cosgrave's essay on Griffith in J.R.H. Weaver (ed.), *Dictionary of National Biography 1922-30* (London, 1937), pp.364-8; Margery Forester, *Michael Collins: the Lost Leader* (London, 1971), p.15; M.G. Valiulis, *Portrait of a Revolutionary: General Richard Mulcahy and the Founding of the Irish Free State* (Cork, 1992), p.14; Desmond FitzGerald, *The Memoirs of Desmond FitzGerald 1913-16* (London, 1968), pp.2-4.

3 *Poblacht na hÉireann*, 14 August 1922.

4 *Arthur Griffith, Michael Collins Commemorative Booklet* (Dublin, n.d.), p.54.

5 Cited in Seán Ó Lúing, *Árt Ó Gríofa* (Dublin, 1953), p.403.

periodical *Studies* by Griffith's foremost biographer, Séan Ó Lúing, and a few newspaper items were all that recalled him in 1971.

He was born in the heart of Dublin and was a quintessential Dubliner who knew and loved his native city intimately. His close friend from schooldays, H.E. Kenny (who wrote under the pen-name Sean-Ghall) attested to this:

> In later years he would 'trot' round (his own phrase) old Dublin, which he passionately loved, from Faddle Alley to Weavers' Square, from the Coombe to Thundercut Alley, from Blackpitts to Kilmainham. He would illuminate the way with tales of Dean Swift and Bully Egan, Emmet and Lord Edward, Davis and Mitchel. The clay-pipe industry of Francis St would move him to eloquence. His stock of street ballads was inexhaustible. 'Do you know "Dead Mate", Sean?' 'Have you heard the "Long and Short of It"?' Then we would have an uproarious time comparing memories of these and other worthies who trolled street songs when we were young.[6]

The multifarious Dublin 'millennium' in 1988 made no mention of this so influential third-generation Dubliner. Yet a building society poster on public display that year purported to depict famous people of the capital - it included Charles Stewart Parnell of Avondale, Co. Wicklow, and James Larkin of Liverpool, England! Similarly, Dublin's year as cultural capital of Europe, and Trinity College's quatercentenary exhibition (1992) highlighting 'The Dublin Experience', were just as unmindful of Griffith's existence.

Another reason for a reappraisal of Griffith is that since the two previous full-length studies of his life were published in the 1950s new material has become available and much further research had been carried out. These offer new insights into the man's life and writings that encourage fresh interpretations.

In the preface to his valuable synthesis of post-Famine Irish history, F.S.L. Lyons referred to a revolution having taken place in Irish history writing between 1930 and 1970.[7] This revolution was in methodology rather than in the amount of attention given to the study of 20th-

6 Cited in Padraic Colum, *Arthur Griffith* (Dublin, 1959), p.49.

7 F.S.L. Lyons, *Ireland since the Famine* (London, 1971; paperback edition, 1973, cited in notes), p.7.

century Ireland. 'If it was a striking achievement of an impressive generation of Irish historians to "exorcise passion"[8] from the study of Irish history, it did so largely by evading the challenge of contemporary history', was how J.J. Lee explained the phenomenon.[9]

This explains why twice as many works on the 1900-1922 period were published after 1970, as appeared before that date. With this increase, interpretations of Griffith's role have expanded.

There is another reason why 1970 should have proved a watershed in Irish history writing. Lee cited Lyons on the difficulty of the historian of modern Ireland having 'to make bricks without straw'.[10] The quantity of straw had greatly increased since Lyons did his research, Lee rightly remarked.[11]

Gearóid Ó Tuathaigh, in a review of Irish history writing of the 1970s, observed that the 1900-1922 period had been 'the subject of a rather vast amount of important historical writing' during that decade. That new primary sources had surfaced contributed to this, and Ó Tuathaigh singled out for special mention Keith Middlemas's edition of Tom Jones's *Whitehall Diary.*[12] This was a truly influential source in altering how Griffith's role in the Treaty negotiations came to be perceived by historians.[13]

Ó Tuathaigh felt that some of the most innovative work came from non-Irish historians - British, European, North American and Australian.[14] Indeed, Griffith's three most recent students, Richard Davis, Calton Younger and Virginia Glandon, are all non-Irish. They have brought fresh perspectives to bear on his place in Irish history.

The 'nationalist' or anti-British genre of history writing has largely vanished. In regard to the history of 20th-century Ireland, this has been largely a post-1970 phenomenon, for the reasons already outlined. The decline in the anti-Treaty approach to writing about Ireland could only have led to an enhancement of Griffith's standing, and so it has proved.

8 The phrase is taken from Aidan Clarke, 'Ireland, 1534-1660', in J.J. Lee (ed.), *Irish Historiography 1970-79* (Cork, 1981), p.34.

9 J.J. Lee, *Ireland 1912-1985: Politics and Society* (Cambridge, 1989), p.xiv.

10 Lyons, *Famine*, p.7.

11 Lee, *op. cit.*, p.11.

12 M.A.G. Ó Tuathaigh, 'Ireland, 1800-1921', in Lee (ed.), *loc. cit.*, p.95.

13 See Part IV.

14 Ó Tuathaigh, *loc. cit.*, p.108.

He has had little chance yet to occupy his newly-acquired pedestal with any measure of security. With the decline of anti-Treaty history there has sprung up an aggressive, left-wing style of writing which has made fiercer dents in Griffith's reputation than anything effected by Dorothy Macardle and her successors. This new strain has appended labels like 'imperialist', 'racist' and 'anti-Semite' to Griffith, charges that would have shocked even the most entrenched exponents of the anti-Treaty line. This strain is surely post-nationalist, in that many of the faults it sees above all in Griffith are flaws it detects in the creed of nationalism itself.

Although he died 75 years ago, what Griffith did and what he thought are of particular value and relevance today - a further reason why he needs to be revalued.

He waged a relentless war in his newspapers on corruption and jobbery in public life, an endeavour which was badly needed since the public bodies set up under the 1898 Local Government Act had quickly become a byword for corruption.[15] It seems that little has changed. During the 1991 local elections campaign, the media vigorously attacked the degree of fraudulence over which Irish local bodies presided. The Telecom and Greencore scandals, and the iniquities uncovered by the 'Beef Tribunal', have revealed the scale of corruption that still exists at the heart of Irish public life.

Griffith was a Europhile long before the idea of close European cooperation gained currency, this while espousing a nationalism which has often been stigmatised as inward-looking. The model of the dual monarchy, which he thought could be applied to British-Irish relations, he took from the history of Austria and Hungary, and his advocacy of economic nationalism was based on the German, Frederick List. During the 1913 lockout in Dublin, he urged a study of labour conditions and problems in countries more akin to Ireland, such as Norway and Denmark, instead of looking to England and the United States, where the situation was very different. His newspapers, especially the *United Irishman* and *Sinn Féin,* contain a wealth of articles on aspects of life in European countries similar to Ireland, such as Norway, Sweden, Denmark and Switzerland. European integration would not have worried Griffith in the least, so long as there remained the separate Irish identity which he so helped to define.

His suggestion for settling industrial disputes was also well ahead of

15 Lee, *Irl. 1912-85*, p.161.

his time. He was the first in Ireland to repeatedly recommend arbitration courts or conciliation boards to deal with industrial unrest, an approach that has become the norm in his country.

Griffith's proposed solution to the dreadful slum problem in Dublin was also later taken up - a housing development away from the inner city, the recommended location being a site owned by Dublin Corporation some twenty miles by tram from the city centre. His suggestions were not adopted at the time but later inner-city Dublin communities were indeed transplanted to outlying areas. However, the dehumanising tower-blocks and sprawling estates without proper amenities bore no relation to Griffith's vision of cottages near the mountains or the sea, with individual front and back gardens for flowers and vegetables.

Griffith had an optimistic view of Ireland's industrial potential and of the value of its natural resources. In *Sinn Féin*, in 1911, when writing about the success of Pierce's Ironworks in Wexford, he painted a glowing picture of a future manufacturing country with a large industrial workforce, sustained by a doubled agricultural population. Sadly, this dream has never been realised, but his detailed ideas on protectionism as an economic policy, the creation of an Irish consular service and merchant marine, and afforestation, bore fruit to some extent in the 75 years since his premature death.

A committee, presided over by him, produced four *Irish Year Books* (1908-1911), which had contributors from all walks of Irish life and dealt with every facet of the country's being. He did not have the means to continue this monumental endeavour, but his devotion to the idea shows an affinity with the economic planners, who have been such a part of Irish public life since the 1948-51 inter-party government.

Women's rights was another important Griffith concern. He supported the vote for women from the beginning of his political journalism, and his organisations were unique in accepting women as full members. Maud Gonne, Countess Markievicz and Jenny Wyse Power were perhaps the most prominent of those women associated with his newspapers and movements.

An additional reason for a new study of Griffith is to examine what light he can shed on current Irish problems. The ferocious impasse in Northern Ireland is still present. Griffith stood out among Irish nationalists of his time in attempting to allay unionist mistrust. His dual-monarchy proposal he saw as a road to Irish independence which would maintain the unity of the country. Similarly, his attitude to the use of violence to achieve political ends has relevance to a perennial and intractable state of Anglo-Irish relations and to the peace process of the past two years.

There is a vital feature of Ireland today to which Griffith's ideas relate. High unemployment, due mainly to the closure of businesses, is a major problem. The bulk of the firms which have closed have been multinationals, and in some ways this has been seen as the failure of the process begun in the 1960s. The much vaunted *Culliton Report*, and Richard Douthwaite's thought-provoking book, *The Growth Illusion*, have argued for greater reliance on indigenous industries. This is something of a return to Griffith's philosophy of self-reliance or Sinn Féin (We Ourselves). How far has Ireland departed from what Griffith proposed? Was he right after all?

In the last decade of the 20th century in Ireland, therefore, it might be instructive to look back at the first decade through the medium of Arthur Griffith's thought.

The reasons just outlined have a rather abstract quality. A reappraisal of Griffith must try to represent the rich, enigmatic nature of the man. He was a gifted and prolific journalist, who not only edited his own newspapers but wrote most of the material for them, and could deliver articles on a staggering variety of topics. With only a limited formal education his command of language rivals that enjoyed by the best.

It is difficult in the present age to relate to his contempt for money, physical comfort, self-advancement or fame. A journalist in the cause of Irish nationalism throughout his working life, he subsisted on a meagre weekly income with which he managed to support his wife, two children and his mother. He had lucrative offers, for example one of £1,000 (£70,000 in today's figures) a year from an American newspaper magnate, and another from the *Freeman's Journal*, Ireland's widest-selling daily at the time, but he refused these.

The de Valera private papers for the 1916-21 period contained a letter from Griffith, following his appointment as Dáil Minister for Home Affairs in April 1919, forgoing the ministerial salary. He was then editing *Nationality*: 'As the time given will not interfere with my ordinary business or diminish any income therefrom, it is unnecessary for me to draw the salary or any portion of the salary sanctioned, and I therefore shall not do so'. Despite this he intended to give at least three days per week to his Dáil work!

He has been described, not without some justification, as enigmatic, paradoxical and ambivalent, both personally and politically. The basic sources for an understanding of him are the newspapers that he produced from 1899 until his death in 1922. His private papers are sparse and fragmentary, hence his status as an elusive figure.

There are some particular curiosities about him which challenge the biographer. Although he argued that the fall of Parnell (whom he idolised) demonstrated that the Irish nationalist movement must never again become dependent on the personality of a strong leader, he himself believed firmly in the *avatar* (at first William Rooney, and later de Valera, followed by Collins). Although he had a circle of intimate literary friends who were clearly awed by his knowledge and delighted in his wit and humour, other literati regarded him as an obscurantist and a philistine, devoid of a sense of humour. Although reared in poor circumstances and a poor man all his life, he believed in the entrepreneur's right to a reasonable profit, and was never attracted to the socialist panacea. Although he preached a philosophy of non-violent resistance, the fierce antipathy to Britain which his writings aroused must have convinced some that only physical force would prove effective in the end.

These and other paradoxes entice one to look anew at his life and writings, and make him a fascinating subject for analysis.

Part I

The Person

'He was, and he remains, an enigma.
The future will not guess his riddle.
It will not prove or disprove him.
He will be measured against no other event,
nor tried in any other fires than
those he lived through.
What were his capacities? We do not know.
How would he have borne himself
or grown in the exercise of power?
We do not know, and we shall never know.
His anonymity is impenetrable to us.
He is, as he was, a name
and a secret.'

James Stephens, Arthur Griffith: Journalist and Statesman, p.26

CHAPTER I

THE SOCIAL MAN AND THE FAIRER SEX

What sort of person was Arthur Griffith? The personal qualities of people may be seen in their words and actions, in what their friends, acquaintances and co-workers have said about them, in glimpses of their private, family lives, whether they had a sense of humour or not, and so on. Because so many of those associated with Griffith were writers, and because he himself was a journalist, we are reasonably well placed to learn something of his personality, pastimes, working life, relationships and his literary ability.

Physically he was not striking. He was short, about five feet five inches in height. His hair, originally fair, turned brown as he got older but it retained some fair streaks. The poet Seamus O'Sullivan (James Starkey), a long-time friend from their first meeting in 1902, has left the following description:

> He was low-sized, but the broad shoulders suggested immense strength. The eyes behind the pince-nez were of a striking colour, a sea-blue... He had a strong, well-set jaw-bone which gave him a rather stern, even to those who knew him but slightly, or as antagonists, a rather militant, even a belligerent expression.[1]

Griffith had a slight deformity - his Achilles tendons were contracted which caused him to walk on the balls of his feet. Because of this the heels of his boots had to be raised. But this did not prevent him from being a strong and enthusiastic swimmer, walker and handballer. His unusual gait together with the squareness of his build, meant that he tramped along like a sailor, according to another friend and his first biographer in the English language, the poet Padraic Colum.[2]

These descriptions are confirmed in a childhood recollection by the writer Terence de Vere White. He recalled 'a small (even to a child's eyes) square figure with eyes that looked piercing behind thick spectacles; a sturdy block of a man with a slightly swaying gait'.[3]

Between 1897 and 1899 Griffith spent eighteen months in South

1 Seamus O'Sullivan, *Essays and Recollections* (Dublin, 1944), pp. 104-5.

2 Padraic Colum, *Arthur Griffith* (Dublin, 1959), p.5.

3 *Irish Times*, 14 October 1972.

Africa. While there he worked for a period as a mine supervisor in Johannesburg. The native workmen under his control called him 'Cuguan'. When he asked what it meant he was told 'a dove'. This pleased him at first until he was told it was because he had a waddling walk. 'And so he had!' declared another friend, Liam Ó Briain, who fought in the 1916 Rising and was later Professor of Romance Languages at University College, Galway.[4] 'Cuguan' was one of the many pen-names Griffith used as a journalist.

In a tribute written shortly after his death, his friend and physician, the poet Oliver St John Gogarty, referred to 'the straight lines in [Griffith's] forehead that Lavater knew to be signs of genius and leadership'.[5] An interesting addendum to Gogarty's comment was provided by Kathleen Napoli-McKenna, private secretary to Griffith during the Treaty negotiations in London.

She told how a group of them were out walking one evening in the vicinity of St Paul's when they happened upon 'the consulting rooms of certain phrenologists'. They persuaded Griffith to go in with them to have their 'bumps' examined:

> The two ancient sisters, Stackpool or O'Dell, I do not remember which, were astonished at the cerebral capacity of Arthur Griffith's skull.[6]

Pastimes

Griffith grew up in what would now be regarded as 'inner-city' Dublin, in an area just north of O'Connell (then Sackville) St. His family lived at various times in Upper Dominick St, Little Britain St, Capel St and Summerhill. In his writings he recounted a little about his youth. One of his favourite pastimes as a boy was to watch street dancers and listen to ballad singers, of whom there was then an abundance.

One singer in particular, and her song, remained vivid in his memory:

> I mind me of a time when I was a little fellow and listened to a strange fierce old woman, some of whose blood is in my veins – a

4 Liam Ó Briain statement, 6 September 1973, in library of late Nevin Griffith, Dublin.

5 *Free State*, 19 August 1922. J.K. Lavater was an 18th-century Swiss physiognomist, poet and theologian, who believed a study of facial features revealed much about personality.

6 Kathleen Napoli McKenna, 'In London with the Treaty delegates', in *Capuchin Annual* (Dublin, 1971), p.324.

> very old, old woman who saw the dogs of Thomas St lap up a martyr's blood - listened to this old woman while she sang a song she heard often in her father's house sung by men who died on the scaffold or fell in the field, rotted in the dungeons or perished across the sea. I can see her yet sitting in her rocking-chair with her little hands crossed in her lap and a glint of godlike fire in her ancient eyes, singing, singing, 'When Erin First Rose'. Peace to her soul.[7]

Griffith's name first appeared in print in June 1885 when he was fourteen years old. The Young Ireland Society, a literary society founded in the early 1880s, held written exams in Irish history for young people and awarded prizes. Presentation of these prizes was something of an event. They were awarded at the Rotunda with the Lord Mayor of Dublin presiding.

Among those present at the prize-giving in June 1885 were MPs T.D. Sullivan and Michael Davitt. Griffith received third prize which consisted of John Mitchel's *History of Ireland* and *Jail Journal* and Charles Gavan Duffy's *Ballad Poetry of Young Ireland.* No doubt the young man valued these prizes, for books were hard to get as there were no public libraries in those days.[8]

A junior branch of the Young Ireland Society was set up at 10 Upper Abbey St, Dublin, with Griffith as assistant-secretary. *The Nation* newspaper, for which his father worked as a printer, recorded the younger Griffith reading a paper on Mitchel before the branch in February, 1886, the first public reference to any written work of Arthur Griffith.[9]

A comrade of Griffith at the time, who described him as 'a born companion who could discuss almost any subject without obtruding himself', recorded how after Sunday mass a group of them used to go walking through the Dublin hills or along the canals, or swimming in the Blackrock baths, or for long cycles.[10]

The young Griffith was an avid reader. He and his friend from earliest boyhood, Henry Egan Kenny, used to haunt the second-hand bookshops and bookcarts on the Dublin quays 'and spend there their tuppences and sixpences and rare shillings'.[11]

7 Ms. 22,293 NLI.

8 *ibid.*

9 *ibid.*

10 Letter from James Moran, 10 September 1951, in library of late Nevin Griffith, Dublin.

11 Statement of Liam Ó Briain, *loc. cit.*.

The Christian Brothers of St Mary's Place and Great Strand St provided his schooling. He finished school around the age of twelve or thirteen and went to work as an office boy for the Underwood Company of Eden Quay, a small, family-run printing business. He decided to follow his father's trade of printing and did his apprenticeship as a compositor in the offices of his father's employer.

Griffith and his acquaintances spent much of their leisure time participating in debating societies. They hired rooms and read papers to each other, mainly on literary topics, which they then discussed. The Eblana Debating Society was the first in which he was involved. No record of its proceedings has survived but the minute book of its successor, the Leinster Debating Society, is still available.

The Society was formed in 1888 and Griffith's name is first minuted in November of that year. His first paper read before the Society (12 April 1889) was entitled 'That ancient civilisation is superior to modern civilisation'. He was elected vice-president on 3 January 1890 and president ten months later.

He resigned from the Society in November 1892 because someone whom he opposed was elected to membership. A large number of the long-standing members followed his example the next week and the Society dissolved itself on 12 December.[12]

Eblana was the handwritten, fortnightly journal of the Leinster Literary Society from 8 February to 4 May 1889. Its editor remarked that the Society was composed of 'hardworking young men of humble circumstances who formed a society for their mutual improvement'. He referred to the journal's contents as 'the maiden efforts in literature' of these young men who were offering their 'honest and unprejudiced opinions', and who were 'strangers to cant and hypocrisy'. To the first edition Griffith contributed an article entitled 'Irish street ballads'. He revealed a wide knowledge of street ballads from the 18th to the end of the 19th century and lamented that they were dying out. He also contributed poetic parodies, usually in street-ballad form.[13]

In the early 1890s Griffith became involved in the Young Ireland League, formed in September 1891 at a meeting at the Rotunda presided over by the old Fenian, John O'Leary. Membership of this introduced Griffith to a wider stratum of Irish society such as the poets

12 Ms. 19,935 NLI

13 Ms. 3493 NLI.

W.B. Yeats and Anna Johnston, Michael Cusack, founder of the Gaelic Athletic Association (GAA), and William Redmond MP.[14]

William Rooney, who had been a member of the Leinster, formed a new society in February 1893 called the Celtic Literary Society (CLS) which was to be the most enduring and influential of those debating clubs. Griffith joined about two years after its foundation. He was then absent from Dublin for a year and a half in the late 1890s, but in September 1899 he was elected vice-president, and a year later president, of the Celtic.[15]

George A. Lyons has provided a brief flavour of what CLS meetings were like. Although they were open to the public, it was usually the same group of faces that were seen there every week. The lectures were on historical or political topics with sometimes biographical sketches of Anglo-Irish literary figures. The Society issued a monthly manuscript journal, *An tSeanchaidhe* (The Storyteller), which was edited by Rooney. It gave those who were shy of public debate or were indifferent speakers an opportunity to show how well they could write.

It was at meetings of the Celtic, according to Lyons, that many young Dubliners first learned that there was such a thing as the Irish language and first heard of Wolfe Tone, Mitchel and Thomas Davis. It was here they received their first warnings about the 'evils' of anglicisation and were first urged to support Irish manufactures.[16]

Friends

Griffith had many friends who have left behind them their impressions of him. A lifelong friend was Sean-Ghall, who has left a poetic testament:

> He had a genius for friendship. In an eastern tale the well of pure cool water in the desert was covered by a huge rock which could be moved only by the elect. Griffith's mask of impassivity was as that rock to the world external. Those who had the blessed privilege of making it roll away came in touch with as rare, as beautiful a soul as ever walked in the haunts of men. I do not remember any public man

14 Minute Book of Young Ireland League in library of late Nevin Griffith, Dublin; Marcus Bourke, *John O'Leary: a Study in Irish Separatism* (Tralee, 1967), p.215.

15 Ms. 19,934 NLI.

16 G.A. Lyons, *Some Recollections of Griffith and His Times* (Dublin, 1923), pp.2-4.

in Irish life who evoked so much reverence and even passionate love as Arthur Griffith.[17]

Probably Griffith's closest friend was William Rooney, a man of similar background and two years his junior. They were in the Leinster and Celtic Literary Societies and the Young Ireland League together in the late 1880s and throughout the 1890s, and they set up the *United Irishman* jointly. Griffith idolised his younger companion, regarding him as the Thomas Davis of their generation and describing him after his death, at the tragically young age of 27, as 'the greatest Irishman I have known or can ever expect to know'. [18]

His death came as a terrible personal blow. Yeats wrote to Lady Gregory that it had 'plunged everybody into gloom. Griffith has had to go to hospital for a week, so much did it affect him'. The loss was such a disaster for Griffith because he believed Rooney might have become the greatest leader in Irish history.[19]

Seamus O'Sullivan first met Griffith in 1902 through Padraic Colum: 'The first meeting was the beginning of a friendship which lasted for many years, and when I went to live on the north side of Dublin, my rooms were a favourite place of call for Griffith'. By that time the Griffith family were living in Summerhill, Dublin, where O'Sullivan was a regular visitor: 'Sometimes I would accompany him to that old house ... and talk far into the night amidst the chaos of books with which his room was heaped'.[20]

A number of Griffith's letters to O'Sullivan have survived. In one of these (it is undated but on *United Irishman* notepaper and so sometime between 1902 and 1906) Griffith thanked O'Sullivan for contributing a story to his paper and asked him to visit the Royal Hibernian Academy to do 'a paragraph' on a current exhibition there: 'Now I can admire and appreciate good pictures, but I know too little of the subject to criticise them with any confidence'. In the event that O'Sullivan might be unable to oblige, Griffith expressed himself willing to 'strive to muddle through'.

Another undated letter told O'Sullivan (always addressed as 'Dear Starkey' or 'My dear Starkey') of Oliver Gogarty's invitation to 'the Tower' (the Martello Tower in Sandycove which Gogarty leased), and urged him to follow after him as quickly as possible because, 'I am

17 Ms. 23,516 NLI.

18 *United Irishman*, 18 April 1903.

19 Richard Davis, *Arthur Griffith and Non-Violent Sinn Féin* (Dublin, 1974), p.15.

20 O'Sullivan, *Essays*, pp.104-6.

helpless and alone'. This final remark reveals something of the closeness of the friendship.

Griffith wrote to his friend from Gloucester Jail (17 October 1918) sympathising with him on the death of his father. There is a reference in this letter to their favourite haunt, the Bailey restaurant and pub in Duke St ('I suppose all our friends who sometimes foregathered with the two BLs are well'). Griffith described the prison atmosphere as 'very sick and tired ... nothing like the bracing ozone of Sliabh Ruadh, Lugnaquilla' and other places in the Wicklow and Dublin mountains, indicating another of their favourite pursuits.[21]

Joseph Holloway, the inveterate Dublin theatre-goer, left behind a copious diary, which gives glimpses of the Griffith-O'Sullivan relationship: 'I had tea with the Montgomerys.... Griffith, Seamus O'Sullivan and others are now off whiskey. When last Monty met them they were having a bottle of Burgundy and talking as brilliantly on that beverage'. The date of this intriguing entry was 3 March 1918.

Another, dated 2 November 1923, suggests that the Treaty caused a rift in the friendship:

> Seamus O'Sullivan now thinks Griffith was never a republican. He got very cross before his death with those who could not see eye to eye with him and he was accountable for the destruction of the Four Courts. Some think that he died of a broken heart when he found out how things were going. Some thought that O'Sullivan should not have deserted Griffith after the Treaty; whereas it was Griffith that deserted him.[22]

Another friend close to Griffith for most of his life was the medical specialist, poet, raconteur and wit, Oliver St John Gogarty. They first met one another in An Stad, a tobacco shop which was a popular meeting-place for Irish-Irelanders at the turn of the century. Gogarty was soon writing for the *United Irishman.* One of Gogarty's biographers, Ulick O'Connor, believed Griffith was his closest friend and avowed that Gogarty admired no one more. AE (pseudonym for the poet and agricultural revivalist, George William Russell) was said to have remarked that Gogarty's tongue spared neither the Maker of the Universe nor his creatures, but he never joked at Griffith's expense.

From 1905, when Gogarty spent his summers in the Martello Tower in Sandycove, Griffith used to stay weekends with him. Other visitors to the Tower were Padraic Colum, Seamus O'Sullivan and James

21 Ms. 10,872 NLI.

22 Ms. 22,293 NLI.

Stephens. These weekends were the only respite Griffith took from his work. He greatly enjoyed the swimming, boating, sunbathing, but probably most of all the witty conversation available at the Tower.

Griffith's favourite hostelry was the Bailey which he frequented, according to Gogarty, because Parnell had been entertained there. 'I always thought it detracted somewhat from Griffith's sense that he should judge a hostelry by its old patrons rather than by its mellow beverages', Gogarty remarked.[23] A special room upstairs in this establishment was set aside for Griffith and his companions. Griffith was unofficial chairman at these Bailey evenings. He seldom spoke but was an avid and hugely entertained listener. Most of those present shared his political outlook but not all. Tom Kettle, poet and Professor of Economics, was a Home Ruler. Others there were Joseph Boyd Barrett, a doctor and a classical enthusiast, James Nolan Whelan, a barrister and inveterate gambler on horses, George Reddin, a Protestant supporter of Sinn Féin who wrote satirical poetic pieces on contemporary events, Seamus O'Sullivan and Padraic Colum. Also present was James Montgomery, famed in Dublin for his wit.[24]

The companionship at the Bailey meant a great deal to Griffith. While in London as leader of the Treaty delegation in 1921 he often remarked to fellow-delegate, Eamon Duggan, that he wished he was back there with his friends.[25]

The death of William Bulfin in February 1910 was a big blow to Griffith. He had been a close friend and staunch supporter for ten years. A number of Griffith's letters to Bulfin are extant, mainly expressing gratitude for articles for the *United Irishman*.[26] Each year the two went together to the Gaelic League Feis Charman in Wexford. They also enjoyed long walks together in Wicklow. Bulfin spent his early years in Argentina where he became a successful journalist, establishing his own newspaper, the *Southern Cross*, for which Griffith wrote from time to time. His book, *Rambles in Erin*, is a delightful account of his travels by bicycle around Ireland.

In the late autumn of 1909, Bulfin and The O'Rahilly went to America to raise funds in an endeavour to save Griffith's *Sinn Féin* daily

23 Oliver St John Gogarty, *As I Was Going Down Sackville Street* (New York, 1937), p.64.

24 Ulick O'Connor, *Oliver St John Gogarty* (London, 1964; paperback edition, 1981, cited in notes), pp.100-1, 103-6, 149-52; J.B. Lyons, *The Enigma of Tom Kettle* (Dublin, 1983), p.203.

25 Piaras Béaslaí, 'Arthur Griffith', in *Leader*, 16 December 1944.

26. Ms. 13,810 NLI.; Seán Ó Lúing, *Art Ó Ó Gríofa* (Dublin, 1953), pp.208-9; Marcus Bourke, *The O'Rahilly* (Tralee, 1967), pp. 37-8.

but to no avail. The cold weather in the United States had a fatal effect on Bulfin's always indifferent health. He became ill not long after his return to Ireland and in February 1910 he died at the age of 45. Griffith was deeply affected:

> Since the day we heard that Willie Rooney was dead, we have not had sadder news than this... William Bulfin is dead. It is hard to believe, with the sun high in the sky as we write this, that that great Irishman, whose heart and mind were full of the light of the sun, is parted from us forever.[27]

The tobacco shop at number 1B North Frederick St, An Stad, was a favourite haunt of nationalists as has been mentioned. Its owner, Cathal McGarvey, was a strong advocate of Irish culture, especially the language, music and games. Discussion went on well into the night and when McGarvey closed his shop the group often adjourned to Griffith's home nearby to continue their debates.

It was here The O'Rahilly first met Griffith. From June 1904 to May 1905 he was a regular contributor to the *United Irishman*. He then went to America, but from his return in 1909 he plunged into activity on behalf of Sinn Féin. He wrote an enormous amount in the short-lived *Sinn Féin* daily and gave financial support. He returned to America late in 1909 to try to collect funds to save the paper.[28]

O'Rahilly was a founder-member of the Irish Volunteers in late 1913. When he supported the appointment of John Redmond's nominees to the provisional committee of the Volunteers in June 1914, he had to face accusations of betrayal, some sent anonymously by post. O'Rahilly was disturbed by the criticism of his motives but, in the words of his biographer, 'a few days later came a short but magnanimous note from his intimate friend, Griffith'. Although Griffith referred bluntly to the 'timid and blundering' action of the committee, he expressed his sorrow that O'Rahilly was taking the criticisms personally. Nobody doubted that his intentions were for the best, declared Griffith, and although some friends might keep their distance, there was 'no justification for an error of judgement severing personal relationships'. It was time to plan for the future, not to dwell on the past, Griffith urged. His letter heartened O'Rahilly.[29]

Michael Noyk, a solicitor who belonged to the Irish Jewish community, was introduced to Griffith by Seamus O'Sullivan around

27 *Sinn Féin*, 5 February 1910.

28 Bourke, *O'Rahilly*, pp. 31-9.

29 *ibid.*, p.83.

1910. 'Griffith and myself became very close friends and I spent many evenings in his home where I got a very intimate knowledge of his character', Noyk has recorded. They often spent time in the IRB man Tom Clarke's little shop at the corner of O'Connell St and Parnell St. Noyk recalled walks with Griffith, the future judge Charles Wyse Power and O'Sullivan:

> Griffith was very fond of walking round the Liberties of Dublin, being an old Dublin-born man...and he could always point out places of great historical interest from a national point of view.[30]

Noyk was solicitor to both Griffith and his son, Nevin, and the two families were very close.[31]

The well-known essayist, Robert Lynd, who was of Ulster Presbyterian background, was a Sinn Féin supporter and friend of Griffith. His essay, 'The Ethics of Sinn Féin', published in Griffith's *Irish Year Book* (Leabhar na hÉireann) for 1909, advocated a passive resistance very similar to that preached by Mahatma Gandhi in India. Griffith was Lynd's political mentor and the subject of one of his essays, 'Arthur Griffith: the Patriot'.[32] The two parted company when the First World War began because Lynd argued that Britain and France should be supported against Germany, whereas Griffith was totally opposed to Irish involvement in the war. Cathal O'Shannon, the journalist and Labour activist, recorded how Lynd visited Griffith and himself in Wandsworth where they were imprisoned after the 1916 Rising.

He gave Griffith some books, among them *War and Peace*. 'This friendly and unexpected scene was the more impressive because a year or two previously Griffith, in the heat of war controversy, had rather harshly damned Lynd as "a philosophical radical" and not a nationalist at all. Griffith was wrong in that, as he sometimes was in expressing his judgement of friends with whom he did not always see eye to eye; and indeed that harshness was not lasting', wrote O'Shannon.[33]

While Griffith was in London at the end of March 1922 he received an invitation from Sylvia Lynd, Robert's wife, to dine with them. She said they 'would like so much to see' him and if he did not have time to spare for dinner to come later and have coffee.[34] Although their differing

30 Ms. 18,975 NLI.

31 Interview with Mrs Ita Gray, daughter of Arthur Griffith, Dublin, 22 August 1995.

32 Robert Lynd, *Galway of the Races* (Dublin, 1990), pp.21, 107-10.

33 *Irish Times*, 17 March 1951.

34 Sylvia Lynd to Griffith, 30 March 1922, in library of late Nevin Griffith, Dublin.

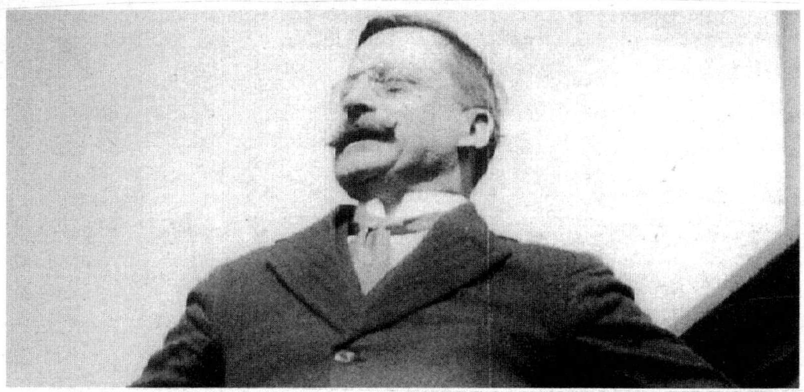

Griffith addresses a public meeting at Sligo, 16 April, 1922

attitudes to the First World War caused a rift between them, the Lynds clearly retained warm feelings for Griffith.

Two somewhat curious converts (the historian and Sinn Féin activist, P.S.O'Hegarty, described them as 'queer birds')[35] to the cause of Irish nationalism after 1916, Darrell Figgis and John Chartres, both established a close rapport with Griffith. Figgis used to meet Griffith daily for tea during the 1919-20 period, and his letters to him began 'My dear Art'.[36] Griffith's daughter, Ita, although very young at the time, remembered Figgis visiting their house. She recalled him because of his vivid red beard and his kindness to her.[37] Chartres, who served in the intelligence section of the British Ministry of Munitions during the First World War, was Griffith's choice as one of the secretaries to the Treaty delegation. He afterwards wrote that Griffith's 'humanity and temperament of humour, his essential kindness and friendly faith, his love of sympathetic conversation, his tremendous sense of anything like a personal obligation, whether important or of the most trifling kind, all these qualities, lying just below the surface, required only the combined stimulus of friendship and occasion in order to manifest themselves'.[38]

Walter Cole, who owned a fruit market, was a lifelong friend and supporter of Griffith. He was on the Sinn Féin executive from the start and was an alderman on Dublin Corporation for many years. 'Mr Cole

35 Ms. 22,288 NLI.

36 Darrell Figgis, *Recollections of the Irish War* (London, 1927), pp. 257-8; Ms 18,851 NLI.

37 Mrs Gray interview,

38 Ms. 23,516 NLI.

comes to see me. He was a very old friend of Arthur's', wrote Mrs Griffith to a friend four months after her husband's death.[39]

Women

Among his friends, acquaintances and co-workers, Griffith counted a number of women. His attitude to women and their rights was well ahead of contemporary opinion. He was a consistent supporter of greater rights for women in his various newspapers. In his first journal, the *United Irishman*, at the beginning of the century, he welcomed the 'new spirit which regarded women as human beings rather than as unthinking dolls'.[40] Referring to the changing role of women, he described them as 'intellectual comrades and helpers in various concerns of public life...in morals, no stronger and no weaker in the main than men, and worthy of frank, full confidence and trust, and of the highest and best education'. Women were not allowed to become members of the CLS. But the first organisation that Griffith formed, Cumann na nGaedheal, was set up in 1900 to link small groups like the CLS and Inghinidhe na hÉireann (Daughters of Ireland), an organisation for women established that same year by Maud Gonne. Indeed, Griffith unintentionally provided the inspiration for the formation of the Inghinidhe.

A group of women met in the CLS rooms after twelve o'clock mass on Easter Sunday 1900, among other things to collect money to buy a strong blackthorn stick with a silver handle to replace Griffith's South African sjambok (a whip made of dried hide) with which he had assaulted the editor of *Figaro*, a Dublin gossip journal, which had published an article declaring Maud Gonne to be in the pay of Dublin Castle. (Griffith was jailed for two weeks for his action.) Out of this meeting grew the new organisation.

In an article which praised women generally and the Inghinidhe in particular, Griffith declared: 'I wish Irish women would take over Ireland and run it for us'.[41] Later he wrote: 'If in the course of time we in Ireland...came to live under a gynocracy, I should not repine. I am weary living in a world ruled by men with mouse-hearts and monkey-brains, and I want a change'.[42]

39 Mrs Griffith to Ms Kate Kelly, 14 December 1922, Ms. 8411 NLI.

40 *United Irishman*, 26 January 1901.

41 *ibid.*, 24 August 1901.

42 Virginia Glandon, *Arthur Griffith and the Advanced-Nationalist Press: Ireland, 1900-1922* (Kansas, 1985), p.139.

Although members of Inghinidhe na hÉireann were more militant than Griffith, most of them had respect and admiration for him. This was because he encouraged the active participation of women in public life and his various organisations made no distinction between men and women. It is interesting that the Inghinidhe did not support the female suffrage movement even though the right to vote was the main women's issue of the day. Griffith did support it, and he saw no incompatibility between membership of Sinn Féin and of the suffrage movement.

He strenuously objected to the police beating women who took part in suffragette demonstrations in Dublin. Hannah Sheehy-Skeffington was dismissed in 1912 from her teaching job at Rathmines College of Commerce because of her militant tactics on behalf of women's suffrage. Griffith denounced her dismissal in his newspaper *Sinn Féin* and named the people responsible for the injustice.[43] At the momentous Sinn Féin convention in 1917 he made an important statement on women's rights.

Inghinidhe na hÉireann established its own newspaper, *Bean na hÉireann* (Woman of Ireland), in November 1908. Again, this did not support the women's franchise movement. Griffith gave the new journal generous backing, referring to it frequently in his own paper and writing for it from time to time.

He first met Maud Gonne in the rooms of the CLS and, like so many of the young men of his generation, he was immediately attracted to her. His pet-name for her was 'Queen' and they cooperated closely until her voluntary exile after her divorce in 1904. She wrote for the *United Irishman* and they campaigned against recruitment for the British army during the Boer War and against the visit of Queen Victoria in 1900. Margaret Ward remarked about his attack on the editor of *Figaro*:

> It was an indication of Griffith's deep devotion to Maud that the taciturn young journalist could be provoked to such an uncharacteristic act in defence of her reputation.[44]

Cumann na nGaedheal was set up to coordinate the activities of groups like the CLS and Inghinidhe na hÉireann and its programme was drawn up by Griffith, Rooney and Gonne. She and Griffith visited Paris in late 1900 to meet John MacBride who had fought on the side of the Boers. This was her first meeting with MacBride. Griffith had known him for some time. The following year she and MacBride went

43 *Sinn Féin*, 28 September 1912; Edward Norman, *A History of Modern Ireland* (London, 1971), p.244, baldly asserted that Griffith 'was actually opposed to female suffrage', which is totally incorrect.

44 Margaret Ward, *Maud Gonne: Ireland's Joan of Arc* (London, 1991), p.62.

on a lecture-tour of the United States, during which she collected funds for the *United Irishman.*

When they reached Boston she received a telegram from Griffith announcing the premature death of Rooney. Her reply showed a surprising lack of sympathy; she said the only consolation she had ever found for sorrow was redoubled work. But in Philadelphia she got a heart-rending letter from Griffith, detailing the circumstances of Rooney's death from overwork. Griffith spent a week in hospital himself, close to a complete breakdown. Another missive reached Maud in St Louis, imploring her to return soon.[45] When it became known that she intended to marry MacBride, Griffith pleaded with her not to do so:

> Queen, forgive me. John MacBride, after Willie Rooney, is the best friend I ever had; you are the only woman friend I have. I only think of both your happiness. For your own sakes and for the sake of Ireland to whom you both belong, don't get married. I know you both, you so unconventional - a law to yourself; John so full of conventions. You will not be happy for long. Forgive me, but think while there is time.[46]

Maud Gonne returned to Ireland after the execution of her estranged husband for his part in the 1916 Rising but she was never again as active in politics as she had been in the opening years of the century. Elizabeth Coxhead believed she was very opposed to the Treaty but seemed to accept it in December 1921:

> She was, after all, a lifelong friend of Griffith, who had the ungrateful task of leading the Treaty delegation to London, and she had no particular attachment to President de Valera, who had stayed at home and then disowned his delegation's work.[47]

In fact, she seemed to have supported or at least remained neutral on the Treaty right up to Griffith's death. This must have been difficult for her because her young son, Seán, joined those who took up arms against it. Her letter to Griffith in April 1922 about distress in Donegal concluded:

> God forgive me for troubling you with all this. I know how hard your task is and how unnecessarily hard it is being made for you by

45 Ward, *Gonne*, p.69.

46 Maud Gonne MacBride, *A Servant of the Queen* (London, 1938), p.349.

47 Elizabeth Coxhead, *Daughters of Erin* (London, 1965; paperback edition, 1979, cited in notes), pp. 68-9.

people who should know better. May you have the strength to carry your great and unselfish work to completion.[48]

Griffith's death was one of the reasons why she changed her stance on the Treaty; she no longer had any bonds of friendship with the pro-Treaty side.[49] Another woman who became well-known in the independence struggle, Countess Markievicz, also worked with Griffith. No friendship grew between them. She herself stated that it was the discovery of a bundle of old newspapers in 1905, among them copies of Griffith's *Sinn Féin*, which first alerted her to the possibility of political action. (The paper in question must have been the *United Irishman* as *Sinn Féin* did not replace it until 1906.) She first met Griffith at a soiree given by AE.[50] She joined Inghinidhe na hÉireann in 1908 but was regarded with suspicion.

Her 'bossy manner and high-pitched Anglo-Irish accent' were not liked.[51] She joined Sinn Féin the same year but she and Griffith failed to see eye-to-eye on a number of issues. 'We never became close friends', she has been recorded as saying, 'for I never thoroughly trusted or understood him and often disliked his methods'.[52] She was more militant in her attitude than he. She set about forming a boy scout movement which could be trained in military tactics and form the basis of a future army to fight for Irish freedom. Griffith was not enthusiastic. When the group - Fianna Éireann - was formed, his refusal to admit it as an adjunct of Sinn Féin angered her.

She was elected in 1909 to the executive of Sinn Féin and there was another clash with Griffith, this time over the question of female suffrage. She criticised the Irish Women's Franchise League for seeking the vote from Westminster without putting the demand for an Irish parliament first. In a letter published in *Sinn Féin* she wrote that Griffith and others had tried to impress on her that Sinn Féin women could participate in the suffrage movement but that she 'firmly but peacefully' rejected this view.

In an editorial note to her letter, Griffith stated that the Countess had

48 Ms. 22,761 NLI.

49 Ward, *Gonne*, p.133.

50 Ward, *Gonne*, p.133. AE, pseudonym for George Russell, was a poet, philosopher and activist on behalf of Horace Plunkett's Cooperative Movement whose newspaper, *The Irish Homestead*, he edited.

51 Marie O'Neill, *From Parnell to De Valera: a Biography of Jennie Wyse Power* (Dublin, 1992), p.64.

52 Coxhead, *Daughters*, p.87.

not pointed out any conflict between the principles of Sinn Féin and those of the Franchise League, that if there were any dichotomy the women in his organisation would feel free to leave, but that in the meantime he would not condemn any group which served 'to awaken civic and national consciousness in Irish women'.[53] Markievicz also disagreed with Griffith's entertaining an approach from William O'Brien of the Irish Parliamentary Party (IPP) in 1909. This did not prevent him from protesting at the way she was treated in Aylesbury Prison after the Rising.[54] Holloway's diary for 3 March 1918, however, suggests that Griffith remained unimpressed by her activities:

> Countess Markievicz was down in Clare lately telling all the ladies they should all become scouts and learn to climb trees. They were amused at this as there are few or no trees about Ennistymon where she gave this advice. When she saw the mistake she had made she suggested telegraph poles instead. This was all the funnier seeing that the lady leader down there was over eighteen stone weight. Griffith would like to silence the Countess, but such a thing would be taken as a division in the camp, so she is allowed to go on making idiotic revolutionary speeches.[55]

Hardly surprisingly, Markievicz took the opposite side on the Treaty to Griffith. Another co-worker and enduring friend was Jennie Wyse Power. She was active in Irish politics from the time of the Ladies' Land League at the beginning of the 1880s. She owned a restaurant in Henry St which served only Irish produce, and Griffith was a regular customer. At the first convention of the National Council (28 November 1905), usually regarded as the beginning of Sinn Féin, she became a member of the new organisation's executive and went on to occupy various positions on it. She did not agree with Griffith's dual-monarchy policy, preferring a republic, but she worked with him none the less. In 1909 she became joint-treasurer of Sinn Féin. Her attitude to the Women's Franchise League was similar to Griffith's and she opposed Countess Markievicz on the question.

On 8 January 1922, the day after the Treaty was ratified by Dáil Éireann, Jennie wrote to her daughter about what she had witnessed in the Dáil the previous day: 'The Dazzler [code name for Griffith] was superb and was the one speaker on that side that seemed to impress the opposite benches'. Her long, close working relationship with Griffith

53 *Sinn Féin*, 27 March 1909.

54 Seán Ó Lúing, *Cork Examiner*, 17 August 1972.

55 Ms. 22,293 NLI.

influenced her attitude to the Treaty.[56] After his death, Wyse Power co-administered his children's State allowances along with Patrick Bradley (Padraig Ó Brolcháin), another old friend.[57]

Another woman who wrote regularly for Griffith's papers, and for whom he formed a deep attachment, was Mary Butler (Máire de Buitléir). There was an unusual character to the friendship. Butler had been raised in prosperous Dublin Castle circles (her family were landed gentry from Clare) while Griffith was a printer's son who often could not afford to buy a meal for himself or a second pair of shoes. In her memoirs, she referred to the social gap she perceived between him and her own class:

> He was in those early days shy and extremely retiring. He had no taste for society and the reason we did not urge him to visit at our house was that we realised he would be bored and suffer from malaise if any of our unionist friends and relatives turned up. They were incapable of appreciating him and he would have disliked them intensely, so although we would have considered our house honoured by Griffith's presence, it was scarcely feasible to meet him except at his office. In those days our drawing-rooms at Upper Fitzwilliam St were still crowded by West-British acquaintances.

She pointed up the gap rather graphically in her description of Eoin O'Gara, the hero of her novel *The Ring of Day*, based largely on Griffith, where it is evident she believed that Griffith did not trust her fully. Fourteen years after they first met she was still uncertain of his confidence in her as she spoke to him about some people who called themselves nationalists. 'He condemned them bitterly and I agreed but when he went on to include in his list of wobblers one or two nationalists whom I believed to be staunch (subsequent events proved his estimation to be the true one), I grew impatient and thought him unjust. "You seem to doubt many people; perhaps you have doubts of my nationalism", I said hotly. "Not the smallest", he replied quietly. My heart smiled with pride at that tribute'.[58]

Seamus MacManus was another close friend and collaborator.[59] One summer's day he and Mary Butler and Griffith cycled through the Phoenix Park to visit Mary's family who were staying in a house near the Park. According to MacManus, Griffith said to him on the way

56 O'Neill, *Wyse Power*, pp.57-8, 60-62, 132, 139.

57 Interview with Mrs Ita Gray, Dublin, 22 August 1995.

58 Mairéad Ni Chinnéide, *Máire de Buitléir: Bean Athbheochana* (Dublin, 1993), pp.68-9.

59 MacManus, a writer, was a director of the *United Irishman* Publishing Company.

home: 'If we had a thousand like Máire de Buitléir it would be easy to create a new Ireland'. Mary herself also referred to that day in her memoirs:

> It was always at his office we had our best talks with Griffith in those days. Only once was he at our house. Seamus MacManus brought him to see us on that occasion. My mother conceived for him a warm regard which never wavered. Of all our democratic acquaintances he was the one who stood highest in her esteem and of his genius she was convinced from the start. None rejoiced more than she when at length his weary years of uphill struggle were rewarded and the country adopted the policy he had advocated.

There is no evidence that Mary played an active part in the Sinn Féin movement, apart from spreading the gospel of its leader in her writings (her primary interest was in the Gaelic League). Most of all it was Griffith's personality that impressed her and those of his traits that appealed to her - his idealism and indifference to personal advancement - are well illustrated in *The Ring of Day*, published in 1906.

When Griffith got married in 1910, Mary and her sister Belinda, both delegates to the first Sinn Féin convention in 1905, contributed to the purchase of a house for the newly-wed couple. Although there was some suspicion of Griffith after 1916 because he had not taken part in the Rising, the respect Mary had for him never lessened. In 1919 she wrote: 'Arthur Griffith is the most remarkable of the many remarkable men I have met. Ireland owes to him more than many of her children realise. As time goes on I think he will be better appreciated'.[60]

On 12 May 1921 Griffith wrote from Mountjoy Jail to Belinda, now Mere Columba Butler OSB, commiserating with her on the death of her sister. He credited Mary with giving the name Sinn Féin to his movement and continued:

> I am very sad when I reflect on how many of my old friends have gone, but it consoles me to think that our generation of Irishwomen and Irishmen have done more to redeem Ireland than any other and that it has been privileged to see what was denied to the patriots of former generations, the end of the long black night and the break of bright day.[61]

Sydney Gifford wrote for *Sinn Féin* under the pseudonym 'John Brennan'. Her sister, Grace, is well remembered because of her

60 Ni Chinnéide, *de Buitléir*, pp.77-8.

61 Ms. 4577 NLI.

marriage to Joseph Plunkett on the night before his execution in 1916. Sydney first met Griffith when he was having a holiday at the Martello Tower with Gogarty and O'Sullivan, who had invited her and her sisters with the promise that they would be taken out in a boat. This led to a case of mistaken identity when Griffith appeared on the scene.

The sisters saw a small man walking towards them with a slow plodding gait. Because of his sun-tanned face, fresh complexion, sun-bleached moustache and bright blue eyes they mistook him for a sailor. Sydney thought he looked friendly and humorous with kindly, smiling eyes. O'Sullivan having introduced them they all got into the boat and Griffith took the oars. He rowed them round the bay for the whole afternoon, and he and O'Sullivan vied with one another telling amusing stories and making up rhymes about incidents at the Tower.[62]

Of course, *the* woman in Arthur Griffith's life was his wife, Maud Sheehan. He first met her when she and her sister, Annie, who were both musicians, performed at a Leinster Literary Society music-evening. Because he lived on the same side of the city he escorted them home. He got on best with Maud, then only fifteen. The Sheehans lived in a large house in Belvedere Place. They were well off and in the big front rooms of their house they gave musical afternoons. In the newspaper office where he worked Griffith was on duty all night on Wednesdays or Thursdays. After finishing, rather than going home to bed he used to call and take the sisters for a morning walk in the Phoenix Park, getting them home in time for eight o'clock mass which they attended before going to school.

There is little surviving evidence of their relationship. One of Griffith's few extant letters is addressed to Maud and it is from an early stage in their association:

> Jan.18th,'94
> Dear Miss Sheehan,
> *The Lily of Killarney* is announced for Saturday night. Do you remember your promise? If you are not better engaged for that evening, I would be delighted to meet you at, say, a quarter past seven o'clock at the corner of Winetavern St and Merchant's Quay.
> Sincerely yours,
> Arthur Griffith.

'The shyness that was so noticeable in Arthur Griffith is in this note',

62 Sydney Czira ('John Brennan'), *The Years Flew By* (Dublin, 1974), pp.29-30, 32-33.

Padraic Colum remarked.[63] They became engaged in 1904 but because of his meagre earnings (he was also supporting his mother) he was not in a position to marry until 1910 when he was 39 and she 29. They had two children, a son, Nevin, born in 1911 and a daughter, Ita, born two years later. They got married on 24 November. On that date in 1916 he wrote the following letter to his wife from Reading Jail:

> Dearest, my love to you on the anniversary. We will spend it happily hereafter. Tell Nevin and Ita to kiss you for me. Did the children like the picture I sent? It was done by Milroy, a fellow-prisoner here, for them. We are all well. I hope Clontarf storms are past and you are having a calm time again....Love to yourself and the children...[64]

He spent half of the last six years of his life in prison, and he was so preoccupied while free that his wife and young children saw very little of him. For the three months before his arrest in November 1920, he did not sleep at home; his house was raided several times a week and on one occasion his son was roughly treated.

He was particularly fearful of the effect the violence would have on the children. 'That the two children...never really knew their father was, naturally, a source of great regret to Mrs Griffith, and, indeed, a loss to the children themselves', observed Colum, who knew the Griffiths well, and who has left the following vignette of their family life:

> Ita, then a little girl, remembers a man who used to come into the house, and standing before her, his hands behind his back, would ask her which hand she would take. She might expect to get a 'lucky bag' - little packages of sweets with a small toy - in one. But the lucky bag was always in the other hand and this vexed the little girl.[65]

His pet-name for his wife was Mollie. Just after he arrived in London as leader of the Dáil delegation he sent her the following undated letter (probably 10 October 1921):

> Dear Mollie,
>
> My address is 22 Hans Place SW. The weather here is insufferably warm. Yesterday we motored to Reading, where I had the first view of the town that I lived in for so many months.
>
> I was at mass at Brompton Oratory. Today we are hard at work and

63 Colum, *Griffith*, p.30.

64 *ibid.*, p.164.

65 *ibid.*, p.238.

tomorrow we meet the other side.

I enclose some cards for Ita and Naomhan.

Love,

Arthur[66]

Kathleen Napoli-McKenna recalled a lunch she had during the Treaty negotiations with Griffith and Fr Augustine OFM Cap, who had been her 'childhood spiritual counsellor'. They talked about Griffith's imprisonment after the Rising and particularly about the night before his probable execution.

'If the worst happens', he had said to Fr Augustine, 'go to Maud and tell her I died thinking of her'. McKenna described Griffith as in a happy mood that day because Maud was coming to join him in London in a day or two.[67] Despite the stress of the negotiations he did not forget their eleventh wedding anniversary: 'Dear Mollie, I am sending a little token to you of the day eleven years ago'. The token was a telegram they had received on their wedding-day wishing them well.[68]

Four months after her husband's death, in the course of a letter to a friend, Mrs Griffith remarked: 'The children now are company and too young to realise the Daddy's loss. He was cheated of their company and all that meant home'.[69]

It was a shared interest in music that brought them together and certainly music meant a lot to him. His colleague in the CLS, George A. Lyons, recognised that music and song 'held a large place in his life'. Griffith himself was convinced that 'a good song is worth a dozen pamphlets'.[70]

He was keenly interested in the Oireachtas or annual Gaelic League gathering, as well as the feis ceoil concerts. He regularly attended orchestral concerts and oratorios. He often sang comic songs at parties. His knowledge of Irish ballads was encyclopaedic and Lyons described his 'Ballad History of Ireland', which ran in the *United Irishman* from January 1904 until February 1905, as among his 'most important and most beautiful achievements'.[71]

Ernest Blythe, a fellow-prisoner in Reading in 1916, referred to his

66 Letter in library of late Nevin Griffith, Dublin.

67 McKenna, *Capuchin Annual*, p.324.

68 Note and token in library of late Nevin Griffith, Dublin.

69 Ms. 8411 NLI.

70 NLI Labour Pamphlet Collection, Ir 941 p30.

71 Lyons, *Some Recollections of Griffith*, pp.60-62.

dazzling knowledge of Irish music. He had only a reasonable voice according to Blythe, but he had a miraculous ear and could whistle thousands of Irish tunes superbly.[72] Another fellow-inmate, this time in Gloucester in 1918-19, Robert Brennan, declared that he loved opera and sang snatches from *The Barber of Seville* and *Faust.* Brennan saw him as 'a typical Dubliner in his fondness for Wallace and Balfe'.[73] His principal respite during the Treaty negotiations was *The Beggar's Opera* at the Lyric Theatre in Hammersmith.'He loved its old airs and old-time atmosphere and went to see it many times', fellow-delegate Eamon Duggan told Piaras Béaslaí.[74]

Some of those evenings were spent playing cards or singing, according to Napoli-McKenna. She described Griffith as having 'a sweet, weak singing voice' and spoke of his fondness for patriotic love-songs like 'The Foggy Dew' and 'Moya My Girl'[75] He wrote a number of ballads himself, the most famous being 'Twenty Men from Dublin Town'. These were collected by Piaras Béaslaí and published by Waltons of Dublin.[76]

72 Ó Lúing, *Ó Gríofa*, p.274.

73 Robert Brennan, *Allegiance* (Dublin, 1950), p.203.

74 Béaslaí, *Leader*, 16 December 1944.

75 McKenna, *Capuchin Annual*, p.324.

76 Piaras Béaslaí (ed.), *Songs, Ballads and Recitations of Arthur Griffith* (Dublin, n.d.).

Chapter II

Personality and Humour

Traits

Despite his willingness to lecture and debate in public Arthur Griffith was a shy person. A fellow-apprentice told Colum that as teenagers when they paired off with girls Griffith often startled his companion by spouting 'To be or not to be' or 'The quality of mercy is not strained' from Shakespeare, or 'I saw her like a morning star' from Burke. Colum believed this 'display of erudition was as much to cover his shyness as to make an impression'.[1]

Seamus O'Sullivan's strongest impression from the start 'and, indeed, when I met him for the last time a little before his death, was that of an innate and unconquerable shyness'.[2] This view was shared by James Stephens: 'He is...exceedingly sensitive, and he is possessed of, not afflicted by, an invisible shyness which he himself can scarcely overcome, and which the stranger or casual acquaintance cannot hope to penetrate'.[3]

It was the continuous reading and research, according to George A. Lyons, and the long periods of solitary writing that made Griffith shy and retiring. As a result he appeared cold and unsocial to those who did not know him very well. Lyons cited several reasons why he often failed to notice people or greet associates. One was that he had very poor eyesight (he confessed as much to Lyons). Another was his preoccupation with his thoughts. But the main one, Lyons believed, was that he never felt people sought recognition from him - he considered himself unknown and unnoticed.[4]

Griffith forgot his shyness in the company of children. When Queen Victoria visited Ireland in 1900, a 'children's treat' was held in the Phoenix

1 Colum, *Griffith*, p.19.

2 O'Sullivan, *Essays*, p.105.

3 James Stephens, *Arthur Griffith: Journalist and Statesman*, (Dublin, n.d.), p.21.

4 Lyons, *Some Recollections*, pp.60-61.

Park. Inghinidhe na hÉireann responded by giving a 'patriotic children's treat' in Clonturk Park. Lyons has left a striking recollection of that day:

> It was characteristic of Griffith to be happy among children. That shyness and reserve of manner which so many mistook for coldness or aloofness, was entirely missing when he was found surrounded by children. The bronze and the marble fell away and he moved with a sense of abandon which made the most timid child feel at home in his presence. Those of us who were to see him in after years, blessed with children of his own and at play with them amid the breezes of the Bull Wall or among the rustling leaves of the 'Green Lanes', always called to our minds that happy day in Clonturk when he gambolled about with a paper hat upon his head and the little children scattered like flowers around his feet.[5]

Gifford also remarked on his gentleness with children. She and her sisters were staying in a farmhouse in Avoca, Co. Wicklow, and they invited Griffith and O'Sullivan down to meet the farmer's son who was about ten years old and whom they regarded as a remarkable child because of his amazing knowledge of Irish history. 'I can still picture the scene as Griffith, his eyes shining with pleasure, sat at the table opposite to the child, listening to him answer correctly and without hesitation questions about every period of Irish history'. When he was leaving he told the child he was 'a grand little chap' and promised to send him a present from Dublin. A few days later the present arrived - an edition of *Jail Journal* inscribed by Griffith.[6]

Another quality of the man which people around him noted well was that he was quite imperturbable. Frank O'Connor told the following story. Once Griffith mistakenly took a brand new hat and coat from a restaurant where he had lunch. The owner, a young man from the country in Dublin on his honeymoon, spoke to the men at the table where Griffith had sat. Because he had eaten in silence they convinced the young man that Griffith was a notorious pilferer of hats and coats. The newly-wed was in a state of distress when Griffith re-entered, replaced the hat and coat, put on his own and 'disappeared in the same awful silence. Not a smile! Not an apology! A man of iron...'[7]

When Piaras Béaslaí first met Griffith, in the office of the *United Irishman*, he was thrown by his impassive manner. Béaslaí was young

5 Lyons, *Some Recollections*, pp.32-3.

6 Czira, *Years*, p.33.

7 Frank O'Connor, *Michael Collins and the Irish Revolution* (1937; revised edition, Dublin 1965, cited in notes), pp.11-12.

and enthusiastic at the time and had been 'thrilled by his patriotic writings'. The little, stocky, bespectacled man who listened silently to the youth's impassioned rhetoric with an expressionless face, or made the odd nondescript remark, was not what he had expected. He could not believe that this was the man 'who wielded so brilliant, so trenchant, nay, sometimes so savage a pen'. But some years later he recalled Griffith as saying: 'I always try to keep clear and cool-headed. We have a cunning and powerful enemy to fight, and we cannot afford to have our judgements swayed by our emotions'.[8]

Robert Lynd, who worked with Griffith, was aware of this trait in his personality: 'He seldom made any display of enthusiasm, and he did not take the display of enthusiasm by other people very seriously....He was one of the most profoundly emotional men in Ireland, but his emotions were kept under iron control'.[9]

Looking back in 1945 on the Irish independence struggle in which she had taken part, the historian Dorothy Macardle wondered: 'Were we fanatics?' Most were, she concluded, but not Griffith, who was 'a lifelong realist'.[10] Terence de Vere White felt the same:

> He had, what is rare in Ireland, the power to dedicate himself without fanaticism. There was no mysticism in Griffith. Passion he had most certainly. Great devotion is not easy without passion, but it was the passion of a man who sees life steadily and sees it whole.[11]

Allied to his impassiveness was a tendency to distrust oratory. Sean-Ghall was able to see this: 'He was the one strong, silent man in a blatant land. For oratory, as such, he had a profound disgust, for he knew it was the devil's fatal gift to the Irish race'.[12] This disposition in Griffith also struck Lynd, who thought that he regarded eloquence as one of the vices of his countrymen, and felt that Ireland would be much better 'if speech-making ceased and demonstrations with bands and banners were abolished'.[13]

He was a poor public speaker, Sydney Gifford believed, because he did not have 'the dynamic force and flow of oratory that made the

8 Béaslaí, *Leader*, 16 December 1944.

9 Lynd, *Galway of the Races*, p.107.

10 NLI Labour Pamphlet Collection, p1304. Macardle's book, *The Irish Republic*, was strongly anti-Treaty.

11 *IrishTimes*, 14 October 1972.

12 Ms. 23,516 NLI.

13 Lynd, *Galway*, p.107.

popular leader'. She thought that as a lecturer he often spoiled a good paper by poor delivery because his voice was monotonous and indistinct, and he lacked the ability to sway a crowd with a dramatic gesture or turn of phrase.[14]

But the historian Desmond Ryan considered him quite an effective orator at times:

> Sometimes a great cheer sent the roof of a Dublin hall sky-high when Arthur Griffith spoke, but that was not often, for Griffith disliked crowds and his speaking voice was low and indistinct.
>
> At the Rotunda I can see him now halted in his speech by roaring waves of applause and stormy echoes, and as he stands quiet and proud and cliff-jawed. He has touched the heart of Dublin with a word as he always can at a pinch, and as it roars in response perhaps Griffith fears he is becoming an orator, and does he not scathe all orators in every issue of his paper?[15]

Perhaps because of his physical appearance, perhaps because of his innate shyness - whatever the reason - Arthur Griffith was a modest, self-effacing person. Gifford had been writing for *Sinn Féin* for some years before she met or even saw him.

She commented on how he kept very much in the background and could pass unnoticed through any political gathering, seldom even presiding at public meetings of his own organisation: 'Yet in the first ten years of the century, this obscure man, whose very appearance was unknown to many of his countrymen, was setting the country pulsating with new ideas, and was changing the whole course of Irish history'.[16]

Although Griffith's manner was reserved,'no man was more free from pride or social exclusiveness', according to Piaras Béaslaí. Béaslaí happened to be travelling with him on the way to the London negotiations in October 1921. They were travelling first-class and were standing on deck chatting when Griffith was surrounded by a group of young women who begged him to sign their autograph albums. He was doing so when Béaslaí noticed a girl who was travelling second-class trying in vain to pass the barrier and approach Griffith. When Béaslaí mentioned this to him, Griffith immediately passed the barrier to the

14 Czira, *Years*, pp.29-30.

15 Desmond Ryan, *Remembering Sion: a Chronicle of Calm and Storm* (London, 1934), p.88. Ryan took part in the 1916 Rising. His father, W.P., was a fellow-editor of Griffith with whom he had many a joust.

16 Czira, *Years*, p.29.

second-class section, signed this and other girls' albums, and remained chatting with them for some time.[17]

D. Carolan Rushe wrote to Sean-Ghall shortly after Griffith's death with some information about his Monaghan ancestry. He began his letter, 'The late Arthur Griffith' and added in brackets, 'It would be an indignity to the memory of the great man to style him Mr'.[18]

Griffith was unusually determined as a person. James Stephens observed that even as a young man 'his will was already set into something of the granitic quality that later became...one of his most noticeable characteristics'. He recalled an occasion when they were discussing the illness of a friend and Griffith remembered a personal experience while he was in South Africa. There was an outbreak of fever and he awoke one morning with a number of the symptoms. He got up and played a solitary game of handball for about six hours until he was not able to play any longer. Then he crawled back to bed and fell asleep: 'He awoke in the morning without any fever, and, indeed, fever never dared to threaten him again'.[19]

'One had only to look at his abnormally developed jaw muscles and his square, powerful shoulders to realise the strength of will that lay behind his habitual quietness', thought Lynd, who observed that it required more than ordinary willpower to set out with any optimism on the road he chose. He had neither money nor a large following and the few who had heard of his paper did not expect very much from him. The fraction of supporters he did have were dubbed 'rainbow chasers' or 'cranks and soreheads' and most of the country was totally unaware of their existence.[20]

P.S. O'Hegarty, who was in Sinn Féin from the beginning, likened Griffith to 'a rock, a beacon, which no depression, no setback, no threat and no bribe could divert from his purpose'.[21] He described the organisation's policy as a long-term one which neither Griffith nor the most optimistic of them expected to see realised quickly or easily. Indeed, he had Griffith's own words in mind: 'We will win through to

17 Béaslaí, *Leader*, 16 December 1944.

18 Letter, 3 September 1922, from D. Carolan Rushe to Henry Egan Kenny, in library of late Nevin Griffith, Dublin. Rushe was secretary of Monaghan County Council for some years and Griffith had some contact with him. Kenny was intended to be Griffith's first biographer but his work never came to fruition.

19 Stephens, *Journalist and Statesman*, pp.9-10.

20 Lynd, *Galway*, p.107.

21 *Sunday Independent*, 12 August 1945.

our goal. Before that goal is attained, many will have fallen and all will have suffered. But - we will win through to our goal'.[22]

The slow, tenacious slog envisaged was well described by O'Hegarty:

> The Sinn Féin movement was educational, practical and political. It sought to educate the people in the knowledge of their land, its history, traditions and resources. It taught them that speeches and resolutions and patriotism were not enough, that of themselves they would not save the nation, that the nation could be saved only by effort, only by the slow rebuilding of the national life in Ireland itself, a rebuilding of individual and group effort until such time as power over our own affairs could be resumed....
>
> It was a call to a long-term effort. It envisaged...a long and necessarily slow construction effort, through the local boards and the General Council of County Councils. It had no doubt of itself. But in the Ireland of that day there was nothing to warrant anybody believing that the conversion of a majority of the people to the Sinn Féin policy could be considered anything but remote, and nobody did so believe.[23]

But Griffith was confident of reaching his goal - and in the shorter rather than the longer term: 'I have no doubt of the acceptance of the Sinn Féin policy as the policy of all Ireland in the near future and no doubt of its ultimate triumph', he wrote in 1906.[24] This 'relentless doggedness' was seen by Robert Kee as Griffith's 'one great characteristic: it is this...determination to persist in working out and maintaining an alternative ideal of Irish nationalism to that so successfully promoted by the Parliamentary Party, that gave him ultimately his historical importance'.[25]

There were setbacks, but he did not lose hope. Part of 1910 was a dark time in his life. His long-time friend and helper, William Bulfin, had died; his *Sinn Féin* daily had failed; his movement had split; scarcity of funds was a constant problem; with the IPP holding the balance of power in the House of Commons and Home Rule an inevitability, the Sinn Féin message was making less and less of an impact. He did not despair: 'We have to contend with apathy and disillusion, but not with

22 Arthur Griffith, *The Resurrection of Hungary* (3rd edition, Dublin, 1918), p.163.

23 P.S. O'Hegarty, *A History of Ireland under the Union* (London, 1951), pp.653-4.

24 *Sinn Féin*, 17 October 1906.

25 Robert Kee, *The Bold Fenian Men* (Volume II of *The Green Flag*, London 1972; published in 3 volumes, 1976), p.156.

a living faith opposed to our own', he wrote in *Sinn Féin* on 18 June 1910.[26]

In the years before 1914, it seemed that a large measure of Home Rule was on the way. 'In the bright promise of those days, Griffith must have sounded like the bad fairy at the christening', remarked de Vere White,[27] but still he persisted.

Sinn Féin was suppressed by the authorities at the end of 1914. 'Entering the year 1915 and approaching his forty-third year, Arthur Griffith was a man out of work. His household, never well off, was now impoverished. And those moments of despondence that a man who had undertaken a long enterprise must pass through and come out of with self-reliance, must have occurred to him over and over again', Colum wrote.[28]

Yet again he carried on and survived through the long periods of imprisonment between 1916 and 1922. He was the first to decide that he would sign the Treaty on the night of 5 December 1921, which drew from Austen Chamberlain, one of the British delegates, the tribute: 'Arthur Griffith was the most courageous man I ever met'. Of this Gogarty remarked: 'He who had met the most outstanding persons of our generation said Arthur Griffith was the most courageous'.[29]

Associated with this dogged, determined streak was an inclination towards individualism. This caused him to be wary of organisations. 'He knew that organisations are apt to develop into tyrannies, and to be deflected from the intentions of their founders', O'Hegarty avowed. A good example of this was Cumann na nGaedheal, the first organisation he helped to set up in September 1900.

In the *United Irishman* (15 March 1900) he had called for the establishment of a central body to coordinate the activities of the various clubs and societies which he thought were doing good work. What he envisaged was a loose federation rather than any sort of rigid control. 'Personally, I would be strongly in favour of limiting its scope, and allowing every association which recognised it, the utmost liberty of action consistent with the maintenance of the policy which the central body should promulgate'.[30]

Similarly with the National Council set up in 1903 to oppose the visit

26 Ó Lúing, *Ó Gríofa*, pp.208-9.

27 *Irish Times*, 14 October 1972.

28 Colum, *Griffith*, p.132.

29 Gogarty, *Sackville Street*, p.236.

30 O'Hegarty, *History*, pp.637-9.

of Edward VII to Dublin. It was not an organisation in the usual sense, with a constitution and rules, but a loose banding together of individuals all over the country. It was kept in existence after it had achieved its immediate purpose - preventing the presentation of a loyal address by Dublin Corporation. O'Hegarty was sure that 'Griffith always hankered after something of this sort, a voluntary association rather than a rigid, rule-bound organisation'.[31]

Following the great interest aroused by *The Resurrection of Hungary*[32], there was much pressure on Griffith to launch the policy advocated in it formally and to establish a new organisation to carry it out. His long, detailed address to the annual convention of the National Council at the Rotunda on 28 November 1905, was afterwards published in pamphlet form as *The Sinn Féin Policy*. Griffith was hoping for a central body only, without branches, like the existing National Council. When the issue was discussed at the convention, the Dublin delegates, who were close to Griffith, favoured the idea of a central body and attempting to promote the policy by individual effort only, but the provincial delegates opposed this and the convention decided to set up branches.[33]

Another outstanding quality was his honesty. According to Sean-Ghall, Griffith was known to his schoolmates as 'honest Dan', because of his utter honesty.[34]

The Church of Ireland rector, Canon J.O. Hannay, who used the pseudonym George A. Bermingham, wrote for Griffith from time to time. Griffith defended Hannay against the accusation that his novel, *The Seething Pot*, made fun of a Westport priest. Hannay said of Griffith: 'He was a man of absolute honesty and no idea of self-glorification or self-advancement ever seemed to enter his head'.[35]

Oliver Gogarty called Griffith 'honest Arthur'. And among the British delegates in London Griffith's judgement to Gogarty was that 'Chamberlain was the best of the whole lot. A clean and honest man'.[36]

31 O'Hegarty, *Irl. under Union*, pp.643-4.

32 This pamphlet urged Ireland to try to achieve independence in the manner in which Hungary had won its freedom from Austria between 1849 and 1867. The constitutional model it suggested for Britain and Ireland was a dual monarchy.

33 *op. cit.*, pp.650-51.

34 Ms. 23,516 NLI. The provenance of the nickname Dan is not clear.

35 George A. Bermingham, *Pleasant Places* (London, 1940), pp.187-8. He wrote this after he had become disillusioned with nationalism and, to some extent, with Griffith himself.

36 Gogarty, *Sackville St*, pp.259, 275.

O'Connor described Griffith as 'incorruptible', and Margery Forester asserted that his predominating quality was integrity.[37]

Generosity was also typical of him. O'Hegarty encountered this at their first meeting, in the offices of the *United Irishman* in August 1903. Griffith showed 'his very remarkable and characteristic kindness to a raw young man' that day. He took O'Hegarty to lunch and arranged to meet him that evening in Mooney's of Abbey St. They then went to a Gaelic League *fáilte* in the Mansion House and on to Griffith's home in Summerhill.[38]

'Arthur Griffith was one of the most generous men I have ever known', declared Robert Brennan, who worked with him on the *Irish Bulletin* during the Anglo-Irish war. After the sack of Balbriggan in October 1920, he was in Griffith's office when a young man entered in a terrible condition - wet, muddy and shivering with cold. He told them he had just managed to escape the Black and Tans, had scribbled a report of what he had seen of the destruction of the town and was anxious that Griffith would see it safely delivered to Collins. As he was about to leave, Griffith gave him his overcoat. Brennan pointed out that he had not even taken his things out of the pockets. This drew the characteristic response: 'In any case, there is never anything worthwhile in my pockets'.[39]

Gearóid Ó Lochlainn, who was private secretary to Griffith as President of Dáil Éireann, described him as always generous to people in need. Ó Lochlainn remembered his actions when people were fleeing the pogroms in Belfast. A number of times he gave money from his own pocket to unfortunate people who came to the Mansion House seeking help. He used to say to Ó Lochlainn: 'Find out the circumstances; see if it is a genuine case of hardship'. If Ó Lochlainn verified it was, then Griffith contributed personally.[40]

After Griffith's death in August 1922, a stranger arrived at the family home in Clontarf. He had seen Griffith's picture in the papers and he recognised it as the same man from whom he and his companions in prison had received a cake and a bottle of whiskey at Christmas, 1920. He explained that he had been a criminal prisoner at the time, that a man he did not know came over and gave them those things, and that

37 O'Connor, *Collins*, p.11; Margery Forester, *Michael Collins: the Lost Leader* (London, 1971), p.73.

38 *Sunday Independent*, 12 August 1945.

39 *Irish Press*, 26 January 1956.

40 'Eolas ar Art Ó Gríofa', 14 September 1957, Ms. 23,516, NLI.

he had no idea who he was until he saw his picture and news of his death in the papers. He had come to the house to extend his sympathy.[41]

There has been some serious adverse comment about Arthur Griffith's personality as well. One of Gogarty's biographers, J.B. Lyons, thought that a number of Griffith's faults were magnified in his subject: both could be assertive and narrow-minded and susceptible to strong dislikes; 'neither was prepared to concede much to an opponent's arguments, or change his own even when facts seemed to have gone awry'.[42] Hannay referred to Griffith's 'humourlessness, taciturnity and frigidity of manner'.[43]

Griffith's first biographer, Séan Ó Lúing, believed that he was stubborn and unreceptive to advice. Bulmer Hobson, who was in Sinn Féin from the beginning, expressed a similar view:

> Arthur Griffith was a man whose sincerity and devotion to the cause of Irish independence commanded respect and admiration. On the other hand, his views were often narrow and reactionary and he was dogmatic to a very unusual degree. He did not easily tolerate any opinion which differed from his own and this made it very difficult to work with him. In the Sinn Féin organisation his attitude caused many of the most active members to withdraw and work in other organisations. This happened, I think, about 1910, and the Sinn Féin organisation did not long survive their departure.[44]

Of course there were important ideological reasons, as well as personal ones, why the separatists left Sinn Féin in 1910.[45]

The most notable criticism of Griffith was that published by Patrick Pearse in 1912 in his short-lived weekly, *An Barr Buadh*. Pearse wrote of him in Irish:

> You were too hard. You were too obstinate. You were too narrow-minded.You were too headstrong. You did not trust your friends enough. You trusted yourself too much. You over-estimated your own opinion. You distrusted people who were as loyal as yourself. You would follow no one's advice except your own. You preferred to prove to the world that no one else was right except yourself.

41 Ó Lúing, *Ó Gríofa*, p.353.

42 J.B. Lyons, *Oliver St John Gogarty: the Man of Many Talents* (Dublin, 1980), p.110.

43 Bermingham, *Pleasant Places*, p.187.

44 Ó Lúing, *Ó Gríofa*, p.207; see also Bulmer Hobson, *Ireland Yesterday and Tomorrow* (Tralee, 1967), p.4.

45 See below, Part II, Chapter II.

It was a harsh judgement, even if Pearse acknowledged his many virtues. There was little contact between them although Griffith helped Pearse some years before when he was seeking the editorship of *An Claidheamh Soluis*, the Gaelic League newspaper. Pearse never had much sympathy for Sinn Féin.[46]

One of Pearse's biographers, Ruth Dudley Edwards, certainly had a low opinion of Griffith as a person. She described him as 'aggressive, harsh, pugnacious', and referred to his 'suspicious nature and difficult personality'.[47]

Kevin O'Higgins worked with Griffith after 1916, and especially between 1919 and 1922. He believed him to be a bad judge of men. He thought likewise of Cathal Brugha. Whenever someone seeking a job presented a testimonial signed by Brugha, O'Higgins would remark: 'Now if only that had been signed by Arthur Griffith as well, we could be certain it was safe to refuse the application'.[48]

Humour

Hannay thought Griffith devoid of humour. Those who knew him but slightly would have found his shy, reserved manner offputting and may have considered him humourless. His writings demonstrate, as do those who have written about him that there was a palpable strain of humour in the man.

As an apprentice printer he was well known to his fellow-workers for the skits he composed in verse on those around him. It was a case of the child being father to the man, as will be seen.[49] One of his early contributions to *Eblana*, entitled 'The vagaries of the printer', was an amusing look at how printing errors could be deadly. He took this example from the *Daily Telegraph* account of the battle of Majuba Hill in South Africa: 'After the death of Sir George Colley, the laughter was dreadful', where 'laughter' should have read 'slaughter'. He found another gem in the same newspaper: 'Mr Chamberlain's voracity was unquestionable', where 'voracity' should have been 'veracity'. The

46 Ó Lúing, *Ó Gríofa*, p.216.

47 Ruth Dudley Edwards, *Patrick Pearse: the Triumph of Failure* (London, 1977), pp.72, 153, 158-9.

48 Terence de Vere White, *Kevin O'Higgins* (London, 1948; paperback edition, 1966, cited in notes), p.49.

49 Ms. 22,293 NLI.

London *Morning Post* offered up 'Sir Robert Peel and a party of fiends have gone to shoot peasants in Ireland'![50]

Griffith was editor of the *Middleburg Courant* in the Transvaal for part of 1897. One of the features of his editorship was a lightness of touch as evidenced in the following:

> When it is impossible to blame the printer, it is the recognised custom of a journalist to blame the pen, as if some subtle devil had possessed it. 'Owing to an unaccountable slip of the pen', writes the journalist, 'we were made to express the opinion last week that Colonel Blank is the meanest man in South Africa. Of course, as our readers must have been fully convinced, it was the exact opposite that we intended to convey. The Colonel visited us during the week and requested us to rectify the slip. We hasten to do so. The Colonel is six feet, three inches in his stockings, carries a brace of revolvers, and hits like a sledgehammer. Under the circumstances we are at a loss to understand how such a misleading statement crept into our columns.

'Griffith liked to sit in the Transvaal with a few pals over a drink, so like the Griffith of Dublin', wrote M.J. Lennon, who visited Middleburg at the end of the 1940s. He found a few veteran Boers there who remembered him as the outspoken, fearless little Irishman. One Englishman who read the *Courant* of Griffith's day recalled with pleasure his jovial style of writing.[51]

Seamus O'Sullivan testified that Griffith wrote a great many pieces 'of a delightful humour, which are scattered anonymously through the various journals which he edited'. Some of the best were to be found in the series of satirical articles published anonymously under the title *At the Poets' Agency.* Griffith's lighter writing was 'full of a very delightful humour which seemed to spring from an almost inexhaustible source'.[52]

Some of the scattered pieces to which O'Sullivan referred were collected by Piaras Béaslaí, who thought that Griffith's sense of fun and humour, so richly displayed in the *United Irishman*, was an aspect of the man which many ignored. These pieces took both prose and poetic form. One prose passage is aimed at D.P. Moran, editor of the *Leader*, an early sparring-partner of Griffith's. It is an account of an imaginary dinner given in honour of Moran, of the speeches made and the letters

50 Ms. 3493 NLI.

51 Ms. 22,293 NLI. M.J. Lennon carried out extensive research into Griffith's life and writings.

52 O'Sullivan, *Essays*, pp.106, 108.

of congratulation received from unlikely people like Sir Horace Plunkett, who was often the butt of Moran's polemics.

Another is the story of an old man who spoke only Irish and who was brought up before a well-known Dublin magistrate. The old man claimed to be Dualtach MacFirbhisigh, a great Irish genealogist of the 17th century. The magistrate sent for Professor Atkinson of Trinity College (supposedly compiling an Irish dictionary) to translate the old man's Irish. Atkinson translated what he said as 'Potatoes will not grow on telegraph poles, and the earth will shiver in his bones, when Johnny comes marching home'.

He refused to translate any more because the old man's remarks were 'positively indecent'. Atkinson had earlier declared that there was nothing in Irish literature which was not either silly or indecent. 'Griffith's skits are so full of topical allusions that they would be unintelligible to the younger generation without copious footnotes', Béaslaí rightly remarked.[53]

Griffith's best known satirical composition is 'The Thirteenth Lock', a song from a short play he wrote called *The Conspirators*. The play pokes fun at Professors Atkinson, Mahaffy and Traill of Trinity College, who were well known for their hostility to the Irish language and whom Dr Douglas Hyde took to task. In the play Traill and Mahaffy stow away on a coal-boat that plies the canal between Dublin and Athy in Co. Kildare. They have heard that Hyde would be walking by the thirteenth lock at midnight and they plan to surprise and kill him there. But they are discovered by the skipper of the boat who has them thrown in chains below deck.

The skipper gets drunk and sings 'The Thirteenth Lock' during Act II. The lock is a very terrifying place to which the sailors fear to voyage. One of the sailor's sweethearts begs him not to go because of the unlucky number and day:

'Oh, Pat, beware!' cried a damsel fair,
'Sail not today, my dear.
We warn - don't scorn - 'tis Friday morn,
The day true mariners fear.
And what would I do, Pat, if I lost you?
Sure my heart couldn't stand the shock'.

But her beloved is brave and reassuring:
'Cease, love, these sighs, dim not your eyes
With beauty-killing tears.

53 *Irish Independent*, 19 August 1964.

You may be bound I'll come back sound,
So calm your woman's fears;
And I'll bring to thee a chimpanzee,
A parrot, a jabberwock,
A kangaroo and a cockatoo
From the wilds of the thirteenth lock.'

At the Poets' Agency Ltd was an elaborate and amusing piece, revealing a philistine's views on poetry. In it Griffith gave some examples of what the philistine regarded as 'true poetry'. The first example, 'The Primal Light', the philistine declared was 'as beautiful a thing as ever I read':

As in contemplation and meditation
For recreation at evening's close,
I wandered gaily down by the Bailey
Where night and daily the water flows.
Old Sol resplendent in the ascendant
Shed his transcendent, effulgent rays;
And I mused and pondered as I idly wandered
On the lights they squandered in the Primal Days.

I heard a n'ise and I raised my eyes and -
May I be pysoned! but I saw a sight
Whose awful wonder took my legs from under,
And broke asunder my powers of flight.
'Twas no grim gnome or wild spectral roamer
But ancient Homer, I'll take my oath,
That took a notion to leave the ocean
And with agile motion popped onto Howth.

He wore that morning no jewels adorning
His barber-scorning dark locks of hair,
Nor raiment shining, with golden lining
And gems entwining through everywhere;
Nor nice and cosy no shoes with bows he
Wore on his toes, he just let them sprawl.
Oh! let truth be spoken, though gently broken
- Resave the token he wore at all....

Another example was supposed to be a love-poem by Atkinson, who had earned notoriety by his declaration that there was nothing written in Irish which was not either 'silly or indecent'. But the piece was directed more at the 'west-British' snobs of the period than at Atkinson. It was entitled 'Lucinda'.

Oh! lovely Lucy Lanigan, my distant twinkling star!
She walks in beauty every day through haughty blue Rathgar,
She wears a frock from Chester and a London blouse and hat,
And she owns a British pugdog and a doaty Manxland cat.
Oh! Lucinda!
My beaming, gleaming star,
I would that I were good enough
To dwell in dear Rathgar.

Lucinda's so respectable the only songs she'll sing
Are 'Genevieve', 'They Follow Me' and 'Heaven Bless the King!'
She reads the penny novelettes, the *Leader*, too, she'll scan -
But she shudders at the mention of the horrid *Irishman*.
Oh! Lucinda! (Repeat)

Her pa's a nice old gentleman, he lives beyond the gates
Of Dublin, where his business is, that he may dodge the rates*.
Her ma collects old clothes and tracts for heathens in Hong Kong,
And her brother says 'Bay Jove!' and plays at croquet and ping- pong.
Oh! Lucinda! (Repeat)....

(*In those distant days, Rathmines and Rathgar were outside the jurisdiction of Dublin Corporation).

There was a serious side to these verses as well. Many of them were written during the Boer War, in which Griffith took a special interest because of his recent residence in South Africa and association with the Boers. One of his poems was called 'The Little Black Coffins of Different Sizes'. In the later stages of the War, Boer women and children were rounded up by the British and put into concentration camps where large numbers of them died.

In the Christmas number of the *United Irishman* in 1901, Griffith wrote: 'The good English Christians will sit down to their dinners at ease this Christmas Day. To aid their digestion, I dedicate to them this rough and imperfect translation from Edmond Rostand, the author of *Cyrano de Bergerac*...who had addressed to the children of Europe the *Ballad of Christmas*:

See! the Day comes when Children reign,
For 'tis the day their Prince was borne them,

And lo! the children writhe in pain
And helpless women watch and mourn them!
The little ones of heroes lie
Huddled in fever camps to die;
Their gentle eyes gaze forth in vain -
No sweet old man, toy-bearing, rises
But spectre foul, and in his train
Little black coffins of different sizes!...

Ten Thousand Coffins - 'tis the gift
To Childhood from the British nation.
Oh! Herod from your tomb uplift
Your voice in praise and admiration!
And shall we heedless dance and sing
While coffin-makers' hammers ring?
Or laugh when loud the women's wail
Up from the Pit of Slaughter rises
While down the sobbing old men nail
Little black coffins of different sizes.[54]

Griffith sometimes included humorous nuggets as fillers in his newspapers: 'If a man be a featherless biped, is not a plucked chicken a man?' Or: 'By a striking coincidence the chief witness for the prosecution in the case of the Board of Works versus the Gaelic Athletic Association was named Woodenhead and the police magistrate's decision in favour of the Board was delivered on All Fools' Day'.[55]

When his first child was being baptised, the priest asked Griffith what his name was to be. When he replied 'Nevin', the priest remarked that he had never heard the name before and asked was there a St Nevin. 'I don't know if he was a saint', replied Griffith with a glint in his eye, 'he was a bishop, anyway.'[56]

A libel action by a Limerick parish priest led to the winding up of the *United Irishman* in 1906. After the court case, Griffith remarked angrily to fellow-editor, W.P. Ryan, that the priest in question was the sort of person who would have burned his enemies in the Middle Ages.[57]

Griffith was able to see the humorous side to the serious political

54 Beaslai (ed.), *Songs, Ballads and Recitations*, pp.6-9,14,18-19,20,30.

55 *Sinn Féin*, 30 March 1912; *United Irishman*, 11 April 1903.

56 Ó Lúing, *Ó Gríofa*, p.211.

57 *ibid.*, p.159.

Griffith arriving for a Dáil meeting, 1921

issues of the day. Some six months after the Irish Volunteer movement was set up, under the leadership of Eoin MacNeill, Griffith had the following passage under the heading 'Moral Benefits of Volunteering':

> Sir Edward Carson has assured some Englishwomen that he regards the National Volunteer Movement with a rather favourable eye. It is a moral regenerating factor. Better, he says, these people should come out and drill in the open than maim cattle, burn houses and murder the inoffensive unionists. There is something in this. It is a fact that since Professor MacNeill became a Volunteer he has not assassinated a single person nor even cut off as much as a cow's tail.[58]

Sean-Ghall said of Griffith: 'He had a mind densely packed with quaint anecdotes, odd reminiscences and rich jokes. On holidays, far from the haunts of men, he would be as frolicsome as a child, a madcap boy at that. Then he was chatty, prank-playing and altogether delightful'.[59] He tended to regard prison as a holiday. After the 1916 Rising he was initially incarcerated in Dublin's Richmond Barracks, where his sense of humour did not desert him. He reported the following conversation overheard between two London soldiers on guard duty:

58 *Sinn Féin*, 30 May 1914.

59 Ms. 23,516 NLI.

'Eh, mate! these 'ere blokes aren't 'arf as bad as we were told'.
'Wot are you talking abaht? These 'ere are only the city blokes.
The 'ill tribes 'aven't come in yet'.[60]

Griffith spent the last part of his post-Rising sentence in Reading Jail. Ernest Blythe, a fellow-inmate, wrote to Padraic Colum about Griffith's time there: 'He behaved like the leading spirit in a party of holiday-makers more or less isolated on a ship during a long voyage. He appeared to be out to enjoy himself during his enforced separation from his work'.[61] He organised pastimes and was friendly with everyone. He pretended he was a seer with magical powers of divination. He learned where things were and then 'sensed them out' for the other prisoners who could not find them.

There was what Blythe termed an honest roguery of that kind in him. The inmates kept a jail journal and Griffith wrote a lot for it - mainly exaggerated detective stories mocking the genre and satirical ballads about prison life. He boosted morale in many ways.[62]

On Sunday mornings most of the prisoners went to mass in the chapel and Blythe's task was to have breakfast ready when they came back. One Sunday Griffith slept it out and called Blythe to his cell just as the other prisoners were returning. He got Blythe to fetch the Protestant Bible and sit with him at a table with it open in front of them. When the others came shouting to his cell to ask why he had not gone to mass he replied that he had finished with mass and was taking instructions from Blythe.[63]

Griffith was imprisoned in Gloucester Jail in 1918-19. From there he wrote to his friend Lily Williams about the people of Gloucester: 'Some disappointment, we hear, was occasioned to the citizens when they discovered that the Irish prisoners were white in colour and did not possess tails. But stringent precautions are still observed against the possibility of our breaking out and devouring the children'.[64] Once again he composed ditties about his fellow-internees. The following two limericks relate to Robert Brennan and Sean MacEntee:

Said Rita, 'As you know I hate men, Anne,
I've loathed them since I was ten, Anne.

60 Ó Lúing, *Ó Gríofa*, p.269.

61 Colum, *Griffith*, p.159.

62 Ó Lúing, *op. cit.*, pp.273-4.

63 Colum, *op. cit.*, p.162.

64 Ms. 19,924 NLI.

I would not even wive
With the last man alive
Unless that last man were Bob Brennan.

A committee appointed to see
Who most patient of all men might be,
After searching the globe
Gave 'commended' to Job
And first prize to Sean MacEntee.[65]

Brennan described Griffith as 'easily the most cheerful man amongst the dozen internees' in Gloucester. Many of the prisoners took advantage of their incarceration to study but Griffith insisted on regarding his stay as a holiday and he refused to take prison life seriously. He even played pranks on the bridge-players, who took their games too seriously.[66]

65 Mss in library of late Nevin Griffith, Dublin.

66 Brennan, *Allegiance*, pp.201, 223-4.

Chapter III

Journalist and Acolyte

Literary ability

Arthur Griffith was a journalist. As a propagandist for Irish nationalism, he needed the verbal dexterity to persuade and move his readers. He had no formal literary training yet he had an innate and natural ability to express himself in writing.

This ability was evident from early on. Among his contributions to *Eblana* were poetic parodies, usually in street-ballad form; an essay in praise of James Clarence Mangan; another on 'The Gracchi' of ancient Rome, and one on Sir Richard Steele. In the final number of the journal, the editor awarded first place in literary ability to Griffith, describing him as 'the life and soul of the journal', and commenting that 'the literary excellence of his prose and poetry leaves nothing to be desired'.[1]

The two major literary influences on him were John Mitchel, the Young Irelander, and Jonathan Swift.

> Mitchel's *History of Ireland* is the very best book an Irishman could study. All my life I have worshipped Mitchel. The proud, fiery-hearted, electric-brained, giant-souled Irishman who stood up to the might of the whole British Empire has always been to me the greatest figure we have amongst us. Even in these degenerate days we owe to him more than to any other man. The nation capable of producing a Mitchel can never become the contented slave of the huxtering English.[2]

He was very familiar with Swift's works and liked particularly his ideas on trade and industry. He quoted him in his very first editorial in the *United Irishman*: 'To be perfectly plain, we believe that when Swift wrote to the whole people of Ireland 170 years ago that by the law of

1 Ms. 3493 NLI. Mangan was one of the most well-known 19th-century Irish poets. Steele was an Irish essayist and dramatist of the 17th and 18th century.

2 Ms. 22,293 NLI.

God, of nature and of nations they had a right to be as free a people as the people of England, he wrote common sense.'[3]

Stephen Gwynn was among the first to contend that in literary skill Griffith ranked with Mitchel and even Swift.[4] P.S. O'Hegarty agreed that Griffith 'was the master of a style of political writing which was trenchant, logical and compelling, the most effective style of any Irish political writer after Swift and Mitchel'.[5]

Griffith used to wander in the evenings around the vicinity of St Patrick's Cathedral where Swift had been Dean, collecting ballads and folklore. The discovery of any new story about Swift in the oral tradition of the people particularly delighted him.[6] But there was more than influence and imitation at play, a point well made by F.S.L. Lyons:

> That the *United Irishman* made the impact it did was largely due to the editor himself....Griffith was an inspired journalist who combined style and temper in a way no one else could match. He recalled both the savagery of Swift and the ruggedness of John Mitchel, but to these he added his own intensity and his own intimate knowledge of the political and economic environment about him.[7]

Griffith's impressive style sprang from his mastery of language; his political writing is attractive for its style as well as its content.[8] Mere Columba Butler OSB recorded that George Moore ('the most severe of critics') said to her sister Mary: 'Griffith has the power of putting life into the worn-out English language'.[9] John Chartres praised his skill as a writer with the felicitous phrase, 'His pen ran pearls ready threaded'.[10]

James Stephens had no doubt about Griffith's literary skill. He was astonished at the variety of his input into his newspapers:

> We must have been a difficult lot to collect copy from, and when

3 *United Irishman*, 4 March 1899.

4 Stephen Gwynn, *The Students' History of Ireland* (Dublin, 1925), p.289. Gwynn was a Home Rule MP and historian.

5 O'Hegarty, *Irl. under Union*, p.637.

6 Ulick O'Connor, *A Terrible Beauty is Born* (London, 1975, paperback edition, 1981, cited in notes), pp.24-5.

7 Lyons, *Famine*, p.248.

8 O'Hegarty, *op. cit.*, p.636.

9 *Irish Weekly Independent*, 17 August 1946.

10 Ms. 23,516 NLI.

the necessary matter was not forthcoming, he would write the missing articles himself, and write them much better than anybody else could. His pen was equal to any task that might be set it. He would turn out, with equal ease, an article on Red Hugh O'Donnell, an appreciation of Raftery, a biographical notice, a comic ballad, or a parody of any person whom fate, at that moment, had doomed to his treatment.

His was one of the easiest pens that ever took naturally to ink, and at its best his prose was actually masterly. He was, in my opinion, the greatest journalist working in the English tongue, with an astonishing lucidity of expression, and with a command of all the modes of tender or sarcastic or epigrammatic expression, and always that ample, untroubled simplicity of utterance which ranks him among the modern masters of the English language.[11]

He wrote some of his best passages about places he visited while working in South Africa:

One cannot thoroughly appreciate or understand *The Arabian Nights* until he has visited an Arab city - until he has wandered through the narrow, tortuous streets with palaces towering to the sky, until he has sauntered through the crowded bazaar and watched the tailor and the turner, the jeweller and silversmith and the other deft craftsmen plying their trade....Arab life was not entirely new to most of us, but Zanzibar more vividly recalled Bacboue and Ali Baba to our minds than any other place.

Sometimes we went into the courtyards of the princely merchants, even as the fugitives of the beloved storybook of our childhood were wont to do, and cooled ourselves under his palm-tree; sometimes we mingled with the whirling streams of Arabs, Swahilis, Singhalese, Egyptians, Japanese, Banians and Parsees in the bazaar, and sometimes we explored the narrow, dirty back streets, scarce three feet wide, lit by occasional lanterns....

Somehow, when we had visited the fish-market and the slave-market and a mosque or two and the grave of some great man which our guide warned us not to go too near lest the genii who guarded it might destroy us, we felt we had done enough for our reputations and we sallied into the African Hotel to take our ease....I stayed a moment to glance at the wares of a curio-seller and when I followed my companions in I saw their eyes flashing and their faces flushed. 'Listen, rebel Irelander', said one of them laughing excitedly, 'Kitchener has smashed the Khalifa and killed 20,000 dervishes.

11 Stephens, *Journalist and Statesman*, pp.18-19.

What do you call that?' 'Murder', said I. My companions laughed heartily. They were all either English or Scotch. 'Ah', said one, 'you Irish will never look without bias at what we do. Gentlemen, Gordon is avenged. Hip, hip, hurrah!' And a wild, vengeful cheer broke from the lips of every English and Scotchman there. They were very pleasant fellows, as travelling-companions, but like all Britishers, each had a tiger sleeping in his heart - and the Irish people in the glow of the Saxon smile often are too dazzled to see the beast crouching for a spring.[12]

The following extract would delight a romantic novelist, but it contains Griffith's usual tilt at the English:

> Night and Astarte dimming in her smile the Cross - no dimple on the ocean's silvered face save where the love-singing wind from western heaven kisses it as it passes. Peace breathed upon the waters and our hearts were softened. 'On such a night' - it is better to think Shakespeare than to quote him....
>
> Along the deck comes Fritz and his new wedded wife. How ugly she is! I wonder why the villainously handsome ruffian married her? I wonder if she had known the beautiful scoundrel better would she have married him? Of course she would. He married her for her money, and she married him for his face. This is thinking and arguing like a rascal Englishman, but I cannot help it.
>
> They stand before me. I wish to Hymen they would clear out of my way, and let me gaze upon the moon. She lifts up her face to his, and love makes her beautiful. Her eyes are shining and her lips trembling with her love for this ruffian. My heart weeps for her. I turn my eyes on him half savagely, and lo! a miracle. I knew him a beast - and now he is a god. Transcendently beautiful is his face, divine the light in his eyes, as he kisses the woman by his side. How great must be their happiness! Shall I ever for one instant feel the divine joy of this one-time vilest of men, who loves and is beloved? I gaze entranced at those whom love has transformed. I hear a sound behind me, and instinctively I mutter, 'Is it not beautiful?'
>
> A vulgar laugh and a vulgar Cockney voice: 'What ridiculous fools Fritz and his frau are!'
>
> 'What hideous, ignorant creatures you English are', I say irritably, and the Cockney, with a surprised grin, sheers off to tell his comrades that the Irishman is temporarily insane again.

12 Ms. 22,293 NLI.

For three hours I meditate what the object of the good God was in creating the English, and then, brain-weary, I give it up for ever.[13]

But most of Griffith's prose was polemical in tone and an attack on the English presence in Ireland. Desmond Ryan and C.P. Curran referred to his 'relentless and acid propaganda', in which 'satire and irony...were his habitual weapons'.[14] Ryan caught the flavour of Griffith's aggressiveness:

Down in Fownes St, Dublin, sat the man with a pen as sharp as Mitchel and an eye upon dastards and bellowing slaves to be flayed in the columns of *Sinn Féin.* Sometimes Arthur Griffith flayed the just with the unjust. George Moore was arrested by his fierce and icy words and summed him up as a ram in mind and person because he butted England with admirable persistency in his paper week in week out...[15]

Máire de Buitléir once attended a party in London at which she was the only Irish person present. The conversation turned to Ireland and someone referred to that dangerous movement, Sinn Féin. Another speaker denied it posed any threat and dismissed it as being run by 'a lot of nobodies' with 'only an insignificant weekly leaflet to voice their ideas'. To this the editor of a large English daily newspaper responded: 'I would be very glad to have the man who edits that leaflet on my staff if he would only come over. He has the power of killing his adversaries with the point of his pen'.[16]

In the opening number of his first journal, Griffith made his intentions clear: 'There is a vile, skulking, servile spirit abroad - a lying, dastardly spirit - sometimes disguising itself as a patriotic spirit....We shall strive to exorcise that spirit and to make its harbourers loathsome as leprosy in the eyes of the people'.[17] This singular, uncompromising language was to be reproduced week after week in the years to come.

Pretence, platitudes and hypocrisy were attacked mercilessly:

Cant and humbug are dying hard in Ireland, but it is cheering to know that they are dying. We expect the coming County Council

13 *United Irishman*, 12 May 1900.

14 Ryan, *Sion*, p.45; C.P. Curran, 'Griffith, MacNeill and Pearse', in *Studies*, LV, 217, Spring 1966, p.21.

15 Ryan, *op. cit.*, p.88.

16 Ni Chinnéide, *de Buitléir*, p.67.

17 *United Irishman*, 4 March 1899.

elections to afford a gauge of their vitality....All the old shibboleths and many new ones are heard in the camps of the armies which will meet in confused, if bloodless battle on 6th April. A violent attachment to 'the undying principles of Irish nationality' is being evinced by gentlemen who wear the letters JP as a pigtail and toast the Royal Family and the Empire at their festive gatherings; an ardent desire for the establishment of a Catholic university is exhibited by candidates whose intellectual inability to argue on the matter may be taken as a point in its favour...

Out on this sickening, infamous humbugging of the people! What has Irish nationality, the Union, Home Rule or Catholic higher education to do with the choosing of men to administer honestly and ably so much of the petty affairs of their districts as the Irish Local Government Act...has placed under their control? Will the people - the patient people - be duped into electing ignorant ranters on their cry of Home Rule and a Catholic university?...The reptile press in Ireland is doing its utmost to bewilder and bulldoze the people, to persuade them that great and grave national issues depend on the casting of their votes; but the only issue, other than local ones, before the Co. Council electors is whether they shall call their consciences their own or surrender them again into the keeping of the politicians and exploiters.

We say to the people there are no national issues before them. The elections are of local importance only and local interests should decide them. We ask the people to note how every day the Home Rule press is insulting their manhood by declarations such as that these elections will form 'a test of their fitness for self-government', that 'the *English* people will watch keenly how they conduct themselves', that the return of certain candidates 'will constitute a proof, to the *English* people, of their attachment to Home Rule', and so forth. A plague on the slaves who preach that Irishmen should be influenced in their actions or conduct by English opinion...[18]

Those who idolised the British royal family were frequent targets of Griffith's scathing satire:

The snobs of Dublin were badly sold on Monday. A rumour spread amongst them that the Duke of York would condescend to look in at the Royal Hibernian Academy....They flocked into the Abbey-street temple of art and disturbed by their chattering and rude and vulgar conduct the few decent people in the place. The young man did not pay his expected visit and some of the

18 *United Irishman*, 25 March 1899.

disappointed toadies demanded their admission-fee back. What should be the fate of such savages?[19]

Irony is the scalpel of the satirist and the following passage bristles with it. Entitled 'The Queen's Speech', it is an imaginary address by Queen Victoria:

> My Lords and Gentlemen - I regret to say that my attempt to exterminate and plunder the Dutch Republicans and South Africa has not been successful. Consequently my arrangements for occupying Delgoa Bay and seizing Madagascar - thus securing for me the dominion of the Indian Ocean - are off.
>
> I have been deeply impressed by the fact that my call to the Yeomanry and Volunteers to aid me in hammering Paul* has evoked a response from 6,000 - including the blind and the lame - out of an available force of 190,000 men. When these gallant fellows have been instructed as to which end of a rifle shoots, and have been fully equipped with running-shoes and white flags, they will be sent as near to the front as they can be prodded into going.
>
> I am deeply grieved that a number of my English soldiers have been killed and wounded. Happily, however, my generals have so arranged matters that for every Englishman hit three of my Irish hirelings have fallen. I have no doubt that as long as these helots are available they will be sent to do the fighting and screen my countrymen from harm.[20]
>
> (*Paul Kruger, President of the Transvaal.)

He described Victoria as 'this woman, during whose reign more than four millions of our people have perished of British-made famine, or suffered expatriation, and who now in her dotage is sent amongst us to seek recruits for her battered army'.[21] Her visit in 1900 provoked some of his most devastating prose:

> The British banners and the triumphal arches which the British garrison will float and erect, and which the British police will guard night and day from destruction by the Irish people, represent the loyalty of the vermin who thrive on the decay of the Irish nation....But...the voice of the Irish people will not be heard, save to curse the curs and slaves who hail this woman to our land....The dastards who will hail her know full well that if the power of

19 *United Irishman*, 22 April 1899.

20 *ibid.*, 3 February 1900.

21 *ibid.*, 17 March 1900.

> England was not here to guard them they dare not mock the men of Dublin with their flags and arches for the Famine Queen.
>
> Know, then, freemen of the world, that it is not the people of Ireland but the English garrison of Ireland who will proclaim this woman - this 'virtuous' woman as they call her. What, in God's name, have we got to do with the woman's virtue? We care more about one poor Irish girl driven by British rule to a hideous life and a hideous death than about the most virtuous of English women. To the evicted mother, dying in the ditch, gazing on her sons and daughters, was it sweet to know that though her sons might die accursed in a devil's war on the devil's side, and her daughters become outcasts on the streets, the Queen of England in her castle, arrayed in purple and fine linen, was virtuous!
>
> And because she is virtuous, snivel the crawlers, we should bow before her. Pray, what were the mothers who bore them? Year by year we are robbed of millions of money. We see cattle grazing where men once dwelt - we see the land becoming a wilderness - we hear the wail of the famine-stricken, and the voices of women weeping, and we see the beggar in his rags everywhere.
>
> Our manufactures - they scarce exist - our trade and commerce, let Diogenes light his lamp and find them. The Queen of England is responsible....For all the blood and tears of the past six decades, for the artificial famines, the Exodus and the countless evictions - she is responsible. The men who died for Ireland in prison, in exile, on the scaffold - the poor who perished by famine in the land of plenty - the Queen of England slew them all.[22]

When he came to contemplate the lapsed Irish, those who were capable of a misplaced sympathy with England, he could be merciless. The 1914 *Sinn Féin* editorial, 'The Slave Mind' is a masterly example:

> England is fighting for her life - the same England that we Irish for generations past have charged with all the crimes that one nation can charge against another. We have charged her with the destruction of our national and political institutions, we have charged her with the assassination of our people, we have charged her with the suppression of our trade and commerce, we have charged her with the wasting of our fields and the enforced ignorance that has left us today the most backward people in western Europe. We have professed to hate her. And if the charges we made against her were true, we would be curs if we did not hate her....
>
> Now either our charges against England are true or they are false. If

22 *United Irishman*, 24 March 1900.

they are false, we are a nation of liars, and we deserve all that England has done to us. If they are true, then to affect friendship with England today is mean hypocrisy. Either England is our tyrant or we Irish have slandered and libelled England. Which is the truth?

There is in Ireland a breed of beings which can reconcile heaven and hell.... England is the enemy with them until England gets into serious trouble and then they find something in the character of England's opponent to prevent them doing aught but support England....What, though all Europe, all Asia, all America, all Africa rang with the clang of arms and drank in blood, should Ireland dream of - think of - work for? Her own freedom, her own restoration to the sovereign nationhood the arms of the Volunteers won for her in 1782, and the treachery of envious England struck down when Ireland laid down her arms. Since that time England's most effective garrison in Ireland has not been her soldiery.

It has been mainly the writers of our press and the orators of our platforms whose prudence is cowardice, whose statesmanship is evasion, compromise and surrender, and who, slaves themselves to the menace of English authority or the inducements of English wealth, have bred and fostered in this country that mental and moral obliquity - that slave mind - which has today unfortunate Irishmen dying on foreign battlefields to uphold the power of their country's tyrants, and which has other Irishmen ignorantly prating of Germany as a despotism, while the dried blood of the unarmed men, women and children shot down in the streets of Dublin by England's soldiers is still darkly visible on the doorposts of Bacherlor's Walk.[23]

There were many clashes between Griffith and his rivals. The liveliest was with D.P. Moran, editor of the *Leader* and himself a master of caustic prose. The causes they championed were mostly the same - the Irish language and Irish manufactures in particular - as were the targets of their attack. But Moran was convinced that the Gaelic Irish were the purest and truest Irish, and he pushed the Catholic religion, unlike Griffith. For example, in his 'Prophets of Patriotism' in the *United Irishman* (10 June 1899), Griffith rejected Moran's racial nationalism, his distinction between 'the Pale and the Gael', and accused him of trying to

23 *Sinn Féin*, 19 September 1914. The mention of Batchelor's Walk refers to an incident that occurred after the Irish Volunteers successfully landed a consignment of arms at Howth, Co. Dublin, in late July, 1914. A contingent of British soldiers, sent out to intercept the weapons and who failed to do so, was jeered by a crowd of civilians on its way back into the city. The soldiers opened fire on the crowd, killing three and wounding many more.

'arouse the suspicions and antipathy of the Irishmen of fifty generations against the Irishmen of five'.

Although Griffith welcomed and praised the *Leader* when it first appeared he took Moran to task when he saw fit:

> Our contemporary, the *Leader*, has done some good work in certain directions in Ireland. For this reason we regret the sly, pro-English sentiments which its columns are being used to propagate. Gentlemen like Mr Hodgson Pratt and Mr Robert Elliot are probably very estimable persons, but they are Englishmen; and to find a journal which assures its readers that it is truly Irish, and professes itself to be strenuously opposed to the anglicisation of Irishmen and women, publishing lectures to them on nationality and respectability from the pens of Britishers would be amusing if it were not sad.
>
> Are we never to get rid of humbug in Ireland? Week after week we have this journal denouncing English-speaking Irishmen as mere Britons, while the person who pens the denunciation in the Saxon tongue is as ignorant of the Irish language as any of his Saxon contributors. Last week an article appeared protesting that the *Leader* was a truly national journal, which would, if it could, sever the last link binding Ireland to England. On the next page we find an appeal to the lowest, basest and meanest passion in man - religious bigotry...[24]

Sometimes he worked out his differences with Moran in a light-hearted way. He defended *Pebbles from a Brook*, written by John Eglinton, against attacks made on it in the *Leader*. That journal, he wrote, devoted 'the whole of an angry and alliterative article to the annihilating of the author':

> Here let us pause and inform the Editor of the *Leader* that, whilst admiring his style, we understand perfectly well 'how it is done'. By a careful use of the strongest adjectives to be found in the English language, by never forgetting to call your adversary a scoundrel at the beginning or end (for choice the beginning) of an argument, and by calling in what Pope called 'Apt alliteration's artful aid', you can, without much difficulty, turn out whole pages of *Leader* articles....
>
> In no time at all you will be able to talk about 'concertina cads', 'bumptious bounders' and 'cackling counterjumpers'. Henceforth, you will write of the English tourist as the 'British bounder', and of

24 *United Irishman*, 12 January 1901.

> the dispirited unionist as the 'skulking sourface'. With a courage born of the knowledge that your style is irresistible, you will smite the 'Orange orang-utan', and the 'sniggering Shoneen', the 'cringing Castlehack' and the 'Trinity toadies'. At sight of you the 'prurient prowler' will hide his head, and the 'music-hall mudlark' slink off abashed. We like this kind of writing ourselves, we must admit, but - in moderation.[25]

Moran watched Griffith and Sinn Féin with a careful and critical eye. In 1907 he accused them of claiming a monopoly on Irish self-reliance, an issue Moran asserted he had advocated, along with the name Sinn Féin, before Griffith came on the scene. He charged Sinn Féin with being anti-clerical. He denounced Griffith for urging the people to follow foreign political and economic examples (Hungary in politics and in economics the German Frederick List), and dubbed Sinn Féin 'the Green Hungarian band'. Moran emphasised how few people had the right to vote in Hungary, how powerful its rich landlords were, how poorly paid were its agricultural workers, and that its laws were made by its landed gentry and its civil servants.

Although it was the political methods of the Hungarians that Griffith argued could be applied to Ireland, Moran accused him of condoning the unjust and oppressive policies implemented by the Hungarian leaders in their own country. Griffith left himself open to such criticism because he had over-simplified the comparison between Hungary and Ireland in order to press the idea of a dual monarchy between Britain and Ireland.

The reason for Moran's antipathy was because he saw Griffith as competing for the very audience he himself wished to reach. To Moran, the Sinn Féin movement consisted of 'irresponsible extremists' who refused to be guided by older and wiser elements in the Irish-Ireland movement, and he blamed them for dissuading older nationalists from joining the Gaelic League.[26]

Within a few months of the outbreak of the First World War, Griffith's paper, *Sinn Féin*, was suppressed by Dublin Castle under wartime regulations. So he conceived of the idea of extracting or rewriting sections and articles from other newspapers, and sometimes even from novels, and publishing these together. His new journal, *Scissors and Paste*, was 'a journalisticic *tour de force*', according to Richard Davis who pointed out that opponents of the Vietnam War in many

25 *United Irishman*, 25 May 1901. John Eglinton was the pseudonym of W.K. Magee, a librarian in the National Library of Ireland and a literary critic.

26 Glandon, *Griffith and Advanced-Nationalist Press*, pp.59-61.

countries much later in the century resorted to similar tactics to avoid censorship.[27] When Francis Sheehy-Skeffington learned that Griffith was the editor, he remarked, 'I thought I recognised his style'.

The first number of *Scissors and Paste* contained a leading article entitled 'Ourselves':

> It is high treason for an Irishman if he demands with the sword the same right for his own little country as is being demanded for Belgium or Serbia or Hungary. And at present if he demands it with his pen, his printer's machines will be smashed. So, as long as England is fighting for small nations, Ireland has to resort to *Scissors and Paste*. The English government in Ireland has not yet banned the sale and use of these goods.

The journal lasted from 12 December 1914 until 27 February 1915.

Up to the Easter Rising, nationalists who did not follow the IPP respected Griffith as their leading spokesman. The *Spark*[28] conducted a poll in February 1915, based on the question, 'Who is the Irish nationalist whom Dublin wishes most to honour?' Griffith was the first choice, followed by MacNeill and Alderman Tom Kelly, a longtime Sinn Féin representative on Dublin Corporation. 'The name of Arthur Griffith has been chosen by a majority of readers of the *Spark*.... What Ireland owes to Griffith, to his patriotism, to his self-sacrifice, and to his ability and earnestness, will one day be told. The man's modesty prevents it being known to his contemporaries.'[29]

A measure of Griffith's success as a polemicist may be gauged from the grudging admiration he won from a most formidable opponent. Augustine Birrell was Chief Secretary of Ireland between 1908 and 1916. On one occasion, while informing the cabinet of the dissemination of subversion throughout Ireland by means of newspapers, leaflets and speeches, he described the general character of the weekly *Sinn Féin* as appalling and Griffith as 'an extraordinarily clever journalist'.[30]

27 Richard Davis, *Arthur Griffith* (Dublin, 1976), p.18.

28 A small Dublin weekly paper edited by John Doyle, under the pen-name Edward Dalton, and for which Griffith wrote regularly.

29 *Spark*, 7 March 1915; Ó Lúing, *Ó Gríofa*, pp.256, 261.

30 Leon Ó Bróin, *The Chief Secretary: Augustine Birrell in Ireland* (Connecticut, 1970), p.120.

Devotion to Parnell

Griffith's devotion to Charles Stewart Parnell was beyond doubt. On 28 November 1890, as president of the Leinster Literary Society, he moved a resolution that the Society express complete confidence in Parnell, call on the Irish MPs to support him and 'reject dictation from any English party'. The Society sent an address two weeks later to the electors of North Kilkenny, where there was a by-election, urging them to support Parnell's candidate. In a paper read before the Society on 6 February 1891, Griffith demonstrated from past experience how fatal the influence of priests in politics had been in Ireland and abroad (obviously in the context of the Parnell controversy where the Catholic bishops had come out against him). During the summer of 1891, the Society sent an address of support to Parnell. Its meeting on 9 October adjourned as a mark of respect on his death. The members marched in his funeral procession two days later.[31]

Before Parnell's death, Griffith had done something which showed his fidelity to 'the Chief'. He believed Dublin remained faithful to Parnell (his candidates had lost three by-elections outside of the capital) and he thought that if Parnell himself were to be elected to a seat in Dublin, this would set an example which the rest of the country would follow. One of the Dublin seats was held by T.M. Harrington, who had been in America, had not participated in the disputes surrounding the leadership, and had remained a Parnellite. Griffith visited him and tried to persuade him to resign his seat so that Parnell could stand, but to no avail.[32]

Colum drew attention to the dichotomy in Griffith's thinking which has already been mentioned: he wanted to break the dependence on the fallible leader yet he believed in the avatar[33], attributing almost messianic qualities to Parnell, Rooney and later Eamon de Valera. The following is from an address Griffith gave in 1910:

> In all the political movements that succeeded the Union in Ireland, no institutional rallying centre for the nation was found, and so defeat always meant rout. Ireland found temporary substitutes in great men - having no institutional centre to form round, she formed round an O'Connell or a Parnell, and her safety depended on the man being impervious to the terrorism and cajolery of her enemies, and

31 Ms. 19,935 NLI.

32 Colum, *Griffith*, p.24.

33 *ibid.*, p.26. The avatar in Hindu belief is the incarnation of a deity.

> superior to the jealousies and follies of her friends.
>
> We have seen in our own time the intrigue of England and the jealousies of Irish human nature break a Parnell. Against an institution such intrigues and such follies have less power of destruction, and the conclusion that the study of Irish affairs forces on me is that we cannot successfully defend ourselves until we find and form within ourselves a central point from which we may advance, beyond which, if repulsed, we cannot be driven back. It is obvious that such a centre cannot be a party one - it must be national or it will be ineffective. It must be the centre of minimum agreement.

This passage contained Griffith's 'master-idea', a consensus via 'a minimum of agreement', operating through a collective body, and not dependent on an individual who must have within himself the possibility of downfall.[34]

How did Griffith reconcile his adoration of Parnell with Sinn Féin's campaign against the Irish fondness for dictatorial leaders? As Oliver MacDonagh speculated: 'Perhaps a Dublin working-boy's hero-worship simply lived on, secured like the fly in amber by Parnell's death'. Griffith often used to recall a handshake with the Chief, who was on his way to the election meeting at Creggs where he caught a fatal virus.[35]

Griffith so admired Parnell because he stood up to the English and forced them to treat him as an equal. He believed that from the time of the 16th-century Ulster chieftain, Shane O'Neill, to Parnell's time, Swift and Davis were the only Irishmen that the English really feared. 'Parnell outmatched all her statesmen, outgeneralled all her diplomats', he wrote in *Sinn Féin* (7 October 1911).

Griffith praised Parnell for not believing in a 'union of hearts' with England and quoted him as declaring: 'I do not believe in conciliating the English. Conciliate them to the Day of Judgement and you will not get the breadth of a nail from them'. He felt this attitude justified Parnell retaining his leadership after the divorce scandal. To him the private morals of a politician were of no concern to the electorate.[36]

Another Parnell legacy which was difficult to accommodate was attendance at Westminster. It was a fundamental plank in the Sinn Féin programme that Irish MPs sitting in the British House of Commons gave legitimacy to the Act of Union, and withdrawal from

34 Colum, *Griffith*, pp.102-3.

35 Oliver MacDonagh, *States of Mind: a Study of Anglo-Irish Conflict* (London, 1983), p.61; see also *Ireland: the Union and its Aftermath* (London, 1977), p.77, by the same author.

36 Davis, *Non-Violent Sinn Féin*, pp.103-4.

Westminster was regarded as the vital first step in the struggle for Irish independence. Yet Griffith attempted to explain away Parnell's attendance there.

He argued that the obstructionism practised by Parnell and other Irish MPs in the 1870s, in order to disrupt the work of the House of Commons, was akin to the passive resistance to British rule in Ireland which Sinn Féin preached. He also maintained that Parnell's involvement in Westminster was conditional and that he was prepared to abandon action in the British parliament as soon as he became convinced it was no longer useful.[37]

He interpreted Parnell's action in 1881-2 as an example of this. Gladstone's second Land Bill (1881) placed Parnell in a dilemma. If he supported the measure, he risked losing the support of those in Ireland who would not benefit from the Bill (tenants in arrears with their rents and leaseholders), while if he rejected it, those who stood to gain from the measure (more prosperous tenants) might desert him. So he temporised: he managed to get himself expelled from the House of Commons so that he would not have to vote on the Bill, and he managed to get himself arrested in Ireland for making a controversial speech.

Griffith was in no doubt as to Parnell's intentions: 'Parnell proposed to his followers to abandon the British House of Commons altogether and, following the Hungarian precedent, return to Ireland and carry on the Home Rule government *de jure*. His parliamentary followers refused to follow him - they held that they would gain Home Rule quicker by action in Westminster - and they are there still, and Parnell is dead'.[38] While Griffith's contention here hardly corresponds with the facts, it did enable him to include Parnell among Sinn Féin's forerunners.

When rejected by the majority of the IPP after the divorce case, Parnell turned to the Fenians. This showed the true Parnell to be an opponent of ultimate action at Westminster, Griffith believed. So, the Chief could be claimed as a patron saint of subsequent Sinn Féin which repudiated attendance at Westminster. 'At the same time, the realisation that his hero...had been willing to try every means in the Home Rule struggle may have encouraged the tactical flexibility discernible in Griffith's later career', Davis maintained with good reason.[39]

The memory of Ireland's 'uncrowned king' remained with Griffith

37 Mac Donagh, *States*, pp.61-2.

38 *Sinn Féin*, 29 June 1907.

39 Davis, *Arthur Griffith*, pp.5-6; the whole question of Parnell's influence on Sinn Féin is examined in depth in Davis, *Non-Violent Sinn Féin*, pp.99-110.

almost to the end of his life. In May 1917, when Sinn Féin was attracting more and more support, he published in *Nationality* short didactic paragraphs entitled 'What Parnell said'. The following month he wrote:

> Twenty-seven years ago I attended a meeting in the Leinster Hall, Dublin, at which the members of the Irish Parliamentary Party pledged themselves unanimously to support Parnell as leader of the Irish Party. Ten days later, the men who spoke thus in Dublin were clamouring in London for Parnell's resignation. The men who spoke in the Leinster Hall, Dublin, on that night spoke sincerely.
>
> What evil miracle happened within a week to make them forswear all they had said? An English statesman wrote them a letter telling them they must choose between him and the Irish leader to whom they had pledged themselves at the Leinster Hall. Parnell had committed a moral offence. Had the people of Ireland deposed him for that offence the people of Ireland would have been within their right. But when his party, having condoned the offence and pledged him fealty, deposed him at the request of an Englishman they killed forever Parliamentarianism as a possible effective policy for Ireland. It was all over with Parliamentarianism as a policy, but it took a quarter of a century for the bulk of the people of Ireland to realise the fact...

William T. Cosgrave was the Sinn Féin candidate in the Kilkenny by-election in mid-1917. During the campaign, strangers interested in the new movement were constantly calling at 6, Harcourt St, Dublin, Sinn Féin headquarters. Griffith was recalled looking very happy standing outside the counter of his office at No.6, in the middle of a group of country people, and saying: 'Reports are excellent. The country people are with us. The cities and towns stood by Parnell. We lost in the country districts. Now that we have the support of the country districts the result is certain'.[40]

Nationality continued to have references to Parnell for some time but after February 1918 he ceased to be featured in its columns. However, Griffith returned to him again at the height of the Anglo-Irish War in 1920. The British Prime Minister, Lloyd George, in a speech at Caernarvon, declared he at no time saw anything from Griffith protesting at the killings in Ireland and he warned of the dangers if Ireland were granted either a republic or Dominion Home Rule (as H.H. Asquith had recommended). In the course of his reply, Griffith said: 'This day twenty-nine years ago I followed the coffin of Charles

40 Ms. 22,293 NLI.

Stewart Parnell to its tomb. Callous and short-sighted politicians thought on that day that it was the Irish nation they had struck dead'.[41]

T.M. Healy had been a Home Rule MP for many years and was one of Parnell's bitterest critics at the time of the divorce scandal and leadership crisis. In 1922, there was a prospect that he would be Governor-General of the newly-independent Irish Free State. Shortly before Griffith's death, Oliver Gogarty has recorded him as saying confidentially to Gogarty himself: 'I don't want Healy; he betrayed Parnell'.[42] Griffith remained a faithful follower of 'Avondale's proud leader' to the end.

41 Ms. 22,293 NLI

42 Gogarty, *Sackville Street*, p.97.

Chapter IV

Ireland, Ireland Over All

Primary allegiance

There are many testimonies to Griffith's indifference to material wealth and to his modest, hard-working life in the cause of Irish nationalism. His first organisation, Cumann na nGaedheal, was well described by O'Hegarty, one of its members:

> ...it recruited few but people of good character, good intelligence and sober. There was nothing in its proceedings to attract the idler or the seeker after cheap enjoyment; its intelligence content was high, and members cheerfully gave up their evenings and weekends to forwarding all sorts of national activities. It was a sober and a sparsely smoking movement, very much in earnest, and rather puritanical, which was one of its great strengths....
>
> Drink was discouraged because it ruined the character, and tobacco because it paid duty to the British Exchequer. When either was availed of, it was a point of honour not to drink foreign drinks, and Gallagher's tobacco was preferred to any of the English brands....In everything it was studied how best to advance Ireland.[1]

During a dispute Griffith had with W.B. Yeats[2] the poet defined a nationalist as one 'who is prepared to give up a great deal that he may preserve to his country whatever part of her possessions he is best fitted to guard'. Griffith rejected such a definition as inadequate: 'He who is prepared to give up a great deal for his country is no doubt a good man, but unless he is prepared to give up all, we do not deem him a nationalist'.[3]

Griffith remained poor all his life and turned down offers of power, position or money. He had reached middle age before he could afford to marry. As soon as a few of his close friends heard he was going to get

1 O'Hegarty, *Irl. under Union*, p.640.

2 It was over J.M. Synge's play, *The Shadow of the Glen*, in 1903. See Part V, Chapter II below.

3 *United Irishman*, 10 October 1903, 17 October 1903.

married, they formed a secret plan to present him and his wife with a house. 'Be sure you have a legal document drawn up in such a way that he will not be able to sell it, otherwise he and his good lady will be in some back tenement room before long', was what Sean-Ghall advised the others.

A few months later, Griffith broached this matter with Sean-Ghall, telling him he believed he and Walter Cole were 'at the bottom of this plot. I have the best girl in the world as a wife; we would be happy anywhere. If I had the money that was given for this house I could put it into the paper and so help forward the movement. It is a shame tying me up so'. Sean-Ghall replied: 'Well, Dan, we did so because we knew your utter selflessness. We wished to see your noble wife in a house and in a neighbourhood worthy of her. You did not care where you lived. Now, as always, you regarded yourself as nothing'. To which Griffith responded: 'You are a bachelor, Sean, you know nothing of conjugal felicity. "Stone walls do not a prison make nor iron bars a cage"'.[4]

'Poor Dan could never make money!', his widow told Séan Ó Lúing.[5] His refusal of an American editorship has already been mentioned, as has his rejection of a ministerial salary.[6] When his first child was born, Sean-Ghall told of receiving a telegram from him which read: 'Send me five pounds. You will never get it back'.[7]

At a private session on 17 June 1919, Dáil Éireann received a directive from its departing President, de Valera, who was going to America, appointing Griffith as Deputy-President, and recommending that 'the Deputy-President should be requested by the cabinet to accept his salary, as in effect he will be giving all his time to the work'.[8] Griffith still refused to draw any Dáil salary.

He ran his various newspapers on a minimum of capital. After the death of William Rooney he carried on the *United Irishman* virtually alone. Oliver Gogarty said he regarded his body 'merely as an indispensable engine of communication and beyond that he had little respect for it'.[9]

4 Ms. 23,516 NLI.

5 Interview with Seán Ó Lúing, Dublin, 18 April 1995.

6 Ms. 23,516 NLI. *Evening Herald*, 20 November 1991.

7 Ó Briain statement, 6 September 1973, in library of late Nevin Griffith, Dublin.

8 *Dáil Éireann: Minutes of Proceedings of First Parliament of Republic of Ireland 1919-21* (Dublin, n.d.), p.112.

9 O'Connor, *Gogarty*, p.101.

Seamus MacManus remembered Griffith as editor of the *United Irishman*:

> If I live for another few lifetimes, never can I forget the Griffith of those difficult days. It is hardly believable now, but often then this man, who could have commanded the best-paid post in journalism, I saw in the dirty little hole that was his 'office' in Fownes St...saw him there at work with toes showing through broken shoes, elbows out of his faded jacket, frayed at coat cuffs, ragged at trouser ends, working twelve hours a day, and sometimes sixteen, eighteen, twenty hours - sustained by an absorbing passion for his country. And these were hard-labouring days, not a few of when he went not out for a meal - because he had not the price.[10]

A letter has survived from Griffith to Patrick MacManus in Argentina (it is undated but the year was probably 1911) which gives further insight into the difficulties he experienced conducting his newspapers. Griffith wrote that the proposed Home Rule Bill had given the IPP a new lease of life and that this had reacted on Sinn Féin. He could not keep the paper going much longer as great sacrifices had been required for the previous eighteen months.

However, he was optimistic for the future of Sinn Féin if it could survive until the Bill went through or was rejected. The weekly loss of the paper was small but the legacy of debt from the *Sinn Féin* daily threatened to submerge it.

He thought that £200 would save the paper. He told how his house was purchased three months previously for £300 and offered this as security for a loan of £200 which he explained he could not try to repay for at least three years. The worst crisis in the history of the paper faced him, he concluded.[11]

The Guardian Bank was a cooperative bank in Dublin which accommodated small businesses. In 1910-11, Griffith was a regular Friday caller there. He got a loan of £25 or £30 to be repaid the following week. This was needed for weekend expenses and until he collected from his advertisers.

He always repaid the amount borrowed. Being more secure by 1912, he marked the last transaction by saying to the bank secretary with whom he had been dealing: 'I am glad to have met a businessman that is so straightforward as never to ask me to sign a paper'. The secretary

10 *Irish Press*, 18 August 1947.

11 Ms. 18,578 NLI.

replied: 'I know by a man's look whether he can be trusted or not, and I knew that we would never be at a loss through you'.[12]

Griffith had founded Sinn Féin and nurtured it for many years but at its annual convention in October 1917, he stepped down as its President in favour of de Valera.[13] Piaras Béaslaí paid tribute to him for this:

> For many years he had toiled in poverty and obscurity, giving the best work of his brain to the cause of Ireland. His ideas had prevailed, and at the very time when he saw the country converted to the Sinn Féin policy, of which he was the pioneer, he surrendered the leadership to a new, almost unknown man in order to avoid any cleavage in the national ranks. His self-abnegation will be all the more appreciated when it is pointed out that in the case of a contest he would certainly have defeated de Valera, as was proved by the results of the election of an Executive Council, when Griffith's supporters headed the poll and the IRB candidates were either defeated or came in at the foot of the list.[14]

Robert Brennan recounted the following incident from his sojourn with Griffith in Gloucester Jail in 1918-19. Brennan expressed his anger about Darrell Figgis's *The Economic Case for Irish Independence*, which had been published in Ireland, because it was plagiarised from Griffith's newspaper articles. Griffith's comment was that the book was not bad. When Brennan complained aloud to another cellmate, Griffith said: 'Well, don't you think it is good to see someone getting the public to pay for it?'

> It was not merely his partiality for Figgis that was exhibited in this attitude. He was most unselfish and he never cared who got the credit if the work was done. He actually shunned personal publicity....During all his adult years, except for the last few, he slaved for four days a week at his paper which, for a long time, he not merely wrote, but set up as well.[15]

Frank O'Connor referred to Griffith's 'lifetime of impoverished integrity', and created a memorable image of him as he was about to

12 Colum, *Griffith*, p.103.

13 The organisation had changed and become considerably larger by that time. See below, Part II, Chapter IV.

14 Piaras Béaslaí, *Michael Collins and the Making of a New Ireland* (Dublin, 1926), Volume I, pp. 172-3.

15 Brennan, *Allegiance*, pp.206-7.

make the most important speech of his life - that which called on the Dáil to accept the Treaty:

> Griffith moves the ratification of the Treaty; the little, cool, stolid journalist who laid it down in penny papers that hardly anyone bought. It was the occasion of his life. Had he been a dramatic type he could have told them of many days and nights of desperation, ignored by England and Ireland, listening in restaurants to young men chattering and laughing while his diligent, humourless mind pursued its endless train of thought. He could have told them of his poverty and of those offers which would have made a rich man of him had he chosen to accept them. But he had no time for passion, for heroics or self-pity. A big man from the heart out, this Mr Griffith, with his granite face, his papers, his orderly, dispassionate mind.[16]

To de Vere White, Griffith left behind him 'an unmatched record of selfless devotion to his country', while O'Hegarty declared that 'his whole being was single-minded patriotism, and to the service of his country his life was devoted'.[17] But it was Sean-Ghall who paid the warmest tribute, in a beautiful passage imbued with the love of deep friendship:

> To die daily, even hourly, for your country; to dwell in the slums when you might have lived in the light, laughing places of the world; to go clad as the very poor are clad when purple and fine linen might have been yours; to eat dry bread, and not much of that, when you might have feasted full; to act thus, not for one year, nor for ten, but for more than a generation - that is heroism of which few but God's great are capable, and that was the heroism of Arthur Griffith.[18]

Death

Although Arthur Griffith had worked hard and lived frugally all his life he had enjoyed very good health and was an avid walker and swimmer. Yet he was relatively young, only 51, when he died on 12 August 1922. How did this happen? How does one account for the apparent rapid decline in his health so swiftly followed by death? One reason must be that he spent half of the last six years of his life in various prisons - Wandsworth, Reading, Gloucester and Mountjoy.

16 O'Connor, *Collins*, p.147.

17 de Vere White, *O'Higgins*, p.27; O'Hegarty, *Irl. since Union*, p.636.

18 *Arthur Griffith, Michael Collins: Commemorative Booklet* (Dublin, n.d.), p.12.

After the Easter Rising he spent some time in solitary confinement in Wandsworth before being transferred to Reading, a low-lying, unhealthy place with restricted exercise yards. The prisoners had a number of daily chores to perform: sweep floors, wash dishes, clean tables and keep cells in order. They were up at seven, breakfasted at seven forty-five, exercised in a yard from ten-thirty until midday, then had dinner, were sent out into another yard from two till five, then had tea and, daylight permitting, were allowed out into a yard again for an hour or so. Lights were extinguished at ten. They could write two letters and receive one food parcel per week. The food was poor and scarce. The prison became very cold in winter and, because of the lack of space and air, many prisoners became ill. Thick, smoky fog was commonplace around the prison.[19]

Griffith experienced many hardships in Gloucester Jail from May 1918 to March 1919. The prisoners often received private letters weeks after they were sent because the authorities kept them back, and all letters to and from prisoners were examined and censored. Some books sent to Griffith he never got. He told an *Irish Independent* reporter shortly after his release that what troubled him most was the lack of air. There were only two small yards for exercising.

Gloucester was a gloomy place and some prisoners suffered from depression. Standards of hygiene were poor as evidenced by the practice of cooking food in the toilet area. The terrible 'flu epidemic of 1919 hit the Gloucester prisoners hard. 'The air of the prison stank with the odour of the plague', was how one internee described it. Griffith was among those stricken by the 'flu.

During the Anglo-Irish War he was under close surveillance. This affected his family, which worried him greatly. Little Ita used to walk to school past a police barracks where she would be joined by a friendly policeman who accompanied her the rest of the way. He chatted to her amicably. She nicknamed him 'Saucepan' because he had asked her how to spell that word.

One day at home she mentioned 'Saucepan'. Her mother quizzed her about him. It turned out that he was asking about her father - had he spent the previous night at home or did she know where he was. From then on she went by tram and the conductor was asked to make sure she did not get off until she was at the school gates.[20]

For the three months before his last arrest, Griffith did not sleep at home but in various offices and friends' houses. From the late summer

19 Ó Lúing, *Ó Gríofa*, pp.271-2.

20 Interview with Mrs Ita Gray, Dublin, 22 August 1995.

of 1920 his house was raided several times a week and on one occasion his son was roughly treated. Griffith dreaded the nervous shock it would be to his children to be caught up in the violence of his arrest.[21]

His final period of incarceration was in Mountjoy for seven months, ending in June 1921. His daughter recalled vividly the circumstances of his arrest after 'bloody Sunday'. She remembered looking out of her bedroom window and seeing him tied to a tree in their front garden while the Black and Tans ransacked the house; one of them searched her room, ripping her mattress with a bayonet and even checking out the chimney (he told her he was looking for Santa Claus). She remembered her worried mother asking where they were taking him and the reply: 'To be hanged or shot, which he jolly well deserves'. That was all she recalled. She collapsed and was very ill for some time.[22]

Leading the Treaty delegation in London was an enormous responsibility. After seven plenary sessions, the meetings took the form of subconferences. The total number of subconference meetings attended by the individual Irish delegates was as follows: Griffith twenty-two, Collins nineteen, Robert Barton three, George Gavan Duffy two, Duggan two. Nine informal meetings were held between the Irish representatives and Tom Jones, assistant-secretary to the British cabinet. Collins attended two, Duggan three and Griffith all nine.[23]

One of Collins's biographers, Rex Taylor, revealed that during the conference Griffith was unwell. On 17 November, Collins wrote to his friend, John O'Kane: 'Griffith is a good man. Only, I fear, much the worse for the strain of a life spent in toil and trouble'. Most of the responsibility was on the shoulders of Griffith and Collins as the main negotiators. In another letter to O'Kane (undated), Collins wrote: 'Griffith and I had a lonely meeting - a house almost empty of customers - and talked and talked. He confessed that he was far from well and asked me to assume leadership of our party even if unofficial....I agreed. Griffith is in poor health and further burdens will do no more than greatly exaggerate his condition'.[24]

'The first thing I noticed in London was his hair turning white', Mrs Griffith wrote to her sister just after the signing of the Treaty.[25] Sean

21 Colum, *Griffith*, p.238.

22 Mrs Gray interview.

23 Rex Taylor, *Michael Collins* (London, 1958), pp.161-2.

24 *ibid.*, pp.166, 170. O'Kane was an Irish businessman then living in the Hampstead area of London.

25 Letter reproduced in Ó Lúing, *Ó Gríofa*, facing p.385.

Milroy saw Griffith in Hans Place (where most of the Irish Treaty delegation resided) on the morning after the signing. He wrote: 'There seemed to be an air of immeasurable weariness about him. He looked to me like a man who had expended his last ounce of energy in some titanic struggle'.[26] When Griffith got off the boat in Dun Laoghaire that evening there was to be no fanfare welcoming him home but instead a peremptory summons to an urgent cabinet meeting. After the exhausting experience in London, further wrangles lay ahead. His children did not see him for three more days.[27]

Back in Dublin he revisited familiar haunts and renewed acquaintance with old comrades. On one occasion he saw an old friend and beckoned him over to where they normally used to sit. But this man was opposed to the Treaty and there was very little conversation between them. This was how Colum commented on the incident:

> But so hurt was Arthur Griffith that he spoke of the estrangement to Mrs Griffith at a time when public affairs were overwhelming. For all his outside imperturbability, Arthur Griffith was sensitive in matters of friendship; he was deeply attached to people in his circle, and the defection of this or that one meant something gone out of his life. In accounting for his later debilitation, one has to include the psychological effect of separation from certain friends, the discovery of public enmity where he looked for supporting friendliness, with the burdensome nights and days that the establishment of an opposed government exacted.[28]

After his election as President of the Dáil on 10 January, difficulties and problems began to pile thick and fast upon him, until they weakened his strength, broke his heart and hastened his death, Ó Lúing declared. People who had worked with him and helped him for years tried to hinder him in every way possible.[29] His wife bore witness to his inexorable deterioration:

> I was the one person who saw his death coming. For four months beforehand I had to watch him declining day by day and he as quiet and accepting in the face of death as he had been during his life....The poor man, he was tortured and tormented to the edge of the grave by people who were once his friends, if they are to be believed. I am glad

26 Colum, *Griffith*, p.306.

27 *ibid.*, p.309.

28 *ibid.*, pp.309-10.

29 Ó Lúing, *Ó Gríofa*, p.394.

> that he escaped from them in the end. As long as I live I will see before me that poor, exhausted face...[30]

It really oppressed him to hear himself referred to as a 'traitor' and as 'an amateur diplomat that Lloyd George had twisted round his finger'. Younger colleagues, who never had occasion to condemn political trimmers, were not bothered by such denunciations. One such colleague, Ernest Blythe, wrote: 'Those of us who were younger and came into prominence after the Treaty could hear ourselves described as murderers and traitors without feeling more perturbed than if we had been told that the weather forecast about the anticyclone had turned out to be incorrect'.[31]

It weighed heavily that his intentions were misinterpreted. 'He always did his best and was killed (a slow death), broken-hearted that anyone could misconstrue his motives', his widow wrote to a friend a few months after his death.[32] What killed Griffith, according to Oliver Gogarty, was 'envy and jealousy and calumny, which can be deadlier than prussic acid, and, what is more mortal to a martyr, ingratitude. He had not the armour with which I, for one, was invested, be it irony or motley. His sincerity was a bow and his belief an arrow which, if deflected, slew his faith'.[33]

Gearóid Ó Lochlainn recorded how deeply troubled he was by the Treaty split and how his oppression grew as things got worse. He felt a republic had been achieved except in name only. The rebellion broke his heart and the Civil War destroyed his health. He feared the anti-Treaty militants were destroying the country's chances, that this would enable the English to come back and, if they did, they would never let go. 'It cut him to the marrow that it was a section of our own people that was endangering our freedom', Ó Lochlainn wrote.[34] It seemed as if the traditional British propaganda that the Irish were not fit to govern themselves was being justified.

A delegation of women was received by Griffith, Collins and Cosgrave at Government Buildings on 1 July, a few days after the fighting had started. According to Louie Bennett, who was part of the

30 Ó Lúing, *Ó Gríofa*, p.403.

31 Colum, *Griffith*, p.342.

32 Ms. 8411 NLI.

33 Gogarty, *Sackville St*, p.188.

34 Ms. 23,516 NLI. Translated by the writer. Ó Lochlainn was private secretary to Griffith while he was President of the Dáil.

women's group, 'Griffith was utterly depressed; an old, broken man'.[35] Such was the extent of the calamity for him.

O'Hegarty, who spoke to Griffith two days after the attack on the Four Courts began, found him very unwell and said it was clear he was sick in body and soul. He sat, heartbroken, writing now and then, with none of the humour or laughter left in him, but like someone waiting for what could not be avoided.

Blythe informed Ó Lúing that Griffith's health was not good at any time after the attack on the Four Courts. He remembered his cabinet colleagues asked Griffith to draft a manifesto, but he was not at all his usual skilful self and they could not accept the draft.[36]

From the outbreak of civil war, Griffith had to stay in Government Buildings for his own security. He had to traverse his native city with an official guard, something that greatly disturbed him. He had to harden his heart and give orders against people who had been his close friends for years. There was no escape from his confinement - no healthy ramble through the Wicklow hills or swim in Dublin Bay. He was suffering from insomnia. He was under the care of Gogarty, who urged him to take a break beside the sea, as he was worn out. But he refused, saying he had too much work to do.[37]

Griffith was greatly weakened in July by a bout of 'flu followed by a severe attack of tonsillitis. In August Gogarty decided that where he was staying was totally inappropriate for a sick man. 'You're going to be decorated for the first time in your life with carpet slippers', he told Griffith and he got General Headquarters' permission to move him to the Sisters of Charity's private nursing-home at 96 Lower Leeson Street.

Complete rest was prescribed. Even then he insisted on carrying out some official duties. 'A man like Arthur Griffith looks upon disease or illness as a nuisance and something to be shaken off as we shake off an importunate bore', Gogarty observed. On the morning of 12 August Gogarty was called to the nursing-home urgently. When he got there Griffith was already dead. He had collapsed on the landing outside his room while bending down to tie his lace. The cause of death was cerebral haemorrhage.[38]

James Stephens captured superbly the mood of shock induced by his death:

35 Ward, *Gonne*, p.133.

36 Ó Lúing, *Ó Gríofa*, pp.398-9.

37 *ibid.*, pp.399-400; Colum, *Griffith*, pp.360, 373.

38 Gogarty, *Sackville St*, pp.185-8; Lyons, *Gogarty*, p.123.

> Arthur Griffith could die! Not one person believed Arthur Griffith could die, not one speculated an instant on an event that seemed as remote as any event could seem. And when the information stabbed up at the mind from the posters in the street, men halted almost as though the blow had been a physical one, and resuming their paths, they went bewildered.[39]

Terence de Vere White considered it 'a cruel trick of fate' that Griffith should have been allowed reach his goal and then die in the midst of a civil war.[40] But Stephens did not think so, as will be clear from the following moving passage he wrote shortly after Griffith's death:

> He had lived without any fuss, and so he died - noiselessly, uncomplainingly, undiminished. How many thousands and hundreds of thousands have gone before him whose hopes were set in the star that he had reached, and to attain which they gave their all! He had not only seen the longed-for, the despaired-of land, he had touched it and become its national symbol.
>
> All who looked on him saw the President of Ireland, and when he looked on himself, if only in a glass, he saw the first citizen of his nation. He saw a free Ireland, which he had helped to free, and which had no more to free except the future, that is never fearful.
>
> The future that is always to be hoped for, which is the eternal springtime in the mind of man. To him there can never come the anguish that draws at last on men and statesmen, when they discover that the times have gone beyond them and that their usefulness is at an end, for he has vanished in full activity and on the very consummation of his work.[41]

39 Stephens, *Journalist and Statesman*, p.24.

40 *Irish Times*, 14 October 1972.

41 Stephens, *op. cit.*, pp.25-6.

Part II

The Great Debate:

Independence and how to Achieve it

'Independence, said Davis, was the goal
of the national movement; but the achievement
of this ideal was not an end in itself, but the all
important means for the building up
of a new, united and happier country.
For this reason Davis, like Tone before him,
cared little for the political abstractions
that divide.'

Nicholas Mansergh, The Irish Question, p.250.

Chapter I

Theory: Physical Force or Passive Resistance?

Introduction

How was Ireland to achieve its freedom and, having achieved it, what form of government should the country adopt? Was physical force the way forward or was passive resistance the better way? Which would be the more effective form of government for the country - a republic or a dual monarchy? These were the questions which dominated Arthur Griffith's public life and writings from the turn of the century to the day of his death.

For most of Griffith's life the debate was waged at a theoretical level. Those engaging in the debate until 1916 were a minority to whom most of the people of Ireland paid little attention. But after the Rising the debate took on a greater urgency as support progressively shifted away from the IPP and Home Rule. With the annihilation of the IPP in the 1918 general election the debate moved firmly into the realm of reality and did not become resolved until the tragedy of the Civil War in 1922-23, if even then.

Griffith did not initiate this debate. It had raged for a hundred years before he became active in nationalist politics. But he gave it a new dimension. More than that, his theories were put into practice, although not in the way he had envisaged.

It is necessary to examine the physical force/passive resistance, dual monarchy/republic debate. Although closely related and overlapping issues, they will be treated separately. It is also necessary to consider Griffith's interaction with the foremost organisation to advocate a republic and physical force in his lifetime, the Irish Republican Brotherhood (after 1916 the IRB and the Volunteers). His attitude to and position after the 1916 Rising, and especially during the independence struggle between 1919 and 1921, as he strove to maintain his original policy, will also be explored.

Griffith was sceptical about the efficacy of force to achieve political ends. That much is clear from his public activity, from his writing and from what has been written about him. As M.Q. Sibley wrote many years later, he 'saw in the non-violent movement in Hungary a model which he hoped his countrymen would emulate in their struggle with Britain'[1]. What is not immediately clear, however, is whether he was opposed to its use on practical rather than principled grounds (believing it justifiable in certain circumstances) or whether he was a convinced pacifist, opposed to using violent means under any conditions.

From Physical-Force Republican to Passive Resister?

When Griffith began his career as a publicist and propagandist on behalf of Irish nationalism in 1899, the choice facing him and others at the time was between constitutionalism, as exemplified by the IPP, and physical force, as represented by the IRB. His own reading reflected this dichotomy in Irish history. He had read and admired the 18th-century Protestant patriots, Jonathan Swift, Henry Grattan and Henry Flood. This reading would have drawn him towards constitutional action. But he also admired Wolfe Tone and the United Irishmen, Robert Emmet, and the Young Irelanders. His problem was how to accommodate the constitutional and violent approaches.

He named his first paper the *United Irishman* associating himself immediately with the Young Irelander, John Mitchel, who had a journal of the same name in the 1840s, and with Wolfe Tone, the father of Irish republicanism and one of the founders of the United Irishmen in the 1790s. In his first editorial, Griffith declared: 'Lest there might be a doubt in any mind, we will say that we accept the nationalism of '98, '48 and '67 as the true nationalism and Grattan's cry of "Live Ireland - perish the Empire!" as the watchword of patriotism'.[2]

The reference to the dates of republican risings seemed to herald Griffith's adherence to the physical-force tradition. But to link Grattan with this tradition in the same sentence introduced an ambiguity into his historical attitudes and political philosophy. Grattan called for, and achieved in 1782, legislative independence for the Irish parliament but with the common Crown linking the two islands, and he condemned the physical-force republicanism of his young contemporary, Tone. The latter grew to despise 'Grattan's parliament' and died in the effort to

1 M.Q. Sibley (ed.), *The Quiet Battle: Writings on the Theory and Practice of Non-Violent Resistance* (New York, 1963), p.138. This book printed a large extract from *The Resurrection of Hungary* in which Griffith described the passive-resistance tactics of the Hungarians under Francis Deak against Austrian rule from 1849 to 1866.

2 *United Irishman*, 4 March 1899.

destroy it. Thus two opposing figures of late 18th-century Ireland were telescoped by Griffith's view of history.[3]

He believed that the attempt to pursue parliamentary means alone had been degraded since the fall of Parnell, and he was an unrelenting critic of the IPP. Yet he was flexible in that first editorial; he was certainly not absolutely in favour of physical force and against constitutional means. In fact a compromise might have been worked out but for the unfortunate clash in 1900 in the South Mayo by-election. Michael Davitt had resigned his parliamentary seat in South Mayo in protest at Britain's part in the Boer War. Griffith and Rooney put forward a protest candidate, the IRB man John MacBride, who was fighting on the side of the Boers at the time.

The newly-reunited IPP could have given him a free run, as his election would have been declared invalid, and the party could then have taken the seat. Instead it used the might of its constituency organisation, the United Irish League, to crush the MacBride challenge. Cooperation did occur on the Transvaal Committee which campaigned against recruitment to the British army and organised demonstrations against the Boer War, and on which Griffith and Maud Gonne sat, as well as the MPs, William Redmond and T.D. Sullivan.[4]

The Boer War (1899-1902) taught Griffith that it would be madness for a small nation to go to war against a powerful adversary.[5] He expressed this sentiment memorably and emphatically: 'We believe that the four-and-a-quarter millions of unarmed people in Ireland would be no match in the field for the British Empire. If we did not believe so, as firmly as we believe that the eighty Irishmen in the British House of Commons are no match for the six hundred Britishers opposed to them, our proper residence would be a padded cell'.[6]

The ambivalence as to the means to be adopted to achieve independence may be seen in Cumann na nGaedheal. It had no clearly agreed policy. Its aims were to examine the resources of Ireland and support Irish industry; to study and teach Irish history, language, music and art; to encourage Irish games and characteristics, and to discourage anything that would spread English influence in Ireland. Members had to promise 'to aid to the best of their ability in restoring Ireland to her former position of sovereign independence', but whether that meant the

3 Donal McCartney, 'The political use of history in the work of Arthur Griffith', in *Journal of Contemporary History*, VIII (January, 1973), pp.6-7.

4 Davis, *Arthur Griffith*, pp.7-8.

5 Ó Lúing, *Ó Gríofa*, p.80.

6 *United Irishman*, 30 March 1901.

independence of Grattan's parliament under a shared monarch with Britain, or the republic sought by the United Irishmen, Young Irelanders and Fenians was not specified.[7]

There have been two schools of thought among historians concerning Griffith's attitude to physical force. The majority have held that his opposition to its use was on practical grounds rather than on grounds of principle, and that he did not rule it out completely. However, a minority have suggested that he was a convinced pacifist to whom violence was abhorrent in all circumstances.

R.M. Henry was the first to put forward the former viewpoint. He maintained that the lesson Griffith drew from the armed risings of 1848 and 1867 was that Irish independence could not be won by force. Henry saw Sinn Féin as different from Young Ireland and the Fenians in that it renounced as a matter of practical politics the use of physical force to achieve its ends, while still holding that a nation subjected against its will by another nation was justified in regaining its independence in any way it could, including resort to force. Griffith's renunciation of physical force differed from O'Connell's, observed Henry, in that although Griffith believed that it was not the practical way to win Irish freedom, he never denied that it was a legitimate way to secure national rights.[8]

George A. Lyons, writing shortly after Griffith's death, was adamant that he was no pacifist. He saw Griffith's policy as aiming to use all the energies and resources of the Irish people. He recalled him as often saying that he would not subscribe to O'Connell's doctrine and would never advise the people to renounce force under any circumstances. Though a man of peace, he never feared war, Lyons wrote.[9] Many other commentators have taken the same view of Griffith's position.[10]

On the other hand, Frank Pakenham has contended that Griffith was widely regarded as a lifelong pacifist and a political moderate because he

7 Kee, *Bold Fenian Men*, p.150.

8 R.M. Henry, *The Evolution of Sinn Féin* (Dublin, 1920), pp.41, 50-51.

9 Lyons, *Some Recollections of Griffith*, pp.48,75.

10 Figgis, *Recollections*, p.2; Ó Lúing, *Ó Gríofa*, pp.78,80; Edgar Holt, *Protest in Arms: the Irish Troubles 1916-23* (London, 1960), p.24; Michael Laffan, 'Sinn Féin 1916-21', in *Capuchin Annual* (Dublin, 1970), p.228; Lyons, *Famine*, p.249; Forester, *Collins*, pp.24-5; MacDonagh, *Union*, p.77; Michael Tierney, *Eoin MacNeill: Scholar and Man of Action 1867-1945* (Oxford, 1980), p.70; J.M. Curran, *The Birth of the Irish Free State 1921-23* (Alabama, 1980), p.3; Calton Younger, *Arthur Griffith* (Dublin, 1981), pp.1,15; Glandon, *Griffith and Advanced-Nationalist Press*, p.83.

hated bloodshed and its consequences for the nation.[11] Although an early member of the IRB, he later opposed physical force totally, and envisaged a disciplined, well-led nation marching forward to its goal on passive-resistance lines, Robert Brennan asserted.[12] And Charles Townshend has put forward the view that Griffith advocated non-violent means because he abhorred violence and bloodshed.[13]

Although those who have argued the second case above are in the minority, some significant support for their position may be found in the autobiography of Maud Gonne. Her organisation, Inghinidhe na hÉireann, strongly discouraged Irish women from associating with men in the British army, and Inghinidhe members used to distribute leaflets to this effect in O'Connell St in Dublin at the turn of the century. In her memoirs she recalled 'with relish' that almost every night there were fights as the brothers and boyfriends of Inghinidhe members were called on to protect the women against attack by angry soldiers, with passers-by often joining in the scuffles. Griffith, she pointed out, hated this activity, although he dutifully took part.[14]

Towards a Theory of Passive Resistance?

The most conclusive evidence is provided by what Griffith himself wrote on the subject. In an early issue of the *United Irishman* he wrote that he accepted both constitutional and unconstitutional action as legitimate. He ruled out unconstitutional agitation at that time because of British strength but refused to exclude it indefinitely:

> I urge the establishment of a national organisation with the openly-avowed ultimate objective of ending British rule in this country, fearlessly asserting its intention of securing that object at all hazards and by any means, but honestly acknowledging its present inability to lead Ireland to victory against the armed might of her enemy; confining herself, *for some time*, to the disciplining of the mind and the training of the forces of the nation, whilst impressing

11 Frank Pakenham, *Peace by Ordeal* (London, 1935; paperback edition, 1972, cited in notes), pp.29,81.

12 Brennan, *Allegiance*, p.210.

13 Charles Townshend, *The British Campaign in Ireland 1919-21: the Development of Political and Military Policies* (Oxford, 1975), p.1. Townshend made a number of mistakes in his brief biographical footnote on Griffith. Griffith was born in 1871, not 1872; he edited *Nationality*, not the *Nationalist*, and did so in 1915-16 and 1917-19, not just in 1916; Griffith was not 'President of the Provisional Government'.

14 Margaret Ward, *Unmanageable Revolutionaries* (London, 1983), p.54.

> on it that, in the last resort, nothing save the weapons of free men can regain its independence.[15] (Writer's italics)

The phrase 'for some time' indicates that he envisaged the preparatory stage to any possible armed conflict as a protracted one. The preparation was to consist of 'the disciplining of the mind and the training of the forces of the nation'. An identical attitude is revealed in something he wrote a few years later. He was describing a meeting at the Rotunda where the statement that the English could not be driven out of Ireland by force of arms at that time was met with cries of dissent:

> We admire the spirit that prompted this dissent; it would be the death-day of the Irish nation were that spirit exorcised, but, nevertheless, [the] statement is incontestable. We cannot drive the English out of the country by force of arms at present, since we have neither (*sic*) the morale, the discipline, nor the leaders necessary for such a desirable object. We do not despair of acquiring them in the future, and to hasten that future the means at our hand is education. 'Educate that you may be free', was the watchword of the men who sixty years ago aimed at restoring Ireland to her position amongst the nations. It is the watchword of Irish nationalists today. When tyranny and knowledge meet, one of them must die, and an educated Irish people cannot remain in political slavery.[16]

So education was to be the means of disciplining the mind and training the forces of the nation. The purpose of all this preparation was to reach the desired and necessary level of 'efficiency'. This was the title of an article by Griffith in late 1912 on Bulgaria's success against Turkey in the Balkan War. In this article he looked at the necessity for a people not to lose 'the will and power to engage in physical combat', and pointed to instances in history where superior civilisations fell to more up-to-date weaponry:

> Behind all civilisation and all political independence stands the armed man - a menace and a guardian. The political state falls after it becomes incapable of active resistance to its opponents. The nation survives the fall of its political expression so long as it can maintain passive resistance. When there is neither active nor passive power of resistance left in a people they either die out or are absorbed into the body of their opponents. Ireland fell as a political state due to her inefficiency [out-of-date arms]. The Irish nation survives because

15 *United Irishman*, 29 April 1899.

16 *ibid.*, 28 March 1903.

> although Ireland has lost all power of effective physical resistance on her own soil, she still maintains some power of passive resistance.[17]

He believed that the dream of settling Ireland's account with England by force was idle until Ireland reached the same stage of efficiency as Bulgaria had attained:

> And before Ireland can attain a Bulgarian efficiency she must, like Bulgaria, have passed through preparatory generations of passive resistance. She must have recovered her language and thus inspired in the Irish character a good conceit of itself. Until she has gone through that travail it will not be possible for her to dream of dictating her terms to the beaten English at London as the Bulgarians are dictating their terms to the beaten Turks outside Constantinople.[18]

Do these statements suggest that Griffith was tending towards a purely passive-resistance stance? Was he saying - you must prepare and discipline yourself so that you will be able to endure whatever your opponent inflicts on you without retaliating; eventually you will win the respect of your opponent and cause him to hate his injustice and oppression? Probably not. It is doubtful that he was ever an exponent of absolute non-violent resistance. However, early Sinn Féin did take a few tentative steps in the direction of a policy of non-violence.[19]

Griffith was very aware of the Indian nationalist movement of his time and kept in touch with several Indian journals which were similar to his own. He considered the 'Swadeshi' movement in India which, among other things, rejected British-made goods, as exactly like Sinn Féin. Indian writers, equally interested in the efforts for Irish independence, had praise for their Irish counterparts. Griffith's pamphlets were published in a number of Indian languages.

The young Jawaharlal Nehru, who became the first Prime Minister of an independent India, and who visited Dublin in 1907 during his holidays from Cambridge University, wrote to his father that Sinn Féin was akin to the advanced section of the Indian Congress Party. Griffith was especially impressed by the views of the Bengal leader, Bipin Chandra Pal, a forerunner of Gandhi, who urged Indians not to hate the British but to develop an attitude of 'benevolent indifference' to them.

P.S. O'Hegarty, looking back from 1924 on pre-1910 Sinn Féin,

17 *Sinn Féin*, 23 November 1912.

18 *ibid.*, 7 December 1912.

19 Davis, *Non-Violent Sinn Féin*, pp.91-2.

wrote: 'Although Griffith, and indeed all of us, wrote bitterly and scathingly about England and the Irish Parliamentary Party, we had no hatred for either'.[20]

Robert Lynd represented the closest Sinn Féin came to doctrinaire non-violence. He argued that non-violent methods, as well as preserving the unity of the country, would make it much more difficult for the British, who could easily put down a violent rising with superior force, but who would inevitably fail when brought face to face with an Irish character stronger than British guns.[21]

The great Russian novelist, Tolstoi, a strong advocate of passive resistance, declared that what militated most against non-violence as a belief was 'divisive nationalism'. By emphasising the Irish language and ancient Irish myths, members of the Gaelic League were behaving much like their contemporary European, particularly German, linguistic patriots. They believed that Irish was a purer language with a greater literature than English and that only one language was firmly implanted in the individual. Griffith, who was relatively weak in Irish, was too honest to take an extremist approach on the language question. He held that though a national language was desirable, it was not a prerequisite for nationality, as Switzerland and the USA showed.[22]

Many nationalists, who did not know Irish, depended on Standish O'Grady's translations of the ancient sagas. These epics, such as the *Táin Bó Cualigne*, glorified violence. The Gaelic revival encouraged a more aggressive and violent nationalism. However, Griffith's use of history in his writings drew attention to the non-Gaelic and Protestant patriotic tradition as well.[23]

There were many precedents for passive resistance. Swift advocated a dual monarchy and methods of non-cooperation. Thomas Davis, though he insisted (like Gandhi) on the right to bear arms, implored that peaceful methods be used as long as they had any chance of success. He stressed the need for national self-improvement and the conciliation of opponents. He believed also that Ireland could share a monarchy with England while maintaining her essential independence.

O'Connell was the only major Irish leader to reject bloodshed unequivocally. He provided what Richard Davis called 'valuable

20 R.P. Davis, 'Griffith and Gandhi: a study in non-violent resistance', in *Threshold*, Volume III, No.2, Summer 1959, pp.35-6.

21 Robert Lynd, 'The Ethics of Sinn Féin', in *The Irish Year Book: Leabhar na hEireann* (Dublin, 1909), pp.356-68; summarised in Davis, *loc. cit.*, pp.36-7.

22 Davis, *Non-Violent Sinn Féin*, p.94.

23 *ibid.*, p.95.

theoretical precedents' for Griffith's Sinn Féin. O'Connell declared the Act of Union a breach of the Renunciationi Act and therefore illegal; he proposed a Council of Three Hundred to act as the actual government of Ireland, and he made some attempts to boycott Westminster.[24]

One can see a similar attitude at work on Griffith's part in relation to the Irish Volunteer movement which was established towards the end of 1913. According to The O'Rahilly, Griffith was left out of the reckoning when the Volunteers were set up in case the leadership might smack too much of Sinn Féin.[25] He joined the new organisation as an ordinary private:

> A private in the ranks, with hat cocked on one side like a Boer commando and rifle in hand - it is Griffith. His gaze, as always, is removed from the scene; the greatest intellect in Ireland is meditating the nation's interests, 'till at the word 'Shun!' from Captain Thomas Markham, the heels click and Arthur Griffith stands as taut and alert as the youngest soldier of them all.[26]

Griffith's attitude to the Volunteers was in line with his passive-resistance. He saw them not as a force to win a military victory over the British and drive them out of Ireland but as a means of improving Irish character. The formation of the Volunteers 'enables Irishmen to realise one of the highest duties of citizenship - the defence of their country and the right to bear arms'.[27] He dismissed the idea that the Volunteer movement would prove the equal of the British armed forces and would deliver Ireland quickly from all her political ills:

> What it is going to do if it be guided manfully is to put a public opinion with backbone in it into the country, to make men more conscious of their duties as citizens, to associate the ideas of order and discipline with the idea of liberty, to bring the manhood of Ireland in touch with realities and to make it clear-seeing and fearless - to create, in fact, an atmosphere in the country in which the gasbag and the flapdoodler will cease to be possible.[28]

And in a similar vein:

24 Davis, *Non-Violent Sinn Féin*, p.97, and pp.91-7 *passim*.

25 Colum, *Griffith*, p.120. O'Rahilly was one of the main moving forces behind the formation of the Volunteers.

26 Aodh de Blacam in *Sunday Independent*, 11 September 1949.

27 *Sinn Féin*, 22 November 1913.

28 *ibid.*, 6 December 1913.

> It is quite true that we must work through public opinion in the circumstances of Ireland rather than through force of arms but he is a poor thinker who does not realise that that public opinion which lacks the confidence, the calmness, the steadiness, the judgement, the resolution and the understanding which training in arms gives a people is a poor weapon to rely upon in times of crisis.[29]

The two great 19th-century expressions of pacific politics, Repeal and Home Rule, were firstly aimed at Britain. They mobilised Irish national sentiment in ways which suggested equality of status with Britain, but without bloodshed or a dangerous severing of the link. The basic aim of the pressure built up in this way was to induce Britain to offer to negotiate. Up to a point, Griffith's Sinn Féin was similar, with dual monarchy playing the role which Repeal and Home Rule had played.

But Sinn Féin went further in two vital ways. Firstly, Irish self-government was not going to wait for a British-Irish agreement but was to be put into action, in as many practical ways as possible, but not through the use of force; at the same time, this would weaken British morale and make them more susceptible to withdrawal from Ireland. Secondly, because Sinn Féin was a loose movement rather than a tightly-run party, a variety of tactics could be employed, and concern was as much about what would happen *within* Ireland as externally.[30]

There were many useful ambiguities in Sinn Féin. Its immediate programme of passive resistance to British rule could have equal appeal to parliamentarians, who had lost faith in action through Westminster after a decade of Conservative rule and IPP disunity, and to IRB men who saw no hope of a successful physical-force campaign against British rule in the near future. The means which Griffith suggested passive resistance could adopt had a potentially wide appeal.

Withdrawal from Westminster and the establishment of a parliament in Ireland could be interpreted as an ultra-typical constitutional gesture or as one that was a departure from constitutionalism. Not even going that far, but simply using local government bodies to lay the bases for native self-government, and undertaking campaigns to promote Irish-made goods, could be represented as either stages on the road to severing the connection with England, or else giving simple expression to a practical patriotism which even public-spirited unionists could support. Thus Sinn Féin was all-embracing in its political usefulness.

Griffith's nationalism was as fierce as any Fenian's, but he opposed violent revolution as both hopeless and wasteful. He advocated: (a)

29 *Sinn Féin*, 20 December 1913.

30 MacDonagh, *States*, p.70.

withdrawal from Westminster and the establishment of a native parliament; (b) the assumption by this body of such executive powers as were possible so that eventually British administration would decay and collapse through lack of use; (c) mass popular action through civil disobedience and passive resistance, and voluntary support for the native parliament in order to cripple the foreign administration. Sinn Féin thus anticipated and probably inspired some of the characteristic devices of anti-colonialism in the middle decades of the 20th century, as Oliver MacDonagh has pointed out.[31]

31 MacDonagh, *States*, pp.63,65; MacDonagh, *Union*, p.77.

Chapter II

Theory: Republic or Dual monarchy

The Hungary of the West

When exactly Arthur Griffith began reading Hungarian history is not known but that he did should occasion no surprise. Links between Hungary and Ireland go back to medieval times. The Young Irelanders, especially John Mitchel and Michael Doheny, were particularly interested in the similarity between Hungary and Ireland in their struggles for political freedom,[1] and Griffith read extensively in their writings, editing publications of their works during the First World War. He revealed an interest in the analogy as early as April 1899, but had more praise for the physical-force republican, Louis Kossuth, who led an armed uprising against Austria in 1848-9, than for Francis Deak, the leader of the successful passive-resistance campaign against the Austrians from 1849 until 1867.[2]

Griffith called at the time for the formation of a new national organisation which should require of its members that they advocate a republic. However, this was not an absolute condition: 'Possibly there be a few persons amongst us who, while subscribing to the doctrine of national independence, are not republicans. If such there be I would remind them, as Mitchel did their fathers, that the time has passed when Jehovah anointed kings; but though I am a believer in republican systems of government, I am ready, as I believe is every other Irish nationalist, to accept any form of native government in preference to alien rule'.[3]

The organisation which resulted, Cumann na nGaedheal, was basically a front for the IRB. It lacked a political policy probably because any attempt to take part in open political action would be

1 Thomas Kabdebo, '*The Hungarian-Irish "parallel" and Arthur Griffith's use of his sources*' (Maynooth, 1988), pp.1-11.

2 *United Irishman*, 22 April 1899.

3 *ibid.*

frowned upon by IRB men who were sworn to a physical-force struggle to establish a republic.[4]

Griffith's extensive reading in 19th-century Hungarian history gave him a new perspective on Irish history. Practical-minded in everything he did, he read history for its political lessons. He was struck by the parallel he saw between Hungary, a small country linked with a great empire, and Ireland, and believed that its history contained an important lesson for the Ireland of his own time.

At the October 1902 convention of Cumann na nGaedheal, the Cork Celtic Literary Society, an affiliated body, proposed a motion condemning the IPP for betraying the Irish republican tradition. Griffith, holding that 'sovereign independence' was a more suitable aim than a republic, proposed an amendment calling for an end to the 'useless, degrading and demoralising policy' of Irish attendance at Westminster and the substitution of the policy of the Hungarian deputies of 1861. He called on the IPP to refuse to attend Westminster or recognise its right to legislate for Ireland but instead to remain at home 'to help in promoting Ireland's interests and to aid in guarding its national rights'.[5] This was his first public advocacy of what came to be known as 'the Hungarian policy'.

Griffith was instrumental in the formation in 1903 of the National Council, which waged a successful campaign to prevent the presentation of a loyal address by Dublin Corporation to Edward VII, who visited Ireland that year. This was his first experience of working with people who were not republicans. He was growing somewhat disillusioned with Cumann na nGaedheal, and welcomed the prospect of a different type of organisation. People joined the National Council as individuals rather than as members of affiliated groups. All who were 'opposed to the British government in Ireland', a wide definition, were eligible to join. In this way, Griffith moved towards a less exclusive nationalism.[6]

He was asked by readers of his paper in 1903 to outline the Hungarian policy in greater detail and he promised to do so. Meanwhile, he kept a close eye on current events in Hungary where the party which favoured complete separation from Austria was in control. The two departments of government in favour of retaining the slight link with Austria had been abolished. He thought it unlikely that complete separation would occur while Franz Josef lived, due to the extent of respect and sympathy

4 Davis, *Non-Violent Sinn Féin*, p.18.

5 *ibid.*; O'Hegarty, *Irl. under Union*, pp.641-3.

6 *op. cit.*, pp.20-21.

for him in Hungary. But the Emperor was an old man and once he died it was almost certain that a republic would be proclaimed in Hungary:

> And the matter for Ireland to reflect on is that fifty-four years ago Hungary lay crushed and bleeding at the feet of this Austria - seemingly as powerless as Ireland at the same time after the Famine debacle. The Hungarians resorted to a manly policy of passive resistance and non-recognition of Austria's right to rule - the Irish resorted to parliamentarianism, implying recognition of English right to rule this country. And one nation today is rich, powerful and able to defy her whilom conqueror, while the other is poor, weak and more tightly held in the conqueror's grasp.[7]

In December 1903, in the course of a book review, he considered the question whether an Irish nationalist could be a monarchist. This was his view:

> There are few Irish nationalists who do not believe with Mitchel that the time has passed when Jehovah anointed kings, but we doubt whether a majority of them would prefer a republican to a monarchical form of government in an independent Ireland - for the Celt is a hero-worshipper, and the Celt predominates, whatever the admixture of alien blood, in the breasts of Irishmen from Howth to Aran and from Cape Clear to the Giant's Causeway. For our part, we care little whether our government be republican or monarchical so long as it be Irish, independent and just.[8]

A series of 27 articles appeared in the *United Irishman* between 21 January and 2 July 1904 under the title 'The Resurrection of Hungary'. 26 of them dealt with the history of Hungary and the last drew the parallel between Hungary and Ireland. It noted how Grattan and the Irish Volunteers had won an independent parliament for Ireland in 1782, and how the Renunciationi Act of 1783 declared that for all time Ireland could only be bound by laws enacted by the King and parliament of Ireland. Thus the Act of Union of 1800 was illegal and the 1782 constitution was as legal in 1904 as it had been in 1783. 'This is simply a statement of constitutional law. The fact that England has ignored the law and Ireland has forgotten it does not affect the matter in the least'.

Ireland's position was exactly analogous to that of Hungary in 1848 when Austria illegally suspended its constitution: 'Deak stood for eighteen years insisting that it was not abolished - since it could not be

7 *United Irishman*, 3 October 1903.

8 *ibid.*, 5 December 1903.

abolished save with the consent of the whole people of Hungary'. The Act of Union was illegal and unconstitutional. Attendance at Westminster did not render an illegal enactment legal, but was a 'temporary acceptance' of it, misrepresenting the position of Ireland to the world and confusing the minds of its own people. Griffith recommended that the Irish MPs withdraw from Westminster and set up a 'Council of 300' which would lay down a national policy which would be implemented by the local bodies and obeyed voluntarily by the people.[9]

Towards the end of the final article Griffith expressed the belief that the continuance of the connection between Ireland and Britain in any form was not for Ireland's good, but he recognised 'a large mass' of Irish people who felt that provided each was independent of the other and equal in status, the rule of a common monarch was acceptable. Nationalists could cooperate cordially with such people: 'A demand that England shall observe her own compact with the parliament of Ireland, and keep her own law, and obey her own constitution - all of which she has violated this 104 years past for the purpose of plundering this country - involved no abandonment of principle on the part of those who desire to see Ireland a sovereign independent state'. No Irish nationalist could in principle accept less, 'though he may seek more'.[10]

The Hungarian articles were published in pamphlet form in November 1904. The publication was financed by John Sweetman.[11] In order to save money, he wanted only the last section of the pamphlet (which described the practical programme for Ireland) and the 1782 constitution to be printed, but Griffith, promising to be concise, believed that 'the parallel rather than the logic' would appeal to the people. By thus minimising the 1782 constitution, which many advanced nationalists had rejected as an objective, Griffith hoped to tread a middle way between parliamentarianism and republicanism.[12]

The pamphlet, *The Resurrection of Hungary*, sold 5,000 copies within 24 hours, 'a record in the Irish publishing trade'[13] which may still stand. In March 1905 the *United Irishman* claimed that more than 20,000 copies

9 O'Hegarty, *Irl. under Union*, pp.645-6.

10 *United Irishman*, 2 July 1904.

11 A large landowner from Co. Meath, chairman of Meath Co. Council, soon to be chairman of the General Council of Co. Councils, and an ex-Home Rule MP.

12 Davis, *Non-Violent Sinn Féin*, pp.22-3.

13 Lyons, *Some Recollections of Griffith*, p.62.

had been sold within three months of its publication.[14] No political pamphlet before or since aroused the same amount of interest in Ireland. McCartney rightly described it as 'one of the seminal documents of modern Irish history'.[15]

Historians have not thought highly of Griffith as a practitioner of their discipline. F.S.L. Lyons considered his understanding of 19th-century Hungarian history 'sketchy', while McCartney regarded it as 'rather questionable'. *The Resurrection of Hungary* contained 'some dubious historical interpretation', according to Robert Kee. Davis believed it treated Hungarian history 'lightly and flippantly'. But most condescending of all was Edward Norman, who judged the pamphlet the fruit of 'slight but excited readings' in Austro-Hungarian history. He thought it was full of inaccuracies and conveniently ignored the subsequent misgovernment of Hungary by the Magyar landowning class. 'The book also revealed all the reverence for history which characterises those who have never quite understood historical scholarship'.[16]

There is a contrary view to theirs. The German Celtic philologist, Kuno Meyer, who frequently visited Potsdam in eastern Germany, and who might be expected to be familiar with eastern European history, offered this opinion on the *Resurrection* shortly after its publication: 'Nor can it be denied that the victorious struggle of the Hungarians for their national existence affords many lessons which may usefully serve the cause of an Irish-Ireland. A series of brilliantly-written and instructive articles on the recent history of Hungary in the columns of the *United Irishman* has but lately drawn the attention of its readers to the subject'.[17]

A Hungarian scholar, Thomas Kabdebo, examined in detail the sources Griffith himself mentioned as consulting, as well as others that would have been available to him at the time. This is what he discovered from an exploration of Griffith's *Resurrection* and his sources:

> All in all, by championing the Hungarian cause, by reflecting what Hungary, through its national historians and benevolent foreign observers, wished to project, Griffith built up a picture of a country in east central Europe which was authentic if over-optimistic...No

14 Ó Lúing, *Ó Gríofa*, p.125.

15 McCartney, 'Political use of history', p.9.

16 Lyons, *Famine*, p.252; McCartney, *loc. cit.*, p.9; Kee, *Bold Fenian Men*, p.154; Davis, *Non-Violent Sinn Féin*, p.11; Norman, *History of Modern Irl.*, p.242.

17 *An Claidheamh Soluis*, 3 December 1904.

doubt he did make political use of history but writing political history is, *ab ovo*, a selection of events and views that reflect the historical period depicted in a certain contemporary light. Griffith's summaries portrayed the main issues also centrally portrayed by contemporary historians. In terms of Hungarian history they were vital issues; in terms of Irish events, decisive ones. It should be noted that subsequent editions of the *Resurrection* were classified by the library of the British Museum 'Hungarian history - appendix' which shows that they had taken the historical authenticity of the work seriously.

Kabdebo's conclusion was clear: 'In summary we may unequivocally state that Arthur Griffith presented...a clear and authoritative document to the Irish nation drawn upon facts and views of Hungarian history as chronicled by Hungarian historians and foreign observers of Hungary. His mistakes were few, his argument was valid'.[18]

Griffith's purpose in writing the *Resurrection* was propagandist and not historical. It would be a mistake to read it as history because it was a parable, a myth, 'an arousing myth' as Colum rightly held.[19] To form a policy based on this myth would require hard toil and discipline:

> If we realise the duties and responsibilities of a citizen and discharge them, we shall win. It is the duty of a free citizen to live so that his country may be the better for his existence. Let each Irishman do so much, and I have no fear for the ultimate triumph of our policy. I say 'ultimate' because no man can offer Ireland a comfortable road to freedom, and before the goal is attained many may have fallen and all will have suffered.[20]

The settlement of 1867, which gave Hungary a parliament independent of Austria but retained the link of the monarch between the two countries, was known as the *Ausgleich* (Compromise). Although Griffith may have underestimated the complexity of this arrangement, he grasped the central lesson of the Ausgleich for Ireland - that it had been won by a superb display of parliamentary non-cooperation.[21]

Griffith's Hungarian analogy represented both equality and the

18 Kabdebo, 'Hungarian-Irish parallel', pp.12-13,16-24,29.

19 Colum, *Griffith*, p.78.

20 Arthur Griffith, *The Sinn Féin Policy* (originally published 1905; published as an appendix to *The Resurrection of Hungary*, 3rd edition, Dublin 1918), p.163.

21 Lyons, *Famine*, p.251.

minimal link between Britain and Ireland, and was a moderate aspiration. His arguments against the Act of Union were, (a) that the Renunciation Act of 1783, whereby Britain formally renounced its claims to pass or influence laws for Ireland, had never been repealed; (b) that the Act of Union was invalid because it had been passed as the result of bribery; (c) that the Act was *ultra vires* as the Irish parliament did not have the power to vote itself out of existence. Perhaps none of these contentions was strictly sound, but they had plausibility, which was all Griffith needed. Furthermore, the phrase 'the King, Lords and Commons' of Ireland was reassuring to Irish conservatives, whatever party they supported.[22]

Towards the Dual-Monarchy Option?

Griffith received an extensive correspondence about his Hungarian articles pressing him to take on the role in Ireland that Deak had played in Hungary. He responded to this request as follows:

> Apart from all considerations of character and capability, the suggestion is impossible of being acted on for one simple reason. The Irish Deak must be like his Hungarian prototype - a man who can say, honestly, that he desires no more - while he refuses to accept less - than the acknowledgement of the 'constitutional' rights of his country, that is, in Ireland's case, the restoration of the Constitution of 1782, and the consequent governing of this country in all its affairs, and the direction of its policy, internal and external, by the Irish people, but with the proviso that, as Swift phrased it, 'The people of England having obliged themselves to have the same monarch as ourselves, we oblige ourselves to have the same monarch with them'. The Irish Deak must be a man who can accept an Ireland linked with England just so far as Hungary is linked with Austria as a final settlement.

Griffith declared he could not do so 'without being untrue to his own convictions'.[23] This response, P.S. O'Hegarty believed, showed that Griffith was a republican at heart and not a dual monarchist, even though he saw no reason why republicans could not support dual monarchism. It was O'Hegarty's view that Griffith was a separatist, an

22 MacDonagh, *States*, p.62.

23 *United Irishman*, 23 July 1904.

IRB and physical-force man, but that he saw no chance of a military victory.[24]

This view is open to dispute. Griffith did indeed support the Hungarian republican, physical-force leader, Kossuth. But Kossuth realised after the failure of the 1848-9 rising that it would be impossible for some time to wage war on Austria, and backed passive resistance. Griffith declared that Ireland was in an exactly analogous position, and that action must come from within the country itself and not from abroad at Westminster. Though he suggested that Irish revolutionaries need give only partial support to a Deak-like policy, he had already shown a personal preference for non-violence by arguing that Hungary could declare full independence from Austria without bloodshed after the death of the reigning emperor.[25]

When the IPP refused to be converted to the Hungarian policy, and no Irish Deak emerged, Griffith reluctantly accepted that he would have to launch the new policy himself, and he did so at the first annual convention of the National Council on 28 November 1905 (usually taken to be the beginning of Sinn Féin). In a very detailed speech, he worked out how the policy could be adapted to Irish circumstances. This speech was published shortly afterwards in pamphlet form as *The Sinn Féin Policy.*

No doubt he was relieved to discover the Irish words 'Sinn Féin', which not only sounded much more native than 'the Hungarian policy', but also summed up more appropriately, his idea of national self-reliance.[26] The young Home Rule MP and intellectual, Tom Kettle, described Griffith's work as 'the largest idea contributed to Irish politics for a generation', but criticised him for not having worked it out in adequate detail to persuade prudent men to try it.

The Sinn Féin Policy was Griffith's political and economic programme for Ireland. A Council of 300, composed of Irish MPs and members of local government bodies, would oversee the carrying out of this programme which involved such areas as education, protection of Irish industries, a mercantile marine, a consular service, a national civil service, law courts, stock exchange, banking system and afforestation.

There were now three organisations in existence with more or less the same policy and with overlapping membership: Cumann na nGaedheal and the National Council in Dublin, and the Dungannon Clubs in the north-east. The first Dungannon Club was formed in Belfast in March

24 O'Hegarty, *Irl. under Union*, p.649.

25 *United Irishman*, 3 October 1903; Davis, *Non-Violent Sinn Féin*, p.18.

26 McCartney, 'Political use of history', p.12.

1905 with Bulmer Hobson in the chair and nine others present, including Dennis McCullough and Padraic Colum, and the inspiration for its founding was clearly Griffith's writings.

At this first meeting, the attendance of Irish MPs at Westminster was deplored and the objects the Club set itself - restoring the 1782 constitution, preserving and spreading Irish culture, encouraging Irish industries - adhered closely to Griffith's thinking. Even the name of the new body was intended to evoke memories of the Volunteer movement of 1782 and the winning of legislative independence in that year. It was strange that the Dungannon Club, formed from IRB men, should initially have stood for the restoration of the 1782 constitution, but when the Club published its *Manifesto to the Whole People of Ireland* later in 1905, reference to that constitution was omitted.[27]

The discussions that preceded the amalgamation of the three organisations into Sinn Féin in August 1907 show that the process of reaching agreement was by no means a smooth one. Griffith's differences with the Dungannon Clubs, and especially with Hobson and O'Hegarty, have been well dealt with elsewhere,[28] and need not be repeated here, but the main theme of the debate was the 1782 constitution (dual monarchy) versus a republic. Forms of government as such held little interest for Griffith. In response to a discussion that went on in the correspondence columns of his newspaper about the best form of government for an independent Ireland, he wrote:

> The Sinn Féin platform is, and is intended to be, broad enough to hold all Irishmen who believe in Irish independence, whether they be republicans or whether they be not. Republicanism as republicanism has no necessary connection with Irish nationalism; but numbers of Irishmen during the last 116 years have regarded it as the best form for an independent Irish government. What the form of an Irish national government should be is an interesting but not a material question. It is the thing itself, regardless of its form, that Ireland wants.[29]

Griffith wished to get the largest possible number of Irish people behind his policy and he believed that the dual-monarchy concept was the most likely way of achieving this. P.S. O'Hegarty believed he was willing to forgo his separatism in the interests of unity and the widest possible appeal. 'I am a separatist. The Irish people are not separatists. I do not think that they can be united behind a separatist policy. But I do

27 Davis, *Non-Violent Sinn Féin*, p.26.

28 *ibid.*, pp.26-36 *passim*.

29 *Sinn Féin*, 18 May 1907.

think that it is possible to unite them on this policy', he told O'Hegarty. Against him it was argued that dual monarchy would attract few unionists and that he could not afford to alienate separatists who formed the vast majority of the rank and file of the movement.[30]

The impetus to unite Cumann na nGaedheal, the National Council and the Dungannon Clubs first came from John Devoy, leader of the Irish-American Fenian Clan na Gael, who set unity as a condition for further funding. It was given added urgency by the resignation in mid-1907 of the Irish MP, C.J. Dolan, who decided to try to recover his seat in North Leitrim as a Sinn Féin candidate.

Unity was achieved at the August 1907 convention. The constitution of the new organisation, which was called Sinn Féin, was quite explicit about the 1783 Renunciation Act: '...no voluntary agreement would be entered into with England until the British government recognised the compact made between the parliaments of Ireland and Britain, and which stated that the only authority competent to make laws binding on the people of Ireland was the parliament of Ireland - a right which was acknowledged by Great Britain to be established and not questioned at any future time'.

There seems little purpose to dwelling upon the arguments of the different sections which combined to make up the new movement. The IRB had no hope of success from insurrection at the time. The arguments about physical force and passive resistance were academic. Griffith's central position made those outside Dublin anxious to limit his influence.[31]

The 1907 constitution was a compromise. It declared that the object of Sinn Féin was to re-establish the independence of Ireland (it was not stated what *form* that independence was to take); that Ireland was a distinct nation; that no agreement would be made with England until she recognised the 1783 Renunciation Act, and that Ireland would use any powers she had to achieve independence (obviously not ruling out physical force). This compromise has rightly been seen by historians as containing an ambiguity which was ominous for the future.[32]

Griffith did not want to fight the North Leitrim by-election in 1907-8. He believed the setting unsuitable for Sinn Féin's first electoral contest. He declared that if they won 1000 votes they could count it a victory. It was an eight-month campaign. As well as Dolan and Griffith, P.T. Daly, Sean MacDermott, Sean T. O'Kelly, Tom Kelly,

30 O'Hegarty, *Irl. under Union*, pp.650-53.

31 Davis, *Non-Violent Sinn Féin*, pp.32,34-6.

32 Lyons, *Famine*, p.256; see also Kee, *Bold Fenian Men*, p.163.

Hobson and Anna Parnell (sister of Charles Stewart) helped the Sinn Féin side. While fighting this election, Griffith realised the vital need of a daily paper. All the Irish dailies were opposed to Sinn Féin. They needed to be answered but once a week was not enough.

The Young Ireland branch of the United Irish League provided the fiercest opposition to Griffith. Among its members were Tom Kettle, Cruise O'Brien, Francis Sheehy-Skeffington, Rory O'Connor and Liam Lynch (the latter two later became the most fanatical converts to republicanism). Dolan was duly defeated but he polled over 1000 votes. What Griffith wrote after the election was prophetic: 'Ten years more and five-sixths of Ireland - Catholic and Protestant - will be banded together in national brotherhood and the epitaph for foreign rule in this country will be in the graving'.[33]

The North Leitrim defeat spurred Griffith to quickly establish a daily paper which would spread the Sinn Féin message to rural Ireland. He knew that such a venture would be financially viable only if it appealed to a wider public than the separatists. His new conciliatory approach contrasted strongly with his earlier exclusive nationalism. Instead of rejecting those who failed to seek full Irish independence, he now judged people by how consistent their actions were with their own political beliefs. All who served Ireland in their own individual way were welcomed in the daily *Sinn Féin*.[34]

Yet he must have known that separatists like Hobson and O'Hegarty would not allow any departure from orthodoxy. Sinn Féin opinion on the daily was divided. The moderates thought it excellent, the separatists thought it good but inadequate in its expression of nationalist views. Sufficient funds were not forthcoming from America to keep it going, mainly because Devoy was in touch with Hobson and those close to his views, who were dissatisfied with many aspects of it.[35]

When the dissident MP, William O'Brien, was establishing the All-for-Ireland League in 1909, with the aim of unifying all parties against extreme unionists on one side and the parliamentarians on the other, he tried to get support from Sinn Féin. His power-base was Cork and if he secured Sinn Féin backing he felt he could win some seats in Dublin. O'Brien claimed that all the young men in the national movements in Cork were helping him: the Gaelic League, the GAA, the Young Ireland Society, the Land and Labour Association and Sinn Féin (Terence MacSwiney, Tomás MacCurtain and J.J. Walsh).

33 *Sinn Féin*, 29 February 1908; Ó Lúing, *Ó Gríofa*, pp.165,169-78.

34 The *Sinn Féin* daily lasted from 23 August 1909 to the 21 January 1910.

35 Davis, *Non-Violent Sinn Féin*, p.60.

He sent Captain John Shawe-Taylor to talk to Griffith. Griffith had in the past been critical of O'Brien's opposition to Parnell and later to John MacBride in the Mayo by-election in 1900. But now he listened to his proposal and was not altogether hostile to it. One reason for this was his desperate need of financial support for the *Sinn Féin* daily - O'Brien was willing to give this support in return for the paper's backing.

The basic sticking-point was attendance at or abstention from Westminster. The suggested compromise was that elected members would attend Westminster on certain occasions and be subject to the control of a national council in Dublin. A special meeting of Sinn Féin was held on 20 December 1909 to consider the proposal, which almost caused an open split, but it was decided to reject it because it was contrary to Sinn Féin's most basic principle. Some Griffith supporters like T.S. Cuffe, Milroy, Wyse Power and Kelly, were in favour of the proposal, but others, like Cole and Sweetman, were against. William Sears, who was at the meeting, wrote that Griffith was in favour of cooperation if possible.[36]

When O'Hegarty publicised this meeting in *The Irish Nation and Peasant* (23 December 1909), a bitter dispute between Griffith and himself ensued. O'Hegarty later told Ó Lúing that he believed Griffith entertained the O'Brien proposal because he was so desperate to keep his daily going.[37]

His attitude to O'Brien's approach was not the only reason why IRB men were discontented with Griffith. When the Conservative-dominated House of Lords rejected the Liberal government's budget in late 1909, the prospects for Home Rule looked considerably brighter. Griffith declared Sinn Féin's willingness to stand aside and allow the IPP a clear run in order to secure the best possible measure for Ireland. To the IRB men in the organisation, this was not good enough. Since the return of Tom Clarke to Dublin in 1907 the IRB had been undergoing a steady revival with the infusion of new, young blood, and some of its members now felt strong enough to openly challenge Griffith's dominance of Sinn Féin.

There was a number of contentious issues down for discussion at the Sinn Féin executive meeting of 24 January 1910. Sean Milroy's motion condemned 'the action of members...assailing their fellow-members' - clearly aimed at O'Hegarty. O'Hegarty himself recommended that the movement should separate itself from Griffith's paper, and that Griffith

36 J.V. O'Brien, *William O'Brien and the Course of Irish Politics 1881-1918* (University of California, 1976), pp.193-4.

37 Ó Lúing, *Ó Gríofa*, pp.199-205.

should no longer proclaim his paper the official publication of the movement. The upshot was that most of the IRB men left Sinn Féin and set up their own paper, *Irish Freedom*, which openly proclaimed the republican tradition of Tone, Emmet and Mitchel. Countess Markievicz, who disliked Griffith, should have left with Hobson (with whom she organised Fianna Éireann) but stayed on because Sinn Féin was the only organisation admitting women (as she herself said).[38]

It is interesting that Eamon Ceannt, who was also in the IRB, defended Griffith for considering a rapprochement with the parliamentarians:

> ...all parties can and should work together to secure those reforms on which they are agreed. To this end Sinn Féin has always preached the necessity of uniting about such matters as the industrial and language revivals, the temperance movement, nationalisation of the railways etc. etc....No charge of inconsistency, therefore, lies against Arthur Griffith for introducing to the executive of Sinn Féin proposals aimed at cooperation amongst brother nationalists... neither Arthur Griffith nor the National Council were false to their political professions in entertaining proposals of union with a section of our nationalist countrymen whose methods are not ours.[39]

When the IPP again held the balance of power in Westminster after the 1910 election, and were in a position to force the Liberals to introduce a Home Rule measure, Griffith frankly recognised that whatever support had been slowly coming Sinn Féin's way was now returning to the party. In such circumstances he passed what he called a 'self-denying ordinance' on himself and his movement in order to give Redmond a fair chance to achieve the best possible measure of freedom he could by his own methods.

But he warned that if the IPP were to fail, 'Sinn Féin must be ready to form the rallying centre of a disappointed nation'.[40] Sinn Féin wanted Home Rule as much as anyone else in Ireland, stated Griffith, not as the ultimate answer to Irish demands, but because it could be used to Ireland's advantage.[41]

His attitude to the Third Home Rule Bill could be described as vigilant watchfulness. Redmond called a great meeting in Dublin for the end of March 1912 to demonstrate the Irish demand for self-

38 Ó Lúing, *Ó Gríofa*, pp.205-7; Davis, *Non-Violent Sinn Féin*, p.68 and pp.59-69 *passim*.

39 *Irish Nation and Peasant*, 5 February 1910.

40 *Sinn Féin*, 8 October 1910, 14 October 1911.

41 *ibid.*, 27 November 1912; Kee, *Bold Fenian Men*, p.160.

The Lord Mayor of Dublin, Laurence ('Larry') O'Neill (centre) sees part of the July 1921 Dáil delegation off from Dublin. From left: Griffith, Barton, Plunkett and de Valera

government, and all important representative people in Ireland were invited to come and speak at it. Griffith and Sinn Féin were included but turned down the invitation, explaining that their attitude was 'wait and see'. When the details of the Bill were published Griffith wrote in the *Irish Review* in May 1912: 'If this be liberty, the lexicographers have deceived us'.

He published two pamphlets, *The Finance of the Home Rule Bill* and *The Home Rule Bill Examined.* He secured 15,000 signatures demanding that the new Irish parliament should have the right to collect Irish taxes and keep them for use in Ireland. These he sent in a petition to Redmond but received no reply. However, by January 1914, he felt that the most would have to be made of the measure of freedom the Bill gave and that it could be gradually extended.[42]

Pearse's criticism of Griffith in *An Barr Buadh* in 1912[43] reveals the problems he faced trying to hold Sinn Féin together during 1910-12, with the prospect of Home Rule on the horizon. The physical-force men had little faith in either the IPP or the British government and what they regarded as empty promises. They found Griffith's 'wait-and-see' attitude intolerable.

His practical politics lagged behind his capacity as a man of ideas. His

42 Ó Lúing, *Ó Gríofa*, pp.218-9,221-2,239.

43 See above p.42.

power lay in his pen. Through his papers and the Sinn Féin movement he inspired many younger Irishmen, but he failed to persuade those of them who revived the physical-force movement of the value of constitutional methods and a gradual disciplined advance to Irish freedom.[44]

Yet there remained a tacit acknowledgement that the only source for republicans was Griffith and his organisation. Although the IRB started its own paper in 1911, the organisation lacked the strength or confidence to make a political impact on its own. It needed a front through which to work, and if not through Griffith's Sinn Féin, it seemed to have nowhere to go.[45]

A Convert to Dual Monarchy?

Griffith's first biographer, Sean Ó Lúing, argued that he was not a dual monarchist and that no one in Ireland was more against any connection between the English royal family and the Irish state. Padraig Ó Caoimh, a close friend and supporter, when asked was Griffith serious about the dual monarchy, replied with characteristic vigour: 'That was all bloody eyewash!'[46] The evidence suggests otherwise.

The attitude to *The Resurrection of Hungary* of those who were later to join Sinn Féin was varied. It converted Sweetman and Dolan from parliamentarianism. Sweetman thought the 1783 Renunciation Act Ireland's *Magna Charta* and saw no reason why all Irish nationalists could not work together in insisting that there would be no agreement with England until she recognised her own act of parliament. 'I think a republican could agree with that view without giving up his principles', he wrote. But IRB men totally disagreed. Hobson thought the Act useless because it was so soon repealed by the British parliament, and saw it having no appeal to the younger generation. Devoy regarded the Irish-Hungarian comparison as unsound.

Terence MacSwiney drew attention to the difficulty of establishing a movement where the members were striving towards very different goals. In 1911, he asserted that those who believed in full freedom and those who believed in only partial freedom could not work together without ending in stalemate and mutual accusation. 'Let not the hands of the men in the vanguard be tied by alien King, Constitution and Parliament', he urged. The term 'Vanguard' has a Leninist ring and

44 Glandon, *Griffith and Advanced-Nationalist Press*, pp.88-9.

45 Kee, *Bold Fenian Men*, pp.163-4.

46 Ó Lúing, *Ó Gríofa*, pp.127-8.

suggests a small, disciplined elite rather than the broad movement Griffith envisaged.[47]

Griffith was in a quandary in getting such a movement under way. He felt he could not play Deak's role in Ireland and sought a leader who could. Sir Thomas Grattan Esmonde was probably considered. He came from an ancient Co. Wexford family, was chief whip of the IPP, was interested in the 1782 constitution, and had resigned from the party with Dolan in 1907. But he was coaxed back into the parliamentary fold. Griffith's alternative leaders between 1905 and 1910, Edward Martyn and John Sweetman, were not so well equipped. Martyn, a wealthy landowner and dilettante, was ineffectual, and Sweetman had twice failed to regain his parliamentary seat and had the appearance of a loser.

By taking on the presidency of Sinn Féin himself in 1911, Griffith was acknowledging the failure of his original intentions. O'Hegarty and MacSwiney maintained that, unable to find a moderate to play the role, Griffith was forced to accept the limited objective he had originally suggested to others.[48] He was, of course, criticised for being too devoted to dual monarchy even when Martyn and Sweetman were occupying the leadership position Deak had had in Hungary. His becoming president of his own organisation in 1911 may have been what finally decided him to leave the IRB the previous year, although there is some dispute about this date.[49]

There is another reason to claim that Griffith became a convert to the dual-monarchy idea. He was akin to 19th-century European nationalists in his preoccupation with finding precedents in history. If Ireland had no equivalent of the Hungarian iron crown of unquestionable age, history had to be combed to produce one. In an article he wrote in 1909 Griffith maintained that since the time of Rory O'Connor, High-King of Ireland at the time of the Norman invasion, there had been only five rightful kings of Ireland.

These were the Scot, Edward Bruce, because he was crowned King of Ireland and accepted as such by the nobles and people between 1315 and 1318; Henry VIII, because the Irish parliament had acknowledged him King of Ireland; Charles I, because the Confederation of Kilkenny 1642-9 had done likewise for him; James II, because the Irish parliament between 1689 and 1691 had accepted him as King of Ireland, and George III, acknowledged King of Ireland under the 1782-1800 Irish constitution. To Griffith, under the 1782 constitution, the King of

47 Davis, *Non-Violent Sinn Féin*, p.118.

48 *ibid.*

49 See Chapter III, section i below.

England's claim to be King of Ireland *because* he was King of England was given up. Although the Irish parliament of that time did not give full rights to Catholics, it had to be differentiated from the Irish constitution which made Ireland an independent state, in Griffith's view.[50]

Starting from this position, Griffith soon became an open admirer of Grattan's parliament and praised it in 1905 for giving Catholics the right to vote, by which it recognised the Irish nation. He eventually came to see the United Irishmen's rising of 1798 as a mistake and he was accused of quietly removing Wolfe Tone from the Sinn Féin pantheon. In a series of articles in *Sinn Féin*, from January to May 1911, entitled 'Pitt's Policy', Griffith contended that William Pitt[51], because he feared the Irish commercial competition that the independent Irish parliament had stimulated, took care to provoke the 1798 rising so as to suppress the Irish parliament and thereby keep Ireland in economic bondage.

According to this argument, Tone was deceived into serving British interests. The republicanism of the United Irishmen was even seen by Griffith as part of Pitt's scheme: 'the republican idea found no flaming response in the heart of the Gael, essentially a believer in aristocracy'.[52] The right of the 1782-1800 parliament to impose tariffs to protect Irish manufactures, Griffith considered more important than any possible limitations on its independence.[53]

When Griffith first published *The Resurrection of Hungary* he was careful to point out that he opposed any connection between Britain and Ireland, and so could not be considered a follower of Deak. But when he republished his pamphlet in 1918 he removed this passage. This was his own mature presentation of his policy.

Republicanism was no longer seen as indispensable. 'He seems to have understood from his new reading and from the events of history (Franz Josef died in 1916 and the Hungarians did not declare a republic) that even Kossuth was no republican until he was forced into exile, and he was increasingly convinced that the composition of Irish society would hardly allow a ready transition of Catholics and Protestants into a united republican Ireland', Kabedo perceptively concluded.[54]

The issues of dual monarchy/republic and passive resistance/violence

50 Davis, *Non-Violent Sinn Féin*, p.119.

51 English Prime Minister at the end of the 18th century.

52 *Sinn Féin*, 4 February 1911.

53 Davis, *op. cit.*, p.120 and pp.117-20 *passim*.

54 Kabdebo, 'Hungarian-Irish parallel', p.28.

divided Griffith and the IRB group led by Hobson and O'Hegarty. It is unlikely that he was in any way enthusiastic about the English royal family, but he 'considered that dual monarchy provided an historical basis for Irish nationalism and a platform on which to unite the country', as Davis remarked. Griffith did not put the dual-monarchy concept before the people in its purest form. Had he done so, they could have seen it offered a larger measure of independence than Home Rule - of the type, in fact, that Ireland achieved after the enactment of the Statute of Westminster in 1931.

Davis wrote: 'The 1782 constitution with its king, lords and commons obscured the central issue and allowed opponents to sneer at a retrogressive desire to retain the wigs and snuff-boxes of the 18th century.' As a result, although the third Home Rule Bill fell far short of the 1782 constitution, the Irish people in general were not tempted to abandon the IPP. And before 1914 the parliamentarians seemed to have an excellent chance to achieve their goal. On the other hand, it was unrealistic of separatists not to consider any link whatever with Britain.[55]

'Had separatist Ireland paid more attention to Griffith's belief that ceremonial acceptance of a British monarch, descended *inter alia* from Brian Boru, was a worthy compromise, and that the gun was not the answer to Ireland's internal problems, much future suffering might have been avoided', was Davis's view, which it would be difficult to dispute.[56]

55 Davis, *Non-Violent Sinn Féin*, pp.124-5.

56 *ibid.*, p.126.

Chapter III

Theory Merging into Practice: The IRB and the Rising

Relations with the IRB

Arthur Griffith was a member of the IRB. He probably joined as a young man while employed by the *Irish Daily Independent*.[1] However, historians disagree as to when and why he left the IRB, and what his overall attitude to it was. Some have held that he gave up his membership in 1906,[2] while others believe that 1910 was the correct date.[3]

Davis was in two minds on the subject. He offered the opinion that 1910 may well have been the date, and that Griffith's departure then could have been related to his assuming the presidency of Sinn Féin the following year. Elsewhere he cited W.T. Cosgrave as vouching for 1906 and thought there was a logic to this, as the political Sinn Féin movement had just been established and Griffith was insisting on a dual monarchy as a minimum settlement, while an IRB group wanted a republic to be its objective.[4]

Padraig Ó Caoimh, one-time secretary of Sinn Féin, denied that Griffith ever left the IRB - he just ceased to attend meetings. According to Ó Caoimh, some IRB men wanted to put pressure on him to make *Sinn Féin* the official organ of the IRB but he was not going to be tied by anyone.[5] Leon Ó Bróin's view was that Griffith used to attend an IRB circle up to 1904-5. The publication of his

1 Because of contact with IRB men also working there, especially Fred Allen, leader of the organisation at the end of the 19th century. Glandon, *Griffith and Advanced-Nationalist Press*, p.84.

2 Taylor, *Collins*, pp.114-15; Kee, *Bold Fenian Men*, p.162.

3 Ó Lúing, *Ó Gríofa*, p.103; Colum, *Griffith*, p.123; Forester, *Collins*, p.79; Younger, *Griffith*, p.41; Glandon, *op. cit.*, p.85.

4 Davis, *Non-Violent Sinn Féin*, pp.118-19; *Arthur Griffith*, p.10.

5 Leon Ó Bróin, *Revolutionary Underground: the Story of the Irish Republican Brotherhood 1858-1924* (Dublin, 1976), p.150.

Resurrection of Hungary in 1904 marked some kind of rift between the IRB outlook and his own. Some doctrinaire republicans even called him a traitor for advancing his idea of a dual monarchy.[6]

Whether Griffith parted company with the IRB because he opposed its aims and methods, or whether no such conflict existed, is an issue also in dispute. Piaras Béaslaí maintained that no such divergence obtained, but that the IRB realised that its secrecy limited its ability to spread national propaganda, and welcomed an open, non-revolutionary movement, which taught sound doctrines of nationality, as a means of increasing its membership.[7]

P.S. O'Hegarty also argued that Griffith had no qualms about IRB objectives and departed from the organisation because, after he launched Sinn Féin, he found the IRB rule that the Supreme Council (the executive of the body) had the right to dictate policy to members in public organisations irksome. The Brotherhood never quarrelled with Griffith, according to O'Hegarty, but always worked with him and recognised him as 'the greatest separatist force in the country'.[8] Griffith's biographers all agreed with Béaslaí and O'Hegarty.[9]

Griffith defended secret societies as a means of opposing unjust rule, but with some reservations: 'I do not believe that secret societies are in themselves good things, but I do believe they are often very necessary'.[10] Michael Noyk stated that Griffith often said to him, when referring to the movements behind the 1848 and 1867 Risings, that 'they were honeycombed with spies and informers'. To Noyk this was why he objected to any physical-force movement, fearing the same results would follow if another rising took place.[11]

Robert Brennan remembered Griffith telling his fellow-inmates in Gloucester Jail the story of Joe Poole to illustrate the dangers of secret societies. It concerned two opposing factions in the IRB. A member of one saw one of the other side, a stonemason, going into Dublin Castle. He was simply going in to do some work, but his opponents concluded that he was informing and sentenced him to death. Poole heard of this and, believing the man innocent, went to warn him, but got lost in some back-streets and could not save the man. Poole himself was

6 Ó Bróin, *Revolutionary Underground*, p.150.

7 Béaslaí, *Collins*, i, p.18.

8 P.S. O'Hegarty, *The Victory of Sinn Féin* (Dublin,1924), pp.133-4.

9 Ó Lúing, *Ó Gríofa*, pp.251-2; Colum, *Griffith*, pp.123-4; Younger, *Griffith*, pp.41-2.

10 *United Irishman*, 19 May 1900.

11 Ms. 18,975 NLI.

arrested, tried and hanged for the murder, having kept silence during his trial.[12] Because the affair involved the deaths of two innocent men, it made a deep impression on Griffith and affected his attitude to the use of force by men who, however patriotic their motives, were responsible only to themselves for their actions.[13]

Dennis McCullough[14] described Griffith's relationship with the IRB as very close. He stated that it had absolute confidence in Griffith, who was a member, shared its sentiments and saw himself aiming at the same target, except that he put forward passive resistance to British rule as having a better chance of success than recourse to arms. McCullough claimed that there was no question of any incompatibility ever existing between Griffith's Hungarian policy and the frank republicanism of the IRB; they trusted in his integrity as a separatist and if there was any difference, it arose over some temporary or personal issue. When McCullough was in the IRB it was not pledged to physical force only but was willing to support any man or movement with separation from England as the final goal, which was indeed what Griffith ultimately wanted.[15]

Some IRB men did make known their difficulty in working with Griffith. One of these was Hobson. O'Hegarty complained that Griffith wanted the members of Sinn Féin to follow him unquestioningly at the expense of their own opinions. But Eamon Ceannt defended Griffith's position and praised him for trying to heal nationalist divisions over Home Rule. And *Irish Freedom*, the organ of the separatists who supported physical force and found other nationalists' methods inadequate, lauded three men for doing most to lead Ireland along the road to freedom, Griffith, Douglas Hyde and AE, and found Griffith the greatest of these.

A shared desire to separate Ireland from Britain linked Griffith and supporters of physical force, and many men participated in both Sinn Féin and the IRB, differing only on the means by which separation should be achieved. Griffith offered the alternative of passive resistance as a way of winning dual monarchy, believing Irishmen of all creeds could support this, while gradually evolving towards greater political and economic control.

By contrast, the IRB were pledged to work for an Irish republic, using physical force if necessary, despite the unlikelihood of a military

12 Brennan, *Allegiance*, p.211.

13 Ó Bróin, *Revolutionary Underground*, p.95.

14 One of those responsible for the IRB's revival in the early part of the century.

15 Glandon, *Griffith and Advanced-Nationalist Press*, p.39.

victory over the British. The IRB lacked the detailed policy which Griffith had worked out, and in spite of their disagreement over methods, there was mutual respect between Griffith and the advocates of physical force. He sometimes needed IRB finance to subsidise his papers, and the IRB had need of his journalismic skill from time to time.[16]

His first paper certainly received IRB funds. Indeed, for the first decade of the century Griffith was far more a rallying point for active republican thinking than the IRB. Devoy's Clan na Gael in America provided substantial sums to keep the *United Irishman* going in its early days, and John MacBride wrote to Devoy at the time: 'The *United Irishman* at present supplies the place of organisers in Ireland and is at least equal to a dozen'.[17]

Griffith was connected from very early with the veteran Fenian, Tom Clarke, who acted as agent for the *United Irishman* in New York. He recommended Clarke for a position on the Dublin Corporation in 1900 and expressed his regret when he did not secure it.[18] Clarke and Devoy arranged meetings and lectures for John MacBride and Maud Gonne when they toured the United States in 1901 at Griffith's urging. Clarke returned to Ireland in 1907 and became active in Sinn Féin in Dublin, being chairman of the North Dock Ward branch by 1909.

Sydney Gifford recorded an interesting conversation she had with Clarke in 1912 about the relative merits of Sinn Féin and IRB policies. She argued that what Sinn Féin stood for was more practical and involved less hardship, but Clarke's vehement reply was that 'Sinn Féin would never succeed, because it was too plodding for the Irish temperament'.[19]

Griffith had little contact with the IRB between 1910 and 1914, but after the war in Europe began he started to work closely with the organisation again. The newspapers which he edited between October 1914 and February 1915 were financed by Clarke and the IRB, and *Nationality*, which ran from June 1915 to March 1916, was actually owned by the Fenian organisation. Griffith told Liam Ó Briain that he had been asked to rejoin the IRB, and its Supreme Council, in

16 Glandon, *Griffith and Advanced-Nationalist Press*, p.83.

17 Kee, *Bold Fenian Men*, p.162.

18 *United Irishman*, 18 August 1900, 6 October 1900.

19 Czira, *Years Flew By*, pp.71-2.

September 1914, but declined because he wished to be free to act and write as he saw fit.[20]

When the IRB was planning the publication of *Nationality*, Sean MacDermott, IRB secretary, objected to Griffith as editor, but Clarke persuaded him that no one better could be found to do the job and that Griffith would adhere to IRB ideals. So, Griffith was made editor of the only official separatist republican journal in Ireland at the time. But he turned out to be somewhat unmanageable and radicals like Pearse were forced to place their articles in the unofficial separatist paper, the *Spark*.[21]

The Terrible Beauty

Eamon Ceannt, on behalf of the IRB, invited Griffith to a meeting in the library of the Gaelic League at 25 Parnell Square on 9 September 1914. Also present were James Connolly, Pearse, Clarke, Thomas MacDonagh, MacDermott, MacBride, Joseph Plunkett, S.T. O'Kelly, and William O'Brien of Labour. It was decided to stage a rising if a German army attacked Ireland, if an attempt was made to introduce conscription, or if the war was coming to an end and there had been no rising. It was also decided that when a peace conference was called at the end of the war Ireland would demand representation there. It was Griffith especially who recommended the latter course.[22]

It is doubtful that he ever supported the concept of a sacrificial rising. He did not think any gesture was necessary before the end of the war to justify Ireland's participation in the peace conference. Instead, he came up with the idea of 'suppressed sovereignty', a concept which he argued was recognised in international law, and that was *after* the actual Rising had taken place. At that September meeting it was agreed that no decision on a rising would be made before the group reassembled, which it never did.

The Easter Rising was planned by a secret group in the IRB known as the Military Council. On the Good Friday before, Piaras Béaslaí called to the office of *Nationality* looking for Sean MacDermott and met Griffith there. Béaslaí knew that Griffith was not privy to the plans for the Rising but wondered if he suspected anything because much of the planning was done in that building. It was clear from Griffith's conversation that he suspected nothing. He told Béaslaí that he was very satisfied with the way things were going. 'As long as the

20 Ó Bróin, *Revolutionary Underground*, p.160.

21 Glandon, *Griffith and Advanced-Nationalist Press*, pp.85-6.

22 Ó Lúing, *Ó Gríofa*, pp.72-3.

Volunteers remain on the defensive, we are winning', he declared. 'The one thing that would ruin us would be to take any offensive action'.[23]

On the following day Griffith was summoned with others to Dr Seamus O'Kelly's house on Rathgar Road by Eoin MacNeill.[24] They were asked to go to various places around the country with MacNeill's countermanding order to the Volunteers, who had been ordered to turn out for manoeuvres without his knowledge or permission. Griffith went to Bray early on Easter Sunday morning with the order for the Volunteers in that area. The Rising went ahead on the following day.

To what extent was Griffith responsible for this major event? Henry argued that he had from the outset proclaimed Irish independence, albeit not an Irish republic, and had renounced armed force because of the certainty of its failure, but had not done so in principle, and had defended an appeal to arms in certain circumstances.[25]

M.J. MacManus believed, and he was surely correct, that there was a wide gulf between Griffith and the men of the Rising, because not only was he convinced that he could achieve all that he wanted without resorting to force, but his separatism was not akin to that of Pearse and Clarke. Griffith thought the Rising unnecessary but, according to MacManus, he prepared the way for one more than any other man of his time: 'there seemed to be no limit to his anti-Britishness and he made more "rebels" than any leader of public opinion since John Mitchel'.[26]

Although Griffith was not actively involved in the Rising, some of the leaders were his close associates and some his disciples. The insurrection was labelled 'the Sinn Féin rebellion' by Dublin Castle, and while there is a certain irony in this in view of Griffith's preference for non-violence, the description was in a sense merited. He was one of many arrested by a government which considered his propaganda had been largely responsible for creating that frame of mind which had made insurrection possible.[27]

It is widely believed that Griffith was opposed to the Rising but that once it had begun he, like his friend The O'Rahilly, decided he must play his part. During Easter week he seems to have got a message to the GPO offering his services as a private soldier and to have been requested

23 *Leader*, 16 December 1944.

24 MacNeill, historian and founder of the Gaelic League, was President of the Volunteers.

25 Henry, *Evolution*, p.213.

26 M.J. MacManus, 'The riddle of Arthur Griffith', *Sunday Press*, 21 January 1951.

27 McCartney, 'Political use of history', p.15.

to save himself for the future as the cause's most effective publicist and propagandist. He is then reputed to have made his way to MacNeill's house to try to get him to call out the rest of the Volunteers to come to the rescue of Dublin.[28]

But P.S. O'Hegarty doubted this version of events. He declared that like the vast majority of Irish people Griffith opposed the Rising: 'It cut across his conception of an orderly and evolutionary movement, and the consequences of a bad failure were always present in his mind'. He took no part in it, continued O'Hegarty, and when 'the great change' occurred, when those who fiercely opposed it at the time began to boast about their own role in the Rising, he was attacked as being afraid to fight, and defended as having been ordered to save himself by the leaders. As far as O'Hegarty knew, Griffith himself never referred to the matter, but O'Hegarty believed he regarded it as a mistake and kept out of it.[29]

But there is evidence to suggest that Griffith *did* actually refer to his having tried to get involved in the insurrection. Michael Noyk recorded that when Liam Ó Briain was appointed to the Chair of French in University College Galway in 1917, his friends gave a farewell dinner for him in Vaughan's Hotel, Parnell Square, at which Griffith was the guest of honour, and at which he gave a speech. He spoke 'with great emotion'. He said the reason he had not fought in the Rising was that he was asked to remain out by the leaders because 'he was more useful outside by carrying on propaganda through his papers and otherwise'.

Ó Briain, who had fought and had been interned in Frongoch, confirmed this in writing for Noyk when the latter was preparing his submission for the Bureau of Miliary History. Ó Briain wrote: 'He said he had sent in a message to the GPO telling them what he thought of them for leaving him in the dark (contrary to promises), but that he would join in'. Gearóid O' Sullivan provided the only confirmation Ó Briain ever got of this. O' Sullivan, who was in the GPO, said he

28 Lyons, *Some Recollections of Griffith*, pp.75-6; Figgis, *Recollections*, pp.141-2; Pakenham, *Ordeal*, p.29; Brennan, *Allegiance*, pp.209-10; Ó Lúing, *Ó Gríofa*, p.266; Taylor, *Collins*, p.115; Colum, *Griffith*, pp.149-51; Holt, *Protest*, pp.103-4; Calton Younger, *Ireland's Civil War* (London, 1968), pp.25-6; Lyons, *Famine*, p.381; Edwards, *Pearse*, pp.306,325-6; Tierney, *MacNeill*, pp.220-21; Younger, *Griffith*, pp.55-6,58; Glandon, *Griffith and Advanced-Nationalist Press*, pp.86-7; Bourke, *O'Rahilly*, p.118; Davis, *Arthur Griffith*, pp.20-21.

29 O'Hegarty, *Victory*, p.45.

remembered Sean MacDermott saying: 'We have got a very nice letter from Griffith'.[30]

Davis asserted that it mattered little whether Griffith offered his services as a private soldier or remained aloof. The real issue was whether his original policy might have led to a happier and more united Ireland than actually emerged.[31] This is one of the imponderables of Irish history, but it is nevertheless worthy of consideration.

There is also dispute about whether Griffith changed his view about the Rising. Béaslaí was witness to what he believed was 'the nearest approximation I ever heard from him to a retraction of his earlier view'. In the speech at the Ó Briain meal he recalled him saying that he was not an emotional man, but that when he heard in his prison cell that certain of his friends, who had spent their lives in the service of Ireland, whom he knew and loved, had been shot by the British, he felt great rage and longed for vengeance.

Béaslaí also pointed out that when Arthur Lynch protested in the House of Commons about Griffith's imprisonment, alleging that he had dissociated himself from the Rising's leaders, Griffith wrote to reprimand him and to declare his association with 'brother-Irishmen, now dead or in prison'.[32]

On the other hand, Brennan maintained that Griffith could never admit that 1916 was the turning-point in Irish history, holding instead that the great change was bound to come sooner or later, and seeing the Rising as merely hastening the inevitable.[33] This view is plausible. In Griffith's comments on the Rising during his address to the Sinn Féin convention in October 1917, Davis described how he argued that public opinion began to swing to Sinn Féin after Redmond 'had rejected Irish history' in 1914 by declaring England's war Ireland's. Although Griffith admitted that without the insurrection the country would not have come over so completely to Sinn Féin, the implication was that it would have happened anyway.[34]

In 1917, when the prisoners in Mountjoy Jail went on hunger-strike in support of their demand for special status, and the prison authorities

30 Ms. 18,975 NLI; Hobson's statement, *Irl. Yesterday and Tomorrow*, p.77, that Griffith received a mobilisation order on Easter Monday reads strangely at first, but perhaps all Volunteers in the Dublin area received such an order.

31 Davis, *Non-Violent Sinn Féin*, pp.73,126.

32 Béaslaí, *Collins*, i, pp.121,123-4,133-4.

33 Brennan, *Allegiance*, p.209.

34 Davis, *Arthur Griffith*, pp.22,24.

resorted to forced feeding, large protest meetings were held in Dublin and addressed by Sinn Féin leaders, including Griffith. He did not hesitate to make clear, when addressing these meetings, that he had disapproved of the Rising.[35]

It has been argued by some historians that but for the existence of Griffith's movement the 1916 protest in arms would have come to nothing, that Sinn Féin's social and political availability in the aftermath of the Rising was crucial. It was one of Griffith's achievements that he never compromised his basic ideal that independence must be won in Ireland and not bargained for at Westminster, and this formed a foundation for the national Sinn Féin organisation of 1917.[36]

Others have said that Sinn Féin would have disappeared had there been no Easter Rising. Dorothy Macardle avowed that old Sinn Féin was moribund by 1916, and that Griffith's programme was useless while it lacked 'an inspiring motive'. While it had an appeal for the imagination of the people, it was without 'the inspiration given to revolutionary movements by the elements of sacrifice and force'. The Rising was seen by Macardle as making good this deficiency in Sinn Féin.[37]

The matter is better understood as a two-way, mutual process. As de Vere White expressed it: 'Pearse and his comrades...provided by their sacrifice whatever mystical and romantic inspiration was lacking in Griffith's work', but 'he had created the political philosophy and hammered out the framework' on which their dream could be realised.

MacDonagh agreed that 'the drama and emotional repercussions' of the Rising gave Sinn Féin the impetus without which it would have been nothing, but he contended as well that mere insurrection would have led nowhere as it had nothing to offer except more sacrifices in new generations: 'In fact, revolutionary republicanism desperately needed something like the Sinn Féin *modus operandi* and the Sinn Féin emphasis upon moral force, civic organisation and legitimation of radical courses by popular sanction at the polls if any further headway were to be made.'[38]

35 Robert Kee, *Ourselves Alone* (Volume III of *The Green Flag*, London, 1972; published in three volumes 1976), p.32.

36 O'Hegarty, *Victory*, pp.10-11; Emil Strauss, *Irish Nationalism and British Democracy* (Connecticut, 1951), p.260; Davis, *Non-Violent Sinn Féin*, p.153.

37 Dorothy Macardle, *The Irish Republic* (London, 1937; paperback edition, 1968, cited in notes), pp.188,62.

38 de Vere White, *O'Higgins*, p.27; MacDonagh, *Union*, p.85; see also MacDonagh's *States*, pp.66-7.

Chapter IV

Theory Merging into Practice: The Great Change

New Sinn Féin

The quick swing in public opinion after the 1916 executions did not mean that violence was now suddenly accepted as the key to Irish independence. Catholic churchmen's insistence that the Rising did not meet that church's requirements for a lawful revolt gave many nationalists food for thought. Also, the fact that the British, despite being involved in a deadly conflict elsewhere, had suppressed the insurrection relatively easily, showed how useless a resort to force could be. England's difficulty was not necessarily Ireland's opportunity.

Griffith had no doubt that the old Sinn Féin policy of passive resistance was still relevant, with its aim of establishing a native government with a dual monarchy as a minimum condition. He was determined to revive it as soon as possible. He believed that the Rising had at most speeded up the swing away from the IPP. One of his followers, Herbert Pim[1], was released early from prison and established a new paper, the *Irishman*, which urged the old Sinn Féin policy in full, emphasising it could not be defeated by force, and dissociating Sinn Féin from the Rising.[2]

For some time before the Rising the IPP had been in a state of turmoil. The way in which the Ulster unionists had defied the British government, and the suspension of Home Rule until the end of the war, greatly disillusioned its followers. Its opponents, encouraged by Griffith's propaganda and the setting up of the Volunteers, were making progress. The IPP, though vulnerable, still managed to retain

1 An Ulster Protestant unionist convert to Sinn Féin and a novelist who seemed to have a penchant for racy, sensationalist plots, with titles like *A Vampire of Souls*, *A Man with Thirty Lives* and *French Love*. Ms. 22,288 NLI.

2 R.P. Davis, 'The advocacy of passive resistance in Ireland, 1916-22', in *Anglo-Irish Studies*, III, 1977, pp.37-8.

support. The executions changed all that.[3] The conscription threat, a year-and-a-half later, might have brought this about anyway.

Apart from the mainstream IPP and its constituency organisation, the United Irish League, a number of more extreme nationalist bodies sprang up after the Rising. One was the Irish Nation League (INL), a group of northern nationalists who broke away from the IPP, angered by Redmond's willingness to accept the temporary exclusion of six Ulster counties. Griffith's Sinn Féin was still small and demoralised and suspected by other groups because of its pacifism and willingness to compromise with non-separatists.

It did, however, have considerable influence through its newspapers and propaganda, and many who later attacked Griffith's moderation probably got their separatist beliefs from him before 1916. The widespread use of the name Sinn Féin strengthened Griffith's position in 1917. The IRB remained a small but important group. The Volunteers was by far the most significant body and provided the majority of the activists in the 1917 Sinn Féin revival, but its chief interest was military rather than political.

Little attempt was made during the second half of 1916 to exploit the change in public opinion by organising a party machine. This did not begin until the release of men like Griffith and Collins at Christmas 1916. The by-election for North Roscommon, due on 3 February 1917, gave them the opportunity for political activity. A number of local men decided to run a separatist candidate, Count Plunkett.[4] The Volunteers, old Sinn Féin and the INL supported him. He took virtually no part in the campaign but was elected by a landslide.

Following the Roscommon by-election a committee of five was set up to arrange cooperation between the various groups. This committee comprised Plunkett, Griffith, William O'Brien of the Dublin Trades Council, Seumas O'Doherty of the IRB and J.J. O'Kelly of the INL. In the first half of 1917 an active, broadly-based organisation was built up, making Sinn Féin the major political force in the country.

Disagreement among the leaders almost undid this achievement. The various groups were suspicious of each other (the INL resented Plunkett's pre-eminence and Volunteers like Collins and Brugha distrusted the INL and Griffith's Sinn Féin), but Plunkett's behaviour made matters worse than they might have been. The publicity

3 Michael Laffan, 'The unification of Sinn Féin in 1917', in *Irish Historical Studies*, XVII, 67, (March, 1971), pp.353-4.

4 He was an unusual choice given his wealthy and ascendancy background, but he was chosen because three of his sons had fought in the Rising, for which he had been dismissed from his job, interned in England and expelled from the Royal Dublin Society.

associated with his Roscommon victory went to his head. He came to see himself as the embodiment of Sinn Féin and its predestined leader. Griffith was the more important figure but his interest was in editing *Nationality* and he made no attempt to challenge Plunkett's primacy.

Plunkett lacked judgement. The contentious issues were whether the new organisation should aim formally at an Irish republic, and whether its elected representatives should attend Westminster or not, but people were judged as moderates or extremists solely on the basis of their personalities. Their views on the Rising were considered more significant than their pre-Rising outlook or even their behaviour during the event itself.

Griffith had been the spokesman of Irish separatism for years and many of his supporters in pre-Rising Sinn Féin, men like Seán Milroy, Padraig Ó Caoimh and W.T. Cosgrave, had actually fought in Easter week. Yet he and they were considered too moderate by Plunkett and his followers like Thomas Dillon and Rory O'Connor. Plunkett tended to browbeat those who disagreed with him whereas Griffith was in favour of persuasion, realising that recent converts could only be won over to full separatism by degrees.

Once Plunkett had decided he would abstain from Westminster (*after* his election), his inflexibility on the issue shocked Griffith who had done most to popularise the idea. This especially annoyed the INL who felt abstention should be tactical rather than on principle. This was enough for Plunkett to try to keep them out of the new movement. He called a convention for April 1917 and deliberately excluded them. Griffith found himself caught between Plunkett and the INL and was appalled by the confrontational approach.

Personal dislike strengthened differences between the two men and this was exacerbated when some Plunkettites tried to get rid of Griffith altogether because he was less than enthusiastic about the Rising. Griffith for his part was careful to steer a middle course and refused to join the INL in an anti-Plunkett front. He referred to the Count favourably in *Nationality* and publicised his April Mansion House convention. He put forward a compromise proposal that the INL should agree to abstention until after the postwar peace conference. Plunkett rejected this as insufficient.

Plunkett's convention almost came to disaster. Resolutions on the peace conference, conscription and such like were passed unanimously, but the question of how to reorganise the new movement was bitterly divisive. Plunkett called for a completely new body, the 'Liberty League', thus virtually ignoring Griffith's Sinn Féin, its journal *Nationality* and its branches around the country. It was a blatant attempt to displace Griffith and an organisation already well established locally. Milroy proposed the cooperation of the various groups under an agreed executive which would represent them all, fight future elections, present Ireland's case to the peace conference and form a council of the Irish nation.

Following a debate, Plunkett put his motion to the meeting and it was passed. Milroy complained that he had not been allowed put his amending motion. Griffith then declared that old Sinn Féin would not allow itself to be subsumed into any new body, and would not give up its policy or its constitution.

The fear of a split led to a proposal that Griffith and Fr O'Flanagan confer to try to come to an agreement.[5] They did so on a basis virtually identical to that proposed by Milroy - the various existing bodies were to maintain their separate identities but to be coordinated by a central committee in Dublin. This committee (which came to be known as the Mansion House Committee), elected before the end of the convention, was fairly evenly balanced between old and new Sinn Féin, and proved effective in achieving cooperation between the various separatist factions.[6]

Griffith's propaganda, and local activity mainly by released Volunteers, led to the rapid spread of Sinn Féin throughout the country during the summer of 1917. Eventually all new branches joined Griffith's Sinn Féin. *Nationality* and his pamphlets were widely read and his followers travelled around founding or organising branches. Griffith's organisation became the centre around which the new bodies grouped. A large factor in this was the misapplication of the name (true even before the Rising) to the various separatist organisations opposed to the IPP. Not all the new members favoured Griffith as the leader of the movement.

Plunkett went ahead and set up his Liberty League with the intention of forming Liberty Clubs around the country. But Griffith's organisation was more firmly-rooted, had a well-known name, an efficient central office with two full-time organisers, and two well-known papers (*Nationality* and the *Irishman*). Nevertheless, the Liberty League attracted Volunteer and Cumann na mBan members to its ranks and made especial headway in Cork and Kerry. But the existence of two separate bodies risked splitting the advanced-nationalist movement. So Griffith's Sinn Féin and Plunkett's Liberty Clubs merged in early June.

5 O'Flanagan had been a member of old Sinn Féin, having been first elected to its executive in 1910.

6 Laffan, 'Unification of Sinn Féin', pp.355-68 *passim*.

It was agreed that the Liberty League would join old Sinn Féin and adopt its name, that Griffith would remain as President, and Sinn Féin's constitution would be retained until a convention of the entire new movement would meet in October. Half of the old Sinn Féin executive would retire and make way for the same number from the Liberty League and any other body that might wish to join. Those on the Mansion House Committee were *ex officio* on the new executive; new members included Collins, Rory O'Connor and Joe McGrath.

Released prisoners were co-opted onto the executive during the summer and autumn - de Valera, Cosgrave, Countess Markievicz and others. The INL accepted abstention from Westminster and were effortlessly absorbed into the new Sinn Féin - Griffith's conciliatory approach was wiser than Plunkett's confrontational one.[7]

Both Griffith and Plunkett were eclipsed when the prisoners from Lewes Jail, the surviving heroes of the Rising, returned to Dublin on 18 June 1917. The leaders among these were de Valera and Thomas Ashe and they began to assert themselves once they realised what had been achieved in their absence. Instead of facing a chaotic situation, they were presented with an efficient, well-organised, united organisation.

The influence of the Volunteers increased between June and October and de Valera replaced Plunkett as the leading figure on that side of the movement. Although President, Griffith desired neither power nor authority, as long as he broadly approved of the course being pursued. He had no respect for Plunkett, but admired de Valera, feeling his part in the Rising entitled him to high office. He was more willing to confine himself to journalism and propaganda than he had been during Plunkett's emergence.

Republicans Versus Dual Monarchists

Before considering the discussions that preceded the October 1917 Sinn Féin convention, and the new constitution that emerged, it is worth glancing at how the IRB under Collins schemed against Griffith prior to that event. Collins, who was instrumental in reorganising the IRB after the Rising, mistrusted Griffith because of his emphasis on the restoration, without resort to arms, of the 1782 constitution.

Collins was determined to keep Griffith and the moderates out. Frank O'Connor thought that Griffith's abstentionist policy, which was nominally adopted by the revolutionaries, had far too slow a pace for the

7 Laffan, 'Unification of Sinn Féin', pp.369-73 *passim.*

Irish temperament: 'to one of Collins's temperament, it must have seemed funereal'.[8]

The Mansion House Committee decided to put forward Joseph McGuinness for the South Longford by-election of May 1917. McGuinness was in Lewes Jail for his part in the Rising. A Longford IRB man, he did not want to be a candidate because he felt it would compromise the traditional republican attitude to parliamentary methods. But Collins wanted to assert republican control over the developing movement and he therefore ignored McGuinness's refusal and proceeded to organise his election campaign.

Collins's most pressing need at the time was to rid the movement of Griffith's moderate influence. The two men had been having some 'fierce rows'.[9] Collins wrote to Ashe, his only backer among the inmates in Lewes, urging him to make it clear to the prisoners that he did not want them to think 'Master AG is going to turn us all into eighty-twoites'.[10]

Darrell Figgis, himself very prominent in Sinn Féin at the time, referred to 'a keen rivalry' existing between the Volunteers and Griffith's organisation. Many Volunteers despised the political movement and wanted control of it. The rivalry was between those who believed only in armed force and those who felt force was useless.

Collins and his IRB followers had leading positions in the Volunteers. They wanted rid of those who were not in the IRB and in favour of force, Figgis believed. Their attempts came to a head at the October convention when the IRB circulated a voting list which deliberately excluded a number of people, including Figgis himself. Some IRB nominees were elected to the new Sinn Féin executive but not sufficient to gain overall control. Subsequently, according to Figgis, some of the IRB men on the executive worked actively for Sinn Féin while others, most notably Collins himself, took little part in political work but concentrated on the Volunteers.[11]

Before going to the convention from Wexford, Robert Brennan received a message from the IRB to call on Collins. When he arrived at the address in Parnell Square he found a queue of men from all over the country. Collins was sitting at a table, and when Brennan got to it Collins handed him a list of names the Wexfordmen were to support in the election for the new Sinn Féin executive. A contest for the leadership

8 O'Connor, *Collins*, pp.25,29.

9 Seán Ó Lúing, *I Die in a Good Cause: a Study of Thomas Ashe* (Dublin, 1970), p.122.

10 Kee, *Ourselves Alone*, pp.24-5.

11 Figgis, *Recollections*, pp.217-8.

was expected between Griffith and de Valera and the IRB was supporting de Valera. As it turned out most of the candidates on the IRB list were beaten.[12]

Policy issues had been left undefined throughout 1917. Most separatists probably did not know what their ultimate objectives were. But by the end of the summer, with the movement now united and highly organised, such questions could no longer be avoided. Whether the new Sinn Féin should aim at a republic was the chief issue. The use of force was not considered at all. Many members of old Sinn Féin felt strongly that adopting an Irish republic as the main aim would commit the party to both an impossible and unimportant goal. They also realised that driving unionists and conservative parliamentarians further away would make any ultimate settlement more difficult.[13]

But by 1917 such advocates were in a minority in the new movement and were cautious and restrained, realising that the Rising had made 'the Republic' a popular call, and had strengthened the hand of the extremists. As for the country as a whole, it is likely that for most people the republic was simply a synonym for independence, and that little thought was given to actual forms of government.

The rival groups in the Sinn Féin movement clashed seriously over the issue. Meetings of the executive before the October convention raised again the possibility of a split. Griffith and old Sinn Féin wanted to retain the 1907 constitution[14], while de Valera, Brugha, Plunkett and Collins insisted on a republic. De Valera's compromise formula ('Sinn Féin aims at securing the international recognition of Ireland as an independent Irish Republic. Having achieved that status, the Irish people may by referendum freely choose their own form of government') eventually brought agreement.[15]

O'Hegarty claimed its new constitution committed Sinn Féin to driving England out of Ireland by force. Griffith wanted to go on as before through passive resistance and the gradual assimilation of power. He saw no chance of uniting Ireland behind the demand for a republic, or of forcing or even persuading England to agree to it. He was a disciple of Davis who believed in independence and unity by means of evolutionary self-reliance, brought about by knowledge and education. But he had little chance with the new recruits to Sinn Féin who had the

12 Brennan, *Allegiance*, pp.154-5; Ó Bróin, *Revolutionary Underground*, p.180.

13 Laffan, 'Unification of Sinn Féin', p.376.

14 Laffan wrongly termed this 'a monarchical constitution'. Its proclaimed aim was 'sovereign independence' but it did not prescribe a form of government.

15 *ibid.*, pp.377-9.

fervour of converts and were conscious of nothing but the 1916 Rising and the republic.

The second part of de Valera's formula was superfluous, in O'Hegarty's view, because there was no need to declare that a country may choose its own form of government *after* independence. He thought it must have had some special meaning for de Valera and Griffith, perhaps qualifying the thrust of the word republic. The second part of the formula had a corresponding provision in the original Sinn Féin constitution: a referendum to decide whether Ireland was to be a republic or not.

O'Hegarty believed the second part was intended to provide for the contingency, foreseen by Griffith, that the republic was unattainable and something short of it might have to be submitted to the people for their vote. What de Valera afterwards called 'the strait-jacket of the republic' was adopted by the 1917 convention. O'Hegarty thought that it so paralysed the native intelligence of the Sinn Féin leaders that when Germany lost the war, and a republic was thereby impossible to get, they could not get out of it or have the moral courage to recognise it for the strait-jacket it was.[16]

One of the most perceptive insights into the republic-versus-dual-monarchy debate in post-1916 Sinn Féin was provided many years ago by the historian of the British Commonwealth, W.K. Hancock. He saw the Rising as giving a halo to the abstract theory of republicanism (the republic was sanctified in the blood of the martyrs). Yet in old Sinn Féin the idea of the dual monarchy still remained deeply rooted. 'This represented not so much a constitutional dogma as a working method of achieving national freedom; it was the product of a practical temper aware of the limitations inherent in changing circumstances and unwilling to fix any abstract label on the national struggle and turn that label into a test for patriots'.[17]

When Sinn Féin became the party of most nationalists in 1917, it had to accommodate two very different political propensities. Here is how Hancock described the dichotomy:

> On the one side was the dogma of the undying republic, living in its own right, needing no ratification by popular vote, but needing only resolution and arms. For this living republic Sinn Féin was trustee, claiming full loyalty and obedience. Here in germ was the party-state. But on the other side was nationalistic democracy,

16 O'Hegarty, *Irl. under Union*, pp.715–19 *passim*.

17 This is the best explanation available of what the dual-monarchy idea meant to Griffith and his attitude to forms of government.

equally resolute for Irish independence, but admitting the right of the Irish people to choose the symbolism and forms of government in which that independence would express itself. This theory subjected Sinn Féin itself to the suffrage of the people.

The 1917 Sinn Féin convention found room for both the dual-monarchy and republican points of view in that its constitution spoke of the republic as coming into existence in the future by means of international recognition, but promised the people the right to choose their own form of government. The immediate programme was Griffith's, modified to suit the prevailing international situation - withdrawal from Westminster, the setting up of a constituent assembly in Dublin, and an appeal to the peace conference to recognise Ireland's independence.[18]

A major result of the 1917 Sinn Féin convention was the change in leadership from Griffith to de Valera. Griffith was indifferent to power so long as his course was being followed. He had a high regard for de Valera. As the convention approached it was clear that de Valera would challenge him for the leadership and that both would have strong support.

Griffith did not want a contest. He arranged with de Valera a few days before the convention that he would step down. According to his authorised biographers de Valera asserted he would win any contest because the Volunteers, who were the backbone of the new Sinn Féin, supported him; Griffith agreed and decided to withdraw and recommend him. It was a magnanimous gesture, especially if Griffith was not convinced he would be defeated.[19]

Could Griffith have won? Many historians of the period agree that he had enough support. His people topped the poll at the elections for the new Sinn Féin executive, while the IRB/Volunteer faction did badly. Griffith willingly stepped down for the sake of unity.[20]

18 W.K. Hancock, *A Survey of British Commonwealth Affairs: i, Problems of Nationality 1918-36* (London, 1937), pp.104-5.

19 T.P. Ó Néill agus Padraig Ó Fiannachta, *De Valera*, i, (Dublin, 1968), p.97; Earl of Longford and T.P. O'Neill, *Eamon de Valera* (London, 1970; paperback edition, 1974, cited in notes), p.68.

20 Glandon, *Griffith and Advanced-Nationalist Press*, p.172; Taylor, *Collins*, p.90; Desmond Ryan, *Unique Dictator: a Study of Eamon de Valera* (Dublin, 1936), pp.76-7; T.P. Coogan, *De Valera: Long Fellow, Long Shadow* (London, 1993), p.96.

Fate Takes a Hand

What was the fate of those who, like Griffith, supported non-violence in the 1917-18 period? When he relaunched *Nationality* in early 1917, Griffith referred continually to the Hungarian analogy and the 1782 constitution. Roman Catholic churchmen gave their backing to traditional, non-violent Sinn Féin, and non-violence continued to be advocated while Griffith struggled with Plunkett for control of the new movement.

Even while some Volunteers, most notably Collins, were preparing for a more effective and systematic use of force than in 1916, passive resistance figured prominently in the pro-Sinn Féin press. Although the October convention ratified the Rising, and the demand for a republic, rather than Griffith's dual monarchy, the way was left open for future compromise. The issue of physical force did not feature at the convention.[21]

In his speech Griffith said that British threats of force would not stop Sinn Féin. 'The threats of Mr Lloyd George we despise. We will go forward towards our goal in the way in which we have been going in the past twelve months and we will achieve it'. He was advising against any retaliatory use of force here. Their goal was the postwar peace conference, he declared, but before they got a hearing there they needed their own parliamentary assembly which could speak in the name of the country. This would provide a central leadership round which the country could unite. 'But when we have that assembly in being, we shall have taken a longer step towards Irish independence than has been taken in 120 years'. When Cathal Brugha proposed the new constitution he said that every means would be used to loosen England's grip on Ireland's throat. This language disturbed some delegates. De Valera explained that moral means only were in question, and Brugha added that they did not intend to destroy British oppression by assassination.[22]

Volunteer raids for arms became more widespread in late 1917 and throughout 1918. These were condemned by churchmen, who often quoted Griffith against them. The passive-resistance case continued to be put. The postwar peace conference was cited and even if that failed the Sinn Féin programme could still be implemented. Griffith made it

21 Davis, 'Advocacy of passive resistance', pp.38-9.

22 Ó Néill agus Ó Fiannachta, *de Valera*, p.99; Longford and O'Neill, *de Valera*, p.69.

clear that he had not ruled out force in all eventualities (conscription was certainly one). He simply believed that in 1917 votes were better than bullets.[23]

There was a committed 'Irish Passive Resisters Fellowship' in existence at this time, which argued in terms of perfecting the individual rather than the short-term advantages of force. Little is known about them except that their advertisement appeared in the *Voice of Labour* newspaper on 3 August 1918. One of their heroes was the English philosopher, Bertrand Russell, whom Irish nationalists admired because of his anti-war campaigning and imprisonment. Like Griffith, Russell was not an out-and-out pacifist but believed most current conflicts could be settled non-violently.

There was a fear that the British might deliberately provoke an insurrection in order to undermine a serious Sinn Féin passive-resistance movement. Griffith had long warned about this and linked it to the violence in Ireland from 1919 onwards. The picture for the years 1917-18 is that moderate Sinn Féin members worked out schemes for a passive-resistance campaign while 'hard-headed revolutionaries', who had contempt for the moderate politicians and for whom Sinn Féin was simply a political front, planned guerilla warfare. Griffith, Pim, Figgis and others were perfectly serious in their desire for a comprehensive passive-resistance movement.[24]

But a number of events occurred in 1918 which undermined their position. The threat of conscription had hung over Ireland since the outbreak of the First World War in 1914. So far the British had refrained because the task of enforcing it might be too great. However, with the successful German offensive on the western front in the spring of 1918, they seemed on the point of taking that step.

The reaction in Ireland was predictable, with virtually all strands of society, outside of the north-east, uniting to reject it. In a letter from jail to his friend Lily Williams (29 November 1916) Griffith had said that he expected the British to try to impose conscription on Ireland and added: 'Ireland must fight conscription with tongues, pens, sticks, stones, pitchforks, swords, guns and all the other resources of civilisation'.[25]

The threat of conscription undermined the IPP even further, enabled Sinn Féin to secure control over the new national consensus, and led to its overwhelming victory at the general election which immediately

23 *Gaelic American*, 18 August 1917, 20 October 1917.

24 Davis, 'Advocacy of passive resistance', pp.38-41.

25 Ms. 5943 NLI.

followed the war. A further result of the threat was, in Taylor's words, 'to turn the Volunteers from a political minority into a national army'. Griffith's moderates never recovered from this blow. The fearful population looked to the Volunteers for a lead and thus endowed them with great prestige.[26]

The British proclaimed that Sinn Féin was in secret and treasonous contact with the German enemy. They blamed the organisation for orchestrating resistance to conscription and this was their response. It was decided to arrest a large number of Sinn Féin members under this so-called 'German Plot'. The arrests had one major implication for the future.

Collins received advanced warning of the arrests from an intelligence contact in Dublin Castle and passed the information to the Sinn Féin executive. But the leaders decided to allow themselves to be taken, calculating that this would rebound to Sinn Féin's political advantage. Only the militarists decided to avoid arrest. These included Collins, Harry Boland and Brugha. In this way the organisation was left with a militant and rigidly republican leadership.[27]

Figgis viewed what happened as a tragic irony: the IRB had struggled for control only to be defeated in an open vote at the October 1917 convention. Brugha had fought tenaciously for a constitution in which the republic would be an indisputable fact, but Griffith had succeeded in preventing this by getting inserted the principle that this question must be decided by the people at the ballot box. At the general election at the end of 1918, 'the harvest of these victories should have been reaped'. But the British government by their arrests had enabled those who were defeated to get control of the organisation and use it for their own purposes. The future was to be decided by this irony.

It became clear to Figgis as the general election approached that all those who belonged to what he called 'the Griffith school' were to be excluded as candidates, most especially himself. Before his arrest he was publicly invited to contest a number of constituencies but, because he was unpopular with the IRB, he was not put forward as a candidate. When he read the list of people who were to form the new Dáil Éireann, he could see that most were IRB men and Volunteers, the very result Griffith wanted to avoid. 'It meant a contest less for liberty

26 Michael Laffan, *The Partition of Ireland* (Dublin, 1983), p.59; MacDonagh, *States*, pp.67-8; Taylor, *Collins*, p.32.

27 Kee, *Ourselves Alone*, pp.47-8.

than for a name; it meant rigidity; it meant the shock of violence where violence might conceivably have been avoided.'[28]

In the weeks before the general election Griffith's *Young Ireland* serialised not only *The Resurrection of Hungary* but Lynd's 'The Ethics of Sinn Féin', which was openly pacifist in tone. This was in stark contrast to what the secret Irish Volunteer organ, *An tÓglach*, was urging - that the election was not as important as military organisation for the 'literal' fight which was coming.

Griffith and his supporters were so committed to passive resistance that the militants felt they had to reduce their influence. Figgis was ousted from the Sinn Féin executive by Collins and Boland, and Pim abandoned Sinn Féin and returned to unionism in disgust at the preparations for war instead of constructive programmes for economic recovery.

Although Griffith was in prison, Figgis bereft of influence and Pim gone, Sinn Féin still appeared a non-violent movement to the general public at the end of 1918. By electing 73 Sinn Féin representatives in 1918, the Irish people gave no mandate to wrest a republic from Britain by force. Rather they rejected the IPP as ineffective and they supported Sinn Féin's appeal to the peace conference and policy of passive resistance.[29]

Griffith spent from June 1918 to March 1919 in Gloucester Jail. The Irish internees had a manuscript journal, edited by him, called the *Gloucester Diamond.* One article he wrote provoked a lively debate. It was about types of government, Griffith maintaining that the best so far developed was a monarchy with strong constitutional links. There were republicans among the prisoners who disagreed with this but, according to Colum, 'Griffith's quiet reasoning left practically all present favourable to the abstract principle'.[30]

He always strongly denied that his *ultimate* aim was the 1782 constitution. On one occasion in Gloucester there was a discussion about the Irish word 'Saorstát', which had been used in some statement issued in Dublin. Griffith suggested that they should substitute 'Saorstát' for 'Poblacht', the word then in use by Sinn Féin for 'Republic'. To the Irish it would mean' Republic' but to the British 'Free State', he reasoned. It need not bother the Irish what the British called the country as long as the Irish felt they had what they wanted.

But two of those present asked Griffith what about his dual

28 Figgis, *Recollections*, pp.221-2,225-6,228-9.

29 Davis, 'Advocacy of passive resistance', pp.40-42.

30 Colum, *Griffith*, p.190.

monarchy, which he constantly insisted on in his newspapers. He explained that his point was that the Irish should refuse to negotiate with the British until the latter conformed to their own Act, whereby they gave up their claim to legislate for Ireland and declared that only an Irish king and parliament could do so. When asked was that not dual monarchy he denied it completely, pointing out that when they declared that they would not treat with Britain until it restored a certain kind of government, that did not mean that that government was their final demand.[31]

'With the election of 1918, Sinn Féin finally triumphed politically, and with this triumph, the republican ideal and physical force as the way to obtain it triumphed over Griffith's moderate policies.' This was the rather questionable claim advanced by Glandon.[32] The electorate was certainly not as committed to a republic and the use of force as this would suggest.

Sinn Féin had snowballed into a national movement and enthusiasm tended to overpower reason among its new supporters. Most had no real understanding of its policy. Although they endorsed the demand for self-determination, they were neither convinced republicans nor grasped the full meaning of the party's republican commitment. After all, even party members had reservations or were confused about this. Sinn Féin could not fairly claim to have won a mandate for armed conflict because this question was not put squarely before the voters. The result was really more a vote *against* Britain and the IPP than one *for* Sinn Féin. It was an angry reaction against the executions, coercion, and the threats of conscription and partition.[33]

The election was not a popular mandate for a republic in the strict sense. The term had been loosely employed. Most people understood it as a more aggressive anti-British stance than that of the IPP. Griffith, 'a monarchist by political nature, was seen as a republican in this sense, as John O'Leary had been before him', Townshend wrote. He went on to correctly point out that it was not until the debate over the Treaty that the term was subjected to any scrutiny.[34]

31 Brennan, *Allegiance*, pp.216-7.

32 Glandon, *Griffith and Advanced-Nationalist Press*, p.176.

33 Curran, *Free State*, pp.21-2.

34 Charles Townshend, *Political Violence in Ireland: Government and Resistance since 1848* (Oxford, 1983), p.328.

Chapter V

Practice: The Independence Struggle 1919-21

Passive Resistance: The First Dáil

The Irish independence struggle 1919-21 consisted of two strands. One was Dáil Éireann and the measures which replaced aspects of the Dublin Castle administration. The other was the military campaign waged by the Volunteers against the police and the army. Griffith's support for the first was wholehearted - it was putting into practice what he had been preaching for twenty years.

There is no doubt that he had major reservations about the second. What the relative importance of each strand was in the achievement of independence is a matter of interpretation. It has been popular to dismiss the constructive though unspectacular work of the Dáil in favour of the derring-do of the men of violence.

Griffith smuggled out a letter from Gloucester in January 1919 offering 'a few hurried suggestions... for consideration by the Dáil'. He wanted to discourage any resort to force: 'Keep the country calm, disciplined and dignified. Let it not be provoked by the Castle gang'. He also discouraged any fixation with what *form* the Irish government should take: 'It would not be advisable, either, to go into the details of an Irish constitution at present; just keep the straight question of Irish independence first. The first thing first'.

The letter is remarkable in its outline of the work the Dáil could and should undertake. Securing control of local government was of first importance because of the powers these local bodies had to stimulate industrial, agricultural and fisheries development, and because of their power to contribute to afforestation and the use of libraries and museums for educational purposes. Griffith urged the formation of a committee of experts to explore in full the extensive powers conferred by the 1898 Local Government Act.

He also wanted the schemes which had been worked out by pre-1916 Sinn Féin to be reconsidered, such as those relating to a National Civil Service, the Poor Law and Dublin housing, to see how they could now be applied. The cooperation of the banks would be vital and he mentioned the branches and the businessmen who would be most supportive.

He pressed for the establishment of arbitration courts, the posting of consuls (he named people abroad who could be counted on) and the use of extensive propaganda abroad (he named the editors of sympathetic newspapers). He thought the Versailles peace conference vital and advised using Irish-American representatives (some he named) to plead the national case if Irish delegates could not be sent. He suggested the support of Poland, Czechoslovakia and the small South American states should be sought for Ireland's case at Versailles.

President Wilson's sincerity should not be questioned. Ireland should be fully supportive of him and should portray him as a sincere man struggling against the 'forces of tyranny, imperialism and lusty world power which are seeking to dominate the peace conference'. The poets should be mobilised for this purpose and should remind Wilson that he had the duty and the opportunity of giving the world true and lasting peace, telling him that they regarded him as their 'Man of Hope'.[1]

The idea of withdrawal from Westminster and the setting up of a national assembly in Ireland was one which Daniel O'Connell had first almost casually suggested. Others, including John Dillon, last leader of the IPP, had seriously considered it. But Griffith alone was the one who made it a practical policy.[2]

The setting up of the first Dáil at the beginning of 1919 was revolutionary because it signalled the end of parliamentary agitation through Westminster. The Dáil 'created the rudiments of a new political framework: a focus for the claim of national sovereignty, and an executive body claiming public allegiance', Townshend wrote.[3]

Griffith originated the idea that 'arbitration could and would replace the hierarchy of courts and adversarial trials whose fulcrum was the Bench and Bar', Mary Kotsonouris has pointed out. He became the first Irish Minister for Home Affairs.

A committee chaired by him was set up to prepare a system of arbitration courts. It took a year to report. The decree which established the courts of Dáil Éireann was not identical to the system Griffith had

1 'Important Letter of 1919', in *Capuchin Annual* (Dublin, 1969), pp.330-35.

2 Tierney, *MacNeill*, p.265.

3 Townshend, *Political Violence*, pp.328-9.

outlined, 'with passion if not precision', to the delegates in the Mansion House in 1906, commented Kotsonouris.[4]

These courts were arguably the Dáil's most effective achievement. Even unionists had resort to them and they won praise for their even-handed administration of justice. Considering the success of such administrative measures, it could be believed that Griffith's long-envisaged plan of superseding one government by another, through pressure that was moral rather than military, was workable.[5]

The other area of noted Dáil success was in local government. Pre-1916 Sinn Féin had a strong tradition in local government. By 1911 it had secured twelve of the 80 seats on Dublin Corporation. It was the major opponent of the dominant IPP membership and constantly attacked corruption, patronage and inefficiency. Griffith's editorials regularly denounced the corruption of local government and the inefficiency of the Local Governement Board.

The local elections of January and June 1920 saw Sinn Féin capture the vast majority of the local authorities, and these pledged their allegiance to the Dáil rather than the British Local Governement Board. From the summer of 1920 large numbers of local representatives, rate collectors and even ratepayers, assisted in the establishment of an alternative administration. Mary Daly has written that the Dáil Éireann Ministry of Local Government operated as a real government department, not only trying to keep the local government system functioning despite civil unrest, but also initiating basic reforms which were continued by the government of the Irish Free State.[6]

How successful was this attempt to peacefully replace one government by another? There can be no doubt that the intensification of the war made the continuation of the Dáil's programme more and more difficult. But the Dáil, for all its flaws, governed more effectively than Dublin Castle. Griffith had always argued that the way to independence was to establish a rival administration which would win the confidence of the people. Once this had been done, English institutions in Ireland were bound to gradually become irrelevant.[7]

'To Britain's chagrin, Griffith's programme of national initiative and self-reliance was proving much more than an idle theory', J.M. Curran

4 Mary Kotsonouris, 'The courts of Dáil Éireann', in Brian Farrell, (ed.), *The Creation of Dáil Éireann* (Dublin, 1994), pp.91-2.

5 Colum, *Griffith*, p.216.

6 Mary Daly, 'Local government and the first Dáil', in Farrell (ed.), *Creation of Dáil*, pp.123-4.

7 Younger, *Civil War*, p.92.

wrote in a review of Dáil successes.[8] His view finds support in the warning to the British cabinet of A.W. (Andy) Cope, the Assistant Under-Secretary in Dublin Castle at the time, that the arbitration courts were doing more harm to the prestige of their government than all the assassinations.[9]

Edgar Holt regarded the truce when it came in July 1921 not as a military victory for Sinn Féin, but as the victory of public opinion based on the old Sinn Féin policy of self-reliance. He posed the question: could this result have been 'more quickly' achieved by an organised campaign of civil disobedience and peaceful non-cooperation rather than by employing the means of bloodshed and violence?[10]

J.J. Lee's view was that there would probably have been some guerrilla activity, with or without the Dáil. This might have been put down ruthlessly and quickly if the British did not have to contend with the 'aura of legitimacy' which the Dáil conferred, especially abroad.[11]

The Dáil could have won Irish independence without resort to force. That is how Griffith would have liked to win independence. It might not have been achieved in his lifetime but he would have considered the wait well worth while. But there were other obstacles apart from a belief in violence which hindered the pursuit of the non-violent path.

Pursuing a Mirage?

In his smuggled letter from Gloucester Griffith discouraged speculation on the form an independent Irish government should take. His advice was not heeded. Only 28 of the 69 elected Sinn Féin TDs were present on the opening day of the first Dáil. P.S. O'Hegarty regretted that most of the intelligence was absent when restrained and responsible leadership was called for.

He felt the people had been won over to an objective, the setting up of a native parliament, and had given broad support to the method of achieving it - doing it at home, making British government impossible by non-cooperation. Ireland's maximum demand (a republic) should not also have been its minimum one, O'Hegarty argued. He thought that Griffith was ever aware of the weakness of the complete separatist

8 Curran, *Free State*, p.31.

9 Kotsonouris, 'Courts of Dáil Éireann', p.94.

10 Holt, *Protest*, p.256.

11 J.J. Lee, 'The significance of the first Dáil', in Farrell (ed.), *Creation of Dáil*, p.154.

position in relation to national unity, and that he had a realistic view of what it was possible to achieve.

The Dáil was perfectly entitled to declare a republic, O'Hegarty agreed, but it was also obliged to consider if it were in fact attainable before definitely committing the people to it. There were some grounds for declaring a republic in 1917 when the possibility remained that Germany might win the war, but none in 1919 when the British had won, and it was not to *their* Empire but those of their enemies that self-determination was to be applied.

Hope in the peace conference that Ireland would be admitted under some principle of international law, quickly faded, yet the insistence on the republic continued and soon became impossible to reverse. 'The old Sinn Féin version of an educated, disciplined, enduring people, beginning at ground level and building its way up, slowly but surely, was shelved in favour of the quick victory which the enthusiasm generated by slogans seemed to promise.'[12]

Sinn Féin's theme had been that Ireland should claim before the peace conference the right to decide its own form of government. This was in keeping with the ideals for which the First World War was being fought, and was especially in tune with President Wilson's principles. But it was important not to anticipate or take out of the hands of the peace conference the decision about Ireland's form of government.

Ireland needed to be deferential as an appellant. But to declare a republic *before* going to the conference was to anticipate the judgement before making the appeal, and was to present that body with a *fait accompli*. This was to present the peace conference with a dilemma and allowed Britain to argue that even to *hear* Ireland's appeal was tantamount to recognising it as an independent state. Figgis had no doubt that if the lines of Griffith's policy had been followed, this impossible situation would have been avoided.[13]

Curran agreed with these viewpoints. He suggested that in confirming the demand for a republic on the opening day of the Dáil, the extremists acted unwisely. Things had greatly changed since 1916. Germany had been defeated and however sympathetic the United States or the victor-nations were to Irish aspirations, they could not afford to quarrel with Britain. Sinn Féin should simply have called for national self-determination, leaving open the question of relations with Britain. This would have won strong support in the United Kingdom and the Dominions and left ample room for eventual compromise. But

12 O'Hegarty, *Irl. under Union*, pp.727-30.

13 Figgis, *Recollections*, pp.230-33.

Brugha made it plain that militant republicans were not interested in practical considerations.[14]

Griffith had high hopes for the peace conference which met at Versailles from January to June 1919. He first advanced the subject at the IRB-inspired meeting in September 1914, and he wrote to a friend in November 1916 about Ireland's determination to be in attendance. He also spoke at length on the issue at the Sinn Féin convention of October 1917 where he stated that Ireland's claim to be at the conference was based on the doctrine of international law known as 'suppressed sovereignty'. Ireland could not secure belligerent rights until Sinn Féin became the actual master of the country. Therefore they had to destroy the existing Irish representation at Westminster because it denied Ireland's claim to independence. They had to set up their own constitutional assembly chosen by the whole people of Ireland, which could speak in their name.

Most Irish hope resided in President Wilson. In the event he refused to see Sean T. O'Kelly, the Dáil representative in Paris. When Wilson returned to America there was intense pressure on him from the Irish-American lobby. Griffith wrote in *Nationality* (21 February 1919) that 'even if Wilson had simply been trying to avoid embarrassment in Paris, he could not avoid the embarrassment which the question "What about Ireland?" would cause in America'. But he declared that Wilson should be given the chance 'to make good'.[15] However, Wilson did not prove amenable to pressure and Ireland's case went unheard at Versailles.

While many political events weakened those on the Irish side wishing to avoid violence, the failure of the peace conference to hear Ireland's claim to independence was pivotal. It was a disaster for Griffith's strategy. His hope for international recognition was then transferred to America, whence de Valera had departed in the middle of 1919.

In late September 1919, the US consul in Dublin, Dumont, reported to his government Griffith's view that a settlement satisfactory to de Valera would be vital in the American political situation, that the Irish-American vote was crucial to the Democratic Party, and that the Irish-dominated Roman Catholic Church could force the American administration into declaring support for Irish independence. Even a year later he confided to Dumont that he still expected a decisive move from America. Though the situation looked bleak for Sinn Féin Griffith

14 Curran, *Free State*, p.23.

15 Kee, *Ourselves Alone*, p.65.

maintained that in a few weeks America would be forced to come out in favour of Ireland.[16]

Brugha, the Minister for Defence, introduced a motion in the Dáil in late August 1919 calling on all members and all Volunteers to swear an oath of allegiance to the Republic, and to the Dáil as its government. Those TDs not rigidly adhering to any one particular form of government, and more interested in the substance than the forms of independence, nevertheless took the oath. It was more than a gesture; in the desperate situation the Dáil faced at the time, it was a necessity, Hancock speculated. 'If Dáil Éireann and its officers made no claim to represent a rightful power, they must be what their enemies called them - a murder gang. For they were killing and ordering to kill.'

Hancock's statement is inaccurate. It was not the Dáil that was managing the campaign of violence, certainly not Griffith and like-minded members. Hancock recorded what Griffith said about the oath: 'They should realise that they were the government of the country. This oath would regularise the situation. If they were not a regular government then they were shams and impostors'.[17] Colum found it surprising that Griffith not only agreed to but strongly urged the taking of the oath. After all he had been reluctant to speak of the Republic.[18]

Neither Hancock nor Colum adverted to the real context in which the oath was introduced. Brugha was becoming antagonistic to Collins and his activities with the Volunteers. He demanded that the Volunteers take the oath in order to bring them more under his own control as Defence Minister. Griffith supported Brugha in the hope that by making the Volunteers subject to the Dáil cabinet the extremists could be kept in check. No doubt Griffith and other TDs felt that this step would establish Dáil authority over the Volunteers, although Brugha's primary aim was to destroy IRB power within that body.[19]

Griffith and the Physical-Force Campaign

Differences between Griffith and Collins continued into 1919. The German Plot prisoners were released in March. De Valera had escaped before this and was in hiding. An announcement appeared in the press

16 A.J. Ward, *Ireland and Anglo-American Relations 1899-1921* (Toronto, 1969), pp.225-6,228-9.

17 Hancock, *Survey*, pp.110-11.

18 Colum, *Griffith*, p.207.

19 Curran, *Free State*, p.25.

that a mass demonstration would be held on 26 March to welcome him back to Dublin. Because it was proclaimed by Dublin Castle it was clear that the demonstration could bring violence. Both the old and the new Sinn Féin executives met to discuss the matter with Griffith in the chair. Figgis asked to see the minutes of the executive decision about the demonstration. The matter had not come before the executive.

Collins admitted that the press announcement had been written by him. He said that the decision had been taken by the Volunteers, not Sinn Féin, and that 'the sooner fighting was forced and a general state of disorder created throughout the country the better'. He said he had no respect for those attending the meeting and that they were summoned merely 'to confirm what the proper people had decided'. O'Connor composed a memorable picture of what happened then:

> It was quite plain he did not give a damn for any political organisation which did not subserve the interests of the fighting men. It was just cheek on their part, setting up to dictate policy to their youngers and betters. This was too much for Arthur Griffith. This young man had coolly thrust him out of the presidency of his own organisation and honeycombed it with Volunteers and secret-society men; he had made it elect fourscore dyed-in-the-wool republicans as its parliamentary representatives, to the exclusion of his own personal friends and associates like Figgis; had made that supposed Sinn Féin parliament, some of whose members had never even read the Sinn Féin constitution, declare an Irish Republic instead of a dual monarchy; and now had the impudence to stand up and maintain that even the shadow of a democratic organisation which was left had no right to an opinion of its own. Griffith rose, a picture of outraged majesty, and thundered forth the democratic doctrine: that meeting, and that meeting alone, had the right to decide.[20]

Collins's plan was for the presentation of the keys of the city to de Valera by the lord mayor, Laurence O'Neill, on Mount Street Bridge. The idea appealed to de Valera, who returned from Liverpool ready to give an appropriately fiery speech at the scene of some of the fiercest fighting in 1916.[21] Griffith, as well as stating that the decision about the demonstration was to be taken by the Sinn Féin executive and no other body, said that he was strongly opposed to the whole idea but would accept the decision of that meeting. A fierce debate raged for two

20 O'Connor, *Collins*, pp.43-4.

21 Coogan, *de Valera*, p.131.

hours, the upshot of which was that Griffith was to see de Valera about the matter. This he did and the next morning's papers carried the announcement that the demonstration was off.[22]

Griffith's position during the Anglo-Irish War is perplexing. A number of earlier commentators, like Béaslaí and Ó Lúing, believed the fighting men had his blessing and that he stood over their actions.[23] But some more recent analysts have disagreed. MacDonagh, for instance, maintained that the old Sinn Féin was by no means moribund during the violence. He believed that the campaign of passive resistance and of taking over some British government institutions probably put as much pressure on the British as the actions of the Volunteers.[24]

Béaslaí and some later historians argued that Griffith regarded the Irish resort to force as a defensive gesture, following the suppression of the Dáil in September 1919.[25] Many others believed that he deprecated the violence carried out during the Anglo-Irish War.

Figgis recounted how he often met Griffith during his Dáil presidency, and while the incumbent never discussed what was happening, Figgis could see that 'he was troubled to discover where the nation was being led beyond his sight, to an extent beyond his control'. When the post-Treaty division 'absolved him from the obligation of silence', he told Figgis that he disapproved of many of the things done during those years and referred especially to decisions taken without his knowledge, some of which he first learned about in the papers.[26]

O'Hegarty recalled how he tried to get Griffith to prevent a proposed Volunteer action which he heard about while in Cork, and how he told Griffith that the people would hold him and the Dáil cabinet responsible for such deeds. Griffith responded: 'The military mind is the same in every country. Our military men are as bad as the British. They think of nothing but their own particular end, and cannot be brought to consider the political consequences of their proceedings'.

O'Hegarty understood from this that Griffith was very disturbed at the violent direction the movement was taking, but that he was either not strong enough or determined enough to control the Volunteers

22 Figgis, *Recollections*, pp.242-5.

23 Béaslaí, *Collins*, i, p.328; Ó Lúing, *Ó Gríofa*, pp.340,353. See also O'Connor, *Collins*, p.55.

24 MacDonagh, *States*, p.68; Brian Farrell, *The Founding of Dáil Éireann: Parliament and Nation-Building* (Dublin, 1971), p.78.

25 Béaslaí, *op. cit.*, ii, p.111; Ó Lúing, *op. cit.*, pp.331,351; Glandon, *Griffith and Advanced-Nationalist Press*, p.183.

26 Figgis, *Recollections*, pp.257-8.

while there was still time.'I believe that the shooting and the ambushing and the savagery and the moral collapse which they generated sickened his soul and then his body; I believe that he was glad that the responsibility was not on his shoulders, and that the red policy had been begun while he was in prison.'[27]

Frank O'Connor described Griffith as being 'horrified' at the incident at Soloheadbeg, Co. Tipperary, on 21 January 1919, when local Volunteers attacked and killed two constables who were escorting a load of gelignite to a quarry.[28] Robert Brennan attested to his reaction when they heard about this event in Gloucester Jail.

Brennan made it clear that he himself lauded the action, but Griffith 'was scathing in his comments', being certain that the Dáil had not sanctioned it, and considering it therefore no more than 'outlaw action'. But what Griffith considered the most important point, according to Brennan, was that the British could always defeat them in war if they chose. 'If this sort of thing goes on, we will end up by shooting one another', he said.[29]

He said something similar to Liam Ó Briain one night in 1920 as they were walking home: 'I am old enough to remember the fade-out of the Fenians when they began shooting one another. The danger of an armed movement is turning the guns on one another'.[30] His words were prophetic. Brennan also remembered Griffith's response to the events of 'bloody Sunday'.[31] Brennan was waiting for Griffith in their shared office the following morning and found him 'badly shaken'. Griffith thought the Croke Park killings bad enough, 'but after all that was a British crime'; no better could be expected from them; but the morning shootings! Brennan started to point out that they were not simply British officers but special agents, when Griffith stopped him: 'How can we justify this? The killing of men on a Sunday morning in their homes in the presence of their wives?'[32]

Robert Kee remarked that Griffith's views about the violent campaign organised by Collins 'must...remain something of a mystery'.

27 O'Hegarty, *Victory*, pp.46-8.

28 O'Connor, *Collins*, p.41.

29 Brennan, *Allegiance*, pp.210-11.

30 Liam Ó Briain statement, 6 September 1973, in library of late Nevin Griffith, Dublin.

31 This was 21 November 1920, when in the morning members of Collins's 'Squad' shot dead fourteen British agents in Dublin and, in reprisal, that afternoon the Black and Tans drove into Croke Park and fired on the crowd, killing exactly the same number.

32 Brennan, *op. cit.*, p.287.

Kee surmised that he must have known who was ordering the shooting of Irish policemen, but one could only guess at the extent to which he felt such deeds were necessary, or how much he worried about the condemnation of clerical and lay supporters of Sinn Féin. Kee speculated that perhaps he justified them 'by straightforward revolutionary logic'.

Griffith's main concern was to see set up in Ireland a self-reliant government, economy and judiciary. Kee did not think him a pacifist. He had after all begun his national career as a Fenian and had been a member of the IRB for some time. His conversion to moral force had been more because he considered physical force impractical than from any moral conviction. 'He had the essential political gift of pragmatic adaptability'.

The rest of Kee's argument went as follows: as 1919 went on Collins and the Volunteers achieved some success. Perhaps what had seemed impractical before 1914 or even 1916 was no longer so. Griffith's goal was to sever the link with England in one form or another and perhaps he was able to change his doubts about means, provided the one end was kept constantly in view.

The decision in 1919 that the Volunteers should take an oath of allegiance to the Dáil, however, showed that Griffith and some other leaders felt uneasy about what was happening and thought that it should be regularised in some way. From that time on, although the Volunteers remained under the control of their own executive, and got whatever central direction they had from Collins rather than from the Dáil cabinet, it was easier to preserve the legal fiction that the Volunteers were now the official army of the republic.

'Moderate men could regard what was being done as "responsible"', Kee observed. When the Dáil and Sinn Féin were suppressed at the end of 1919, Griffith could say with some justice in an interview: 'The English government in Ireland has now proclaimed the Irish nation, as it formerly proclaimed the Catholic Church, an illegal assembly'.

By the late summer of 1920, Kee felt that a genuine Sinn Féin government operating simultaneously with, and in some cases more successfully than, the British government, was a reality. It was the violent campaign that made this possible, and this 'inevitably blurred still further such reservations as Griffith and other moderates may have had' about the use of force. As the latter had brought the fulfilment of their own policies, it was no longer easy to distinguish one from the other. It also became easy for Sinn Féin to forget that their political campaign was going on largely because the IRA permitted it.[33]

33 Kee, *Ourselves Alone*, pp.86-7,89,106.

Kee's hypothesis is plausible but open to question on a number of grounds. Whatever the effectiveness of the violence, Griffith believed the same results could have been achieved by other, and better, means. We have the evidence of his reaction of horror to events like Soloheadbeg and 'bloody Sunday'. We have his intervention to prevent bloodshed at the welcome Collins had planned for de Valera at the end of March 1919. Figgis recalled a plan to attack the Viceroy, Lord French, on the first anniversary of the armistice (11 November 1919) as he reviewed a march-past in College Green. When Griffith heard of this he 'immediately interposed his authority' and prevented the assault from going ahead. Blythe described him as moving 'firmly and decisively' on this occasion.[34]

Blythe asserted that Griffith persuaded Brugha that the enactment of partition did not call for 'a desperate campaign of violence in Britain'.[35] There is a reference in the cabinet minutes to a dispute on defence between Griffith and Brugha on 23 October 1920.[36] Brugha had a plan to have members of the British cabinet assassinated and to send armed men into the House of Commons. When he outlined the scheme to the Dáil cabinet, Griffith, in charge of the meeting, was totally against the notion, saying that he would never agree to it, but Brugha told him that they all knew where he stood, had no illusions about him, did not expect him to follow them, and did not want his agreement to anything. But the proposed action did not go ahead.[37]

Griffith's attitude to the men who were carrying out the military actions on the ground is difficult to assess. Most likely he had virtually no contact with them. There is a document in the Mulcahy papers which is very revealing. Dating from late April 1922, it is apparently an intelligence report on the views of the garrison occupying the Four Courts at that time. According to this, the anti-Treaty IRA could justify their demand for their own independent executive because: '...the army was never really the army of the government. That [the Ministry of] Defence was simply a connective link with the cabinet. That the army executive planned the war and carried their plan whether the cabinet was willing or not and that the cabinet and Dáil were often most unwilling. That the cabinet refused to accept

34 Figgis, *Recollections*, pp.274-5; Blythe in *Irish Times*, 17 June 1970.

35 *Irish Times*, 17 June 1970.

36 *ibid.*, 16 April 1971.

37 Terence Ryle Dwyer, *Michael Collins and the Treaty: His Differences with de Valera* (Dublin/Cork, 1981), pp.31-2; Ó Bróin, *Revolutionary Underground*, p.202.

responsibility for the shooting of police early on, particularly Arthur Griffith'.[38]

It was not until March 1921 that the Dáil for the first time formally took responsibility for IRA actions and this was after de Valera had resumed his presidency. Davis expressed the belief that Griffith would have done likewise, but perhaps with more inner misgivings than de Valera who had been far from the scene of the action.[39] But this is to invite the question why Griffith did not indeed do so between the middle of 1919 and the end of 1920 while he was acting as de Valera's deputy.

A detail concerning Erskine Childers is relevant here. When Childers joined the Sinn Féin publicity department he thought it was in severe need of reorganisation. He was particularly disturbed that the political side of the movement had not taken responsibility for the military actions of the Volunteers and he believed that Griffith was the cause.[40]

Griffith's treatment of the British agent provocateur, Francis Harling, from whom he extracted the maximum propaganda value, shows his divergence from the methods of the IRA (whom he preferred to call by the old name of Irish Volunteers). In the spring of 1920 a man calling himself 'Hardy' sought Griffith out. He told him that he had been in jail for smuggling arms into Ireland and had an ingenious plan for capturing the leaders of the British army in Ireland. He would only reveal it to the leaders of the IRA, especially Collins.

Griffith strung him along for a while in order to find out more about him, and came to the conclusion that he was a British agent. He arranged for Harling to be brought to a place known to be a Sinn Féin premises to meet whom he thought were IRA leaders, but who were really Irish and foreign journalists. Harling unfolded his plan to them, a dangerous plan because it involved the IRA leaders revealing themselves. Then Griffith read out the true account of Harling's background and ordered him to be on the boat to England that night.[41]

Griffith's reaction to the peace overtures of late 1920 are instructive as regards his attitude to the campaign of violence. As early as 28 July 1920, Alfred T. Davies, Conservative MP for Lincoln, wrote to Griffith telling him that he believed the British government would give Sinn Féin anything except a republic. Davies informed Griffith that he had spoken to many MPs and that all of them had suggested Dominion

38 Valiulis, *Mulcahy*, p.145.

39 Davis, *Arthur Griffith*, p.34.

40 Andrew Boyle, *The Riddle of Erskine Childers* (London, 1977), p.257.

41 Colum, *Griffith*, pp.227-8.

Home Rule for Ireland.[42] It is not known if Griffith responded to this overture, and Davies was not a member of the British government. But the letter does show that a large body of British political opinion regarded Griffith as likely to be susceptible to suggestions for peace.

The Mayo businessman, Patrick Moylett, has left an account of secret talks he held in London with the British government in October/November 1920. He was a friend of Griffith, was going to London on business at the time, and Griffith requested him to make contact with the British. He met C.J. Philips, secretary to Lloyd George and the Cabinet Committee on Ireland, H.A.L. Fisher, chairman of the latter and Minister for Education, and Brigadier-General Sir George Cockerill, MP, who had been supreme head of British Intelligence during the war, and who had written to the London *Times* suggesting a truce, an amnesty and a conference without preliminary conditions.

Moylett reported to Griffith that the British were anxious for a settlement, and Griffith was heartened, but he wanted Moylett to get the British to recognise the Dáil. Moylett met Fisher and Philips again. They asked if a conference were arranged, would hostilities in Ireland cease, but Moylett thought that before the republicans ceased their actions Dáil Éireann would have to be formally recognised. Philips proposed that the Dáil would nominate three or four, and the British would do likewise, to discuss the basis of a formal conference. At Moylett's suggestion this was put in writing and he was asked to deliver it personally to Griffith.

When Griffith read it he 'actually broke down with emotion'. He immediately wrote a note of reply. 'While writing Griffith was visibly affected by high-wrought emotion, so much so that he could not refrain from laughing whilst the tears coursed down his cheeks. This was a phase of Griffith's character which was new to me. Usually he hid his emotions under a wonderfully calm and restrained exterior', Moylett recorded. Moylett met Griffith and Collins in Alderman Cole's house and Collins, who had been apprised of all the details, was delighted with Moylett's work.

Moylett returned to London and had more talks. Philips asked him how far from a republic the Irish were prepared to go. 'It was plain enough by this time that the idea of a sovereign, independent republic was a political concept that no British statesman could afford to consider. The adamantine attitude on this point had to be met with great caution and finesse', Moylett wrote. He told Philips that naturally the Irish wanted a republic but it would be far from being a threat to England because of its small army and navy. The Irish wanted an army,

42 Letter in library of late Nevin Griffith, Dublin.

complete control of their own affairs, fiscal autonomy and the usual consular services of any country. This talk occurred on 12 November, from which date 'really serious negotiations began', according to Moylett.

The morning after bloody Sunday, Philips asked Moylett to convey an urgent message to Griffith from Lloyd George: 'To ask Griffith for God's sake to keep his head, and not to break off the slender link that had been established. Tragic as the events in Dublin were, they were of no importance. These men were soldiers and they took a soldier's risk'. Detailed negotiations between Moylett and Philips continued after 21 November and got to a stage where Philips felt there would be preliminary agreement within a week. The talks had been carried on in a friendly spirit and in complete secrecy, and Moylett felt that it would be only a number of days before the terms of a truce were made public.

'Then came the deluge!' declared Moylett. Dublin Castle became suspicious that serious moves were afoot and wanted to know with whom the talks were being held. London refused to say, thereby confirming the Castle in its suspicions. The Castle authorities acted unilaterally and arrested Griffith, MacNeill, Duggan and others. Moylett was determined to break off the talks and return to Dublin but Philips begged him not to, as did his friends in London, and he reluctantly agreed to go on. One of the thorniest issues was exclusions from the truce. The British wished to exempt Collins and Dan Breen but Moylett would have none of it and stormed out. The British withdrew the exemptions. They were within seven days of publishing a truce when the British changed tack.

The Dublin Castle government threatened to resign en bloc if London went ahead; Chief-Secretary Greenwood had arranged to meet Archbishop Clune of Perth, who was then in England, and claimed he would get a better deal for Britain from a settlement arranged through him. The Galway Co. Council had passed a resolution for peace and Fr O'Flanagan had sent a peace telegram to Lloyd George. The latter felt the Irish were weakening and this made him more susceptible to Greenwood's urgings. He gave Dublin Castle two months to effect a settlement but Philips was sure that they would fail and that Moylett would be back again after that.[43]

When Griffith saw Clune the sticking-points were the surrender of arms and the right of the Dáil to meet freely. On 15 December, Griffith sent a peace formula to Collins for the Dáil cabinet's consideration. This did not openly insist that the Dáil be allowed to meet freely but stated that both sides would eschew violence with the aim of creating an

43 *Irish Times*, 15,16 November 1965.

atmosphere in which the Irish people's representatives could meet with the object of achieving a lasting peace.[44]

Clune's mediation came to nothing. What is noticeable about Griffith's attitude throughout, though, is his anxiety for the fighting to come to an end and the negotiations to begin.

Overview

Did the setting up of the Dáil and the declaration of independence mean that there was now an elected government with the right to wage war on behalf of the people? The problems about this are: the nature of the mandate provided by the 1918 election; the degree of control exerted by the elected members over the physical-force campaign; the refusal of the Catholic bishops at the time to accept Sinn Féin's right to use violent means. Most Irish people, some TDs (even though handpicked by Collins and Boland for their strong republicanism) and the Catholic hierarchy felt Sinn Féin's mandate was for a passive-resistance campaign.

Griffith's publicly-stated position in the 1919-21 period was that the Dáil and the people had tried hard for most of 1919 to pursue a purely non-violent course, but that British oppression provoked inevitable Irish counter-violence. He continuously publicised this case throughout the Anglo-Irish War in speeches at home and in Britain, in his paper *Young Ireland* and in the *Irish Bulletin*.[45] 'A reader of Griffith's *Young Ireland* before 1921 would gain the impression that an entirely non-violent Irish movement was continually beset by homicidal maniacs in British uniforms', Davis wrote.

The published memoirs of leading Irish guerrilla-war figures, like Breen and Ernie O'Malley, assert that *they* forced the violence on unenthusiastic Sinn Féin politicians. These memoirs demonstrate that a considerable number of supporters of passive resistance did exist. The coming of the Black and Tans and Auxiliaries weakened the influence of the non-violent wing and rendered the physical-force/passive-resistance debate somewhat obsolete.

Both the Griffith British-provocation and the Breen/O'Malley Irish-initiative cases are unsound. It was the divided leadership, not the local enterprise of a few guerrillas reacting against Dublin political control, that led to violence. It had been planned and justified long before the Soloheadbeg incident.

Griffith's position as acting head of the government during de Valera's

44 Younger, *Civil War*, p.120.

45 A mimeographed news-sheet distributed by the Dáil Department of Publicity to the world's press.

long absence in America was incongruous. He had negligible control over men like Collins who were orchestrating the physical-force campaign. He prevented whatever violent incidents he could. He became a split personality, privately condemning certain Irish acts of violence while publicly denouncing British aggression, and at the same time trying to put some of his original passive-resistance policies into practice.

While Griffith's passive-resistance backers found their situation increasingly difficult, their views were still heard throughout 1919. It was sometimes argued, for example, that certain 'crimes' were perpetrated by a dissident minority without the agreement or knowledge of the official Sinn Féin leaders. Breen asserted that some of the Sinn Féin leaders tried to persuade him and his friends to leave Ireland after the incident at Soloheadbeg.

Griffith considered men like Bishop Fogarty of Killaloe a much greater asset to the Sinn Féin cause than men like Breen. Fogarty persistently maintained that Sinn Féin could succeed without violence, no matter how much force the British used.

He wrote to Mrs Griffith after her husband's arrest in late November 1920: 'The world was given to understand that pacific assertors of Ireland's rights were not molested. Mr Griffith was the High-Priest of pacifism in the Sinn Féin movement'.[46]

The 74-day hunger strike of Terence MacSwiney, Lord Mayor of Cork, from August to October 1920, brought the question of physical force or passive resistance to the surface once again. It is true that MacSwiney did not espouse a non-violent approach.

In his *Principles of Freedom*, first published as a series of articles in *Irish Freedom* in 1911, he expressed his opposition to the original Griffith programme. But, as was seen in the case of Gandhi many times, the hunger strike is one of the main weapons of non-violent practitioners. Paying tribute to MacSwiney, Griffith stressed his dictum that those who endured, not those who inflicted the most would win. Perhaps this was as close as he could go in late 1920 to the original non-violent ideas of Robert Lynd.

Even after such intensely violent episodes as bloody Sunday in Dublin and the Kilmichael ambush in Cork, his *Young Ireland* suggested violence was at best only one aspect of national policy and not as effective as industrial expansion. Privately, as has been noted, he did not hesitate to express his horror at the assassination of the British agents on 'bloody Sunday'.

46 Bishop Michael Fogarty of Killaloe to Mrs Griffith, 29 November 1920, in library of late Nevin Griffith, Dublin.

It appears that, through Fogarty, he tried in vain to get the Irish hierarchy to issue a strong condemnation of the British terror campaign. While some nationalist journals of the period sometimes attacked the bishops' attitude, it is significant that Griffith's *Young Ireland* was not conspicuous among them.[47]

Because, on the surface, he appeared to accept the violence of the 1919-21 period, was Griffith not really an adherent of non-violent resistance? A brief look at the career of Mahatma Gandhi, probably the best known non-violent resister in modern history, is instructive in this regard. Gandhi organised an Indian ambulance brigade for Britain during the Boer War and recruited in India for the British during the First World War. When he became fully converted to Indian nationalism after the First World War, he constantly declared that courageous violence was morally better than cowardly compliance. In 1920 he tried his first nationwide civil disobedience campaign based on a refusal to pay the salt tax.

But when it broke into violence, he called it off, arguing that the people as a whole had not been prepared enough and did not fully understand the deeper implications of a campaign of civil disobedience. Despite his great work in the Indian independence movement, Gandhi never succeeded in persuading all of the Indian people to non-violence.

That it is almost impossible to get acceptance of a moral idea, or respect for the law, in any country where a majority of the people live near to the level of mere survival, was an important point made by Davis. Gandhi's heroic self-sacrifice won him enormous popular esteem but he had to continually call off national campaigns because of outbreaks of violence.

The Irish struggle was also marked by heroic self-sacrifice, such as the death of MacSwiney after a protracted hunger strike, and Gandhi was heard to speak in an almost reverential tone about the unconquerable spirit of the Irish people. Though he wished the struggle had not ended in violence, he paid tribute to Griffith, the architect of non-cooperation with the English in Ireland, in his own preparation of India's plan for non-cooperation.

Should Griffith have tried to call off the struggle in Ireland when Gandhi called it off in India? The situations in the two countries were not comparable. Gandhi's mass campaign consisted simply of the sale of banned pamphlets and the refusal to pay the salt tax. But Sinn Féin had won a general election and had set up a government in opposition to the

47 Davis, 'Advocacy of passive resistance', pp.42-7 *passim*. See also Richard Davis, 'Arthur Griffith 1872(*sic*)-1922: architect of modern Ireland', in *History Today*, 1979, 29(4), pp.251-2. And Davis, *Arthur Griffith*, pp.28-32 *passim*.

British government in Ireland. Not everyone at the time believed in non-violence and the choices were cowardly acquiescence or violent resistance when the Dáil was suppressed.

There was nothing inconsistent in Griffith retaining his leadership because by that time it was too late to turn back. 'Had he been granted time to accustom Ireland to his policy, to create a greater feeling of respect for law as distinguished from British domination, and, above all, to orient his movement in the direction of diminishing the widespread and degrading poverty which existed, he might have guided the country which he loved to a peaceful settlement marred neither by civil war nor partition - a consummation not achieved by the Mahatma in India', wrote Davis. He concluded that Griffith and Gandhi unfortunately experienced 'a common failure...when confronted by surprisingly similar obstacles'.[48]

48 Davis, 'Griffith and Gandhi', pp.39-43 *passim*.

Part III

Crossing The Great Divide: Griffith and Irish Unionism

'We anxiously wish to see the day
when every Irishman shall be a citizen,
when Catholics and Protestants,
equally interested in their country's
welfare, possessing equal freedom and
equal privileges, shall learn to look upon each
other as brothers, the children of the same God
and the natives of the same land,
and when the only strife among them
shall be who shall serve
their country best'.

Sinn Féin, 5 May 1906

CHAPTER I

AFFINITES AND ARGUMENTS

Irish nationalism has been subjected to stringent examination by historians in the past 25 years. One of its principal shortcomings has been seen as its immaturity in relation to Irish, and especially Ulster, unionism. Historians have demonstrated a failure on the part of nationalists to make any genuine attempt to come to terms with the fears unionists had of Irish independence from British rule.

The divide-and-rule tactics of political and industrial leaders were leading Ulster Protestants astray; they were merely bluffing in their opposition to Irish self-government; religion was irrelevant to that opposition - these are some of the misapprehensions that have been identified among nationalists in relation to unionism.[1] Did Griffith display any or all of the inadequacies in relation to Irish unionism that historians have uncovered?

Arthur Griffith had an Ulster Protestant ancestry. The Griffith family was originally from Co. Cavan - so he said opening his by-election campaign at Bailieboro in that county on 28 April 1918. He told his election workers that the family had originally been farmers at Redhills, Co. Cavan. There are 18th-century records of lands leased at Redhills by Griffiths (Protestants) who lived at Cornapaste, Co. Monaghan. There is a tradition that his grandfather converted to Catholicism on marriage. His oldest brother, who was born in 1865, was given a very Protestant name, William George, as was his sister, Marcella, born the following year.[2]

Pilib Ó Mordha has shown that Griffith's ancestors most likely came from Laurelhill, Cornapaste and Fastry in Co. Monaghan. Although he found no clear documentary proof of it, Ó Mordha speculated that it was his great-grandfather who converted from Protestantism.[3]

Griffith's first job was with a printing firm owned by a Protestant lady, Ms Underwood, at 12 Eden Quay. He liked to tell a story of one

1 Richard Davis, 'Ulster Protestants and the Sinn Féin press, 1914-22', in *Éire-Ireland*, 1980, XV, 4, p.61.

2 Ms. 22,293 NLI.

3 Pilib Ó Mordha, 'The Griffiths of Laurelhill, Co. Monaghan, and associated families', in *The Clogher Record*, XIV, 4 (1993), pp.111-124.

of the Underwoods, Ms Underwood's father or brother. One day this gentleman noticed the new boy and said: 'Well, my boy! When was the battle of Clontarf?' When Griffith gave the correct answer, his comment was: 'That's right, my boy! Know your Irish history'. Sometimes when passing through the works he would put a question to Griffith jocosely. The incident impressed itself on Griffith and he often used it to illustrate a favourite point: the Protestant unionist was as national as the Catholic nationalist, and the British made use of religious differences in Ireland for their own ends.[4]

At the inaugural meeting of the CLS, its founder William Rooney lectured on the 19th-century Irish poet and antiquarian, Sir Samuel Ferguson. This respect for Ferguson, a political unionist, anticipated a tendency of the subsequent Sinn Féin movement.[5]

The first means by which Cumann na nGaedheal, the earliest organisation that Griffith induced to come into being, aimed to advance the cause of Irish national independence was by 'cultivating a fraternal spirit amongst Irishmen'.[6] There can be no doubt that Griffith had enormous respect for famous 18th- and 19th-century Irish Protestants. His debt to Dean Swift has already been noted and it will be recalled that he had profound admiration for Grattan's parliament of the late 18th century. Indeed at times he declared that Irish Protestant rule was preferable to control from England. The person whom he claimed as his political mentor was the young Trinity College Dublin graduate and Young Irelander, Thomas Davis. Of Davis he wrote: 'He softened our asperities and dispelled much of the bigotry and misconception that kept Irishmen apart, and he opened the way to national reunion....When the Irish read and reflect with Davis, their day of redemption will be at hand'.[7]

Griffith also greatly esteemed the Protestant historian W.E.H. Lecky who died in 1903. Lecky's five-volume *History of Ireland in the 18th Century* is admirable for its lack of prejudice, and Griffith declared that Lecky had achieved the highest honour as an historian.[8]

Sinn Féin, unlike the IPP, supported the Cooperative Movement of the unionist Sir Horace Plunkett, which aimed at a revival in Irish agriculture. Plunkett subscribed money to support Griffith's *Sinn Féin*

4 Ms. 22,293 NLI.

5 Davis, *Non-Violent Sinn Féin*, p.6.

6 O'Hegarty, *Irl. under Union*, p.639.

7 Arthur Griffith (ed.), *Thomas Davis: the Thinker and Teacher* (Dublin, 1914), pp.xii,xiv.

8 *United Irishman*, 31 October 1903.

daily, which so badly needed funds.[9] When Plunkett, who had been chairman of Lloyd George's Irish Convention in 1917-18, called for Colonial Home Rule for Ireland in April 1918, Griffith did not altogether dismiss the idea.[10] He afterwards nominated Plunkett to the first Senate of the Irish Free State.

Griffith condemned the sectarianism of one of his contemporary Dublin newspaper editors, D.P. Moran of the *Leader*. As already noted, in his clash with Moran he accused him of seeking 'to arouse the suspicions and antipathy of the Irishman of fifty generations against the Irishman of five'. He denounced the *Leader* for appealing to 'the lowest, basest and meanest passion in man - religious bigotry'.[11]

The enlargement of university education was a question prominent in late 19th- and early 20th-century Irish politics. Griffith hoped that Trinity College, Dublin, would expand to become a national university, an *alma mater* for the leaders of Ireland, as he put it.[12] He did not want separate universities for Catholics and Protestants, believing that the one type of university that would be of lasting benefit to the nation would be one open to Catholics, Protestants, Dissenters and groups other than these, and that would welcome the children of the poor on an equal footing with the children of the rich.[13] Any settlement of the university question which did not facilitate the child of the poorest person in Ireland and which did not enable Catholics and Protestants to come together on neutral ground was a travesty and denial of true education.[14]

When Birrell's Bill (March 1908) proposed three National University of Ireland colleges for Catholics, Queen's University Belfast for Presbyterians, and Trinity College Dublin for Anglicans, Griffith was vehemently opposed. He urged nationalists to boycott the new universities if they were set up.[15] In the final article of his *Resurrection of Hungary* series, Griffith called on the IPP to withdraw from Westminster and to set up a Council of 300 to formulate national policies which could be put into practice by the county councils and other local bodies. By doing this, he suggested that a form of internal Home Rule, under the

9 Davis, *Non-Violent Sinn Féin*, pp.50,61.

10 *Nationality*, 20 April 1918.

11 *United Irishman*, 10 June 1899, 12 January 1901.

12 *ibid.*, 10 January 1903.

13 *ibid.*, 13 April 1901.

14 *ibid.*, 21 November 1903.

15 *ibid.*, 4 April 1908; Ó Lúing, *Ó Gríofa*, pp.188-90.

British monarchy, could be created in Ireland which could bring together the two opposite traditions: nationalism and unionism.[16]

He saw his dual-monarchy policy as the means of attracting the widest possible support in Ireland as a whole. He explained to O'Hegarty that he was willing to forgo his separatism in the interests of unity. O'Hegarty remarked that Griffith was always aware of the weakness of the complete separatist position in relation to Irish unity, and described him as a disciple of Thomas Davis for whom the unity of all Irish people was of paramount importance.[17] It is certain that he saw the 1782 constitution as a possible basis for unity with the unionists.[18]

He was encouraged when the unionist Standish O'Grady[19] suggested that his Hungarian policy would force unionists to 'shift their ground'. Griffith believed that unionists could only be represented through the Irish nation. They may have had a 'logical excuse for existence' in the days of Repeal, Fenianism and Home Rule. But if they rejected the dual monarchy they showed themselves 'an English garrison maintained by British armed force' who would now, to take O'Grady further, have to 'shift their ground' into England.[20]

Davis was probably right when he considered Griffith 'naive' if he thought he could convert opponents by forcing them 'into intellectual corners'. Davis was also correct when he observed that in any event O'Grady was far from being a representative unionist.[21]

Ulick O'Connor believed that Griffith ranked with O'Connell and Parnell as one of the three great Irish leaders of the post-Union era, because he worked out a way of uniting all Irishmen.[22] A number of other commentators held that he sacrificed his own personal preference - separatism - and put forward the compromise of the dual monarchy to try to conciliate unionists.[23]

But a different view has been advanced. Michael Laffan remarked that Griffith's *Resurrection of Hungary* recognised only two nationalities in the

16 Glandon, *Griffith and Advanced-Nationalist Press*, pp.15-16.

17 O'Hegarty, *Irl. under Union*, pp.652,728-9.

18 Ó Lúing, *Ó Gríofa*, p.143; Colum, *Griffith*, p.135.

19 His translations of the ancient Irish sagas were very well known.

20 *United Irishman*, 21,28 January 1905.

21 Davis, *Non-Violent Sinn Féin*, p.117.

22 O'Connor, *A Terrible Beauty*, p.28.

23 MacDonagh, *Union*, p.77; Tierney, *MacNeill*, p.289; Curran, *Free State*, p.42; Younger, *Griffith*, p.24.

Austro-Hungarian Empire, which he compared to the British and Irish. This ignored the fact, well known to unionists by 1921, that his Hungarian heroes had oppressed their own minorities. This could only have frightened Irish Protestants, Laffan believed.[24]

Laffan, however, elsewhere observed that Griffith's pre-1916 Sinn Féin was 'monarchist', and although few of its followers were avid royalists or thought an Irish kingdom worth toiling for, many felt strongly that to include an Irish republic among Sinn Féin's aims would only further alienate unionists and increase the obstacles in the way of any ultimate settlement.[25] This is certainly how Griffith felt and that is why he put forward his dual-monarchy proposal.

Griffith attracted to early Sinn Féin a number of Protestant supporters who continued to have links with their own communities. The two most interesting were J.O. Hannay, better known as the novelist George A. Bermingham, and the Presbyterian essayist Robert Lynd. Hannay remained on the fringe of Sinn Féin, communicating with Griffith by letter, and sometimes contributing to his papers and year books.

Hannay implored Sinn Féin to pay more attention to genuine Protestant fears over such issues as the *Ne Temere* decree on mixed marriages and the question of state education to which the Catholic Church was so opposed. Hannay contended that it was their fear of the Catholic Church which prevented a number of Irish unionists from becoming nationalists. But Griffith and Sinn Féin were reluctant to take up such contentious religious issues because they were anxious not to provoke the hostility of the Catholic Church.

However, Griffith did condemn the sectarianism of the Ancient Order of Hibernians. The Order 'had given the Orangemen the only explanation for their existence', he asserted.[26]

Lynd was actively involved in early Sinn Féin as a London member of its executive and as a writer of articles outlining a non-violent policy for nationalists to follow. When the First World War broke out, both Lynd and Hannay displayed what Davis described as 'a persistence of ancestral loyalties' by supporting Britain in that conflict. Griffith declared them banished from the nationalist movement as a result.[27] He dismissed Lynd as basically 'an English philosophical radical' and never an Irish nationalist, while Hannay's desertion was explained as a succumbing to

24 Laffan, *Partition*, p.73.

25 Laffan, 'Unification of Sinn Féin', p.376.

26 Davis, *Non-Violent Sinn Féin*, pp.56-7.

27 See 'Down among the dead men' in *Nationality*, 29 January 1916.

material attractions. Both of these early converts to Sinn Féin again supported the Irish right to self-government during the Anglo-Irish War.[28]

Writing about Griffith some years after his death, Lynd expressed the faith he had in his good intentions: '...he had a large-minded conception of nationality and wished to create an Irish civilisation that would be as acceptable ultimately to the old unionists as to the nationalists. Politically, he preached hatred of England, but he looked forward to peace with England as the ideal'.[29]

In *The Orangeman and the Nation* (Belfast, 1907) Lynd made a case which Griffith and Sinn Féin utilised for many years afterwards. Lynd contended that, leaving aside his religious bigotry, the Orangeman was an upstanding Irish citizen who had much better qualities than half-hearted Catholic supporters of the IPP. He lamented how the various vested interests had indoctrinated the Orangeman, and praised his sincerity, dedication and extremism.

Griffith, on occasion, took a similar approach. He respected Irishmen who honestly believed that they were labouring for the good of their own country rather than England; unionists who adhered to Britain in the hope of material benefit, and Irish people who feared that Ireland could not survive alone were condemned by him. He felt that the 'honest' and 'bigoted' Orangeman, who had no love for England but for whom Rome held a terror, deserved more consideration. His sincerity went some way towards compensating for his ignorance and prejudice.

He maintained that the first nationalists had been those Orangemen who opposed the Act of Union and that Daniel O'Connell, because of his close association with Roman Catholicism, repelled them. He was able to demonstrate that even by the mid-19th century, Orangemen were still divided in their attitude to Irish self-government. Anti-papist Orange demagogues, like William Johnston of Ballykilbeg and the Rev. R.R. Kane, actually impressed Griffith and he regretted that British Conservatives, in collaboration with Ulster business interests, had, by means of huge subsidies, weaned Orangemen away from support for Irish nationalism.

He blamed the parliamentarians and the sectarianism of the Ancient

28 Davis, 'Ulster Protestants Sinn Féin press', pp.61-4 *passim*.

29 Lynd, *Galway*, p.109.

Order of Hibernians[30] for provoking the Carson-led campaign against Home Rule.[31]

Griffith's views on Orangeism may seem hopelessly naive now but in the early years of the century they made some sense. An example would be that of the Lisburn journalist, Robert Lindsay Crawford, who tried to combine in the Independent Orange Order extreme Protestantism and moderate Irish nationalism. But the powerful Ulster unionist leaders ensured the destruction of his endeavours. Griffith wanted to cooperate with Crawford but the IRB members of Sinn Féin stymied any such efforts. Crawford emigrated to Canada where, during the Anglo-Irish War, he was an assiduous exponent of Sinn Féin propaganda.[32]

Before Sinn Féin was established, National Council supporters were urged to vote for unionists in Dublin Corporation elections rather than for nationalists who signed loyal addresses.'A foeman is to be fought - he may be respected. A renegade is to be loathed and crushed', declared Griffith.[33]

The result of the North Leitrim election in February 1908 surprised everyone: Meehan (IPP) 3,103; Dolan (Sinn Féin) 1,157. At the 1900 election, the IPP candidate had defeated his unionist opponent by 4,025 to 383. There were an estimated 600 unionists living in the constituency. Dolan's good showing worried the IPP whose spokesman asserted that his votes came from personal supporters and unionists and were not cast for Sinn Féin. But the unionist *Irish Times* dismissed the notion of unionists voting for Sinn Féin because its attitude to England was 'so ridiculous and so disloyal'.

Other accusations of an alliance between Sinn Féin and unionism were made. In Tyrone in 1907 Sinn Féin supporters, it was asserted, had voted *en bloc* for a unionist against the Liberal solicitor-general, who was a Home Rule supporter. In Dublin the following year it was claimed that unionists had been advised to vote for the Sinn Féin candidate, Walter Cole, in an election in the Drumcondra ward to Dublin Corporation.

The *Irish Times'* reaction to the North Leitrim result was interesting. It was very impressed by Dolan's respectable vote in what had been one of the IPP's safest seats. The paper praised the non-political elements of the

30 During his time it was largely controlled by the northern IPP MP, Joseph Devlin, and Griffith came into direct and bruising conflict with it at the North Leitrim by-election.

31 Davis, 'Ulster Protestants and Sinn Féin press', pp.64-5.

32 *ibid.*, pp.65-6.

33 *United Irishman*, 7 January 1905.

Sinn Féin programme, believing the encouragement of Irish self-reliance to be similar to constructive unionism.

Griffith's *Sinn Féin* daily of 1909-10 was criticised for going too far in its attempts to conciliate unionists and its editor was accused by vigilant IRB men of diluting nationalist doctrine to please unionists.[34]

Griffith edited four *Irish Year Books* between 1908 and 1911. In his own words they were 'designed to supply the Irish public generally with information on Ireland in all its aspects'.[35] He hoped that they would build up to an Irish encyclopedia. The response of the contributors, all unpaid, heartened him greatly. It confirmed his faith that 'Irish patriotism is the monopoly of no party, no sect, no class'. He pointed out that 'unionist and anti-unionist, Catholic, Protestant, Presbyterian, Methodist, Quaker, the northern manufacturer and the southern agriculturist, the man of leisure and the man of toil - all are here offering the result of their study or their experience to help their country'.[36]

This showed what Griffith was working towards - a common ideal among Irish people regardless of class, creed or political affiliation, a consensus. The 1782 constitution was important to him, not as an ultimate settlement, but as something around which a consensus could be built. In a deliberative man like Griffith, the desire for a consensus was intense.[37]

The importance of the north-east for the rest of Ireland, in Griffith's thinking, cannot be over-emphasised. It represented what he wished to see achieved all over the country. The ideal to which he hoped his policy would lead was an industrial revolution in the rest of Ireland based on the model of the north-east. The basis of his economic policy was protection of native industries and the imposition of duties on imports.

Given such aims, it was natural that Ulster formed a central part of his thinking. The complete rejection of the idea of Irish self-government by Belfast business interests did not lessen in any way the vital role he envisaged for that part of the country in the Ireland of the future. There was no question of the industrialised north-east being heavily taxed in the interest of the agrarian south. Ulster was, as Emil Strauss put it, 'a precious plant to be nourished by protective duties'.[38]

34 Davis, *Non-Violent Sinn Féin*, pp.48-9; Davis, *Arthur Griffith*, p.15.

35 Ms. 10,872 NLI.

36 Preface to *The Irish Year Book/Leabhar na hÉireann* (Dublin, National Council of Sinn Féin, 1908).

37 Colum, *Griffith*, p.95.

38 Strauss, *Irish Nationalism and British Democracy*, p.219.

But Griffith took little cognisance of the deep hostility of Ulster commercial interests towards his policy of protection. The possibility of economic barriers between Ireland and the rest of the world, and especially between Ireland and Britain, was perceived by them as a serious threat to the material interests of Ulster commerce.[39]

D.S. Johnson argued that Griffith paid little attention in his writings to the economic interests of the people of the north-east. For example, in his *Sinn Féin Policy*, Dublin was referred to fifteen times, Cork five, and Belfast not at all. Also, his 1909 *Year Book* had chapters on the main industries outside the north-east, such as brewing and distilling, and even on the smaller industries, but had nothing on the linen and shipbuilding industries of the north-east.

But it is most likely that unionist opposition to Irish self-government and unity was not inspired mainly by the fear that protectionism would result from them. For example, in 1911, the president of the Belfast Chamber of Commerce, J. Milne Barbour, who was the leading unionist economic spokesman, and who afterwards became Minister for Commerce in the government of Northern Ireland, started his evidence to the Primrose Committee on Irish finance by putting forward the traditional unionist view that Home Rule was feared because of the damage protectionism would do the northern economy. But when he was skilfully cross-examined, especially by the Bishop of Ross, Dr Kelly, he had to admit not only that the motivation behind the opposition to Home Rule was mainly religious but that in fact the spinning sector of the linen industry would definitely benefit from a tariff that stopped or reduced continental dumping. (And Milne Barbour was himself a big linen manufacturer.)[40]

So Griffith's protectionist policy was not altogether inimical to northern unionist economic interests. But he refused to accept the religious dimension to northern unionism's aversion to Irish independence, and that dimension may, in the last analysis, have been the most important.

39 Strauss, *Irish Nationalism and British Democracy*, pp.231-2.

40 D.S. Johnson, 'Partition and cross-border trade in the 1920s', in Peter Roebuck (ed.), *Plantation to Partition: Essays in Ulster History in Honour of J.L. McCracken* (Belfast, 1981), pp.229-30.

Chapter II

Resistance: Unionist and Nationalist

Building Bridges Across a Widening Chasm: 1910-14

When the prospect of Home Rule grew more immediate from 1910 onwards, Griffith frequently addressed unionists and urged them to devise a scheme which would ensure that they would not be treated unfairly in a self-governing Irish state. He also exhorted them to identify their interests with their native country and to press for a genuine measure of independence. Proportional Representation was strongly advocated by him because it would ensure that minorities would not be stifled. This would also be the purpose of the upper house in the new Irish parliament. He further argued that unionists representing the urban north, and Sinn Féin representing the urban south, could make common cause against the agrarian interests for which the IPP largely acted.[1]

As Ulster unionist opposition to Home Rule intensified, he turned his mind to discovering concrete guarantees which would reassure the north-east that it would suffer no discrimination in an independent Ireland. The IPP was urged to stop wasting its time setting the minds of potential *English* opponents of Home Rule at rest, and to concentrate its efforts in this direction on Irish unionists instead.[2] Indeed, Griffith even went so far as to praise the nascent anti-British sentiment being displayed in Ulster, and promised unionists that they would have the support and sympathy of nationalist Ireland in their struggle with the British parliament. What were they doing but putting Sinn Féin policy into practice, he reasoned.[3]

Alternatives to Home Rule were considered by him, such as the proposition of provincial assemblies subordinate to a national parliament.[4] He welcomed the few suggestions for safeguards that

1 *Sinn Féin*, 1 January 1910; 29 October 1910; 24 December 1910.

2 *ibid.*, 11 November 1911.

3 *ibid.*, 24 August 1912; 11 October 1913; 20 December 1913; 28 March 1914; Davis, *Non-Violent Sinn Féin*, pp.55-6.

4 *ibid.*, 6 September 1913.

emanated from the unionist side, and argued that they should be given serious and generous consideration by nationalists.[5] Indeed, from the time that the Home Rule sun (or cloud) appeared on the horizon, he had been repeatedly urging unionists to put forward whatever safeguards they required.

By 1914 he finally accepted that they would not name what they did not want - there was no safeguard against the fact that they would be in a permanent minority in an all-Ireland polity. But though in a minority they need not fear that they would be subject to disabilities, and he believed every effort should be made to remove their fears. So in April 1914, under Griffith's direction, members of Sinn Féin formed the Anti-Partition of Ireland Committee (APIC), and his newspaper published its practical proposals which he hoped would win unionist agreement to a self-governing parliament for all Ireland.

Sinn Féin's APIC proposed to give Ulster representation in an Irish parliament which would reflect the province's comparative importance to the rest of the country, something which the Home Rule Bill did not do. The Committee wanted to amend the Bill to give Belfast, the biggest industrial and business part of Ireland, three more representatives. It also wished to increase the representation of the other urban centres in Ulster with populations between ten and twelve-and-a-half thousand.

It was also proposed to change the Bill in relation to the rest of Ireland to give the dispersed unionist minority a greater voice. Sinn Féin suggested increasing the membership of the new Irish lower house from 161 to 194, of which total Ulster would elect 74. The results of these changes would mean an additional eleven members from the mainly unionist counties; between eleven and fifteen southern unionist representatives would be elected, and borough representation would increase from 34 to 52.[6]

In summary, the rest of APIC's suggestions were:

(a) all of Ireland was to be the unit to elect the upper house of the proposed new parliament and representation of the southern unionist minority was to be ensured by proportional representation;

(b) there was to be no tax on the linen trade without the agreement of the Ulster members;

(c) the Ulster representatives would always choose the chairman of the joint exchequer board;

(d) all posts in the new civil service were to be filled by examination;

(e) the Ulster Volunteer Force was to be retained under its then leaders

5 *Sinn Féin*, 3 January 1914.

6 Glandon, *Griffith and Advanced-Nationalist Press*, pp.49-50.

as part of an Irish Volunteer Force and would not, except in the case of an invasion, be asked to serve outside Ulster;

(f) there would be alternating sittings of the Irish parliament in Belfast and Dublin.[7]

R.M. Henry rightly thought these 'the most statesmanlike and generous proposals put forward on the nationalist side'. The Belfast Trades Council approved them and they were only narrowly defeated at a number of Ulster Unionist Council meetings, but the unionist political leaders ignored them.[8] Extreme republicans did not think too much of them either. Dorothy Macardle declared that they would have given unionists a disproportionate amount of influence in the proposed Home Rule parliament and would probably have proved unacceptable to republicans.[9]

The proposals were the fruit of much thought devoted by Griffith to trying to solve the great problem of the danger of partition, and they were sensible and generous to the north-east.[10] This episode clearly showed how sensitive he was to the Ulster problem and how far he was willing to go to assuage northern unionist fears. Not only would Ulster be significantly over-represented in the new Irish legislature of his design, but its members would have a veto and near autonomy on economic issues.[11] Davis's assessment was that APIC's offer constituted fair terms by any rational criterion, but the flaw lay in the proposals' complete emphasis on economics, to the exclusion of religious considerations. His conclusion that it remained the case that Sinn Féin had no real solution to the Ulster difficulty, while true, was unduly harsh, and did not sufficiently acknowledge the distance Griffith was prepared to go to reassure unionists.[12]

Johnson was strongly sceptical about the APIC proposals. He regarded them as tardy and as being put forward only when it began to seem as if the country might indeed be partitioned. Although they offered a guarantee for the linen trade, they contained no mention of shipbuilding. Overall, Johnson was doubtful about the sincerity of the

7 *Sinn Féin*, 18 April 1914; 25 April 1914; 9 May 1914; 13 June 1914.

8 Henry, *Evolution*, pp.150-51; Glandon, *Griffith and Advanced-Nationalist Press*, p.51.

9 Macardle, *Irish Republic*, pp.99-100.

10 Ó Lúing, *Ó Gríofa*, pp.241-2.

11 MacDonagh, *States*, p.65.

12 Davis, *Non-Violent Sinn Féin*, pp.56-8.

last-minute conversion, especially as the *Sinn Féin Policy* was reprinted unchanged in 1918.[13]

One might respond that, however late the offer was made, at least it *was* made, and it was the only one of substance to emanate from the nationalist side at the time. Furthermore, it must be remembered that from the time Home Rule first appeared a very likely prospect, Griffith repeatedly urged unionists to name whatever safeguards and guarantees they required.

As the northern opposition to Home Rule intensified in the summer of 1914, Griffith condemned the Ulster unionists for demanding a veto on the rights of the whole country: 'There can be no more ascendancy - whatever the cost. The rights, the apprehensions, even the prejudices of the Ulster unionist must be dealt with broadly, fairly and generously in Ireland. But his implied claim to superiority over his countrymen can only be dealt with in one way if it be explicitly put forward'.[14] What that way was Griffith did not specify.

However, he assured unionists that an Irish parliament, meeting alternately in Belfast and Dublin as Sinn Féin proposed, need not hold any fear for them. The two cities would balance each other, he maintained, and as long as the industry, trade and wealth of Ulster were protected from the threat of any other interests, such a balance could be preserved to the satisfaction of all.[15]

Griffith's preoccupation with economics is again seen here. He refused to accept that unionist opposition had any religious basis and consequently made no attempt to address this aspect of the problem. J.J. Lee has recently shown the extent to which the unionist aversion to being ruled by the majority on the island was racial.[16] Griffith refused to contemplate this.

The Home Rule Bill became law in September 1914 but was suspended for the duration of the war. As the war carried on, it seemed that Griffith's attitude to unionist opposition to Irish self-government was hardening. In October 1915 he wrote: 'The only preventative to the exclusion of Ulster is a strong, powerful, well-armed and well-disciplined force of determined Irish Volunteers'.[17] From this Glandon

13 Johnson, 'Partition and cross-border trade', pp.229-30.

14 *Sinn Féin*, 2 May 1914.

15 *ibid.*, 13 June 1914.

16 Lee, *Irl. 1912-85*, pp.2-5.

17 *Nationality*, 16 October 1915.

concluded that by that time 'all possibility of political compromise on Ulster apparently had been abandoned by Griffith and Sinn Féin'.[18]

This is too drastic. No doubt Griffith saw such a Volunteer force as an effective bargaining counter in any future negotiations with the British, just as the Ulster Volunteers had proved for the unionist leaders in 1913-14. It will be seen from what follows that he rejected any notion of coercing the Ulster unionists and that he remained very alert to the need to keep a path to unity with the north always open.

'The Dreary Steeples'

The 1916 Rising and the First World War deepened Ulster unionist hostility to Irish independence. In post-Rising Sinn Féin there were two main strains of thought. One of these aimed at a republic and favoured physical force as the means to attain it. How unionists, who so vehemently resisted a lesser measure of independence like Home Rule, were to be brought to accept a republic, was not considered. The other strain favoured the dual-monarchy compromise as the only hope of persuading unionists to accept a self-governing Ireland, even though it had not so persuaded them before 1914 and dual monarchy would be a wider measure of independence than Home Rule.

One of the main reasons why Griffith opposed a republic as the goal of Sinn Féin in October 1917, and why he was against the first Dáil declaring a republic in January 1919, was that he realised the impossibility of achieving that status for the whole of Ireland. More than anyone else he had always been aware of the threat, for the unity of the country, that the separatist position held.[19]

Faced with pressure from America, Lloyd George convened in the summer of 1917 his Irish Convention, consisting of the Home Rule and unionist leaders, with the aim of reaching a compromise. Sinn Féin did not attend. The Convention continued to meet until the spring of 1918. Its failure to find any common ground finally jettisoned the notion that any arrangement was possible, in the conditions then existing, which would bring about an Ireland that was both united and self-governing.

This was an unpalatable message and it is no surprise that contemporaries did not want to accept it. For another few years, the IPP, Sinn Féin and the British government continued to believe some arrangement could be achieved which would involve all of Ireland. But the persistence of such a belief is hard to understand in view of the

18 Glandon, *Griffith and Advanced-Nationalist Press*, p.51.

19 *ibid.*, pp.176-7.

From left: Duggan, Griffith and Collins, London, October-December 1921

Convention deadlock. It must have been clear by that stage that unionists were not bluffing in their refusal to have anything to do with Home Rule.[20]

There continued to be a lot of ambiguity in nationalist attitudes to Ulster unionism in the 1917-21 period. Griffith rejected any coercion of unionists but at the same time he insisted that they had no right to separate from the rest of Ireland. Irish nationalists faced an almost impossible dilemma. An appeasement approach to unionists could not offer concessions on vital religious issues without antagonising the Roman Catholic Church. On the other hand, an aggressive approach would lead directly to communal war.

Was it possible to find a solution? Griffith thought so. But he chose once again to ignore the religious dimension of the problem. He contended that economic exploitation caused all the difficulty. No religious safeguards needed to be offered. An economic recession would soon make Belfast workers forget the Pope and turn on their employers.

He constantly worked to undermine what he described as the 'myth' of Ulster prosperity. The union with England had been a disaster for Ulster, he argued, reducing its population and rendering it poorer than Leinster. As well as this, English control prevented the development of the province's natural resources. Instead of needing English or Scottish

20 Lyons, *Famine*, p.386.

raw materials, Belfast was situated on a huge, unexploited coalfield and there were many other minerals in the province awaiting exploitation.

Griffith blamed Belfast firms, such as Workman and Clarke, for instigating most of the city's sectarian clashes. Although he condemned the Linen Trust on a similar basis, he so admired the linen industry in the north that he was willing to allow the northern members of any future Irish parliament an absolute veto over any legislation that might affect it. By this means he hoped to meet the fear of Ulster businessmen that protective Irish tariffs would seriously damage the export market for linen. Further, he argued that favourable railway transport rates in Ireland under an Irish government would make flax from all over the country available to Ulster manufacturers and would open up the home market much more.

His arguing in this way clearly had some effect because Sir Edward Carson was anxious to deny the existence of vast, untapped mineral resources in the north-east. But Griffith's economic appeal to the 'hard-headed' businessmen of the north was never likely to succeed in the face of the other difficult aspects of the question and was also partly handicapped by the ambiguity of nationalist approaches.

An intensive campaign of public meetings in the north was one of the none-too-practical solutions suggested to remedy what was lacking in the economic and general education of the Orangeman. Griffith spoke in Belfast, Derry and other northern locations before his election to two Ulster constituencies at the end of 1918, and it was the economic case he particularly stressed. But the unionist papers ignored what he said and only Catholic nationalists would have attended such meetings.[21]

The question seemed so complex and insoluble that during the Anglo-Irish War some nationalists preferred the simple, direct approach of physical force. For example, in an unguarded moment, Eoin O'Duffy, an active Volunteer commandant, remarked that if unionists did not prove amenable, they would have to be 'given the lead', by which he meant that force would be used against them.

By the middle of 1920 the increasing violence had all but overwhelmed Griffith's attempts to keep a peaceful campaign of propaganda in motion. Herbert Pim, an Ulster Protestant convert to Catholicism, who had been working closely with Griffith on his economic propaganda aimed at unionists, defected from Sinn Féin and returned to his original loyalty. The increasing preference he perceived

21 Davis, 'Ulster Protestants and Sinn Féin press', pp.72-4.

among nationalists for violence rather than industrial development dismayed him.[22]

As attacks against Catholics in Belfast became widespread in the summer of 1920, and as some employers required written pledges from their employees that they were not and would not become members of Sinn Féin, the Dáil debated a motion in August 1920 calling for a commercial boycott of Belfast. Some TDs recommended that a complete boycott of Belfast be carried out officially and thoroughly, while others thought that such a course would be a disastrous mistake, and that only the people behind the anti-Catholic pogroms should be boycotted.

Griffith, as acting-President, perceived the dilemma. He pointed out that a total boycott would be the same as one part of the country threatening war on another part, and that it would amount to behaving as if Belfast were outside the country altogether. Instead he counselled ending business with any bank having its headquarters in Belfast, thus putting a stop to the twelve million pounds that were paid into Belfast banks from the other provinces every year. He thought that this would soon bring the instigators of the pogroms to their senses.

He then proposed giving a week's notice to Belfast business people to confirm that they would not ask their employees to sign any more papers against their consciences. If the commercial interests would not agree, then they should be boycotted completely, but a list of companies should be drawn up that did not practise discrimination, and trade should be maintained with these.[23]

The Dáil did not take a vote on the issue and it was left to the cabinet to decide policy. Griffith must have persuaded the other ministers to accept his advice, because what he recommended was put into effect. The Belfast boycott achieved nothing but did much harm in that whatever damage it did to Belfast business was insignificant in comparison to the way that it contributed to a deterioration in north-south relations. It is difficult to understand why Griffith recommended the course that he did, but it is likely that he had to find a *via media* between those who were totally in favour of, and those who were totally against, the boycott.[24]

Davis, Tierney and Curran all referred to Griffith's reluctant support for the boycott as some sort of gesture towards northern nationalists, and as something rendered unavoidable, because of the pogroms conducted

22 Davis, 'Ulster Protestants and Sinn Féin press', pp.77–8.

23 *Minutes of First Dáil / Miontuairisc an Chéad Dála*, pp.191–4.

24 Ó Lúing, *Ó Gríofa*, pp.332–3.

against them.[25] Indeed, Davis believed that there was a certain inevitability about the boycott. The Dáil claimed that it was in response to attacks on, and the murder of, northern Catholics in the middle of 1920, but unionists contended that these were provoked by the killing of police officers, such as G.B. Smyth, an Ulsterman, in Cork, and District Inspector Swanzy in the north itself. (Ernest Blythe later described Swanzy's assassination as 'a deed of lunatic recklessness'.)[26]

There was a similar conflicting interpretation of the effect of the boycott. To Sinn Féin it was selective, applying only to those firms known to discriminate against their Catholic employees, and was having the desired effect. But unionists responded that the firms chosen were the wrong ones and that anyway there was too little trade with the south for it to cause the economic recession which other factors had brought about.

It is difficult to establish the origin of the boycott. Davis described it as 'yet another product of propagandist ambivalence'. It was begun by local communities, such as Tuam in Co. Galway, taken up by the General Council of Co. Councils, and finally sanctioned by the Dáil. Griffith was doubtful about it but his paper, *Young Ireland*, defended the policy later.[27]

The Northern Ireland parliament was officially opened in June 1921. Partition was now a *fait accompli* and the delegation that Griffith led to London at the end of that year was unable to undo it. The South African leader, J.C. Smuts, who met the Dáil cabinet in July 1921, felt that Griffith agreed with his view that partition would have to be accepted as a temporary fact which would mean that the rest of the country could achieve its independence.[28] How the Ulster issue figured in the Treaty negotiations will be examined in Part IV.

The following thoughts from Davis are worth repeating. He believed the Ulster problem so intractable, not because Irish Protestants and Catholics are so different, but because they have so much in common. Both communities are priest-ridden, 'excessively addicted to authority, rather than private judgement', have too much clerical involvement in education and politics, and their fundamentalism has led to sexual repression which has manifested itself in violence:

> It thus appears that earlier nationalists – such as Griffith...who

25 Davis, *Arthur Griffith*, p.33; Tierney, *MacNeill*, p.289; Curran, *Free State*, p.42.

26 *Irish Times*, 4 January 1975.

27 Davis, 'Ulster Protestants and Sinn Féin press', pp.78-9.

28 *ibid.*, p.80.

appeared naive in their apostrophising of Orangemen as excellent Irishmen - were actually approaching the problem of the north from the right angle. Some went wrong in their failure to appreciate that the Orangeman's attitude to his religion was identical to that of the Irish Catholic, and in no sense a matter of 'bluff'.[29]

Terence de Vere White wrote thoughtfully of Griffith 50 years after his death:

> No one has provided a cure for the condition that divides Ireland into two small states. Griffith saw the solution in his Hungarian scheme of a dual monarchy. It gave Ireland independence and at the same time satisfied the monarchical sentiments of those who felt personal loyalty to the Crown. Griffith did not share these sentiments but he was civilised enough to wish to cater for opinions different from his own.[30]

'Griffith's original programme, though open to objection in detail,was at least a serious attempt to achieve Irish independence without partition and without bloodshed. It might have succeeded', was the judgement of Richard Davis.[31] The tragedy for Ireland was that it was never given a trial.

29 Davis,'Ulster Protestants and Sinn Féin press', pp.84-5.

30 *Irish Times*, 14 October 1972.

31 Davis, *Non-Violent Sinn Féin*, p.151.

Part IV

The Dramatic Climax to a Lifetime's Work: The Anglo-Irish Treaty

'Arthur O'Shaughnessy held that
'three with a new song's measure
can trample an empire down'.
Griffith did it with a couple of pamphlets,
for the Treaty of 1921 was the beginning
of the end of the British Empire.
It has found not alone another name
but another nature'.

Dedicatory preface to Bulmer Hobson and Robert Lynd in P.S. O'Hegarty's A History of Ireland Under the Union

CHAPTER I

THE PROTAGONISTS

Introduction

The Anglo-Irish Treaty gave birth to the independent Irish State. For Arthur Griffith, who was the first Irish signatory to the document, it represented the culmination of a life's work. He was not to enjoy its fruits. The Treaty caused a deep division which led to civil war, at an early stage of which Griffith died.

The debate which ran through Griffith's life, and indeed through the previous 125 years, reached a culmination in the Treaty, the debate between those who wanted a republic and those who were ready to accept a form of government remarkably close to a dual-monarchy arrangement.

The Treaty split also revealed a division between advocates of physical force and those who felt that independence could be achieved through gradual and peaceful evolution. The so-called 'Ulster question' played a central role in the negotiations but had virtually no part in the bitter chasm which was to open up in Irish nationalism.

The Anglo-Irish Treaty was the most significant political event in 20th-century Irish history. It is hardly surprising that it spawned pro- and anti-Treaty historians. What is surprising is how much the most entrenched of these had in common. Both schools adhered to a nationalist line in that they faulted the British delegates, especially Lloyd George, with practising deception on their Irish counterparts, but the anti-Treaty exponents tended to be much harder on British tactics during, and especially *after* the negotiations which led to the signing.

There is one obvious difference in the way the two schools blamed the British delegates. Pro-Treaty historians wrote of cynical and worldly-wise men exploiting the integrity of the Irish representatives. Those of the anti-Treaty persuasion saw it as the wily 'Welsh Wizard' (Lloyd George) outwitting the naive and credulous Griffith.

It is impossible to overstate the influence on later historians of *Peace by Ordeal*, the history of the Anglo-Irish negotiations written by Frank Pakenham (who later became Lord Longford), which was first published in 1935. Very few questioned his account. In his introduction to the 1972 edition of his book he claimed that it was an impartial study. Yet he acknowledged that Robert Barton gave him most help with his research. (Barton was a member of the Irish delegation but later repudiated his own signature of the Treaty). Through Barton, Pakenham met Mrs Childers and 'acquired an undying admiration' for her husband, Erskine, who was principal secretary to the Irish delegation and one of the Treaty's most implacable critics.

Pakenham also referred to long conversations with de Valera who, he informed his readers, took pains to avoid imposing his point of view. He admitted that the long-term effect of his book had been 'to correct a widespread bias' against de Valera, and he wondered if 'it had been possible to form a more favourable opinion of his role without thinking the worse of great Irishmen like Griffith and Collins'. Pakenham confessed to not having any deep understanding of Griffith.[1]

In an early review of *Ordeal* Desmond FitzGerald, who took the pro-Treaty side at the end of 1921, believed that Pakenham set out 'with certain preconceived views' and 'strained' the facts to fit. He concluded that this account left 'the historical truth still waiting to be written'.[2]

Fortunately, what has been written about the Treaty does not fall solely into pro- or anti-Treaty categories. The founding of *Irish Historical Studies* in the 1930s marked a turning-point in Irish history writing by taking history out of politics, and a new generation of young historians strove for impartiality 'on the basis of the critical method and the restriction of moral judgements'.[3]

Despite this 'a popular school continued the tribal dance around the ancestral idols', as Lee put it.[4] John A. Murphy began his review of Tom Cox's biography of Erskine Childers with the useful advice, 'Never judge a book by its blurb'. The blurb declared that the book provided a perspective 'for those who would attempt to heal the wounds of Ireland' in the 1970s (it was published in 1975). Murphy believed it did nothing of the sort. There was too much dependence on 'secondary sources that needed updating', Murphy complained, 'out-macardling' the author of *The Irish Republic*. It singled out Collins especially for abuse,[5] but went none too gently on Griffith either.

1 Pakenham, *Ordeal*, pp.8-9,11.

2 *Observer*, 16 June 1935.

3 Joseph Lee, 'Some aspects of modern Irish historiography', in Ernst Schulin (ed.), *Gedenkschrift Martin Gohring* (Wiesbaden, 1968), p.439.

4 Lee, *loc. cit.*, p.440.

5 *Irish Times*, 31 May 1975.

Preliminaries

The hostilities in the Anglo-Irish War ended on 11 July 1921. Next day, de Valera went to London to confer with Lloyd George. Griffith, Barton, Stack, Plunkett and Childers went with him, but he met Lloyd George alone four times over the next ten days, reporting afterwards to his colleagues. What he was offered was Dominion status, the same kind of independence as the British Dominions but with significant limitations. The size of the Irish army was to be limited; voluntary recruitment to the British army was to be permitted to continue; Britain was to be granted air and naval facilities; Ireland was to pay a contribution to the British war debt; the status of Northern Ireland was to be recognised and could not be changed except with the consent of its parliament.

Desmond FitzGerald joined the Irish delegates in London. He found Griffith very hopeful that a settlement could be reached.[6] Austin Stack wrote a personal account of the lead-up to the Treaty while on hunger strike in Kilmainham during the Civil War, more than two years after the events he was recalling.[7] This became the source used by many historians to comment on the Dáil cabinet's reactions to the British July proposals.[8]

Stack related a talk he had with Griffith while they were both part of the July delegation in London. While walking through Whitehall, Griffith asked him if he would like to take home to Dublin a certain building he pointed to. When Stack saw it was the Home Office (he was Minister for Home Affairs), he interpreted the question to mean that Griffith was satisfied with the British proposals. When Stack responded that surely he did not think they should accept the terms, Griffith replied that he thought them 'pretty good'.

Stack also recorded his impressions of the Dáil cabinet's discussion of the proposals. Griffith and Collins were well disposed towards them; Brugha and he were utterly against them, and Barton, too, he understood. But Griffith favoured them except as regards Northern Ireland, and Collins described them as 'a great step forward'. Pakenham thought these expressions of opinion no more than cursory remarks

6 Colum, *Griffith*, p.263.

7 J.A. Gaughan, *Austin Stack: Portrait of a Separatist* (Dublin, 1977). The entire Stack memoir is given in this book.

8 Pakenham, *Ordeal*, pp.71-2,76; Keith Middlemas (ed.), *Tom Jones: Whitehall Diary. Volume III, Ireland 1918-25* (London, 1971), p.90; Ryle Dwyer, *Collins*, pp.40-41.

'into which significance was later read', because the entire cabinet rejected the offer without 'the least hesitation'.[9]

De Valera got Griffith to draft the reply to Lloyd George rejecting the British terms, although Griffith himself regarded them as favourable.[10] But the rejection, which was sent on 10 August, did not end the truce. There followed two months during which fifteen dispatches passed between de Valera and Lloyd George.

Analyses of the preliminaries to the Anglo-Irish conference concentrate mainly on this 'duel'[11] and the positions reached by the respective sides by the time the formal talks began. Anti-Treaty sympathisers hold that de Valera performed well and gave nothing away.[12] Pro-Treatyites argue the opposite.[13]

Impartial historians contend that de Valera's statements at the time did not imply that he would insist on a republic when negotiating. They argue that his failure to declare that a republic was fundamental to the Irish side, while Lloyd George made clear that Irish allegiance to the Crown and membership of the Empire were fundamental to him, left the initial advantage on the side of Britain.[14]

There is no accepted record of the vital discussions among the Sinn Féin leaders during the summer and autumn of 1921. There was a willingness to compromise to some extent, but the degree of compromise some were ready to accept was probably not apparent, as Hancock observed.[15]

All discussion of terms in the de Valera-Lloyd George exchanges

9 Pakenham, *Ordeal*, pp.71-2,76.

10 Coogan, *de Valera*, p.239.

11 Macardle, *Irish Republic*, p.467.

12 *ibid.*, pp.467-8,479-81; Florence O'Donoghue, *No Other Law* (Dublin, 1954), p.183; Tom Cox, *Damned Englishman: a Study of Erskine Childers 1870-1922* (New York, 1975), pp.133-4.

13 O'Hegarty, *Victory*, pp.66-8; Colum, *Griffith*, pp.233-4,268-71,286.

14 Hancock, *Survey*, pp.129-36; Holt, *Protest*, pp.260-61; J.C. Beckett, *The Making of Modern Ireland* (London, 1966), p.452; L.J. McCaffrey, *The Irish Question* (Kentucky, 1968), pp.172-3; Lyons, *Famine*, p.429; D.G. Boyce, *Englishmen and Irish Troubles* (London, 1972), pp.142-54; Kee, *Ourselves Alone*, pp.146-8; J.A. Murphy, *Ireland in the 20th Century* (Dublin, 1975), pp.27-32; D.H. Akenson, *The United States and Ireland* (Harvard, 1973), p.58; Edward MacLysaght, *Changing Times: Ireland since 1898* (London, 1978), p.127; Curran, *Free State*, pp.67-8; Ryle Dwyer, *Collins*, pp.50-51; Terence Ryle Dwyer, *De Valera's Darkest Hour: In Search of National Independence 1919-32* (Dublin/Cork, 1982), pp.73-4; S.M. Lawlor, *Britain and Ireland 1914-23* (Dublin, 1983), pp.99-112; Hopkinson, *Green against Green*, pp.23-4.

15 Hancock, *op. cit.*, pp.129-30.

centred on two issues: Irish allegiance to the Crown and Irish unity. Griffith had realistically accepted that the shared crown was the only feasible Anglo-Irish arrangement for his time, just as it had been for O'Connell and Parnell. The vast majority of the Irish people probably agreed with Griffith in this, but there was what Kee called 'a minority clique of republican dogmatists', in the Dáil cabinet and in the Dáil itself, for whom the republic was sacrosanct.[16]

Many members of the Dáil refused to look some hard realities in the face. These realities were (a) a coalition in Britain dependent on a Conservative majority who would never entertain the thought of full Irish independence and separation from the Empire; (b) the inability of the IRA to resume military action and the unlikelihood that the people would support it following the long truce; (c) most of all, the newly-established and constitutionally-secure Northern Ireland with the consequent determination of the unionists to hold what they had. Extreme republicans in the cabinet and Dáil took no stock of such practical considerations, holding that their mystic, indivisible republic was already in existence, and that any tampering with it would be traitorous.[17]

Pakenham admitted that Ireland had lost important psychological ground by the end of the preliminary exchanges, in that Lloyd George had insisted on Ireland remaining in the Empire, while de Valera had not pressed for a republic.[18] De Valera did not once put forward the demand for a republic, or insist that if the British refused to grant this, negotiation would be over and war resumed. By contrast, the British were totally unambivalent in that no fewer than six times Lloyd George stated that there could be no compromise on Irish allegiance to the Crown. Despite this, the Irish agreed to confer formally, so that it was presumed that they were prepared to give way on the Crown and Empire in the last resort. Griffith was therefore justified in defending himself during the Dáil debate on the Treaty: 'In the letters that preceded the negotiations, not once was a demand made for the recognition of the Irish Republic'.[19]

De Valera's exact position during this period is difficult to define. As S.M. Lawlor observed, 'it was never quite clear what de Valera stood for,

16 Kee, *Ourselves*, pp.146-7.

17 Murphy, *Ireland*, pp.31-2.

18 Pakenham, *Ordeal*, pp.98-9.

19 Hancock, *Survey*, pp.135-6.

or with whom he stood, at least from December 1920 until June 1922'.[20] On the opening day of the second Dáil, 16 August 1921, he said he did not claim that what the Irish people voted for in 1918 'was for a form of government as such, because we are not republican doctrinaires, but it was for Irish freedom and Irish independence'. And on the following day, he declared: 'As far as I am concerned, I would be willing to suggest to the Irish people to give up a good deal in order to have an Ireland that could look to the future without anticipating distracting internal problems'.[21]

Again, on the same occasion, he stated: '...an association that would be consistent with our right to see that we were the judges of what was (*sic*) our own interests, and that we were not compelled to leave the judgement of what were our own interests or not to others - a combination of that sort would, I believe, commend itself to the majority of my colleagues'.[22] And he also warned the Dáil that they were asking the delegates they were sending to London to secure by negotiation what Ireland had been completely unable to secure by force.[23]

The form of association de Valera envisaged between Ireland and Britain was encapsulated for him by the phrase 'external association'. Basically it meant that Ireland would be completely independent in her internal affairs but would associate with the British Empire, or Commonwealth as it was beginning to be called, in external affairs. Ireland would recognise the Crown as head of this association and would guarantee to be neutral in time of war. It was a skilful constitutional concept, but well ahead of its time in 1921, when Dominion status was the absolute limit of British concession.

Griffith's attitude to 'external association' is revealed in what he told P.S. O'Hegarty in April 1922. O'Hegarty enquired of him how the concept first arose. Griffith replied that it was around the time de Valera was pressing him to go to London as a delegate (probably late August or early September 1921). Griffith went into de Valera's office to find Brugha and Stack with him. When he told Griffith that he wanted him to go to London, Griffith replied: 'You are my Chief, and if you tell me to go, I'll go. But I know, and you know, that I cannot bring back the Republic'. It was then de Valera produced the external association idea,

20 Lawlor, *Britain and Irl.*, p.xi.

21 *Dáil Éireann: Tuairisc Oifigiúil: Official Report for the Periods 16-26 August 1921 and 28 February-8 June 1922* (Dublin, 1922), pp.9,14.

22 *ibid.*, p.15.

23 Hopkinson, *Green against Green*, p.19.

From left: Gavan Duffy, Collins, Griffith and Childers in Hans Place, London, October-December 1921

the first Griffith had heard of it, and after half-an-hour's persuasion, Brugha reluctantly agreed to it, while Stack said nothing.

When the other two left Griffith asked de Valera what it all meant and what purpose did he hope it would serve. In his pre-political existence de Valera had been a mathematics teacher, and he liked to illustrate his ideas with diagrams. So he got a pencil and paper and drew a vertical line AB. This he described as himself in the 'strait-jacket of the Republic' from which he wanted to escape. He then drew a diagonal line AC, which he explained was external association, the purpose of which was 'to bring Cathal along'. Finally, he drew a horizontal line AD, which he described as where they would probably eventually get to. Griffith then expressed himself satisfied and said no more about it.[24]

Griffith declared 'in a burst of anger' in the Dáil some months after this period, that before going to London he had been asked by de Valera to get him out of the strait-jacket of the republic.[25] The Labour leader, William O'Brien, corroborated this point. O'Brien and other Labour representatives took part in the Mansion House conference in April 1922 which tried to effect an agreement between the pro- and anti-Treaty sides. O'Brien stated that Griffith again referred to de

24 O'Hegarty, *Victory*, pp.86-7.

25 de Vere White, *O'Higgins*, p.58.

Valera's asking him to get him out of the strait-jacket, and de Valera did not deny doing so.[26]

Lloyd George finally hit on the formula he needed at the end of September 1921. Sinn Féin was invited to send delegates to London on 11 October, 'with a view to ascertaining how the association of Ireland with the community of nations known as the British Empire may best be reconciled with Irish national aspirations'. It was Griffith who drafted the telegram accepting this invitation.

Appointment and Composition of Delegation

The most remarkable feature of the Irish delegation was de Valera's decision not to be part of it. Piaras Béaslaí later declared that de Valera's cabinet colleagues were 'startled' by the announcement. Béaslaí particularly emphasised Griffith's unhappiness, stating that he saw de Valera as 'shirking his plain duty as leader of the Irish people'.[27] When de Valera explained himself to the Dáil at a private session on 14 September 1921, he stressed that he was not shirking his duty.[28] This certainly lends credibility to Béaslaí's account.

Griffith's reasons for wanting de Valera in London were, in Béaslaí's opinion, that the Irish delegation would be handicapped without him, and it would be cumbersome to have to refer every detail to him in Dublin, as he would 'fight tooth and nail over hairsplitting distinctions'.[29]

It was W.T. Cosgrave's unease at de Valera's decision, rather than Griffith's, that occupied the attention of historians. In an oft-quoted image, Cosgrave described the delegates who were being sent to London as a team who were leaving their ablest player in reserve.[30]

Pakenham was at one with Béaslaí in pointing to opposition within his cabinet to de Valera's decision, but disagreed that it was unanimous. In this version of the event, which is the correct one, de Valera used his casting vote to keep himself off the delegation. Ministers were evenly divided - Griffith, Collins and Cosgrave believed he should go to

26 MacLysaght, *Changing Times*, p.127.

27 Béaslaí, *Collins*, ii, p.274.

28 *Suíonna Príobháideacha an Dára Dala: Private Sessions of Second Dáil* (Dublin, n.d.), p.95.

29 Béaslaí, *op. cit.*, ii, pp.274-5.

30 *Private Sessions*, p.95.

London, and Barton, Brugha and Stack supported him. Pakenham saw this division as 'the first small symptoms of the coming rift'.[31]

The truth is that the cabinet was already well and truly riven. Brugha and Stack were deeply hostile to Collins. They both refused to be part of the delegation to London. In fact, Stack regretted that he had gone there the previous July. And we have seen how deeply opposed Griffith's and Brugha's views were since as far back as 1917.

Historians nowadays agree that de Valera should have led the delegation to London. He was the only one with direct negotiating experience of Lloyd George. And no one understood the concept of external association better than he, who had invented it. It simply did not make sense for the ablest player 'to remain a non-playing captain in the biggest match his team was ever likely to play'.[32]

The three ministers who later opposed the Treaty had the opportunity to be delegates and turned it down. They had some responsibility therefore for the actions of their chosen representatives. This was Pakenham's judgement. He contended however that Griffith and Collins had a free hand in choosing whom they wished to accompany them, and had therefore only themselves to blame for any shortcomings they found in their fellow-delegates.[33]

This argument is difficult to accept, and it seems that Pakenham himself had changed his mind about it when he collaborated with T.P. O'Neill on de Valera's authorised biography. In this it is clear that de Valera, in order to make sure that there would be no criticism of the delegation not being 'republican' enough in outlook, determined to send a committed one.[34] In fact, historians for the most part agree that de Valera was responsible for the composition of the delegation.

The Irish delegates were Griffith (chairman), Collins, Barton, Eamon Duggan and George Gavan Duffy. Childers went as their principal secretary. (He was Barton's cousin.) The delegation reflected the coalition character of the Sinn Féin movement. Griffith represented the older members and the constitutionalists, Collins the young militants and IRB men. Barton, Duffy and Childers were sent by de Valera to

31 Pakenham, *Ordeal*, p.83.

32 Lee, *Irl. 1912-85*, p.49.

33 Pakenham, *op. cit.*, p.84.

34 Longford and O'Neill, *de Valera*, p.149.

keep a close watch on Griffith and Collins, to act as a brake on them, and to prevent them conceding too much to the British.[35]

In a letter to Joe McGarrity, de Valera revealed his thinking on the composition of the delegation he appointed. Duggan and Duffy, who were lawyers, he dismissed as 'legal padding'. He felt that Griffith and Collins would accept Irish recognition of the Crown, so Barton and Childers were chosen to counter-balance them. Barton 'would be strong and stubborn enough as a retarding force to any precipitate giving-away by the delegation. Childers, who is an intellectual republican, as Secretary would give Barton, his relative and close friend, added strength'. De Valera told McGarrity his intention was that 'the Cabinet at home should hang on to the delegation's coat-tails', leaving everything safe for a final 'tug of war', which his external association would resolve.[36]

The appointment of Griffith as chairman of the delegation has evoked differing responses from commentators on the Anglo-Irish Treaty. Pro-Treaty historians have argued that de Valera knew when he picked Griffith how far he would go. Griffith made it clear that he would not break off negotiations over the issue of the Crown. It did not make sense to choose him to lead the plenipotentiaries if it were intended to accept nothing less than a republic. An uncompromising republican should have been chairman if this was the intention.[37]

A number of detached commentators have supported this reasoning. Ryan remarked that while Griffith agreed to go, he was adamant that he could not return with a republic and he had always stated openly that he would not break on the Crown.[38] Akenson held that de Valera knew well Griffith's position on the Crown, but still made him chief delegate. His view was that de Valera did so because, and not in spite, of Griffith's willingness to accept the monarchy. This reflected de Valera's willingness to compromise, Akenson thought.[39]

Upholders of the anti-Treaty viewpoint maintained that the obvious leader of a Dáil delegation was the Dáil Minister for Foreign Affairs

35 Strauss, *Irish Nationalism*, p.267; Taylor, *Collins*, p.145; Holt, *Protest*, p.262; Curran, *Free State*, p.76; Garvin, *Evolution*, p.130; Younger, *Griffith*, p.100; Ryle Dwyer, *Collins*, p.47; Ryle Dwyer, *de Valera*, pp.71-3; Hopkinson, *Green against Green*, p.24.

36 McGarrity was a close friend of de Valera who lived in America. The letter is dated 27 December 1921. Ms.17,440 NLI.

37 O'Hegarty, *Victory*, p.74; FitzGerald review of *Ordeal* in *Observer*, 16 June 1935; Taylor, *op. cit.*, pp.144-5; Colum, *Griffith*, p.277.

38 Ryan, *Unique Dictator*, p.240.

39 Akenson, *US and Irl.*, pp.59-60.

(Griffith). They argued that as de Valera had already rejected one British offer, if another were to be turned down, it would be better that this came from one with the reputation of a moderate, like Griffith.[40]

These contentions too have been accepted by some impartial observers. Curran agreed that as Minister for Foreign Affairs Griffith was 'a natural choice' to lead the delegation.[41] That it was better for another British offer to be turned down, if necessary, by a moderate like Griffith, was one of the reasons subsequently advanced by de Valera himself for his not going to London. Both Lyons and Curran accepted it as a valid reason for sending Griffith as chairman.[42]

Many thought Griffith an obvious choice for the position. To Younger it was inevitable that he should lead the delegation in de Valera's absence.[43] Because economic issues would be included in the talks with the British, Lyons considered his selection inevitable.[44] Curran believed it so because he was widely respected and had done well as acting-President. Brugha and Stack both hated his political moderation, but refused to go themselves, and neither challenged his appointment, Curran pointed out.[45]

Ryle Dwyer saw Griffith as a logical choice as chairman, because he had his own personal following in Sinn Féin and had great influence with the older members.[46] Lawlor believed that he was chosen 'as a man of experience, as a popular name, as the father of Sinn Féin'.[47] It would be hard to disagree with Hopkinson's contention that Griffith and de Valera were the obvious men to present the Irish case from the points of view of experience and negotiating ability, in which the Sinn Féin leadership was bound to be lacking.[48]

There is no evidence whatsoever of Griffith displaying any reluctance to go to London. Yet, Younger suggested that he believed profoundly

40 Macardle, *Irish Republic*, p.481; Ó Néill agus Ó Fiannachta, *De Valera*, i, p.242; Longford and O'Neill, *de Valera*, p.146.

41 Curran, *Free State*, p.74.

42 *ibid.*, pp.75–6; Lyons, *Famine*, p.429.

43 Younger, *Civil War*, p.156.

44 Lyons, *op. cit.*, p.430.

45 Curran, *op. cit.*, pp.74–6.

46 Ryle Dwyer, *de Valera*, p.71.

47 Lawlor, *Britain and Irl.*, p.111.

48 Hopkinson, *Green against Green*, p.24.

that the task to be performed in London was for men younger than he.[49] Both Taylor and Hopkinson referred to his poor health during the conference causing him to hand over the running of matters from time to time to Collins.[50] However, neither Ó Lúing nor Colum, Griffith's biographers, made any allusion to this.

The Sinn Féin delegation was not a united team. The Dáil cabinet's divided attitude to the July proposals was given formal expression in the October delegation. De Valera's reasoning on its composition was that he expected Barton and Childers to counteract the influence of Griffith and Collins. Historians agree that Griffith was opposed to the appointment of Childers as chief secretary to the delegation. Ryan referred to uneasy relations existing between Griffith and Gavan Duffy before they went as delegates to London.[51] Taylor described Collins's low opinion of both Duffy and Duggan (this would be at one with de Valera's dismissal of them). According to Taylor, Collins had a neutral attitude to Barton, though his being cousin to Childers did nothing to enhance his suitability in Collins's eyes.[52] Mutual suspicion and distrust did not help the Irish cause, and impugn the reasoning behind the composition of the delegation.

Many historians have commented on the anomaly of sending a moderate delegation to London while the extremists in the Dáil cabinet remained in Dublin. Men like Brugha and Stack, totally opposed to any compromise with the British, were living in an unreal world. De Valera was in that same unreal Dublin situation and 'inevitably applied to the negotiations in London, something of its unreal perspective', as Kee remarked.[53] The distrust and exasperation felt by Griffith and Collins for those who remained in Dublin was to prove of enormous significance.

49 Younger, *Civil War*, p.156.

50 Taylor, *Collins*, pp.166,170; Hopkinson, *Green against Green*, p.24.

51 Ryan, *Unique Dictator*, p.140. Ryan was unique among historians in making this claim. Duffy had been a member of Cumann na nGaedheal and Sinn Féin and had been interacting with Griffith for more than 20 years by this time.

52 Taylor, *op. cit.*, p.152.

53 Kee, *Ourselves Alone*, pp.149-50. See also Lyons, *op. cit.*, pp.430-31; Middlemas (ed.), *Jones*, p.113; Akenson, *US and Irl.*, p.60.; Ryle Dwyer, *Collins*, p.47; Hopkinson, *op. cit.*, p.25.

Chapter II

Confrontation

Strategy. Preparedness. Griffith's Tactics.

The broad Irish strategy was to ensure that if the conference broke down it would do so on Irish unity, and not on Ireland's relationship with the Crown and Empire. The day-to-day strategy, which was devised by de Valera, was to concentrate initially on non-contentious issues and avoid the major areas of disagreement until a harmonious atmosphere had been built up. He hoped that in this way the British could be gradually introduced to the subtleties of external association.

The Irish position on unity was that the six counties of Northern Ireland should accept an Irish administration on the same basis as the other twenty-six. If they refused, Sinn Féin was willing to concede autonomy to Northern Ireland but with overall authority for the area being held by Dublin rather than London.

The Irish delegates were poorly prepared for their task. They did not know what their fundamentals were and had no agreed counter-proposals ready. They took with them 'Draft Treaty A' which was not a draft Treaty at all but a rough outline of external association. It was a memorandum de Valera had compiled after his July consultation with Lloyd George, which he intended to send to him but did not. The plenipotentiaries also had a 'Draft Treaty B', again not a list of terms Ireland was willing to accept but a document which was to be used as propaganda should the conference break down. Nor did they have a written proposal on Ulster with them. This was not forwarded to Griffith by de Valera until six days after the talks began.

There was sense behind the approach of making sure that if the conference collapsed it did so over unity and not Ireland's relationship with the Crown. British Liberal thinking and world opinion was more sympathetic to the idea of Irish unity than to a withdrawal of allegiance to the Crown. Assessments of the soundness of this policy have varied. Pakenham initially expressed the belief that it could have worked. But on radio some 30 years later, he was less assured. And when he coauthored the de Valera biography, he thought it extremely unlikely that it could ever have worked.[1]

Contemporaneously with Pakenham in the thirties, Hancock regarded this Irish approach as double-edged in that, in order to prove the northern unionists unreasonable, Sinn Féin was forced, first of all, to show its own reasonableness, and this was why it offered to be associated freely with the other dominions.[2] John Bowman was the only modern historian to believe that the Irish strategy was 'a shrewd ploy', because it reflected what British ministers were saying in private.[3]

The fact that a parliament and executive actually existed in Northern Ireland was the most important counter to the strategy's success. There is no doubt about what the desirable Irish plan should have been. The issue of unity should have been kept to the fore and the question of Ireland's relationship with the Crown treated as secondary. Both Griffith and Collins regarded unity as the more important concern and so did the vast majority of the Irish people.

However, Béaslaí's comment that some TDs spoke in the Treaty debate as if they would have welcomed an independent republic with the six counties excluded, has to be taken into consideration.[4] Hopkinson vigorously pursued this view later. He held that the Ulster question was 'always likely to be avoided' and that both sides used it merely as a bargaining counter, but did not see it as solvable.

Hopkinson contended that Sinn Féin had never been really serious about unity - the declaration of a republic made unity less likely; Sinn Féin's cultural and economic policy, and especially the Belfast boycott, widened the north-south divide; 26-county independence was more of a priority than 32-county unity. He concluded that it was improbable that the Sinn Féin leadership would have regarded all-Ireland unity as a make-or-break issue of the conference, despite talk to the contrary.[5] Griffith, as we have seen earlier, can be exempted from Hopkinson's contentions.

The Irish strategy was not likely to succeed. It showed a poor appreciation of internal *British* political realities. Sinn Féin had ruled out coercion of the unionists. It depended therefore on the British to

1 Pakenham, *Ordeal*, pp.253-5; Lord Longford, 'The Treaty negotiations', in T.D. Williams (ed.), *The Irish Struggle* (London, 1966), p.110; Longford and O'Neill, *de Valera*, p.151.

2 Hancock, *Survey*, p.142.

3 John Bowman, *De Valera and the Ulster Question 1917-73* (Oxford, 1982), p.61.

4 Béaslaí, *Collins*, ii, p.325.

5 Hopkinson, *Green against Green*, pp.20-22.

put pressure on them to accept unity. But with the enormous support the unionists had in the Conservative Party, which had an overwhelming majority in the House of Commons, this pressure was always likely to be limited.

How well prepared were the Irish delegates for their assignment in London? Anti-Treatyites believed that they were sent to London well prepared for their task. Macardle wrote that they were 'forearmed and forewarned'. Cox asserted that they were 'carefully briefed'; that 'Draft Treaty A', which they took with them, 'was meant to be a dependable frame of reference' to remind them of 'the limits of republican manoeuvre'.[6]

Impartial historians disagreed completely with these views. To Hancock, 'Draft Treaty A' was a 'vague' document. Akenson regarded it as virtually worthless. Curran saw it as a rough sketch of external association. Ryle Dwyer denied suggestions that it was intended to be a draft for a Treaty at all, viewing it instead as 'a partially completed document containing an outline of external association' and 'designed for diplomatic manoeuvring'.[7] The document was actually a memorandum which de Valera had drawn up for Lloyd George after their July consultations, but which he had decided not to send.[8]

The delegation was also given what was called 'Draft Treaty B', which did not contain the terms the Irish were prepared to accept, but was intended for use as propaganda should the negotiations collapse. It was an outline of what the delegates should publish as acceptable terms in the event of a breakdown. De Valera gave incomplete copies of these two documents to Duffy and Childers on the eve of their departure. He intended that the delegation should fill out the details as they went along in London. This can be seen from what he wrote to Griffith a few days after the conference began: 'We must depend on your side for the initiative after this'.[9]

The Irish team was sent to London poorly equipped. Neutral historians argue unanimously that they began the negotiations at a great disadvantage. They had no clear instructions or guidance from

6 Macardle, *Irish Republic*, p.482; Cox, *Damned Englishman*, pp.136-7.

7 Hancock, *Survey*, p.139; Akenson, *US and Irl.*, p.63; Curran, *Free State*, p.78; Ryle Dwyer, *Collins*, p.57; Ryle Dwyer, *de Valera*, pp.74-6.

8 Coogan, *de Valera*, p.256.

9 De Valera to Griffith, 14 October 1921, DE 2/304/8 NAI.

their cabinet; they did not know how much they could concede or what their sticking-point should be, and they had no agreed counter-proposals worked out.[10]

The immediate day-to-day strategy was devised by de Valera. The aim was to discuss less contentious issues first, to create an atmosphere of trust, before tackling the more difficult problems. Pakenham believed that this strategy was wrong: Griffith at the outset should have asserted that Ireland would in no circumstances join the Empire, instead of following the pre-arranged procedure 'to place first things last'.

Later, in his de Valera biography, the same author wrote that the Irish plan was to avoid an immediate clash, and that external association was to be held in reserve while the British proposals were examined. He adjudged that de Valera must share responsibility for this 'circumspect' course, although very early in the conference he tried to check the lengths to which Griffith was carrying it.[11]

But Griffith was actually apprehensive about the tactics to be pursued in London as de Valera had outlined them. Robert Brennan wrote that the normally 'taciturn' Griffith 'kept pelting de Valera with questions' about possible flaws in this approach.[12] In fact, what he wrote to de Valera at the end of only the second day of the conference bears out Brennan's recollection: 'Our tactics have been successful up to the present, but unless we can get in our Treaty proposals by Monday, the initiative will pass to them. If we cannot have the Ulster and other omitted clauses by ten o'clock Monday at the latest, we must fight them on ground of their own choosing'.[13] Hancock's opinion that these tactics 'necessitated a persistence in ambiguities' cannot be disputed.[14]

A number of anti-Treaty authors were unaware that Griffith was following this prearranged strategy in the early stages of the conference. Thus, Macardle viewed the trend of the first week's discussion as 'invidious' to the Irish cause because there was no reference to 'the fundamental question of democratic principle' (by which was meant the republic, presumably), which was the backbone of the Irish case. Instead, the talking was confined to 'details of dominion Home

10 Hancock, *Survey*, pp.137-9; Beckett, *Making of Modern Irl.*, p.452; McCaffrey, *Irish Question*, p.173; Boyce, *Englishmen and Irish Troubles*, p.154; MacDonagh, *Union*, p.97; Curran, *Free State*, p.78; Hopkinson, *Green against Green*, p.26.

11 Pakenham, *Ordeal*, pp.101-2; Longford and O'Neill, *de Valera*, p.150.

12 Brennan, *Allegiance*, pp320-21.

13 Griffith to de Valera, 13 October 1921, DE 2/304/8 NAI.

14 Hancock, *op. cit.*, p.139.

Rule', with Lloyd George's 'finesse' hampering the Irish delegates from keeping the issue of the republic before them.[15]

Cox was much fiercer in his condemnation of Griffith's performance. He complained that Griffith did not present either 'Draft Treaty A' or de Valera's Ulster clause in the opening fortnight in London, and although de Valera was unimpressed when Griffith wrote to him that he believed the British were anxious for peace, nevertheless Griffith persevered, convinced that the talks would succeed if he were given a free hand. This introduced a theme which Cox pursued throughout his whole account of the negotiations - that Griffith was determined from the beginning to act independently and abandon the idea of collective cabinet responsibility.

When Cox declared that Griffith found it easier to attack the British proposals than to stand solidly behind an Irish set, he was ignoring two facts: Griffith was following an approach agreed with de Valera beforehand and an Irish set of counter-proposals had not yet been fully worked out. In Cox's eyes, Griffith *'consistently shunted aside the basics of the agreed Irish position'*.[16] (This last was placed in italics for extra emphasis.)

The opening week of the conference went relatively smoothly. The subject of Irish unity was first discussed on 14 October. Griffith did not have Sinn Féin's proposal on that particular question for this discussion, so his only option was to play for time. Basically, he talked out the session and exasperated Lloyd George. It must have been very embarrassing for him to have to try to present the Irish case without knowing his side's actual policy on the North.[17]

He wrote urgently to de Valera on 14 October requesting him to send on the cabinet's Ulster proposal. In fact, Griffith had been given the task of preparing that proposal, and de Valera kept it in case it needed to be changed. When it was required pressingly in London, he sent it to Griffith, explaining that the other cabinet members in Dublin had not seen it, but that he did not think there would be any dissatisfaction with it in principle, whatever about the wording, and that he himself had hardly altered it at all.[18]

However, Cox was convinced that the Ulster clause was de Valera's, because he declared that Griffith received on 17 October de Valera's 'lengthily deliberated proposals on the Ulster problem'. But Griffith was the author of Sinn Féin's Ulster clause. This is ironic, because had

15 Macardle, *Irish Republic*, p.489.

16 Cox, *Damned Englishman*, pp.150,156-7.

17 Hopkinson, *Green against Green*, pp.26-7.

18 Akenson, *US and Irl.*, p.63; Bowman, *De Valera and Ulster Question*, p.61.

Cox known that it came from his hand, he would certainly not have praised it in the way that he did.

In summary the Ulster clause requested Northern Ireland to give up the arrangement under the 1920 Government of Ireland Act and accept representation in an Irish parliament like any other part of Ireland. If it refused this offer, it would be allowed to retain its subordinate parliament, but the overriding powers would be transferred from the British to the Irish parliament, in which it would be represented. Safeguards for the North were to be reached by agreement within Ireland. In other words, Sinn Féin was offering Northern Ireland a form of Home Rule.

Ulster was again on the agenda when the two delegations met on 17 October. By that time Griffith had received his cabinet's policy on it from Dublin, but he did not present it during the discussions that day. Instead, he requested the British to withdraw and let his side make Northern Ireland a fair offer.[19] Griffith and the Irish delegation clearly wanted to emphasise the Sinn Féin belief (really it was a misapprehension) that British backing for the unionist position was the real source of the problem.

An incident outside the conference now troubled its so far smooth-running course. Pope Benedict had cabled King George to express his hope for a successful outcome to the conference. In his reply, the king stated his wish for a permanent settlement of 'the troubles in Ireland', and the beginning of 'a new era of peace and happiness for my people'. De Valera took issue with the phrases 'troubles in Ireland' and 'my people' in the king's reply, and sent a telegram to the pope to point out that the trouble was *between* Britain and Ireland, and that the Irish people owed no allegiance to the king.

De Valera's telegram to the pope on 19 October had a disquieting effect upon the course of the negotiations as far as Griffith was concerned. He later told Seán Milroy that they had been trying to avoid the Crown issue in the conference until they knew what they would get in return for accepting it in some way, but the telegram put it right at the top of the agenda.[20] It gave Lloyd George the opportunity to make the Crown the central concern of the negotiations, something which the prearranged Irish strategy had sought hard to avoid.[21]

How Griffith coped with Lloyd George's angry reaction in the session following the telegram episode won him praise from various authors.

19 Pakenham, *Ordeal*, pp.133-4.

20 Colum, *Griffith*, pp.291-2.

21 Curran, *Free State*, p.86; Younger, *Griffith*, p.104; Ryle Dwyer, *Collins*, p.66.

Pakenham remarked that it was bad enough for Griffith to have to justify the telegram, which he regarded as a serious mistake, and it was worse for him to see the whole harmonious atmosphere, patiently built up over the previous week, destroyed by it, but that nevertheless he defended de Valera's action. Refusing to be pessimistic about the outcome of the talks, he pointed out to the British that they had begun by finding points of agreement, and if they could reduce those over which they disagreed, they could probably find a way to a settlement.[22]

Colum, Longford and O'Neill, Curran and Younger took the same view. Griffith certainly did not intend to allow the talks to collapse over the issue of the Crown, which would have been greatly to the benefit of the British, and would, also, have meant no hope of unity. He had advocated a dual monarchy for almost two decades for the sole reason that he knew the unionists would never give up allegiance to the Crown.[23]

After the telegram incident Collins crossed to Dublin and tried in vain to get de Valera to join the delegation in London. In the following week, the format of the conference changed from plenary sessions, involving the entire Irish and British delegations, to subconferences involving two or three from either side. The papal telegram incident accentuated the unease Griffith and Collins were feeling both about Childers's activities in London and the role some of the cabinet in Dublin were playing in the conference. It is likely that the initiative for the change from plenary to subconference came from Griffith and Collins.

Historians differ about who instigated the change. The majority believe it was the British. But a minority say it first emanated from the Irish side. The following is Pakenham's account. Cope, through Duggan, asked Griffith and Collins to meet Lloyd George and Chamberlain for a brief private meeting after the seventh plenary session on 24 October. The Irish were given to understand that Lloyd George's reason was his difficulty with some of his own delegates. However, he had not shown that he cared a whit for the opinions of these delegates at the plenaries. His real motives were that he had found the plenary gatherings too big for him to exercise 'the personal touch', and he also wished to exclude Childers, whom the British regarded as a fanatical opponent of the Dominion-status solution.

Pakenham went on to say that at the 3 December Dáil cabinet

22 Pakenham, *Ordeal*, pp.139-40.

23 Colum, *Griffith*, p.292; Longford and O'Neill, *de Valera*, p.152; Curran, *Free State*, p.86; Younger, *Griffith*, p.104.

meeting, Brugha remarked 'provocatively' that in choosing Griffith and Collins, the British chose the two weakest of the Irish team. (What Brugha actually said on that occasion was that the British 'selected their men'.) Pakenham himself believed that it was natural that Griffith and Collins should have been chosen as they were the leaders. However, he thought that there was one sense in which Griffith and Collins could have been seen as the 'weakest' by the British: as the leaders they had more responsibility, and could be expected to be more anxious for a settlement, and more open to compromise. Furthermore, Griffith was reckoned to be a less intransigent republican than his colleagues.[24]

Macardle and Eoin Neeson, both of whom wrote from an anti-Treaty perspective, believed that the British wanted the change from plenary session to subconference. Forester, who wrote from the opposite point of view, saw Lloyd George as resorting to the age-old tactic of divide and rule. She agreed with the two motives Pakenham ascribed to the Prime Minister but she added the novel one that Lloyd George had perceived divisions in the Irish delegation, and wished to exploit these.

She did not state how Lloyd George had come to detect disunity in the Irish team, but she felt that Griffith and Collins may have been as desirous as he was to meet without secretaries, because 'Griffith was personally antagonistic to Childers' and Collins's practical mind found Childers's meticulousness increasingly irritating. She added that both had the uncomfortable belief that Childers was sending 'watchdog' memoranda of his own to Dublin with Griffith's daily summaries.[25]

On the other hand, Béaslaí gave it as his understanding that the subconference arrangement was made at the instigation of the Irish representatives, their reason being that after seven plenary sessions it was obvious that that structure was too unwieldy to do any effective business.[26]

Among recent historians, both Murphy and Younger accepted Béaslaí's view. Keith Middlemas claimed that Cope, at the request of Griffith and Collins, arranged the private meeting with Lloyd George and Chamberlain on 24 October. The British leader welcomed the

24 Pakenham, *Ordeal*, pp.145-6.

25 Macardle, *Irish Republic*, p.497; Eoin Neeson, *The Civil War in Ireland 1922-3* (Cork, 1966), p.38; Forester, *Collins*, pp.225-7.

26 Béaslaí, *Collins*, ii, p.300.

proposal because he was anxious to reduce the size of the meetings and he wanted Childers excluded, because he was regarded as an extremist.[27]

Ryle Dwyer stated that because they suspected Childers of spying on the delegation for de Valera, Griffith and Collins wanted to keep him out of the talks altogether. The rest of the Irish delegation did not realise that the subconference procedure originated with a request from their side, he observed.[28]

Curran agreed with Pakenham that the subconferences came as a result of a British request. The British Prime Minister knew that the Irish leaders would talk more freely at private meetings, according to Curran. He did not explain how Lloyd George acquired this information however, or why Griffith and Collins wished for smaller encounters.[29]

Supping with the Devil? Griffith and Lloyd George

Griffith's interaction with Lloyd George, in subconferences and private meetings was crucial to the whole outcome of the negotiations. Pro-Treaty authors tell the story of an honest and honourable man taken advantage of by the wily 'Welsh Wizard'. Those of the anti-Treaty persuasion depict him as an amateur diplomat outwitted by a devious expert. But the reality was more complex than either of these versions allowed.

Post-1970 authors, in particular, concentrate more on the complex nature of the British domestic politics in which Lloyd George operated. The Prime Minister has been seen as genuinely desiring a settlement of the Irish question, but always conscious of a potential diehard backlash. This perspective has altered how Griffith's role in the whole process has come to be perceived.

A minority group of extreme unionist supporters in the Conservative Party put down a motion, to be debated on 31 October, censuring the government for continuing the Irish talks. At a private meeting on the day before, Lloyd George sought personal assurances from Griffith on the Crown and defence in return for taking on the unionist diehards. Griffith promised to recommend recognition of the Crown if satisfied on all other points. This was embodied in a letter which was sent from the delegation as a whole on 2 November.

27 Murphy, *Irl. in 20th Century*, p.32; Younger, *Griffith*, p.105; Middlemas (ed.), *Jones*, p.141. Jones was assistant-secretary to the British cabinet.

28 Ryle Dwyer, *Collins*, pp.67-8.

29 Curran, *Free State*, pp.89-90.

In return, Lloyd George promised Griffith he would resign rather than resume the war in Ireland if he could not get Northern Ireland to accept the overriding authority of Dublin. But he failed to make any progress with Craig and it appeared he was going to resign. However, he came up with the idea of a boundary commission as a way of putting pressure on Craig and which he hoped would be acceptable to Sinn Féin. Griffith neither accepted nor rejected the proposal when it was put to him on 8 November. Tom Jones urged him to support it because Lloyd George needed his help against Craig and his backers in the Conservative Party, and he presented the boundary commission as a tactic to deprive the Ulster unionists of support in Britain. Griffith agreed not to undermine the Prime Minister's position by publicly rejecting the proposal while Lloyd George was fighting the Conservative diehards.

On 12 November Griffith again met with Lloyd George and agreed not to publicly repudiate the boundary commission proposal in the run-up to or during the Liverpool conference of the Conservative Party on 17 November. On 13 November Jones showed Griffith a memorandum he had drawn up on the Prime Minister's instructions of their meeting of the previous day. Griffith glanced at it and assented to it. This document was produced by Lloyd George on the last day of the conference (5 December) with the claim that it was a pledge from Griffith to accept the boundary commission as a solution to the unity issue.

The above is a synopsis of the interaction between Griffith and Lloyd George between 30 October and 13 November. Pakenham's version of the events of that fortnight has had an enormous influence on later historians. What follows is a summary of Pakenham's interpretation.

Griffith's meeting with Lloyd George on 30 October was the most important encounter of the whole conference. The period from 30 October to 3 November seemed to be Griffith's week, in that he thought he had achieved much, but he had actually given ground. With the diehard motion of censure pending, Lloyd George wanted some personal assurances from Griffith on the vital matters of Crown, Empire and defence in return for putting down the unionist hardliners and fighting on the Ulster issue to secure 'essential unity'.

Griffith promised to recommend recognition of the Crown, if satisfied on all other points. Lloyd George expressed the belief that he could carry a plan for a six-county parliament subordinate to an all-Ireland one (which was Sinn Féin's Ulster clause). Griffith gave his personal assurance in a letter to Lloyd George on 2 November, which he and Collins discussed with the British beforehand. The letter stated that Ireland would be willing to enter into 'a free partnership with the

Commonwealth'. Lord Birkenhead wanted Griffith to change this phrase to 'a free partnership *within* the Commonwealth', but Griffith refused, as this would have meant partnership with the Dominions, as a Dominion. However, the British 'tricked them properly' by getting them to accept 'free partnership *with* the other states associated *within* the British Commonwealth'.

This form of words was acceptable to Griffith and Collins because it meant to them that they would still be associated with the Commonwealth from outside, and no one in Dublin thought otherwise. But the only interpretation of the phrase which made any sense was that Ireland entered a partnership with the other states which, *'like Ireland'*, were associated *'within'* the Commonwealth. Griffith 'was trying to be clever, to shake hands across the boundary line, and he was pulled over without noticing it'.[30]

Lloyd George told Griffith that he would resign if he could not carry an overriding parliament in Dublin, but he did not intend to step down. He failed to make any progress in meetings with Sir James Craig on 5 and 7 November and, as his subsequent moves demonstrated, he cleverly worked his way out of his pledge to resign.

Tom Jones came to see Griffith on 8 November. He professed to be 'infinitely sympathetic' to the Irish cause, wanting to avoid above all else a militant anti-Irish government under Bonar Law (former leader of the Conservatives and a staunch supporter of the Ulster unionists). Jones had a scheme of his own in mind - Dominion status for the South and a boundary commission to delimit the six-county area, if it rejected an all-Ireland parliament. Griffith wrote to de Valera that Sinn Féin would get most of Tyrone and Fermanagh and parts of Derry, Down and Armagh, but he expressed no definite opinion on the proposal.

What Jones said to Griffith was partly but not wholly bluff: the conference could end but, if so, on the right note of Ulster intransigence as far as the Irish delegates were concerned. Griffith still had grounds for optimism: Jones's boundary commission idea required no immediate action.[31]

It needs to be pointed out here that Pakenham was mistaken in his belief that the idea for a boundary commission was Jones's own. Jones's diary, published in 1971, made it clear that it was Lloyd George who thought the scheme up. Jones did indeed present it to Griffith and

30 Pakenham, *Ordeal*, pp.159-60;162-4. The italics are Pakenham's.

31 *ibid.*, pp.165-8.

Collins as if it were his own, and he was so convincing that his account was accepted ever since.

To return to Pakenham's narrative, Griffith made 'startling and secret concessions' four days after the 8 November meeting with Jones. By 12 November Lloyd George had rammed home the tiny advantage gained by Jones's opening of the door earlier. If Griffith had flatly refused to discuss the boundary commission suggestion, Lloyd George would have found it difficult to get out of his promise to resign.

Jones worked on Griffith again on 9 November. He urged that Lloyd George needed support against Craig and his backers and he used the Bonar Law bogey just far enough but not so far as to frighten the Irish off their tactics. Jones presented the boundary commission as a 'tactic' to deprive Ulster of public support in England. Griffith replied cautiously (or so he thought) to the proposal, promising not to queer Lloyd George's position if he used it. This showed 'the ravages effected by Jones's diplomacy' on Griffith.

Jones impressed on Griffith the urgency of keeping Lloyd George in power, and Griffith half consciously prepared to modify his plans to that end. So he was already as good as reconciled to the boundary commission as an alternative to an all-Ireland parliament. It was true that he wrote and thought of it still as a tactic, but if one accepted a policy as a tactic, one almost certainly accepted it in fact as well.

For all Griffith's care in not putting Sinn Féin behind the boundary commission scheme, he 'had agreed not to queer Lloyd George's pitch', and thereby *'he had released him from his obligation to secure an all-Ireland parliament or resign'.* Lloyd George continued to try to win Craig over but more and more faced the possibility of failure and instead employed the other prong of his policy - settling with Sinn Féin directly and separately. But Ulster had been and still was a most useful means of keeping Sinn Féin 'along the course he desired'.[32]

If there had been no 12 November there might have been no Treaty. This was when Griffith met Lloyd George and agreed not to repudiate publicly the boundary commission proposal in the run-up to, or during, the Liverpool conference of the Conservative Party on 17 November. An attempt was likely to be made at the conference to pass a motion opposing the continuation of the Anglo-Irish conference. The evidence for the events of 12 November is unsatisfactory and some speculation is necessary. There were two written versions of Griffith's interview with Lloyd George: Griffith's own in a long letter to de Valera, and Austen Chamberlain's memoir of Lloyd George's account, given to him shortly after the meeting.

32 Pakenham *Ordeal*, pp.167-72. The italics are Pakenham's.

According to Griffith's letter, Lloyd George showed him Craig's correspondence, completely rejecting the all-Ireland parliament solution. Lloyd George stated that his reply would be to offer this again, with Northern Ireland having the right to opt out of its jurisdiction within a year, but if it did so it would have to accept a boundary commission which would delimit its area.

This was to be the last British offer to Ulster, and if it were refused, Lloyd George was to resist the unionists, summon parliament, appeal to it against Northern Ireland, and then either call a general election or pass an all-Ireland act. What this amounted to was that Lloyd George would proceed with the boundary commission without Ulster's consent, and what this meant for Sinn Féin was that what they had accepted as a tactical manoeuvre only was being given substance as a concrete solution.

Griffith insisted that the boundary commission proposal was Lloyd George's and not Sinn Féin's. The Prime Minister replied that while the British were fighting their extremists, they would be lost if Sinn Féin repudiated it. Griffith conceded that they would not do that, but reiterated that it was Lloyd George's suggestion, that if Northern Ireland accepted it they would discuss it with him in the privacy of the conference, but that they could not guarantee its acceptance.

Griffith had got it fixed in his mind that Lloyd George was very satisfied with Sinn Féin and dissatisfied with Ulster (he told de Valera that the Conservative leaders, Birkenhead and Chamberlain, would fight Ulster if necessary at Liverpool). He believed he had committed himself no further than he had to Jones on 9 November (he realised the value of the boundary commission as a tactical manoeuvre and if Lloyd George proposed it they would not queer his pitch). His colleagues, who relied fully on him for information, thought likewise. This was why, three weeks later, they still believed they could stage the break-up of the negotiations on Ulster. But Chamberlain's memoir of the meeting suggested that this option was closed to Sinn Féin from 12 November.

According to Chamberlain, Lloyd George impressed on Griffith the gravity of the situation and also the opportunity. All hinged on the Liverpool conference; if Birkenhead and Chamberlain succeeded, the British would not support an unreasonable Ulster and the way to a settlement would be clear at last. But he could not ask the two Conservatives to risk their careers unless he could be sure Griffith would not let him down. His Ulster offer would be unpopular and would cause a crisis, and his survival counted on his being able to present it as the only compromise acceptable to Sinn Féin. Griffith gave the promise not to repudiate his Ulster proposals, that is, Chamberlain understood, not to break off the negotiations over them. Jones drew up a memorandum of the meeting on Lloyd George's instructions and Griffith assented to it next day when shown it by Jones.

What exactly did Griffith accept by agreeing to this 13 November memorandum? Griffith had been hearing of its contents for some days from Jones and had informed Dublin of them on 8 and 9 November. 'There is no conflict therefore over the *nature* of the terms in which Griffith in some sense acquiesced', but there were two main differences between Griffith's and Chamberlain's readings of the situation. The first was that Chamberlain understood that Griffith promised that he would not find a cause to break over the British Ulster terms, that is, that he accepted them as a concrete solution. But Griffith agreed to them as a tactic only, promising not to undermine Lloyd George while he was fighting the unionist reactionaries.

The second was that Griffith mentioned no document in his report to de Valera. He did see the British Ulster terms in written form but there was no question of any 'intentional concealment' on his part. The terms were the same as those he had already described twice to the Dublin cabinet and it had seemed to him unimportant that he had seen them written down.

The first difference (what Griffith believed he said about the boundary commission proposal and what Chamberlain *understood* him to have said) is harder to explain. But it is a necessary fact for judgement that Lloyd George was able to use Griffith's pledge against him on the final day of the conference as containing a promise not to let him down and after some trouble was able to get him to abandon the prospect of breaking the talks on Ulster.

Griffith's language and the manner of his assent on 12 November could afterwards be used to imply a more far-reaching promise than he meant at the time. Chamberlain saw it in this light from the first, and indeed from 12 November onwards all the British acted on the assumption that if agreement could be reached on the other disputed points, Ulster would present no difficulty because they could go ahead with the boundary commission. Perhaps Griffith was much less explicit about his attitude to Lloyd George on 12 November than he should have been, taking it for granted that the Prime Minister already knew where he stood.

Perhaps Griffith believed he had been as clear as he described in his report to Dublin on 12 November, but afterwards could be made to feel that he had not been, and in fairness felt himself prevented from denying Lloyd George's interpretation. If these conjectures were true, then the existence of the document shown to Griffith by Jones on 13

November was decisive. There, down on paper, were the terms Griffith had acquiesced in, but where were the qualifications he believed he had made? From the point of view of strategy, the scheme of accepting the boundary commission as a tactical ploy only, which was always risky, was finally stymied by Griffith's acceptance of the 13 November document. When the crux came on 5 December, Lloyd George was able to persuade Griffith that he was prevented by a solemn promise from breaking off the talks over Ulster.[33]

In his summary, Pakenham contended that from 30 October onwards, Griffith carried the delegation with him in accepting sacrifices on the Crown and Empire in return for unity. The form that unity took at first was an all-Ireland parliament, which Lloyd George promised to secure, failing which he would resign. But from 9 November onwards Griffith was impressed by the need to keep Lloyd George in power, and to make this possible he accepted the boundary commission as a tactic. However, Lloyd George refused to proceed with it unless he got definite assurances that Griffith would not let him down on it. Griffith gave an undertaken, which he later could be persuaded was more than he thought. Lloyd George was in safe keeping as long as he was pledged to resign, but wormed out of the Irish hold and soon had them on the floor.

Pakenham decided that responsibility for this escape lay with all on the Irish side who knew of the gradual emergence of the boundary commission alternative to an all-Ireland parliament, but most of all with Griffith because of his acceptance of the 13 November document. But for that they could rightly have denied that they were committed to the boundary commission proposal. Griffith should have preserved a complete distinction between the all-Ireland parliament and the boundary commission, and as soon as it seemed likely that Craig would not budge - as it must have from 8 November onwards - he should have gone all out to collapse the conference on Ulster.

Lloyd George's promise to resign was an unexpected piece of good fortune. Griffith should have held him fast to it and discounted 'the illusion of a Bonar Law militarist regime'. (But *was* it an illusion?) This would have preserved the republic and justified the attempt to ensure the conference broke on Ulster to the full.[34]

However, Pakenham was less certain 30 years later. In a radio talk on the Treaty negotiations, he declared that the strategy of trying to stage the break on Ulster 'was a cock that probably would not fight in the end'.

33 Pakenham *Ordeal*, pp.174-81.

34 *ibid.*, pp.181-2,250-55.

However, he wondered if Griffith had not been outsmarted on 12/13 November, would the Irish have got away with it? Not quite, was his own surmise, because they would not have escaped the dilemma confronting them since the talks began - entrance into the Empire or war - but they would 'almost certainly' have got away from London without signing and without internal schism.

'What would have happened then is pure speculation', he admitted. The Free State might have been set up later; there would probably have been no Civil War and no partition. (Surely this was to ignore its actual incarnation in the form of the Northern Irish state, established *before* the Anglo-Irish negotiations began?) 'One has to admit that Irish independence beyond the point already achieved by the middle of 1921 was probably impossible without further heavy sacrifices and further grave suffering', was Pakenham's sober mature conclusion.[35]

There is a recognisably anti-Treaty school of authors who accept fully Pakenham's thesis, but who are harsher on Griffith than he was. Macardle was the first of these. She asserted that Griffith needed to be wary of Lloyd George, but that he trusted to his own wisdom. She saw him as not only cooperating but conspiring with his opponent.[36] Neeson wrote in similar vein: 'Doubtless Griffith hoped to use Lloyd George's difficulties to his own advantage, but he forgot that one needs a long spoon to sup with the devil'.[37] Cox closely followed the course mapped out by Macardle but introduced a Cambrian element into the discussion. He believed Jones to have been of inestimable value to Lloyd George in his 'diplomatic finesse and behind-the-scenes manoeuvring'.

Griffith, Jones and Lloyd George 'had Welsh antecedents, and shared Celtic emotive affinities....Griffith and Jones assiduously cultivated one another'. What Cox found most reprehensible was 'the continuance of Griffith's personal diplomacy'. It was his unrelenting conclusion that Griffith's personal diplomacy 'inexorably' led to the collapse of the Irish position.[38] There is also a pro-Treaty group of authors which acknowledges Pakenham's version, but which is sympathetic to Griffith. In general, from this perspective Griffith is seen as an honest and honourable man, outmanoeuvred by a skilled but devious politician.

Ó Lúing represented Lloyd George as very much the *bete noire*, seeing him as using Colonel Gretton (the leader of the unionist diehard

35 Longford, 'Treaty negotiations', in *Irish Struggle*, pp.111-12,115.

36 Macardle, *Irish Republic*, pp.506,510,512-13.

37 Neeson, *Civil War*, pp.42,44-5.

38 Cox, *Damned Englishmen*, pp.163,166,193.

element in the Conservative Party) and Craig, to soften the Irish delegates. He believed that the Prime Minister had no intention of forcing Craig to give in and that Craig knew this. Jones was portrayed by Ó Lúing as Lloyd George's intermediary who had learned political skills from his master.[39] Davis, Younger and Glandon all agreed with Ó Lúing.[40]

In a review of Frank Gallagher's *Four Glorious Years*, Hugh Delargy, like Pakenham a member of the British Labour Party, provided a counterblast to the view just outlined above. Delargy refused to accept Gallagher's (and by implication Pakenham's) interpretation of events. Delargy noted how Lloyd George had been painted 'the villain' of the Treaty negotiations by Gallagher, and how Jones 'invariably appeared as...the faithful lackey always at the beck and call of his master'. If the story of their inveigling of Griffith were to be taken at face value, then Delargy rightly believed that it led to all sorts of 'disturbing conclusions'.

The main one was that Griffith was 'a fool, who was willing to split Ireland from top to bottom, to abandon the six counties, to risk civil war - all because, mesmerised by Lloyd George, he had given some vague private promise which he himself had forgotten within three days'. Delargy did not consider Griffith to be either a fool or a traitor and so could not accept Gallagher's 'melodramatic account' which 'masqueraded as the history of the Irish Treaty'.[41]

Struggling to Achieve a Settlement? Griffith and Lloyd George

Historians, free from the bias which encumbered those surveyed, writing mainly since the publication of Jones's diary in 1971, display differing approaches and emphases. Many of them accept Pakenham's case that Griffith was outmanoeuvred by Lloyd George, but regard this of less significance that he did. What they stress is that the British genuinely desired to bring about Irish unity but that extremists in both Belfast and Dublin frustrated this.

Hancock, a contemporary of Pakenham's, believed that the British did want to achieve a united Ireland, desiring the unity of Ireland for

39 Ó Lúing, *Ó Gríofa*, pp.370,372-4.

40 Davis, *Arthur Griffith*, pp.35-6; Younger, *Griffith*, pp.107-10; Glandon, *Griffith and Advanced-Nationalist Press*, pp.192-3.

41 Hugh Delargy, 'Give us the truth!' in *Reynold's News*, 13 September 1953. Gallagher wrote under the pen-name David Hogan. He was anti-Treaty.

the sake of the unity of the Empire.[42] This view was borne out by Jones's diary.

Keith Middlemas, who edited the diary, had a different interpretation of Lloyd George's role from that presented so far. The following is a summary of Middlemas's argument. The Prime Minister's threat to resign if Ulster rejected the settlement was genuine. On 30 October Lloyd George wanted documentary proof of Irish acceptance of the Crown and Empire, so that he would be armed against the Conservative hardliners before the party conference. He also needed something of substance with which to approach Craig. The diaries of Lord Riddell and C. P. Scott support the contention that Lloyd George fully intended to resign. (Riddell, a newspaper proprietor, was a confidant of Lloyd George. Scott, editor of the *Manchester Guardian*, which was sympathetic to the Irish cause, was also a close friend of the Prime Minister.)[43]

Griffith's 2 November letter gave Lloyd George sufficient grounds to bring in Craig. But the latter's total obduracy left Lloyd George with little room to manoeuvre. After his meeting with Craig on 7 November Jones reported he had never seen him so depressed since the talks began. He instructed Jones to see Griffith and Collins and to prepare them for a breakdown in the negotiations, avowing that he would resign rather than coerce the South. However, he saw one possible way out of the impasse, the boundary commission, and Jones was to see Griffith and Collins and ask them if they would support him on this.

Lloyd George's first mention of a boundary commission was in no way a ploy intended to ensnare Sinn Féin. (Middlemas did not comment on the fact that Jones presented the idea as if it were his own, but he would not have put this down to any deviousness on Jones's part. He described Jones as 'a true friend of Ireland - self-governing, peaceable, moderate Ireland, not the Ireland of those he saw as the gunmen, the irreconcilable republicans'.) Neither Griffith nor Collins liked the boundary commission proposal but Jones summoned up the terrifying alternative: 'Chaos, Crown Colony Government, Civil War'. When Jones reported on this meeting to Lloyd George, the latter informed him that he had made up his mind to resign, and had told the king, his wife and his secretaries.[44]

On 10 November Lloyd George made a statement that Northern

42 Hancock, *Survey*, p.142.

43 Middlemas (ed.), *Jones*, pp.xii,150,152.

44 *ibid.*, pp.xvii-xvix,xxii,154-6.

Ireland would have to accept increased taxation if it refused an all-Ireland parliament. This disturbed the Conservative unionists. But it was clear that the British delegates and indeed most of the cabinet accepted that moral pressure could be brought to bear on Northern Ireland. Lloyd George wrote 'a long and persuasive' letter to Craig asking him to join the conference. Part to the persuasion was the veiled threat that if Northern Ireland rejected the all-Ireland parliament it could face increased taxation. Craig refused to attend the conference unless the British withdrew their all-Ireland parliament proposal. He also suggested that Northern Ireland be granted Dominion status as well as the South. When Jones showed Griffith Craig's reply on 12 November, he told him that if Sinn Féin cooperated with Lloyd George, Irish unity could be achieved before long.[45]

From Jones's diary Griffith's role emerges positively as one enabling Lloyd George to make progress in difficult circumstances, assured of Irish goodwill. It was Griffith's reasonable stance which swung erstwhile unionists like Birkenhead and Chamberlain behind the Prime Minister in support of the Irish negotiations and settlement. This was how Middlemas viewed it in contrast to Pakenham. One must bear in mind, of course, that Middlemas regarded the Treaty as a worthwhile agreement, while Pakenham did not.

Most authors writing after Middlemas take greater cognisance than Pakenham of the British dimension to the Anglo-Irish negotiations. Paul Johnson, for example, believes that a settlement was extremely difficult to negotiate in the circumstances of the time and that Lloyd George's was the crucial role.[46] Curran stresses Jones's constructive part: he knew Ireland well and sympathised with Irish nationalism; his sympathy, tact, discretion and closeness to his fellow-Welshman, Lloyd George, made him 'an ideal intermediary' with the Irish delegates.[47]

Laffan argues that the British believed initially that they could persuade Northern Ireland to accept the overall authority of an all-Ireland parliament in return for six-county autonomy. Lloyd George then believed that the threat of the boundary commission and higher taxation would cause Craig to yield some ground. Jones noted in his diary that his Prime Minister was considering 'various ways of bringing pressure on Ulster through her pockets'. Laffan describes

45 Middlemas (ed.), *Jones*, pp.158-63,164.

46 Paul Johnson, *Ireland: Land of Troubles* (London,1980), pp.164-5.

47 Curran, *Free State*, pp.79,94-5,102-7.

Lloyd George's 10 November letter to Craig as 'a combination of inducement and veiled threat'.[48]

Lawlor examines Lloyd George's position in some detail. By 1 November, having overwhelmingly defeated the vote of censure in the House of Commons, he had reached the decision to oppose the extreme unionists as long as Sinn Féin would accept the British 'essentials'. In this he had Birkenhead's support, which he considered vital. Perhaps he hoped his threat to resign would bring him the support of most Conservatives and isolate the extremists. He considered the letter that he got from Griffith on 2 November 'the essential document' he needed to confront Craig and the extremists. However, making no headway with Craig he got Jones to sound out Griffith and Collins on the boundary commission idea. He claimed he would resign and had told the king and his colleagues. By 9 November he was more confident about his position, and was more assured that Birkenhead and Chamberlain would back him. Churchill, too, had discouraged him from resigning, arguing that that would mean the government abdicating responsibility.

Lawlor also deals with Lloyd George's desire to bring pressure to bear on Craig, the unease felt by some Conservative ministers about this, and their eventual acceptance that it was permissible to exert 'moral pressure' on Northern Ireland.[49]

Hopkinson holds that while Lloyd George certainly exaggerated his domestic difficulties so as to make an impact on Griffith, the latter's assurance made an impression on Chamberlain and Birkenhead and helped the conference to make progress. Craig was called to London and the advantages of accepting an all-Ireland parliament were impressed on him 'forcefully'. Craig showed himself somewhat flexible at first but afterwards stiffened.

Although Griffith had been careful in how he dealt with Lloyd George, he had been 'outmanoeuvred' by him, according to Hopkinson. He seems to mitigate this judgement by pointing out that 'Chamberlain's and Birkenhead's strong support of Lloyd George helped considerably to nullify potential opposition at the Liverpool conference - they had been impressed by Griffith's conciliatory attitude'.[50]

Hancock was the first to argue that Craig frustrated both British and Irish hopes of unity: 'Against this impressive devotion to the United Kingdom the vision and subtlety of the new imperial statesmanship

48 Laffan, *Partition*, pp.82-4.

49 Lawlor, *Britain and Irl.*, pp.128-32.

50 Hopkinson, *Green against Green*, pp.28-9.

achieved nothing. Ulster had ruined the chances of an Anglo-Irish reconciliation grounded without ambiguity on the reconciliation of a united Irish people'.[51]

Hopkinson is one of a number of later historians who write along similar lines. Lloyd George had hoped to get Craig to consent to an all-Ireland parliament and felt genuine chagrin at Ulster unionist attitudes: he was very happy, however, to settle for second-best in the form of southern agreement to the boundary commission, the more so because Griffith failed to force him to define it more clearly. From a longer perspective, however, the real beneficiaries of these developments were the northern government. They had called Lloyd George's bluff, which Griffith had singularly failed to do.

It could be said in Griffith's defence that his position was much weaker than that of Craig, who was head of a government already in existence and enjoyed substantial support from the Conservative majority in Britain. Hopkinson admits as much by conceding earlier in his book that with coercion ruled out, Lloyd George was very limited in his power to deal with Ulster. He put moral and economic pressure on Craig to come into an all-Ireland parliament, but he had to do so carefully in case he would arouse Conservative opposition and bolster the hardline element. The fact that the Northern Ireland government existed and that there was a Conservative majority in the coalition effectively vetoed an all-Ireland parliament. Lloyd George had first to satisfy his own cabinet in order to negotiate successfully, and this was why Birkenhead, Chamberlain and Churchill were part of the British delegation. Up to mid-November he was very preoccupied with conspiracies against himself, believing Churchill unreliable, and fearing that opposition to any arrangement with Sinn Féin would centre on Law, who was intimately linked with Ulster unionism.

Both Chamberlain and Lloyd George told the Irish delegates of the risks they were taking with their political futures. C.P. Scott told Collins how hard Lloyd George had worked to bring the Tories into line, maintaining that only he, of all British statesmen who had tried to solve the Irish problem, could succeed. When Collins replied that he could only afford to think of Ireland, Scott's retort was that he had to take stock of internal British politics if he wished to achieve anything.[52]

Griffith believed that better terms could have been secured if the Irish delegates 'had not been handicapped by their own fiction' (that the republic really in fact existed and could be preserved). Thus wrote

51 Hancock, *Survey*, p.143.

52 Hopkinson, *Green against Green*, pp.29,22-3.

Joseph Hone some 60 years ago, introducing a new dimension into the debate which was then taken up by later commentators. Noting Pakenham's belief that Griffith was outmanoeuvred by Lloyd George, Hone himself inclined to the view that Griffith and Lloyd George were outmanoeuvred by de Valera and Craig. Hone presented the following case.

Griffith cared more for unity than 'the Republic' and realised that if the talks broke down, it would be a great advantage to Sinn Féin to be able to put the blame on Ulster, because British public opinion would not support a resumption of the Anglo-Irish War to buttress Ulster intransigence. Lloyd George could see Griffith's strategy and supported it. At one point in the conference he was ready to take on the diehards and fight to secure unity, provided that he was assured by Sinn Féin on the Crown. But he never got this assurance as de Valera in Dublin persisted with 'external association' as the limit of Sinn Féin concession on the Crown and Empire.[53]

Pakenham showed how the Irish delegation was outmanoeuvred, and placed definite responsibility on Griffith, but he did not show that Griffith was prevented from achieving unity, because he was 'defending a position he knew to be untenable', argued Frank O'Connor. Griffith would not break on the Crown, nor would Collins in the last resort, but they would both break on Ulster, and their main tactic should have been to demonstrate clearly from the start that 'on the integrity of Ireland they would and could break', and in doing so 'carry a united nation with them'.[54] Lyons agrees with Hone and O'Connor that extremists on both sides greatly hindered movement in any direction. Similarly, Murphy states that Lloyd George got the better of the Irish delegates, but that de Valera and the republican extremists were an even greater bane to them: 'The will-o-the-wisp of sovereignty had been pursued at the expense of unity and in the end neither was served'. But, Murphy rightly wonders whether a more sensible policy would have avoided Irish disunity, given the intensely difficult nature of the Ulster question.[55]

Kee makes the strongest case for this line of argument as follows. The Irish delegation should have insisted rigidly on unity and made whatever concessions on the Crown were necessary to achieve it. The greatest Irish mistake was to allow the issues of unity and allegiance to become mixed up, instead of concentrating on unity, on which the British were more

53 Hone, *New Statesman and Nation*, 24 March 1937.

54 O'Connor, *Collins*, p.137.

55 Lyons, *Famine*, p.432; Murphy, *Irl. in 20th Century*, p.37.

vulnerable and likely to be more amenable. The reason for this maladroitness was that although to most Irish people unity was of more substance than allegiance, the latter was equally important to 'the minority of republican dogmatists, whom the delegates also represented'. As it turned out, they were defeated on both issues.

In terms solely of the tactics which the situation seemed to demand, it is amazing to find that as late as ten days after the conference had begun, the Irish were writing to de Valera through Childers for instruction as to which issue to give more weight to, Ulster or the Crown. When Griffith indicated that his natural inclinations were to offer concessions on the Crown, de Valera wrote back that there could be 'no question of our asking the Irish people to enter an arrangement which would make them subject to the Crown, or demand from them allegiance to the British King. If war is the alternative, we can only face it...'

Lloyd George showed Griffith the potential benefits for Ireland, if the Irish delegates had been fully free to make concessions on the Crown. The two stumbling blocks were (a) Griffith and Collins had only limited room to manoeuvre on the Crown, and (b) when Craig proved immovable as regards any change in the status of Northern Ireland, the British Prime Minister introduced 'a subtle device' (the boundary commission) to extricate himself from the Dublin and Belfast headlocks at the same time.[56]

Historians after 1970 take much more stock than their predecessors of two realities which made the Irish delegates' task particularly onerous. One of these was that the six-county state existed before the Anglo-Irish negotiations began. Partition was a *fait accompli* and Craig had no intention of giving up any of the advantages he had secured. So the Irish delegation's task was not to prevent partition but to undo it, which was an immensely complex assignment as Craig held all the cards: he knew he could not be moved, especially when he had the support of a powerful faction in England.

Lyons expresses amazement that the Irish delegates, and especially Griffith, relied so much on the ability of the British government to coerce Craig. It had not occurred in 1914, 1916 or 1917, and it was even less likely in 1921 with an actual government established in Belfast. Lee holds that it was part of Lloyd George's achievement to have 'bewitched' Griffith into believing that he could deliver unity in the face of the opposition of Ulster unionists backed by the Conservatives. But in this

56 Kee, *Ourselves Alone*, pp.148-9,150-52.

'Griffith merely reflected the immaturity of nationalist thinking about Ulster in allowing himself to be deluded'.[57]

The second 'reality' for Griffith and his colleagues was the danger of a Conservative backlash destroying the conference. Pakenham dismissed this as an illusion. Although Lyons sees substance in the charge that by giving even a cautious promise to Lloyd George concerning the boundary commission, Griffith was thereby releasing him from his pledge to resign, against this must be set the dilemma which Griffith faced: if the Prime Minister's resignation was forced by him, the result would have been the coming to power of obdurate unionism in the person of Bonar Law.[58]

Middlemas also contends that the alternative to Lloyd George's coalition was a Tory government under Law which might have led straight to what General Sir Neville Macready had warned of: 'the military shooting 100 men in one week' in Ireland. Johnson, Lawlor and Hopkinson also believe that had Lloyd George resigned, a coercive Tory government would have replaced him. It was a predicament which the Irish negotiators could not ignore.[59]

A number of modern historians have concluded, unlike Pakenham, that de Valera was no less culpable than Griffith, perhaps more so, for the way the negotiations developed in London. Following his 8 November meeting with Jones, Griffith wrote to de Valera expressing the belief that the proposed boundary commission would give Sinn Féin all of two counties and parts of others. He also told de Valera that he felt the conference might end within a week and, if so, it would be over Ulster intransigence, which would turn public opinion against the North. In his reply, de Valera expressed himself as happy with the prospect of a break in such circumstances, but warned against any concessions on the Crown and Empire. There was no warning against concessions on Ulster, though, Curran points out tellingly.[60]

Bowman draws attention to the fact that Griffith kept de Valera informed of developments, and concludes that de Valera's response would have persuaded Griffith that the extreme republicans in the Dublin cabinet were agreeing to 'the compromises already mooted by

57 Lyons, *Famine*, p.433; Lee, *Irl. 1912-85*, pp.52-3. See also MacDonagh, *Union*, p.97, and Hopkinson, *Green against Green*, p.22.

58 Lyons, *op. cit.*, p.433.

59 Middlemas (ed.), *Jones*, p.xxii; Johnson, *Land of Troubles*, p.165; Lawlor, *Britain and Irl.*, p.124; Hopkinson, *op. cit.* p.22. Macready was the General-Officer-in-Command of the British forces in Ireland for much of the Anglo-Irish War.

60 Curran, *Free State*, p.103.

the Irish delegation in London'.[61] Lawlor records that on 9 November Griffith wrote to de Valera of Lloyd George's boundary commission proposal. On 11 November Collins went to Dublin and two days later attended a Dáil cabinet meeting. No record of Collins's private talks with de Valera exists, but the latter must have been informed of the course that the discussions in London were taking. At the 13 November cabinet meeting, de Valera said that there should be as much cooperation between London and Dublin as possible, but the plenipotentiaries should be totally free, while following original instructions, to take important decisions.

'But the problem, of course, lay in the nature of the original instructions and the delegates' interpretation of them', Lawlor writes, and she points out that, for example, Griffith thought his 2 November letter to Lloyd George consistent with external association. 'So,...the problem for the historian may well have existed for the delegates at the time: how far did de Valera privately encourage the delegates - by manner, hints, omissions, by the very vagueness of his appreciations - to continue the negotiations along the lines as recorded by Griffith and Collins? How far did he acquiesce in their plans and proposals? How far was the record of the cabinet on 13 November a fair indication of his attitude that although Ulster would be the best question on which to break (if a break were "inevitable"), he was neither clear that a break must take place nor on what issue to break. De Valera referred on the one hand to the plenipotentiaries maintaining "a perfectly free hand' and on the other to following 'original instructions'. Griffith seems to have assumed that he was following original instructions."[62]

What were Griffith's and Collins's attitudes to the boundary commission? What did they expect from it? There has been much debate about these questions: whether they had faith in the commission and whether this was due to British prompting or was self-induced; why they did not insist on a more precise definition of its terms; whether it might have led to unity.

Pakenham, who had surprisingly little to say on the topic, believed that but for the Irish delegates' confidence that the boundary commission would bring about a united Ireland, they would never have agreed to sign and there would have been no Treaty. He did not know whether they were wise or foolish in their expectations. Ryan had no doubt that Griffith and Collins were misled by the British.[63]

61 Bowman, *De Valera and Ulster Question*, pp.62-3.

62 Lawlor, *Britain and Irl.*, pp.136-7.

63 Pakenham, *Ordeal*, pp.11-12; Ryan, *Unique Dictator*, p.144.

Collins told P.S. O'Hegarty that Griffith and he were given a personal assurance by Birkenhead and Churchill that Northern Ireland would get only four counties from the boundary commission, and that the British would make four-county government impossible. Ó Lúing, Colum and other authors emphasised Griffith's confidence in the boundary commission.[64] But, according to Lyons, the Irish were only too willing to delude themselves into believing that the boundary commission would deliver the desired result. Akenson describes the Irish delegates' attitudes as 'wishful thinking' but at Lloyd George's prompting.[65]

Tierney attacks the theory that Lloyd George simply hoodwinked the Irish delegates, and especially Griffith. It was 'a supposition dear to those who later opposed the Treaty and who contended that Collins and Griffith were fools or knaves or both'. It has to be said, however, that many Griffith sympathisers, and a number of neutral observers who regarded the Treaty as the best that could have been achieved in the circumstances of the time, upheld this notion of British deception.[66]

Ronan Fanning, Lawlor and Hopkinson all insisted that there was nothing to show that the British delegates gave definite assurances about the outcome of the boundary commission to their Irish counterparts. The following explanation from Curran of this aspect of the conference merits consideration. Griffith and Collins had some faith in the boundary commission but Lloyd George, Chamberlain and Birkenhead led them to believe that border revision would so maim Northern Ireland that Craig would be forced to seek unity. The reason that the British could not state this openly was that it would have led to a Tory rebellion, which would have destroyed the conference, but they conveyed it indirectly through Jones and T.M. Healy (the former Home Rule MP).

'It is easy to dismiss such assurances as a calculated deception, but the truth seem more complex'. The British genuinely wanted unity as the only basis for a lasting peace. They were tired of Craig's intransigence. They could not openly force him, but they probably thought that if they reached an amicable agreement with the rest of Ireland, they would be able 'to apply legitimate forms of pressure, such as higher taxation and the threat of boundary revision, to promote unification'.

Lloyd George told his cabinet in early November that if Northern Ireland was intent on opting out of an all-Ireland parliament, it could not retain Fermanagh and Tyrone. When, after the Treaty, he,

64 O'Hegarty, *Irl. under Union*, p.754; Ó Lúing, *Ó Gríofa*, p.376; Colum, *Griffith*, p.381.

65 Lyons, *Famine*, pp.433,437; Akenson, *US and Irl.*, p.69.

66 Tierney, *MacNeill*, p.347.

Chamberlain and Birkenhead said that these two counties preferred to be united with the rest of Ireland, they seemed to be preparing the way for some dismemberment of Northern Ireland. 'Fulfilment of British pledges, however, depended largely on Sinn Féin's reception of the Treaty'.

If all had gone well and the new government in Ireland had been set up quickly, with the boundary commission meeting soon afterwards in an atmosphere of goodwill between Britain and Ireland, the wishes of the people would have been met and the mainly nationalist areas of Northern Ireland would have been given to the South. The unionists could have done little to prevent this happening. A large reduction in Northern Ireland might not have resulted in unity, but partition would have been much fairer as a result, and the Treaty arrangement would have been reinforced.

'As it happened, however, events took quite a different turn in the post-Treaty period and the boundary commission changed nothing'. Birkenhead's spring 1922 promise to Lord Balfour (made in a private letter not published until 1924), that there was no question of seriously reducing Northern Ireland, was probably 'unavoidable'. This was because Balfour looked for the guarantee at a time when Collins publicly claimed a large northern area, and when there was growing unease in Britain with the Treaty, because of the republican opposition to it.[67]

Colum had many years before put forward the same line as Curran. Concerning Griffith's anticipations from Clause XII (the boundary commission clause) of the Treaty, Colum argued that had there been:

> ...a peaceful transition from a revolutionary to a stable regime, had a united Dáil, which had shown goodwill towards the British people, asked for the boundary commission within a few months after the Treaty had been signed, there is much probability that the northern and Free State leaders would have been brought together to hammer out a settlement, which would have made for Irish unity. But the disturbances on both sides of the border, the opposition to the Provisional Government, the long-continued disorders, the boycott of Belfast, the assassination of Sir Henry Wilson, the killings and expulsions of the Catholics in the North, made impossible any friendly arrangements between the Irish governments.[68]

67 Ronan Fanning, *Independent Ireland* (Dublin, 1983), p.24; Lawlor, *Britain and Irl.*, p.144; Hopkinson, *Green against Green*, p.78; Curran, *Free State*, pp.133-4.

68 Colum, *Griffith*, pp.381-2.

There has to be truth in this contention. And there is evidence to support it from elsewhere. Middlemas pointed out that Tom Jones did not believe that the Treaty made partition permanent, and that Jones's account of the 1922-25 period suggested that but for the Civil War, Northern Ireland might have accepted an all-Ireland parliament. Middlemas wondered was this wishful thinking, based on the experience of the Collins-Craig meetings of early 1922, but he contended that the atmosphere of the 1925 meetings suggested otherwise. 'In spite of outrages, murders and reprisals, the persecution of Protestants and Catholics, Orangemen and IRA, and the intransigence of the supporters on both sides, when the leaders met they were not irreconcilable'.[69]

This issue is certainly 'one of the most fascinating, unanswerable questions in Irish history', as Glandon describes it. Her opinion is that unionists' fears for their future as a minority in the Irish Free State were certainly confirmed by the bitter divide over the Treaty, and the period of upheaval which followed it.[70]

Another important detail relating to the boundary commission clause was recorded by Colum. (The clause stated that the border would be revised 'in accordance with the wishes of the inhabitants' in so far as these 'may be compatible with economic and geographic conditions'.) One of Griffith's party on the journey back to Dublin for the 3 December cabinet meeting was John O'Byrne, a legal adviser to the delegation, who went through the British draft, clause by clause, with Griffith. When Griffith explained to him his expectations from the boundary commission, O'Byrne pointed out that the clause was too vague, left too much power to the commission itself, and he suggested that electoral units should be specified.

Griffith immediately saw the validity of O'Byrne's point, but was uncertain whether it would be possible to have the clause amended at that stage. It was not changed, as it turned out. Colum, in his account of the meeting in Dublin on 3 December, wondered why Griffith did not suggest getting this clause altered, as he had recognised its importance when suggested to him by O'Byrne. Probably because the meeting 'was obsessed with the question of the Crown', was Colum's surmise.[71] The official record of that meeting shows that he was correct in this.

This is how Curran deals with this question. Griffith and Collins

69 Middlemas (ed.), *Jones*, p.xxii.

70 Glandon, *Griffith and Advanced-Nationalist Press*, p.215.

71 Colum, *Griffith*, pp.295-6,298.

might have avoided the eventual outcome of the boundary commission, if they had demanded that its functions be specified exactly, instead of being content with a loosely-worded clause which could be interpreted to the benefit of Sinn Féin. They and their colleagues in London and Dublin, by being shrewder and more insistent,should not have settled for less than boundary revision 'in accordance with plebiscites in specified local units'. They should not have allowed economic and geographic factors to be introduced, as these could override the wishes of the inhabitants.

Safeguards like careful supervision of plebiscites, and Dominion arbitration where there was a dispute over the boundary commission's decision, could have been embodied in the Treaty. If Sinn Féin had sought these, the British could hardly have refused, as the Irish were willing to accept proposals not guaranteeing unity. And as they had promised not to use force against the unionists, they were totally justified in making sure that the unionists treated Northern Catholics in like manner.

It is clear that the question of the oath dominated the 3 December meeting in Dublin, and that this at least partly explains why the Dáil cabinet failed to clarify its position on Northern Ireland.[72] But it is surely more than a partial explanation. The official record of that meeting makes clear that the question of partition received virtually no attention. And the same was to be the case during the long Dáil debate on the Treaty.

72 Curran, *Free State*, pp.134,120.

Chapter III

Divisions and Decisions

Divisions

The Irish delegation could hardly be described as united. De Valera's 27 December letter to McGarrity revealed that situation more than anything else. Personal suspicions no doubt added to differing policy aspirations and approaches. Under the strain of the intense discussions in London, the divisions became more marked, exacerbated as they were by the events arising.

The divisions within the Irish delegation first surfaced over de Valera's telegram to the pope. Pakenham saw it as threatening the settlement for which Griffith and Collins had begun to hope, and he wrote that they were unhappy with the manner of de Valera's intervention. It was this that Colum dwelt on, observing that de Valera did not consult those in London before sending his telegram, and that his wording certainly 'detracted from the authority of the Irish delegation'. When Seán Milroy later questioned Griffith about the incident, he replied 'with an unusual tinge of bitterness', that the delegates in London knew nothing about the telegram until it appeared in the press. Forester surmised that the telegram episode must have reinforced Griffith's and Collins's fears that de Valera was drifting towards the extremists in the Dublin cabinet.

Ryle Dwyer found their annoyance 'understandable' as they were carrying on 'tense and difficult negotiations' and de Valera, without warning, had revived the whole recognition issue 'by insulting the British King in an attempt to chide the Pope'. The episode strengthened the unease Collins was feeling that de Valera was planning to lay all the blame for any compromise on the delegation.[1]

The exchange of letters between Griffith and de Valera around 25 October proved another flash-point in London-Dublin relations. In his report of the 24 October meeting with Lloyd George and Chamberlain, Griffith explained that the British pressed him to say that he would accept the Crown if agreement was reached on other issues. Griffith's

1 Pakenham, *Ordeal*, pp.136-7; Colum, *Griffith*, pp.291-2; Forester, *Collins*, p.224; Ryle Dwyer, *Collins*, p.66.

answer to them was that if they could agree on all other points, he was prepared to recommend 'some form of association with the Crown', but that any kind of Irish connection with the Crown depended on Irish unity being achieved. The British repeatedly stressed to him that peace was impossible unless the Crown was accepted.

Part of de Valera's reply caused uproar in London. 'We are all here at one that there can be no question of our asking the Irish people to enter an arrangement which would make them subject to the British King. If war is the alternative, we can only face it, and I think the sooner the other side is made to realise it the better'. Griffith and Collins regarded this letter as curtailing their powers. They threatened to return home. Collins was in a particular rage, bluntly telling the other delegates that Dublin was trying to put him in the wrong and get him to do 'the dirty work for them'.

A written protest was sent from the whole delegation, pointing out that de Valera's letter was curbing the area of discussion and was inconsistent with their status as plenipotentiaries. If their powers were withdrawn, they would have no option but to return to Dublin immediately. De Valera replied that there was no question of limiting their status. He was simply trying to keep the delegates in London in touch with the views of the cabinet in Dublin on the various matters as they arose in the conference.[2]

Pakenham viewed this affair from de Valera's perspective. He acknowledged that the plenipotentiaries had established the need for the widest possible freedom in discussion, and had recorded and won acceptance of the view that external association involved a form of recognition of the Crown. But they had also recognised the binding force of their instructions and the duty of referring back before taking major decisions. What Pakenham considered most significant was the declaration in de Valera's first letter, and even if he seemed to 'climb down' in his second, he never withdrew it, nor did those in London dispute it: war was to be faced if it were the only alternative to allegiance.[3]

O'Connor regarded the matter purely through Collins's eyes, claiming that the letter was the first sign that Collins had that de Valera did not want to compromise. Until then he had deluded himself into thinking that de Valera had been working to overcome Brugha's and

2 Griffith to de Valera, 24 October 1921; de Valera to Griffith, 25 October 1921; Griffith to de Valera, 25 October 1921; de Valera to Griffith, 26 October 1921, DE 2/304/8 NAI. Curiously, de Valera saw the delegates' powers as being conferred on them by the cabinet and not by the Dáil which was, of course, the superior body.

3 Pakenham, *Ordeal*, pp.149-51.

Stack's opposition to any kind of arrangement, and now 'this extraordinary sentiment from the man whose "dirty work" he felt he was doing, simply bewildered him'.

Taylor's biography confirmed Collins's developing suspicion of de Valera. He quoted a letter from Collins to a friend that his being sent to London was a trap to destroy his reputation in Ireland. Taylor described Griffith as very unhappy with the Dublin-imposed limitations, because he felt that the chances of any sort of settlement were slim enough without being endangered further by interference from Dublin.[4] Forester wrote that de Valera's letter almost terminated the conference and asked: 'Were the plenipotentiaries to become puppets?' She stated that Collins was so angry that only Griffith's persuasion stopped him from resigning.[5]

Childers was instructed by the delegates on 21 October to write to de Valera seeking Dublin cabinet advice on how to deal with the allegiance question. The options, Childers explained to de Valera, were either a total refusal of the Crown, or to express a willingness to discuss it, if satisfied on all other points, in order to gain time and room for manoeuvre. Longford and O'Neill saw de Valera's 25 October letter as his firm response to this and to Griffith's missive of a few days later. They were puzzled that Griffith, Collins and Duggan were angered by de Valera's response about allegiance, since Childers was seeking directions on that very question in *his* letter.[6]

This interpretation is difficult to accept. De Valera always replied promptly to the London letters, and would hardly have waited a full four days to make his response to this particular one. His 25 October letter was his reply to Griffith's of the previous evening, and not to Childers's of four days before.

It was unfortunate that the Dublin cabinet did not reply to Childers's letter. Although Griffith did not mention in his letter what form association with the Crown would take, de Valera assumed he had allegiance in mind. Ryle Dwyer surmised that de Valera's letter must have been especially annoying to Griffith and Collins, because they had got Childers to write to Dublin for advice on how to approach the question, and had received none, but when they adopted one of the courses to which Childers referred, they were reprimanded.[7]

4 O'Connor, *Collins*, p.136; Taylor, *Collins*, p.165.

5 Forester, *Collins*, p.227.

6 Ó Néill agus Ó Fiannachta, *De Valera*, pp.244-5; Longford and O'Neill, *de Valera*, pp.152-4.

7 Ryle Dwyer, *Collins*, pp.66-7;69-70.

Curran considered that their 'violent reaction may well have been caused by the two men's belated realisation that de Valera would not, after all, agree to a Dominion settlement'. But if de Valera had been aware of Griffith's concept of recognition of the Crown, he would likely not have expressed any alarm in the first place. It was John Chartres (Griffith's choice as one of the secretaries to the delegation) who originally suggested the idea to Griffith: even if Ireland was *externally* associated with the Empire, there would have to be *some* form of recognition of the Crown. Once de Valera was fully familiar with this view, he adopted it, made it a basic part of external association, and even got Brugha to agree to it.[8]

In general, historians recorded differences within the Irish delegation in London, and between it and Dublin. Earlier authors concentrated on the former and paid little heed to the latter, but this deficiency has been offset more recently.

Pakenham drew attention to the following flashpoints: the dispute among the Irish in London over Griffith's 2 November letter to Lloyd George; when Lloyd George's first letter to Craig initially reached the Irish delegates, Barton's and Duffy's protest that Griffith was allowing the Prime Minister to delude the unionists into thinking that Sinn Féin would accept the Crown and Empire; the row in Hans Place over the 22 November Irish proposals; the divisions following the meetings in Dublin on 3 December, and Griffith's attack on Gavan Duffy for causing the collapse of their 4 December subconference with the British.[9]

O'Connor wrote that the delegation, never very united, soon began to show signs of division. He believed that the bad feelings between Griffith and Childers were largely responsible.[10] Several authors recognised two distinct factions; Griffith, Collins and Duggan in one, and Barton and Duffy, supported by Childers, in the other. Colum considered that the subconference procedure caused Barton and Duffy to feel that their opinions were being ignored, and they and Childers 'naturally' formed an alliance that became more united as they realised that the British were using the subconferences to exclude them as representatives of 'the extreme section'.

Kevin O'Higgins was in London in late October on his honeymoon and a dinner was given in his honour by the delegation. It soon became clear to him that it was a case of forced gaiety and underlying gloom. He

8 Curran, *Free State*, pp.90-91.

9 Pakenham, *Ordeal*, pp.161-2,173,189-91,212,218.

10 O'Connor, *Collins*, p.138.

was inclined to think that Childers was the source of the disharmony. He sat up at night writing memoranda to Dublin, and some of the delegates had the 'uncomfortable' suspicion that these were critical. But Colum rightly believed that the tension was more broadly based: Griffith, Collins and Duggan went in one direction, and Barton, Duffy and Childers in another.[11]

Forester identified the impasse: while Griffith and Collins were disposed to consider alternatives to the complete Irish demand once they had secured as much as possible from the British, Barton and Duffy were not.[12] Curran highlighted one particular clash. He wrote that although the final 22 November Irish memorandum was very like his original draft, Childers complained that little of it endorsed the Irish claim to complete independence. Barton and Duffy agreed, but an 'outraged' Griffith accused Childers of trying to prevent an agreement. Childers demanded that this accusation be put in writing, and Griffith apologised, 'but his dislike of Childers was doubtlessly intensified'.[13]

The following account from Childers's diary of the Irish delegates' discussion of their 21 November draft proposals vividly illustrated the bad atmosphere that existed among them (in this Childers referred to Griffith by his initials):

> AG attacks me about *Riddle of the Sands* - says I caused one European war and now want to cause another...It is exactly like arguing with the British...Bob [Barton] protests about trade, I about defence. AG insolent to me about secretary altering drafts. I protest and virtually threatened resignation. He climbs down.[14]

Ryle Dwyer also elaborated on a particular instance of discord among the Irish representatives in London. He referred to their strained feelings at the meeting in Hans Place after the 4 December encounter with the British: 'the distrust within the Irish delegation was so strong that each element felt that the other was trying to blame it for the collapse of the negotiations'. Especially gloomy were Barton and Duffy who privately informed Childers that Griffith had 'made fools' of them by manipulating them into the situation where they seemed responsible for the collapse of the conference.

When Childers was typing the report for Dublin, Griffith told him to make known that the British had indicated the possibility of changing

11 Colum, *Griffith*, pp.289,292-3.

12 Forester, *Collins*, p.226.

13 Curran, *Free State*, pp.78,110.

14 Cited in Hopkinson, *Green against Green*, p.26.

the form of the oath, explaining to Childers that he had forgotten to mention this earlier. In the absence of Barton and Duffy, Childers included this in his report, but he consulted the others before sending it. Barton consented to its inclusion, though he could not remember its being said, but Duffy did recall Birkenhead 'rather casually' saying that the oath could be amended. Ryle Dwyer commented on this: 'If the difficulties in drawing up the report of the subconference meeting - which was the only one attended by Barton and Duffy - were anything to go on, then it was little wonder that Griffith and Collins had been anxious to exclude them from the actual talks. But of course by then the atmosphere within the delegation had been poisoned by the distrust brought on by the whole subconference set-up'.[15]

Taylor was the first to emphasise and explain the differences between some of the Irish representatives in London and the remainder of the cabinet (with the exception of Cosgrave) in Dublin. His summary view was that de Valera wanted the delegation to get external association; Collins was thinking in terms of Dominion status; 'Griffith, fully aware that neither a republic nor de Valera's external association arrangement could be got from the British, took the same line as Collins; indeed, it may be said that Collins took from Griffith's lead the line of Dominion status'.

Taylor quoted from two Collins letters written near the end of the talks, when agreement was in prospect. These revealed that Collins believed that the agreement would not be accepted in Dublin, 'not by those who have in mind personal ambitions under the guise of patriotism'. The letters also revealed that he was certain of winning any election, expecting 60% support for the settlement, but Griffith was not so sure, because of what might have occurred while they were in London.[16]

Desmond FitzGerald's reminiscences set the scene from Griffith's and Collins's perspective. They had been given powers to go to London and make a settlement. *They* were to be responsible for the result. They knew that Brugha and Stack would oppose any feasible settlement and that a small number of TDs would support these two. On the other hand, they knew that failure to reach a settlement would lead to national calamity, and that a majority of the cabinet (including de Valera), the Dáil and the people felt the same. De Valera had made his opinions obvious to his colleagues and had gone a long way towards discrediting the extremists. Perhaps he still thought that a settlement would be

15 Ryle Dwyer, *Collins*, pp.91-2.

16 Taylor, *Collins*, pp.172,176.

unanimously approved, but he was definitely intent on postponing any split until after the talks. This was vital, because a premature rift would weaken the plenipotentiaries' position. This circumstance strengthened the extremists as they had to be 'pampered' to keep them from sundering from the majority.[17]

It was Curran's balanced view that while Griffith was impatient with the disagreement within the Irish team in London, he knew the real crux was at home. Collins agreed and was afraid that any agreement would result in their being accused of treason. There was no doubt from Collins's letters that by late October/early November he had concluded that Dominion status was as much as could be achieved for the time being and should be taken as an initial step. 'Yet he did not dare admit this openly at the time' because 'neither he nor Griffith knew just how far they could go with those in Dublin', Ryle Dwyer wrote. They suspected that whatever they agreed to would be seen as 'a gross betrayal or similar act of treachery'.[18]

De Valera's strategy led to clashes between the delegation and Dublin. He argued that by staying in Dublin he could prepare people, particularly Brugha and Stack, for any accommodation, while Griffith and Collins were best equipped to get the British to concede more. Collins in fact saw him as putting Griffith and himself forward as scapegoats, who would have to make compromises which would lead to talk of betrayal. Collins believed that his task was one that his fellow-ministers knew had to be performed, but had not the moral courage to perform themselves.[19]

Nothing better reveals how deep the divisions had become than the 3 December meetings in Dublin involving both the delegation and the remainder of the Dáil cabinet. These meetings were held to consider the final British draft proposals. They lasted for seven hours and were confused and acrimonious. Brugha's comment that the British government 'selected its men', when it chose Griffith and Collins for the subconference meetings, poisoned the atmosphere. An outraged Griffith walked over to Brugha and demanded that he withdraw the remark. Brugha refused at first, and only did so after Griffith insisted that it be recorded in the minutes.

Most of the discussion centred on the oath. De Valera suggested an amendment to it but Barton and Childers, both of whom supported him, afterwards disagreed about what he said, so it is hardly surprising

17 Colum, *Griffith*, p.287.

18 Curran, *Free State*, p.110; Ryle Dwyer, *Collins*, p.72.

19 Hopkinson, *Green agains Green*, p.24.

that Griffith and Collins had little idea of what was in his mind. When they returned to London, Childers insisted that de Valera wanted the first four articles in the British proposals - those dealing with Dominion status - dropped and external association presented again. Griffith, and especially Collins, disagreed vehemently that this was the case.

Some on the anti-Treaty side, including de Valera himself, said later that Griffith gave an 'express undertaking' that he would not sign the British document without first referring back to Dublin. The official record of the 3 December meetings does not mention this at all. However, Barton's version of the events of that day recorded that when Brugha asked Griffith did he not realise that if he signed the document he would split the country from top to bottom, Griffith allegedly replied that he would go back to London and not sign *that* document but refer back to the Dáil.

The extraordinary thing about Griffith's alleged pledge was that it was made a few minutes before the plenipotentiaries rushed off to catch the boat back to England, at the end of the exhausting day-long discussions. This was probably why the official recorder missed the Griffith-Brugha exchange. In any event, Griffith had made his position absolutely clear, and it *was* set down in the official record. 'Mr Griffith would not take the responsibility of breaking with the Crown. When as many concessions as possible were conceded, and when accepted by Craig, he would go before the Dáil. The Dáil was the body to decide for or against war'. What Brugha, Stack and de Valera understood by referring back to Dublin was referring back to *them* but Griffith had no such intention.

According to the official record, the delegates were to return to London to try to get the oath amended. It is noticeable that no attempt was to be made to get the partition provisions in the British document changed. But the delegates were still expected to make sure that the conference collapsed, if it were to collapse, over this issue. They were empowered to meet Craig if they thought it necessary, but Brugha and Stack objected to this.

The official record for 3 December shows that of the delegation, Griffith, Collins and Duggan favoured acceptance of the British proposals, while Barton and Duffy did not. (Childers, who was not a delegate, supported the two last-mentioned.) Griffith, Collins and Duggan returned to London together. Barton, Duffy and Childers travelled on a different boat. It is amazing that so divided and unguided a team should have achieved a result at all. That they achieved what most historians agree was the best possible result in the circumstances is a great tribute to them.

Griffith and Childers

No examination of the divisions on the Irish side would be complete without considering the clash of personalities and policies between Arthur Griffith and Erskine Childers. The latter became directly involved in Irish affairs from May 1919 onwards, but Griffith's unease with him began well before this time. It went as far back as the Boer War when Griffith supported, and Childers fought in arms against, the Boer cause.

Griffith's reaction in a *Sinn Féin* leader of March 1912 to Childers's *The Framework of Home Rule*, was revealing. In this Griffith expressed his belief that Childers was an English imperialist who, unlike most of his fellow-English Liberals, wanted an honest Home Rule settlement for Ireland, not because of any love of Ireland, but in the interests of the British Empire, which was being threatened by Germany and would need Ireland's help to defend itself. Clearly the distrust between the two men had long been there, but increased greatly during the Anglo-Irish talks.

Childers served in the British army during the First World War. Ó Lúing remarked that it was against Griffith's principles to accept into Sinn Féin someone who had been a high-ranking British officer. Colum did not consider Childers's activities between 1914 and 1918 of any great consequence, as thousands of Irish nationalists also fought in that conflict. But he wrote that 'one got the impression that he crossed no psychological boundary in giving such service'.[20]

Ó Lúing noted that Childers had been secretary to Lloyd George's abortive Irish Convention of 1917-18, for which Griffith had little respect. It was to the important role Lloyd George assigned to Childers in his Convention that Cox attributed the beginning of the jealousies and suspicions that Griffith developed of the Englishman. Griffith was jealous of Childers's knowledge of constitutional law, seeing himself as the expert in that area on the Irish side.[21]

Pakenham was the first to observe that it was Griffith who brought Childers into active work for Sinn Féin by sending him to Paris in the middle of 1919 to help the Irish envoys there. Brennan denied that Griffith resented Childers's appearance on the Irish scene, and hated

20 Colum, *Griffith*, p.361.

21 Ó Lúing, *Ó Gríofa*, p.381; Cox, *Damned Englishman*, p.95.

him from the outset because he was an Englishman. Brennan knew this because he introduced them. When he told Griffith that Childers was offering his services to the Irish cause, 'Griffith was obviously pleased'. He is supposed to have remarked: 'He is a good man to have. He has the ear of a big section of the English people'.[22]

Andrew Boyle thought that whatever doubts Griffith may have harboured about Childers's motives for joining the Sinn Féin cause, Collins had no reservations at all. Boyle added: 'To do Griffith justice, he could think of nobody better qualified than Childers, in that summer of 1919, to publicise the Irish case at the peace conference in Paris', as neither Sean T. O'Kelly nor Gavan Duffy, the Irish envoys in Paris, had any training in publicity, and both were delighted to have Childers to assist them.[23]

Forester contended that 'Collins was soon making full use of the new convert, though as a rule he distrusted such people, in contrast to Griffith who tended to welcome them, often to his later discomfort'. She claimed that in the first half of 1920, Griffith seemed to have been as satisfied as Collins with Childers's propaganda work. But this is flatly contradicted by Boyle's account of Collins defending Childers 'against all comers', including Griffith and Brugha.[24]

On 11 March 1921, in the Dáil, de Valera announced that he had appointed Childers as replacement for Desmond FitzGerald (who had been arrested) as Director of Publicity. Padraig Ó Caoimh objected and a long discussion followed as to the constitutionality of appointing a non-member of the Dáil to head a Dáil department. De Valera argued that as Childers was the head of a department - a civil servant - the question was not one for the Dáil to consider.[25] Sean MacEntee disagreed with de Valera and proposed a motion of deferral until the constitution could be scrutinised, but this was not seconded, and de Valera got his way.[26]

Griffith's opposition to Childers's appointment as Director of Publicity, to his becoming a TD in May 1921, and to his being assigned to the post of chief secretary to the delegation going to London was commented on by many authors. They concerned themselves with the motivation behind this disapproval somewhat differently. One reason

22 Brennan, *Allegiance*, p.245.

23 Boyle, *Riddle of Childers*, pp.251,253-4,256.

24 Forester, *Collins*, p.140; Boyle, *op. cit.*, p.254.

25 This was somewhat unusual as all the other heads of Dáil departments were members of the Dáil.

26 *Minutes of First Dáil*, pp.274-5.

put forward by many of them was that Griffith distrusted Englishmen, who involved themselves in Irish affairs, especially in influential positions. Béaslaí wrote that Griffith held it permissible to use an Englishman's help in the struggle against England, but dangerous to place one in a position of trust. Both Pakenham and de Vere White alluded to his advising Childers to remain in England and work for the Irish cause from there.[27]

Colum dwelt at greatest length upon this aspect of Griffith's attitude towards Childers. As argued by Colum, to Griffith's way of thinking, Childers the person was inseparable from a principle which he (Griffith) held very strongly: Childers was an Englishman, and 'an Irish cause, as Irish people felt it, could not be thoroughly his'.[28]

Pakenham was the first to advance another reason for Griffith's antipathy towards Childers. This was that the latter's meticulous attention to minutiae more than once irritated Griffith, who found his formalism ridiculous.[29] O'Connor wrote that because he believed himself responsible for everything, Childers was 'thorough, fussy, nervous', and that Griffith disliked his 'endless memoranda'.[30]

Béaslaí suggested a further reason for Griffith's suspicions of Childers; that he believed him 'a disgruntled Englishman' who had sided with Ireland because of irritation with his own country. This idea was taken up by de Vere White, who maintained that Griffith perceived Childers as an English radical who, seeing no future for himself in England, decided to make his political career in Ireland. Younger developed this view at some length.[31]

There has been some dispute concerning Childers's role in the London conference. Béaslaí, who had little sympathy for him, asserted that from the start he seemed to regard his brief as watchdog for Griffith's and Collins's critics and that 'it almost seemed as if there was a private understanding between him and Mr de Valera on the point'. De Vere White adverted to Childers sitting up late at night, writing long memoranda which he sent to Dublin, and which some of the delegates uncomfortably felt were critical. Burke Wilkinson believed that Griffith

27 Béaslaí, *Collins*, ii, pp.167-8; Pakenham, *Ordeal*, p.252; de Vere White, *O'Higgins*, p.60.

28 Colum, *Griffith*, pp.246-7,266-7. See also Lyons, *Famine*, p.431, and Curran, *Free State*, pp.74-5.

29 Pakenham, *op. cit.*, pp.183,189.

30 O'Connor, *Collins*, p.138.

31 Béaslaí, *op. cit.*, p.168; de Vere White, *op. cit.*, p.60; Younger, *Civil War*, pp.479-81. See also Curran, *op. cit.*, p.75.

became convinced that Childers was simply de Valera's spy, reporting every move to his master by courier or even by telephone.[32]

Ryle Dwyer was the first historian to cite evidence for the *suggestions* of some of his predecessors. He held that Childers's reports home added to the distrust Collins felt of the cabinet in Dublin, because Childers gave his own views even though they were at variance with Collins's, and the latter thought them full of innuendo which created a very false picture. Ryle Dwyer also maintained that Collins suspected that Childers sent secret accounts to de Valera as well. Collins was correct in this suspicion, Ryle Dwyer believed.[33]

He referred to two sources to support this claim. One was a reference in Ulick O'Connor's biography of Gogarty, where the author alluded to Childers making daily telephone calls to de Valera, the nature of which was kept secret from the delegates. O'Connor acquired this information from Fionán Lynch, who was an assistant-secretary to the delegation.[34]

The second source was a reference to secret telegrams from Childers to de Valera in a letter from N.S. Ó Nualláin (assistant-secretary to the government at the time) to Marie O'Kelly, de Valera's personal secretary, dated 27 October 1961. This document is in the Irish National Archive[35], but the writer has been unable to trace the whereabouts of the actual telegrams themselves. Hopkinson agreed with Ryle Dwyer that Griffith and Collins had 'accurate suspicions' that Childers was privately communicating his account of developments in London to de Valera.[36]

On 10 January 1922, at the end of the long debate on the Treaty, Griffith was elected President of the Dáil. When Childers stood up to put some questions to him, Griffith responded that he would not reply to any 'damned Englishman' in that assembly. How various authors dealt with this outburst depended on their points of view.

Béaslaí, who as a member of the Dáil himself at the time tried to get Childers ruled out of order, gave a version that was strongly pro-Griffith. Following his election as President, Griffith announced that he would keep the Dáil and the republic in existence until there could be an election, and he appealed that there be no obstruction as he and his colleagues would have to carry as heavy a burden as ever was laid on

32 de Vere White, *O'Higgins*, p.60; Burke Wilkinson, *The Zeal of the Convert: the Life of Erskine Childers* (New York, 1976), pp.185-6.

33 Ryle Dwyer, *Collins*, pp.67-8.

34 O'Connor, *Gogarty*, p.197.

35 The reference is DE 2/304/2.

36 Hopkinson, *Green against Green*, p.26.

the shoulders of Irishmen. Béaslaí then described Childers arising, 'contrary to all rules of debate', and criticising what Griffith had said:

> There was something particularly irritating in the spectacle of this English ex-officer, who had spent his life in the service of England and English imperialism, heckling and baiting the devoted Griffith, with his lifelong record of unselfish slaving in the cause of Ireland - answering Griffith's moving appeal with his carping criticism. Griffith, usually so stolid and unemotional, lost his patience. He rose, like a sleeping lion roused...[37]

By contrast, Macardle was very much anti-Griffith, declaring that he used the description 'the Englishman' about Childers 'in a moment when his uncontrollable and inexplicable hostility to Childers broke out in the Dáil', indicating Griffith's 'virulent prejudice'. Some were fiercer in their condemnation.[38]

Colum and Wilkinson were more balanced. Concerning Griffith, Colum wrote that being branded 'traitor' and held up by some speakers during the Treaty debate as an amateur diplomat outwitted by Lloyd George, 'produced strains even in his solidity', and led to the Dáil scene under discussion. Colum believed he would not have spoken so had he not felt, as he himself expressed it, 'put in the dock'.

Nevertheless, Colum rightly held that Childers was 'in the right'. His nationality was not relevant to how any other member of the Dáil treated him: 'he was entitled to the courtesy that was due to any deputy, and to deny him this was to reduce the moral authority that, as Griffith more than anyone else knew, had to be upheld'. Colum considered his reaction to Childers's question 'an unparliamentary retort from a man, who through all that trying debate "never did he become personal, never lose his coolness or depart from the solid rock of argument"'.[39] Wilkinson considered the 10 January Dáil scene a sad occurrence. Griffith, in a near-exhausted state after his long ordeal, was putting all his remaining strength into rallying support for a Treaty which would end the republic's life, and Childers's 'gadfly questioning stung him out of his usual calm'.[40]

37 Béaslaí, *Collins*, pp.353-4.

38 Macardle, *Irish Republic*, p.733; Norman, *History of Modern Irl.*, p.271; C.D. Greaves, *Liam Mellows and the Irish Revolution* (London, 1971), p.282.

39 This was a quotation from the *Irish Independent* journalists, John F. Doyle and Padraig de Burca, who covered the Treaty debate and wrote a lively account of it in a pamphlet called *Free State or Republic?*.

40 Colum, *Griffith*, pp.333-4,360; Wilkinson, *Zeal*, pp.202-3.

This idea that Griffith's 'damned Englishman' remark was out of character was also put forward by Ernie O'Malley, a militant opponent of the Treaty, who afterwards wrote that Griffith was 'a man who seldom stooped to personal abuse'. Recent more detached commentators thought so too. For example, Kee put it that 'even Griffith' jeered at Childers as an Englishman in the Dáil, and Johnson pointed out that apart from his flare-up at Childers, Griffith never became personal, lost his temper or deviated from reasoned argument.[41]

There seems little doubt that Childers became something of a preoccupation with Griffith in the last seven months of his life. In Pakenham's opinion, Griffith viewed Childers as an obstacle to the settlement to which he had dedicated his life at the cost of all personal gain, and which once infinitely far off, seemed now close at hand.[42]

It was Colum's belief that by the last months of Griffith's life, Childers had 'come to dominate his outlook', and that he considered him to be behind every attempt to undermine the democratic state for which he had planned and worked all his life: 'If there are things which turn distrust of a person into an *idee fixe*, they are ubiquitousness and busyness'. Griffith came to perceive Childers as being everywhere and doing everything, and he thought Childers was singling him out personally. So, by way of explanation on Griffith's behalf, Colum wrote: 'We have to think of him at this stage as being on guard, indisposed, giving too much of his faculty to consideration of an individual'.[43]

Childers became the leading propagandist on the anti-Treaty side, and it was in this context that Griffith, in late April 1922, accused him of inciting the assassination of the Treaty signatories. He also accused him of having spent his life in the British secret service. Greaves dealt with this incident in fiercely denunciatory terms. Boyle regarded it as a 'venomous assertion', as a gratuitous and damaging insult which was taken up by the press, 'and nobody understood better than Erskine Childers that mud thrown by so eminent a figure as Griffith would be sure to stick'.[44]

The implication here that Griffith was indirectly responsible for Childers's death was stated more bluntly by de Vere White and O'Malley. The former believed that Griffith engendered the suspicion

41 Ernie O'Malley, *The Singing Flame* (Dublin, 1978), p.193; Kee, *Ourselves Alone*, p.169; Johnson, *Land of Troubles*, p.167.

42 Pakenham, *Ordeal*, pp.189-90.

43 Colum, *Griffith*, pp.360,362.

44 Greaves, *Mellows*, p.312; Boyle, *Riddle*, p.308.

and anger which ensured Childers's death when he was captured in the Civil War. (He was executed in November 1922.) O'Malley told how some Free State soldiers, with whom he was engaged in conversation, refused to listen to his defence of Childers, declaring he was and always had been 'a damned English spy'. To O'Malley, this meant that 'Arthur Griffith's bitter words had carried weight'.[45] But Childers was executed because he was one of the anti-Treaty leaders and his side's foremost propagandist. The cabinet which decided on his execution believed that he was leading others astray.[46]

Griffith's 'damned Englishman' remark has coloured the perception of his reputation and has given a misleading impression of the man. It was an outburst which was uncharacteristic.

Why Griffith Signed the Treaty

Arthur Griffith was the first to decide that he would sign the Articles of Agreement for a Treaty Between Great Britain and Ireland on 5 December 1921. Among the reasons for his agreeing to do so, Pakenham laid great stress on the importance of the 13 November memorandum. (This document was a summary of Griffith's meeting with Lloyd George of the day before and contained his promise not to repudiate the boundary commission proposal while the British were dealing with their own hardliners at the Liverpool conference of the Conservative Party.) This contained no definite promise that Griffith would agree to terms before there was a response from Craig, but Pakenham maintained that Lloyd George by now knew a good deal about Griffith, especially his 'passionate self-respect and his abnormal sensitivity to any charge that involved his own or his country's honour'. Griffith cared nothing whether people liked or disliked him personally, but he was determined to give his country a worthy showing 'on her first appearance in the intercourse of nations'.

On the last day of the conference, when Griffith insisted that the Irish would have to know what Craig's response to the British Ulster proposal was, Lloyd George accused him of trying to engineer the breakdown of the talks over the question of unity. He produced the 13 November memorandum which contained Griffith's promise and accused him of letting him down. According to Chamberlain's account of the last day of the conference, when Lloyd George confronted Griffith with his 12

45 de Vere White, *O'Higgins*, pp.61–2; O'Malley, *Flame*, p.193.

46 Valiulis, *Mulcahy*, p.180.

November promise, Griffith simply reiterated it. But Pakenham inclined towards a 'more volcanic' reaction on Griffith's part:

> Shaking his pencil across the table, he repudiated with staggering emphasis the charge that he was breaking faith. 'I have never let a man down in my whole life and I never will'. And then came his simple agreement to abandon all attempt to bring about the break on Ulster.

However, in Pakenham's version of that last day, it still took the British concession of full fiscal autonomy for Ireland, and Lloyd George's threat of the immediate resumption of the war, before Griffith finally agreed to sign.

Returning to consider the matter 'fresh' after 30 years, it seemed to Pakenham that once Griffith had been persuaded to abandon the break on Ulster, the chances were always great that he would agree to sign. 'And so it proved', because his response to the war ultimatum was an immediate agreement to sign.

There are five extant written accounts of what happened on 5 December: Lloyd George's in the *Daily Telegraph* of 23 December 1922; Chamberlain's in the same newspaper of 29 March 1932; Churchill's in a chapter of his book *The World Crisis: The Aftermath;* a detailed memorandum written by Barton on 6 December 1921 at Griffith's request, and a short note written by Griffith himself.[47]

In none of these is there reference to Griffith's heated reaction, as relayed by Pakenham, to Lloyd George's slight on his honour. In fact, in Barton's minute, Griffith signified his willingness to sign *after* the Prime Minister's offer of complete fiscal freedom but *before* he issued his threat of war. This being so, it is remarkable the number of historians who, like Pakenham himself, considered the production by Lloyd George of the 13 November document so crucial.

Anti-Treaty authors followed Pakenham's lead but dealt with Griffith more censoriously. Macardle contended that his 'commitments to Lloyd George had isolated him from the delegation of which he was chairman'. He seemed to realise this, as he gave his decision to sign as personal, she continued, and his 'lifelong loyalty to Ireland, his government, his colleagues, his mission and his republican oath, gave way to his promise to Lloyd George made as a tactical manoeuvre'. Neeson, too, remarked that Griffith seemed 'blinded...to the fact that he was letting down his cabinet colleagues'.

Cox declared that unilaterally Griffith had reached *'a substantive understanding'* with his opponents and that the 13 November

47 Pakenham, *Ordeal*, pp.229-38; Longford, 'Treaty negotiations', in *Irish Struggle*, p.111.

memorandum was 'uncontradicted evidence of it'. Cox wondered how Collins must have felt - that he and Griffith had an agreed plan for a settlement but that Griffith had acted alone, and did this portend a Griffith or a Collins primacy for the future? Lloyd George's coup proved what Barton had feared all along, according to Cox, which was that Griffith was conducting *'a personal operation* for weeks' behind their backs.

Cox pictured Griffith as in a corner, wondering to himself what the Prime Minister's *'next'* move would be. 'To *circulate* that paper (with possibly a signature or a set of initials at its foot) around the room', speculated Cox - clearly forgetting that in his own account Lloyd George had already shown it to Collins and Barton - or to the press next morning? How would Griffith explain it to the Dublin cabinet? Cox held that this was why he repudiated Lloyd George's charge of breaking faith 'with staggering emphasis', and concluded that from then on Griffith voiced no objections worth talking about on Ulster or on any other subject. (All the italics are Cox's.) Longford and O'Neill referred to Griffith 'stung in his tenderest spot, rising to his feet in his excitement' and, shaking his pencil across the table, 'this strong man, usually so quiet, repudiated with staggering emphasis the charge that he would ever break faith'. The result was that the attempt to break on Ulster, on which the whole Irish strategy hinged, had been discarded.[48]

Ó Lúing defended Griffith by stating that no satisfactory answers had been given to the questions: What did he give away that could have been secured? What did he fail to achieve that any of the other four Irish delegates could have won? Not unity, because of the way in which Northern Ireland was firmly established, with its privileges guaranteed by the British Crown and government. Colum fully accepted Pakenham's version,[49] while Davis wrote: 'Whether Griffith was outmanoeuvred is immaterial; he believed in the terms...he acted consistently with his own ideas'.

Lyons, Curran, Younger and Hopkinson all agreed with Pakenham that Lloyd George exploited Griffith's sense of honour on the final day of the conference.[50] This is difficult to understand. After all, at the 3 December meetings in Dublin, Griffith had made it clear that he was happy with the British terms.

48 Macardle, *Irish Republic*, pp.533-6; Neeson, *Civil War*, pp.49-50; Cox, *Damned Englishmen*, pp.180-83; Longford and O'Neill, *de Valera*, pp.164-5.

49 Ó Lúing, *Ó Gríofa*, p.383; Colum, *Griffith*, pp.302-3; Davis, *Arthur Griffith*, pp.36-8.

50 Lyons, *Famine*, p.437; Curran, *Free State*, p.126; Younger, *Griffith*, pp.116-18; Hopkinson, *Green against Green*, p.32.

With the changes in the oath and the concessions on defence, and most of all, with the offer to Ireland of complete control over her own finances (all of which occurred on 4 and 5 December), Griffith's inclinations to sign must have been much stronger. It is significant that Lyons, Curran and Ryle Dwyer all adopted Barton's record of the final meetings, and had Griffith agreeing to sign after Lloyd George's concession of full fiscal freedom and before he issued his war ultimatum.[51]

It has been suggested that one of the reasons why Griffith agreed to sign the Articles of Agreement was because he was prepared to accept the Crown and membership of the Empire. Macardle was actually the only exponent of the anti-Treaty school to emphasise this. She held that Griffith would not have signed had he not 'in his own mind been satisfied with the prospect of an Ireland within the Empire under the Crown'. Others correctly emphasised Griffith's lack of concern with forms of government in this matter. O'Connor argued that the symbols of independence never mattered to Griffith and he was 'as ready to make a success of Ireland under the British Crown as under an Irish president'.[52] Griffith was older than his colleagues on the delegation and had been in the national movement earlier than any of them. There was not the least indication 30 years before that Ireland would secure so many rights as she was now being offered. The substance of freedom meant more to Griffith than any dispute about words, and he realised what a large measure of freedom was being offered. He accepted the oath because he realised that it could afterwards be rendered nugatory, when the time was right, Ó Lúing believed.

McCaffrey and Forester argued along similar lines, as did Glandon, who wrote:

> Griffith had no deep-seated objections to leaving Ireland within the British Empire, if it could have control of its own government, finances and trade. Even as late as 1918, he republished *The Resurrection of Hungary*, which extolled the political framework of dual monarchy. His abiding concern for the essential unity of Ireland undoubtedly prompted this move.[53]

A number of recent historians have suggested a firmer commitment on Griffith's part to his dual-monarchy model for Anglo-Irish relations.

51 Lyons, *Famine*, p.437; Curran, *Free State*, pp.124-8; Ryle Dwyer, *Collins*, pp.95-8.

52 Macardle, *Irish Republic*, p.534; O'Connor, *Collins*, p.135.

53 Ó Lúing, *Ó Gríofa*, p.384; McCaffrey, *Irish Question*, p.175; Forester, *Collins*, p.253; Glandon, *Griffith and Advanced-Nationalist Press*, p.195.

Owen Dudley-Edwards drew attention to some division among those in favour of the Articles of Agreement, at the 8 December Dáil cabinet meeting called to discuss them. Griffith favoured recommending them to the Dáil on their merits; Collins, Barton, Cosgrave and O'Higgins argued for their recommendation because they had been signed. The difference in views should not cause any surprise, Edwards wrote, because Griffith was returning to his old idea of the dual monarchy.[54]

Griffith made a strong showing for external association during the conference, although he himself would have been prepared to accept a settlement based on a dual monarchy. The Treaty negotiations brought to a head the old divisions within Sinn Féin between dual monarchists and republicans. Davis offered many interesting comparisons between the Treaty and Griffith's old Sinn Féin policy. In 1907, Sinn Féin had undertaken not to accept less from England than the constitution of 1782, but the Treaty gave much more than that. It also appealed to moderates who got little chance to express their views during the Black-and-Tan terror, but who were still in a majority in Ireland.

Even the Sinn Féin constitution of 1917 had been realised by the settlement. As the Irish delegates had been accepted as plenipotentiaries, and as a *Treaty* had been signed between the two countries, Irish independence was by implication acknowledged. Griffith stressed this at the Dáil private debate on the Treaty. 'By stretching a point, it recognised the Irish republic, which according to the 1917 Sinn Féin constitution was necessary before the Irish people could decide their own system of government by referendum', Davis wrote. He went on to contend that Griffith had stepped down in favour of de Valera in 1917 as part of a compromise deal, and that he was entitled to feel, in December 1921, that this compromise had at last turned in his favour.

MacDonagh presented this argument with even more force, proposing that the Treaty was 'Griffith's own', because it embodied many of his objectives and attitudes since 1905. Although the settlement was not the dual monarchy by name, constitutionally the type of Dominion status it gave came close to it:

> Every other Dominion was an area of comparatively recent white settlement; Ireland was a mother country. Every other Dominion contained a very large population identifying itself, in spontaneous feeling, as British; truncated Ireland contained only a minute, despairing fragment of such people. In every other Dominion the

54 Owen Dudley-Edwards, 'Facets of Treaty "split" disclosed', in *Irish Times*, 16 April 1971.

> oath of allegiance was simply to the Crown; in Ireland it was primarily to the State, and only secondarily to the King as its titular head.

So the dual monarchy as Griffith envisaged it - 'separate states linked by a common, nominal superior' - was achieved in the Treaty.[55]

In his analysis of the financial clauses of the third Home Rule Bill of 1912, Griffith wrote: 'There can be no real self-government where there is no real control of the purse....Finance is the blood and bones, the heart and bowels, the hand and eyes of Home Rule'.[56] Many historians have drawn attention to his preoccupation with economic independence. Lyons stated that again and again Griffith stressed that real independence for Ireland had to be economic as well as political, and that the development of manufacturing industries and protectionism were the twin prongs of his economic strategy.

Davis affirmed that in Griffith's 'perfect community, labour and capital would submit to governmental regulation; and that would mean in the case of Ireland, hard work and sacrifices from both classes' while industry was developed to the 'take-off' stage. So, Griffith, 'assuming Ireland's fiscal autonomy, did not care about forms of government and titles'. It was MacDonagh's belief that for Griffith economic independence was 'the most critical form of national liberty'.[57]

With this in mind, it is surprising that Pakenham described Lloyd George's offer of full fiscal autonomy to the Irish delegates on 5 December as 'a concession which meant much to Griffith, more to Collins, and most of all to Barton'.[58]

Did Griffith regard the agreement in London as a final and absolute settlement, or did he see it as containing the potential for further development towards complete independence? Pakenham believed that the possibility for evolution which it contained had little influence on Griffith's signing on 5 December. Collins, on the other hand, from his study of the leading authorities on the subject, was convinced that the Empire was developing towards 'a league of free states', and this explained his 'stepping-stone' argument in the Dáil debate on the Treaty. Collins never accepted the Treaty as a final settlement. He

55 Davis, *Arthur Griffith*, p.37; MacDonagh, *States*, pp.68-9.

56 *Sinn Féin*, 9 March 1912.

57 Lyons, *Famine*, pp.253-4; Davis, *Non-Violent Sinn Féin*, pp.152-3; MacDonagh, *op. cit.*, p.64. See also Ryan, *Unique Dictator*, p.143; Strauss, *Irish Nationalism and British Democracy*, p.269; Ó Lúing, *Ó Gríofa*, p.383; Younger, *Griffith*, p.119; Glandon, *Griffith and Advanced-Nationalist Press*, p.194.

58 Pakenham, *Ordeal*, p.237.

intended to use in his own lifetime whatever agreement was reached to enlarge upon Irish independence.[59]

Pakenham was virtually alone in his views on this. It has already been demonstrated that Griffith was aware of the evolutionary potential inherent in the dual-monarchy arrangement. Students of Griffith have rightly portrayed him as an evolutionist in his attitude to the Treaty as well, and this was one of the reasons he signed.

Younger wrote that Griffith was convinced that further negotiations with the British concerning Ireland's status were inevitable. Davis observed that he urged acceptance 'as an imperfect but valuable step towards full Irish independence'. Glandon also believed that Griffith and Collins were aware that Dominion status ensured that there would be future constitutional development, 'a fact which consoled them'.[60]

MacDonagh's conclusion also differed from Pakenham's. Once the British had secured their 'one crucial symbol', they could forget that Ireland's new status was not fixed, but would develop as unpredictably as that of the other Dominions, as these, and especially the most advanced, Canada, acquired more and more independence. 'Griffith was certainly a believer in the march of nations; it was Collins, under his influence, who claimed that the Treaty had won the freedom to win freedom'.[61]

To what extent did an abiding desire for peace and an abhorrence of bloodshed influence Griffith's signature? To a very great extent, in Pakenham's opinion. Griffith was overwhelmingly influenced by the harm the British could and would do to Ireland if the demand for a republic was persisted with: 'No doubt he would have struck a different balance if, like some of his colleagues, he had been a more passionate republican, or a less passionate opponent of war'.[62]

Many authors of various persuasions agreed with Pakenham. Ó Lúing stated that Griffith did not want the extensive warfare which Lloyd George was threatening. Neeson had no doubts that Griffith was influenced by the British Prime Minister's threat of the consequences if Ireland rejected his proposals: 'Hating war, he chose peace'. Younger wrote that Griffith was aware that 'wars that do not end in settlement end in total destruction'. According to Longford and O'Neill, de Valera

59 Pakenham, *Ordeal*, pp.224-6.

60 Davis, *Arthur Griffith*, p.39; Glandon, *Griffith and Advanced-Nationalist Press.*, p.194.

61 MacDonagh, *States*, p.69.

62 Pakenham, *op. cit.*, pp.238,98-9.

saw Griffith 'as a man who at the supreme crisis, put peace before everything'.[63]

Griffith admitted in the Dáil that what persuaded him to sign was the threat of war, but because he regarded the British offer as a good one, he would have recommended it to the Dáil anyway. He was certain that it was a case of peace or war. Glandon believed that while in London Griffith had deeply considered what the campaign of violence had achieved in Ireland, and had concluded that yet again physical force had failed, because the British had not been defeated, and the unionists had not been won over to an acceptance of any kind of independent Irish state.[64]

Ryle Dwyer contended that Griffith and Collins must have realised that Lloyd George's use of Craig on 5 December was not really in earnest.[65] They knew that he had initially intended to give Craig the final British proposals at the same time as he gave them to the Irish leaders, that is on 6 December. But they had insisted on Dublin seeing them before Craig, and were given them early. So, according to Ryle Dwyer, they must have been aware that all the British needed to do was to send a copy of their final terms to Craig by 6 December, not to have a signed agreement by that date.

The ultimatum had little influence on Griffith, Ryle Dwyer argued, because he had agreed to sign before Lloyd George issued it. Griffith and Collins probably played along with the Prime Minister's bluff to make sure that all of their fellow-delegates signed, as this would facilitate getting the Treaty accepted in Dublin. If they did not have Barton's vote, for example, they would probably not get it through the cabinet, knowing that Brugha, Stack and de Valera would be against it. If the majority of the cabinet were opposed,the Dáil might not be given any more say than it had been in the case of the British July offer, which was formally turned down before the Dáil was called to discuss it.

The Dáil had given them the responsibility of negotiating an acceptable settlement, and Griffith and Collins believed that it was their duty to sign when they were sure that the arrangement would satisfy a majority of TDs and a majority of the Irish people. They also believed that their refusal would lead to a war of certain defeat.

63 Ó Lúing, *Ó Gríofa*, p.384; Neeson, *Civil War*, p.50; Younger, *Civil War*, p.198; Longford and O'Neill, *de Valera*, p.198.

64 Davis, *Arthur Griffith*, p.36; Glandon, *Griffith and Advanced-Nationalist Press*, p.193.

65 Lloyd George had held up two sealed envelopes before the Irish delegates and told them that one of them had to be sent posthaste to Craig that night. One signified Sinn Féin acceptance of the British offer; the other, rejection, meant a swift resumption of intensified warfare.

Hopkinson agreed with Ryle Dwyer that Griffith and Collins may somehow have colluded with Lloyd George to force the moment to its crisis.[66]

66 Ryle Dwyer, *Collins*, pp.101-2; Hopkinson, *Green against Green*, pp.32-4.

Chapter IV

Long Talk and Tragic Denouement

The Long Talk

The signing of the Treaty was followed by an acrimonious cabinet meeting in Dublin on 8 December and a bitter debate in the Dáil from 14 December 1921 to 10 January 1922. That debate did not have an auspicious beginning. Time was wasted and ill-feeling engendered in wrangling over the instructions issued to the delegates and whether they were genuine plenipotentiaries. Although de Valera began the debate by stressing that the Treaty be assessed on its merits, he then proceeded to ignore the document and complain that the delegates had not carried out their instructions, a contention that Griffith rejected.

Because de Valera brought up the delegates' instructions, Collins countered by reading out their credentials, which conferred full power to negotiate and conclude an agreement. A dispute then ensued over whether these credentials had been presented to and accepted by the British, and whether Collins was implying that the authority to 'conclude' an agreement was final and did not need Dáil ratification. Griffith's reply to this was brief: the British delegates 'did not sign the Treaty to bind their nation. They had to go to their parliament and we to ours for ratification'.[1]

The Dáil then went into private session for four days where, instead of debating the Treaty itself, there was a lengthy wrangle about various documents issued or not issued to the delegates. This debate also began badly with de Valera expressing his personal hurt that the Treaty had already been signed when he first heard of it, describing himself as the captain of a team which should have played with him to the end, the last word being his.

Both he and Brugha accused Griffith of breaking an undertaking not to sign (obviously referring to the 3 December meetings). Griffith replied that the delegates had sought guidance from the cabinet on 3 December and had got none. He quoted from the official record of that day: his promise had been that when he secured as many concessions as

1 *Treaty Debate*, pp.7–14.

possible from the British, he would go before the Dáil, which was the body to decide for or against war.

De Valera then proposed his alternative to the Treaty, which became known as 'Document No.2'. It was this, rather than the Treaty, that was then debated at length. Griffith argued that the purpose of the meeting was to accept or reject the Treaty, and that there was no third course: 'We took your responsibility and you must take ours'.[2]

Document No.2 was de Valera's idea of external association in a revised form. The British had stressed that the Irish must be in the Empire or the war would continue and de Valera must have known, as well as Griffith, that to offer his alternative to the British would have been to offer something that had been tendered on a number of occasions and had been rejected.

Supporters of the Treaty saw no more in this document than 'a quibble'. Some of those who opposed the Treaty thought likewise. Like the Treaty, it was a compromise which did not provide for a full republic. P.S. O'Hegarty made the point (with which many historians subsequently agreed) that Document No.2, as a proposal coming from the Irish side, would have bound the country not to seek to enlarge upon the measure of independence it contained, but to have accepted it as a lasting settlement.[3]

Document No.2 had advantages and disadvantages. It would have provided Irish neutrality and excluded British symbolism from Irish internal affairs. Dominion status did not fully acknowledge Ireland's nationhood, was not what Sinn Féin had sought, and did not seem appropriate for an ancient nation like Ireland. But it would not have given Ireland fiscal autonomy as the Treaty did. While providing neutrality Ireland would still be tied in matters of common concern, and external association meant that Ireland would not have the self-interested support of the Dominions in disputes which would arise over defence and foreign affairs. It would be more binding as a final settlement than the Treaty which, as an imposed settlement, could never limit Irish political development in the same way as one proposed by Ireland itself could (a point first made by O'Hegarty).

Its worst defect, however, was that the British had rejected it. As Curran remarked: 'It was an ingenious compromise but too novel, subtle and abstract to win either British acceptance or Irish enthusiasm'. From the outset, the British had made it clear that there could be no

2 *Private Sessions*, pp.101,110,104-6.

3 O'Hegarty, *Victory*, p.86.

peace unless the Crown and the Empire were accepted, and repeatedly turned down external association no matter how much it was modified.[4]

Document No.2 was put forward from the outset with little regard for the facts. Griffith, Collins and Duggan believed they had gone as far as they could go towards realising their goal and neither war, which was an option, nor prolonging the talks, which was not, would take them any further. Had they believed that the British would accept such terms as were put forward in de Valera's alternative in preference to the Treaty, they would not have accepted the Treaty. His document could not have been substituted for the Treaty. The only substitute for the Treaty was renewed fighting.[5]

The public session of the Dáil debate on the Treaty resumed on 19 December, de Valera's alternative having failed to win widespread support. De Valera announced that it was now withdrawn and asked that it be treated confidentially. Griffith demurred at this; de Valera had condemned the Treaty in public but was not ready to allow the people to see his alternative. When Griffith moved Dáil approval of the Treaty, he said he would respect de Valera's wishes as far as possible, but would not 'hide from the Irish people what the alternative is that is proposed'.

The journalists Boyle and de Burca, who covered the Treaty debate for the *Irish Independent*, commented on this speech of Griffith's: 'One point he hammered mercilessly. The issue was not between an independent republic and Dominion status. Rather it was between two forms of association with the British Empire'. But they were perplexed: 'We gathered he was referring to something produced at the secret session and were puzzled for the moment'.[6]

In his speech proposing that the Dáil ratify the Treaty, Griffith said that the task the plenipotentiaries had been given was 'as hard as was ever placed on the shoulders of man'. They had not asked that it be given to them, but had taken it on when others refused it, and were prepared to see it through. What they had got was not ideal, but was honourable, and protected Ireland's vital interests.

An attempt was being made to represent to the public that some had stood firmly by the republic but that Collins, 'the man who won the war', had sold the pass. In the pre-conference correspondence, not once had recognition of the republic been insisted upon. The difference between the two sides was between half recognising the king and Empire and going in, as one TD had phrased it, with their heads up.

4 Curran, *Free State*, pp.135-6.

5 Forester, *Collins*, pp.273-4.

6 Colum, *Griffith*, p.317.

This was a quibble and, as far as he could make it possible, 'not one young Irishman's life shall be lost on that quibble'.

He argued that the Treaty's real merit was that it was the first agreement between Irish and English representatives in 750 years, signed from a position of Irish equality; it was the first that admitted that Ireland was equal. Ireland would have its own flag, would see the occupying forces being removed, and would have its own army. It would have full fiscal freedom, would be equal with England and all the Commonwealth countries, and would have an equal say in foreign relations.

The oath in the Treaty could be honourably taken by any Irishman because it was primarily to his own country's constitution and only then a promise to be faithful to the head of the Commonwealth. They had not dishonoured their oath to the republic but had followed de Valera's understanding of doing their best for their country. He did not think that the Irish people would be foolish enough to fight for the name of a republic, having got everything else, but, if they were, he 'would follow in the ranks'. He concluded with the claim of having translated Thomas Davis into the practical politics of the day, that is, not enmity, but equality and friendship with England.[7]

Griffith's opening speech made the case for the Treaty absolutely clear, and those on his side who followed him, with the exception of a few, especially Collins, repeated or elaborated on his points. Each TD spoke in the debate. There was much repetition and not a little rancour. Mary MacSwiney described Collins as worse than Lord Castlereagh, infamous in Irish history for the corruption which led to the passing of the Act of Union. She dismissed the idea of any cooperation between the two sides.

Seumas Robinson sneered at Collins as nothing more than a Fleet Street hero. Brugha's speech set out mainly to belittle Collins as 'one of the heads of a subsection of my Department' who had been the subject of an unwarranted and self-cultivated personality cult.[8] Griffith's contribution to the debate was only one-fifth the length of de Valera's who, whenever he wanted to say something, behaved as if he had the right to determine his own procedure.(In fact, at one stage he declared that he was going to choose his own procedure.)[9]

Despite their length the opposing arguments are not difficult to sum up. On the pro-Treaty side it was contended that while the agreement was not ideal, it gave the substance of freedom immediately and put no

7 *Treaty Debate*, pp.20-23.

8 *ibid.*, pp.347,290-91,325-7.

9 *ibid.*, p.259.

obstacle in the way of further progress. The strongest point was that it was the best bargain that could be secured and rejection meant the return of the war.

Anti-Treatyites contended that the delegates had no right to sign and had betrayed the republic. Dominion status was rejected and the oath was the focus of attack. But no practical alternative was forthcoming. Some even declared themselves ready to take on England once more, but many, including de Valera, argued as if all they had to do was *ask* the British for better terms and they would get them. De Valera said at one stage: 'The sad part of it is that a grand Treaty could at this moment be made'.[10] He did not explain how. For two months the delegates had tried to persuade the British to accept what his Document No.2 contained, and they had been flatly refused.

There were complaints that because de Valera had vetoed discussion of his alternative, TDs were unable to explain to their constituents what it was. De Valera immediately made known his willingness to present it, but only to amend or replace the Treaty. Griffith objected, wanting a straight vote on the Articles of Agreement, and de Valera then refused to allow it to be discussed. On 4 January, following further argument on this, de Valera gave formal notice that he would move his alternative next day as an amendment to the Treaty.

Griffith suggested that he hand it to the press, as they had requested two weeks before. Later the same day Griffith protested again that when de Valera's document was circulated, in preparation for its formal moving next day, six of the 23 clauses of the original had been dropped. De Valera told him he was 'quibbling', that he would present it as he wanted to present it, and that it was then up to the assembly to decide whether to accept it as an amendment to Griffith's motion.

The next day de Valera protested that his original document had been given to the press. Griffith then freely admitted that he had given it to the *Freeman's Journal*. He argued that during the debate he had honoured de Valera's request not to discuss it. This had meant he had had to speak 'as with one hand tied'. But when accused of quibbling over the changes in the latest version, he had thought the time had come to let the people see whether he was quibbling or not.

De Valera tendered his resignation and offered himself for re-election on 6 January. This was an attempt to sideline the Treaty motion and take Griffith on in a personality vote. But Griffith insisted that his motion stood, and until it had been voted on de Valera was out of order. De Valera replied that the government could resign at any time and that an executive was necessary to carry on Dáil business. The Speaker, Eoin

10 *Treaty Debate*, p.26.

MacNeill, ruled that the Dáil was superior to the government, that Griffith's motion stood, but that a motion to suspend standing orders could be accepted. This was debated at length. It ended when Griffith protested that he had to listen for days to his character being attacked and saw no reason why, in the middle of the debate, they should suddenly have to vote on de Valera's personality.[11]

Griffith and Collins were on the defensive during the debate. This was inevitable because they were calling for an end to the republic. Agreeing to keep de Valera's alternative confidential compounded their difficulty. Making Document No.2 public would have demonstrated how far the full cabinet was committed to a compromise and how little difference there was between external association and the Treaty.

A move such as this would have put their opponents on the defensive and undermined them in the eyes of the public. It might also have split supporters of external association and extreme republicans. But Griffith and Collins held back because of their esteem for de Valera and also because, like him, they hoped to avert a split. The result was that supporters of the Treaty had either to apologise for its shortcomings or defend themselves from personal attacks. The true value of the settlement did not emerge. Griffith displayed little emotion, but his solid, forceful presentation had an effect on both the Dáil and the press gallery.[12]

'Delivered after many disillusionments, affronts and repulses', Griffith's winding-up speech, 'in its earnestness, solidity [and] occasional passionate expression, was splendidly characteristic of the man', wrote Colum. One TD had told the Dáil that there was a *prima facie* case for putting Griffith on trial for treason. But Griffith knew how much had been secured:

> A few years ago I found, when I saw the misery and degradation and poverty of my country - when I saw her name forgotten in Europe - I found that the cause of all that was the infamous Act of Union. From the day that Act was passed Ireland became a chaos. In the 120 years since that was passed, we have lost twelve millions of our people; our country has been ravished and ravaged; we have had the emigrant ship and the famine and the prison cell and the scaffold all through that 120 years, because you have had the English army in occupation here; and by your vote are you going to keep the English army in occupation here, because that is what it means? Are you going to put out the English army, the English tax-gatherer, the

11 *Treaty Debate*, pp.217-18, 258-9,266-8,271-82.

12 Curran, *Free State*, pp.156-7.

English West Britons; to build yourself up as a nation again and stand as this Treaty gives you power to stand - on equality with the other nations again - and get your fair name in the world? Or are you going back, without hope of success in this generation at least, to the position in which we were until the heroism and capacity of these young men made England offer terms in July last?

Replying to the anti-Treaty point that this generation could bide its time but the next would achieve freedom, he was passionate:

> Is there to be no living Irish nation? Is the Irish nation to be the dead past or the prophetic future? Have we any duty to the present generation? I say we have. I say it is the task of political leadership, and statesmanship, or whatever you like to call it, to adopt the weapons and circumstances of this time to achieve the best possible result for the country while keeping the honour of the country safe; and I say if leadership does not devote itself to that task, it is not leadership. We have a duty to our country, and our country is the living people of Ireland; we have a duty to our people; we have a duty at least, so far as our judgement goes, not to lead them astray, not to tell them something will happen 'if you do this' - when you know they cannot do it - in order to save our faces at the expense of our countrymen's blood.

But whether the Treaty was accepted or rejected was not Griffith's whole concern. Some TDs had actually challenged the people's capability of deciding. He found himself having to argue on behalf of democracy as well as the Treaty:

> I have heard one Deputy say here that it does not matter what his constituents say. I tell him it does. If representative government is going to remain on the earth, then a representative must voice the opinion of his constituents; if his conscience will not let him do that he has only one way out and that is to resign and refuse to misrepresent them; but that men who know their constituents want this Treaty should come here and tell us that, by virtue of the vote they derive from these constituents, they are going to vote against the Treaty - that is the negation of all democratic right; it is the negation of all freedom....You are trying to reject this Treaty without allowing the Irish people to say whether they want it or not - the people whose lives and fortunes are involved.

Colum regarded Griffith's closing speech as 'the one great speech of the debate'. He put all his experience and singlemindedness into it, spoke for the Treaty as the one who did most to bring it about, and asked for support for it, 'not as a personal venture', but as 'the opportunity to give the people of Ireland a chance to raise themselves in prosperity, responsibility and dignity. 30 years of planning and working was behind that speech. In all that volume of speeches it stands out because it is a testament'.[13]

The *Irish Times* described the speech as 'by far the most statesmanlike utterance that has been made in the Dáil'. Béaslaí thought that Griffith's performance was 'worthy of his record, combining the incisive logic and commonsense of his other utterances and writings with an unwonted fire and emotion, which the exceptional events evoked from him'. Macardle dismissed it as a long and bitter condemnation of opponents of the Treaty.

De Vere White saw Griffith's final speech as 'by far the most effective, reasonable and persuasive of the whole debate'. Despite the taunts of treachery he had to listen to, he did not reply in personalities. De Vere White thought that one of Griffith's comments 'showed a keen appreciation of the spirit that was stirring abroad'. This was his remark about democracy: 'Ah! democracy is, to some minds, very good in theory when democracy fits in with their own ideas; but when democracy bends the reins contrary to their own ideas, they get back into a casuistic vein'. Taylor quoted AE's comment on the speech: 'it was extraordinarily fine; [he] did not think he could speak with such fire and on such a high level'.[14]

Proposals were tabled in early January to try to meet de Valera's objections to the Treaty and to reach a compromise that would avert disaster. One, from the Labour Party, was that the Dáil would give the Provisional Government the necessary authority to function, and the authority to draw up the Free State constitution.[15] The people could then claim that the Dáil, and not the king, was the ultimate authority for that constitution. The king, therefore, would not be seen as the source of Irish independence, or Westminster as having any right to

13 Colum, *Griffith*, pp.325-7.

14 *Irish Times*, 9 January 1922; Béaslaí, *Collins*, ii, p.338; Macardle, *Irish Republic*, p.583; de Vere White, *O'Higgins*, pp.77-8; Taylor, Collins, p.208. A large extract from the speech was included in an anthology of the world's greatest speeches. See Lewis Copeland and Lawrence Lamb (eds.), *The World's Great Speeches* (New York, 1968), pp.223-6.

15 The Provisional Government was to take over the powers of the British government in Ireland under the terms of the Treaty, but was to be answerable to the parliament of Southern Ireland because the Dáil was not recognised by the British. In theory different institutions, the Dáil and the Southern Irish parliament were really the same in practice because the second Dáil had been elected in May 1921, following elections to the Southern Irish parliament under the Government of Ireland Act.

interfere in internal Irish affairs. De Valera initially predicted that this compromise would prove unacceptable to Griffith and Collins, but when he learned that they were in favour of it, he rejected it himself.

He also turned down a similar idea advanced by a group of backbench TDs, some of them his own supporters. On 5 January the group reached an agreement whereby members of the Dáil opposed to the Treaty would abstain from voting on it; only Provisional Government members would be required to sign acceptance of it. De Valera would remain Dáil president and the army and all other services in Ireland would be taken over by the Provisional Government which would derive its authority from the Dáil.

Griffith and Collins accepted this *ad hoc* group's compromise. De Valera immediately turned it down and pressed for Document No.2 instead. This destroyed the prospect of a compromise because the whole issue of the Treaty was once again raised and the anti-Treaty men in the *ad hoc* group withdrew their support from the document they had helped draw up.

On 7 January the Dáil ratified the Treaty by 64 votes to 57. De Valera led his supporters from the house while Griffith was being elected President of the Dáil, the assembly which he, more that anyone else present, had helped bring into existence.

A Definite Constitutional Way?

The curious duality which troubled the country for the following months emerged shortly after the Treaty vote. Griffith was elected leader of the Dáil cabinet and the Provisional Government came into existence with Collins as its chairman. The country appeared to have two governments even if some ministers held portfolios in both.

Pro-Treaty authors such as O'Hegarty, O'Connor and Taylor contended that Griffith and Collins should have brought the Dáil to an end after the vote in favour of the Treaty, because continuing it meant two governments, and gave the anti-Treatyites a forum in which they could obstruct and criticise. An election straight away would indeed have been the most advisable course, but it was impossible. The British had to authorise an election and the anti-Treaty IRA had to be persuaded to allow one to be held.

Prolonging the life of the Dáil simply made the best of the difficult circumstances. It satisfied opponents of the Treaty and made sure an alternative government would not be established. The Provisional Government had time to take root and begin to function. That the Dáil and the Provisional Government existed side by side did not prevent the

Treaty from being implemented: the overlap of personnel and the joint-meetings to agree approaches saw to this. Republicans were not fooled by the facade of the Dáil and it was not a brilliant policy stroke by Griffith and Collins, as anti-Treaty apologists like O'Donoghue and Neeson asserted.[16]

It was a mistaken strategy of de Valera and his followers to give their allegiance to the Dáil and deny it to the Provisional Government, Fanning believed. Whatever the differences between Griffith, Collins and the pro-Treatyites on the one hand, and the British on the other, both were determined to put the Treaty into practice and therefore, in effect, to defeat de Valera and his supporters. The Provisional Government took effective control.

The main reason why the power and influence of Griffith's Dáil cabinet decreased was that from 27 February onwards Dáil ministers were invited to attend Provisional Government meetings, which led in practice, although it was unofficial, to the two systems of government being fused. The Provisional Government was not responsible to the Dáil or any other assembly, and the emasculation of the Dáil worked to the disadvantage of the anti-Treatyites who continued to attend it. In fact, the Dáil cabinet did not meet as a separate body after 28 April.[17]

There was much confusion at the Sinn Féin ard-fheis in late February, when Griffith and de Valera proposed conflicting motions. Collins spoke in favour of the Treaty but appealed to the delegates to preserve unity. The ard-fheis was adjourned to enable the leaders to try to reach agreement. Griffith, Collins, de Valera and Stack eventually agreed a compromise. Basically, this was to postpone an election on the Treaty for three months to give the people the chance to examine both the Treaty itself and the new constitution.

Griffith was not happy with this agreement. He was certain that an election would give a mandate to implement the Treaty, would resolve the ambiguity inherent in the two-cabinet situation, and above all would give the people the chance to express their opinion. That the election was put back until June was both a political and a personal setback for him. However, time was needed to build up an army and police force, to organise the judicial system and to draft a constitution to show the people how much they had won.

But the postponement was, to use Colum's words, 'an evasion, and Griffith was an unevasive man'. On a personal level, it affected his esteem for Collins. He remarked to a friend: 'Have you noticed that all

16 Curran, *Free State*, p.159.

17 Fanning, *Independent Irl.*, pp.8-9.

those people who are attacking Collins are paying compliments to me? They admit that I, at least, have acted consistently so as to strengthen the suggestion that Collins is a traitor. They think, in their small minds, that they can drive a wedge between Collins and me'. The February arrangement did not drive a wedge between them, but it left Griffith more wary of Collins.[18] The British, worried by the agreement to postpone the election, invited Griffith and Collins to London to discuss the situation. Griffith, despite his reservations about it, defended the deal in London. He argued that if the electorate were familiar with the constitution, de Valera could not maintain that the British could reject it if the Irish people had not seen it in its final form. He also held that it would take time to organise an election anyway and the delay would only be six weeks. Another point he pushed was that the Irish cabinet had been given three months' security to prepare for the election.

The pro-Treatyites got the better bargain and even some anti-Treatyites felt this, Griffith told the British. He assured Chamberlain that de Valera would maintain a constitutional path and that the IRA were loyal to the Minister for Defence, Mulcahy. The British agreed to accept the arrangement and Churchill told the House of Commons of his government's satisfaction with the meeting.[19]

At first de Valera was satisfied with the February agreement, but soon he was demanding that the electoral register be updated. This would have necessitated a longer delay than the three months agreed. The issue was first raised in the Dáil on 1 March and de Valera wrote accordingly to Griffith nine days later. Griffith replied that it would take more than five months to revise the register and he would not agree to so long a postponement of the election. De Valera was proving impossible to satisfy and his attitude must have exasperated Griffith. Concessions made to him simply led to further demands.[20]

A conference was held in April, sponsored by the Catholic Archbishop and the Lord Mayor of Dublin and Labour representatives, to try to heal the ever-deepening rift over the Treaty. But the atmosphere was far from conducive to agreement. Brugha accused Griffith and Collins of being British agents, and when the Archbishop asked him to withdraw that remark, he agreed, but added that those who did the work of the British government were British agents. Furiously, Collins asked if he and Griffith were ministers whose blood was to be waded

18 Colum, *Griffith*, pp.336-7.

19 Curran, *Free State*, pp.167-8.

20 Ryle Dwyer, *de Valera*, pp.102-3.

through in defence of the republic (an allusion to a de Valera speech in mid-March). Brugha replied calmly that they were. So deep was the bitterness between the two sides that they eventually occupied separate rooms.[21]

Nevertheless, Griffith and Collins made de Valera several offers. One was a June election on both the Treaty and constitution; Griffith promised to enact the constitution if his side won, introduce full adult suffrage, and hold another election on the constitution in its final form. Another offer was a June election on the Treaty only, followed by a second election on the constitution. A third offer was a plebiscite within a month (all over 21 eligible to vote) supervised by the clergy, the Labour Party and other public bodies. De Valera rejected the first two because they would be held on what he regarded as an invalid register and would be a breach of the February agreement. He dismissed the third as a 'Stone Age' plebiscite.

De Valera knew his side had no hope of winning an election on the Treaty, even with an updated register. Griffith and Collins rightly concluded that the real purpose was to postpone, and if possible prevent, an election. De Valera looked for a six month postponement.[22] He repeated the extraordinary argument, first put forward during his mid-March speaking tour of Munster, that a minority had the right to use force to oppose any attempt to surrender sovereignty. Griffith and Collins did not accept this. The April conference ended in failure.

The Dáil met again on 26 April. Griffith opened by attacking the opposition for being obstructive, for interfering with the rights of the people, for trying to win over the army to their side and frighten the populace. De Valera assailed the cabinet for refusing to accept that the Provisional Government was responsible to the Dáil, and for dividing the army and trying to set up a rival military force. Reference to the supremacy of the Dáil reopened the issue of the Treaty and there was an angry exchange between Griffith and de Valera about who exactly was responsible for surrendering the republic.

Griffith stated during the sitting of the following day that he had kept silent for too long and now wished to give the true background to the

21 Ryle Dwyer, *de Valera*, pp.109-10.

22 Curran, *Free State*, pp.185-6. He had some grounds for complaint about the register. It had been prepared improperly in some places in 1921 and listed many who were dead or had emigrated while omitting others who were entitled to vote. On the other hand, no previous register had been compiled in three months, which de Valera had argued would be an adequate period, and agreement to add 400,000 women to the electorate was sure to complicate the revision. When a new register was compiled in 1922-23, it took more than six months.

London conference. De Valera knew when he sent him to London that he could not bring back a republic. He had asked him to get him out of the strait-jacket of the republic. When he was going to London, de Valera said to him that there might have to be scapegoats, and there was a member of the Dáil present on the opposite side who had heard that remark.[23]

Griffith explained that he was saying all this at that particular time because of an attempt on the life of his colleague, Collins. He said that *Poblacht na hÉireann* (an anti-Treaty newspaper) was edited by an Englishman who had spent his life in the military secret service of England. When Childers protested, he told him he would give the Dáil his record if necessary. He referred to the recent 'wading through blood' speeches of de Valera and to an article in *Poblacht na hÉireann* urging the execution of the Treaty signatories.[24]

Relations with the North

What effect did the signing of the Treaty have in the northern counties? The first move towards better relations with Northern Ireland came with the so-called 'Craig-Collins pact', signed in London in late January 1922. Collins agreed to end the Belfast boycott in return for Craig's promise to protect the Catholic minority and to press for the re-employment of 9,000 Catholic workers who had been expelled from their jobs. It was decided to change the Boundary Commission arrangement by mutual agreement and also to find a better mechanism than that provided by the Council of Ireland in the 1920 Government of Ireland Act, for dealing with all-Ireland problems.

Violent clashes in border areas and in Belfast destroyed their pact. In February, Collins sought further talks with Craig, but the latter declined while the 'Special' Constables, taken in a clash at Clones, Co. Monaghan, were being held prisoners. Craig was informed by Churchill that it was his intention to send him a formal letter inviting Northern Ireland to begin talks with the South, but while the Limerick crisis (see below) remained unresolved, he would go no further for the moment. However, once that had been settled, he informed Craig that he would 'not be disposed to accept a simple refusal from the Northern

23 This was Mrs Kathleen Clarke, widow of the executed 1916 leader, Tom, who confirmed this in the Dáil on 17 December 1921. *Private Sessions*, p.262.

24 *Official Report of 2nd Dáil*, pp.303-6.

government, in view of the heavy obligations in regard to troops and Special Constabulary which we are incurring on their behalf'.[25]

Before long, Collins was cooperating with Liam Lynch, a prominent anti-Treaty IRA leader, in direct action aimed at helping Northern nationalists. Griffith knew nothing about this. Lynch sent rifles to the North, which Collins then replaced with British weapons supplied to the Provisional Government. Griffith was incapable of such deception. Those who accused Collins of putting expediency before principle in this situation had a point.

At the end of March, Griffith, Collins and Duggan signed a new agreement with Craig. The IRA was to cease activity in Northern Ireland in return for the reorganisation of the Belfast police. In mixed districts, half the police force was to be Catholic. The British were to contribute half a million pounds for unemployment relief to ease the pressure on Craig to have Catholic workers reinstated as he had agreed with Collins.

On 4 April, Craig wrote to Collins: 'I am glad to say that the effect of our agreement is beginning to be felt'. The unemployed were to be relieved by means of a programme of public works. One-third of the money available was to be spent in Catholic areas. Steps were being taken to deal promptly with serious crime. Collins's cooperation was sought in setting up a Catholic Police Committee.

He reminded Collins of his promise to release a number of prisoners and requested action on the Belfast boycott. A strong appeal had been made to 2,000 businessmen to re-engage Catholic employees but their willingness to do so depended on a trade revival. He was certain that Collins would recognise that he was 'energetically carrying out the spirit as well as the letter of our Agreement'. But it was the anti-Treaty IRA that was orchestrating the Belfast boycott and there was little Collins could do about it.[26]

The Provisional Government appointed a North-Eastern Advisory Committee (NEAC) in late February to keep it in touch with Northern nationalist opinion. The NEAC met for the first time on 11 April. The horrific murders of five Catholics, following the shooting dead of a Special Constable in Belfast, was the main topic discussed. Collins's furious protests to Craig and demands for an enquiry had been in vain, and he therefore urged a policy of non-cooperation until the Northern Ireland government agreed to three demands: a joint-

25 Calton Younger, *A State of Disunion* (London, 1972), pp.132-4.

26 *ibid.*, pp.136-7.

enquiry into the murders, the end of raiding in Catholic areas by Specials, and the release of prisoners as agreed in the March pact.

There was a discussion at the NEAC meeting about whether the pact with Craig should be broken if, as seemed likely, there was no response from him. Griffith contended that 'the core of the whole question' was that Craig had no more control over extremists on his side than the Provisional Government on theirs. It was an embarrassing reminder to Collins that, as Fanning put it, 'the wild men were out of control south as well as north'.

In actual fact, Dublin could do nothing to protect the most vulnerable Catholics in Belfast. Griffith admitted as much when he said at the same meeting:

> ...we were undoubtedly unable to protect our people in Belfast....Those people are being murdered. We can always take reprisals, you can burn their property. That does not save the lives of the people. If you embark on a war policy, you can make things bad for Belfast, but you certainly cannot make them better for our people....You cannot hit them in Belfast without further exposing our people there to assassination....We have to look at it from one point or another - to save our people's lives or burn the property of our opponents.

He concluded that the pact with Craig, for all its shortcomings, was the most Dublin could do to offer some sort of protection.

The record of this NEAC meeting vividly shows the weakness of the Dublin government's policy of non-recognition of Northern Ireland, not to mention Collins's secret support for the IRA there. The Committee met only twice and achieved very little. At least Dublin was forced to confront Northern realities they had hitherto been able to ignore.[27] To his credit, Griffith questioned the wisdom of non-recognition, arguing that the Treaty recognised the Northern Ireland parliament, and supporters of the Treaty were inconsistent when they did not recognise that parliament. But non-recognition remained the core of Collins's Northern policy until the Civil War began.

'The brief respite between the signing of the Treaty and the outbreak of the Irish Civil War did allow, especially on the pro-Treaty side, several frank statements, whose impact would have been considerably greater had they been openly debated eight years earlier', Davis wrote. Erstwhile advocates of violent methods, like Collins and Eoin O'Duffy, acknowledged that force could not ensure the safety of the Northern Catholic population. Griffith and Collins were not entirely

27 Fanning, *Independent Irl.*, pp.28-32.

off the mark when they contended that the Six Counties could eventually be drawn in by unity and good government in the South.

Carson himself had acknowledged this as a possibility in 1914. The Council of Ireland, which had been provided for in the Treaty, might have been the basis for cooperation on matters of mutual concern, and thus the basis for practical unity. Even Carson was willing in 1918 to consider self-rule for Ireland in a British federal arrangement. Blythe thought de Valera made his gravest error when he refused Craig's proposal in 1921 of two Irish dominions linked by a Council of Ireland.

The Civil War, with its attacks by anti-Treaty militants on Southern Protestants, doubtlessly confirmed Northern Protestants' worst fears. The insistence of Griffith's *Young Ireland* that 'the recent appalling murders' of Protestants in the South did not mean that Protestant civil and religious liberties would be imperilled in the Free State, must have rung hollow in such circumstances. Blythe, himself a Northern Protestant, was convinced that but for the Civil War, the Northern Irish government itself believed it could not have lasted for very long. But the Belfast boycott was reimposed by the anti-Treaty IRA, who were again active in the North, and were secretly aided by Collins who, by this time, was 'almost a split personality', in Davis's opinion.[28]

Fratricidal Strife - All Nonsense?

It was evident when de Valera and his followers withdrew from the Dáil that the time for parliamentary debate was over. What would decide the future was the new government's ability to function. This, in turn, depended upon the army's reaction to the lengthy Treaty debate. The army was the key to survival.

Mulcahy assured the Dáil that the army would remain 'the army of the republic'. What of its unity? It was of course divided, when friends and even families were at odds. Headquarters staff were mainly pro-Treaty but vehement opponents existed, like Rory O'Connor and Liam Mellows. There was division throughout the country as well and some of the strongest commandants, Liam Lynch and Ernie O'Malley among them, were anti-Treaty. The military had a chequered history. The Volunteers had their own executive at first and submitted to the authority of the Dáil only when Brugha insisted that both TDs and soldiers should swear an oath of allegiance to the republic. Now that the republic was without substance, would the army still hold itself bound by the oath?

On 12 January, O'Connor, Mellows, Lynch and Oscar Traynor wrote

28 Davis, 'Ulster Protestants and Sinn Féin press', in *Éire-Ireland*, pp.80-82.

to Mulcahy demanding an army convention which ought to reaffirm army allegiance to the republic and entrust overall control to an executive of its own choice, independent of civil authority. The Dáil cabinet was against this pressure. It was clear, however, that the convention would be held anyway, so Mulcahy accepted the proposal. It was agreed the meeting would be held within two months. Curran believed that giving the anti-Treaty officers the convention they wanted strengthened the pro-Treaty side because it gave it time to build up its own army from Volunteers loyal to headquarters.[29]

IRA division was a personal tragedy for Collins: he had been so instrumental in building the organisation. He became so preoccupied with the dangers of a split in the army that in trying to prevent it his relations even with Griffith suffered. Griffith wanted to scotch any signs of trouble immediately. As the British vacated, their barracks were taken over by IRA units, whether pro- or anti-Treaty was not known at the time. Griffith and Collins had no control over this. There was a flare-up in Limerick in late February and Griffith was for strong action. According to Blythe he was 'driven to desperation' by the 'wait-and-see' approach adopted by the military leaders:

> For the first and only time in my experience, he rose to his feet at a cabinet meeting and made a formal speech. He spoke, I remember, under obvious stress, and with a degree of passion I had never before known him to show. He wound up by saying that if we were not prepared to fight and preserve the democratic rights of the ordinary people and the fruit of national victory, we should be looked upon as the greatest set of poltroons who had ever had the fate of Ireland in their hands.[30]

The situation in Limerick became dangerous. To Griffith the issue was plain and simple: most of the people wanted the Treaty and those opposed would have to accept this; if they would not, force would have to be used against them. He had come to accept that a clash was inevitable; postponing it would only make it worse. At first Collins supported him, as did the rest of the cabinet except Mulcahy. The latter urged caution, arguing that the military lacked readiness for war at the present time.

Lynch wanted a peaceful settlement. Mulcahy knew this and persuaded Collins to go along. The rest of the cabinet were left with no choice but to agree to a conciliatory line. Griffith was uneasy with this

29 Curran, *Free State*, pp.162-3.

30 Colum, *Griffith*, p.339.

approach but it did keep Limerick out of anti-Treaty control and an armed confrontation was avoided which could have destroyed the Treaty. Such is the verdict of Joseph Curran.[31] But one might ask to what extent did postponing the conflict make it wider and worse.

Griffith seems to have grasped instinctively that Limerick was an omen. Just how ominous became apparent in March when the crisis was brought to a head by the government banning the convention for fear of a military junta. Anti-Treaty apologists maintained that Griffith was responsible for the ban even though the decision was a unanimous cabinet one. The convention took place anyway. It was attended almost exclusively by out-and-out republicans, among whom Rory O'Connor emerged as the most intransigent.

The convention declared the army's allegiance to the republic and vested authority in an executive of sixteen officers. O'Connor made it absolutely clear in a special press conference that they would not obey Griffith's cabinet and that they rejected Dáil authority. Was not this military dictatorship? It could be taken in that way, he said. What he meant became clear within weeks with the seizing of the Four Courts and other buildings in central Dublin.

The smashing of the *Freeman's Journal* presses and the repudiation of Dáil authority by the anti-Treaty forces in late March showed their contempt for both civil liberty and democracy. They also tried to prevent the government from laying its case before the voters. They blocked railway lines and roads and cut telegraph wires. Local IRA commandants often proscribed meetings to be held by their opponents. Griffith refused to be intimidated and addressed a meeting at Sligo as scheduled on 16 April.

The stark contrast between physical-force republicans, who felt they needed no popular mandate, and democrats of Griffith's school, was forced brutally on the public's attention with the seizure of the Four Courts and the aftermath. Griffith wanted a regular government responsible to the people. O'Connor's position was tantamount to military dictatorship. Collins was caught between Griffith and O'Connor - having earlier removed Griffith's constitutionally-minded supporters from the Sinn Féin executive, he now stood with Griffith against his former friends. Despite the anti-Treaty IRA seizing the Four Courts, Collins still wanted to deal with it.[32]

A deputation of army officers appeared before the Dáil on 3 May and urged TDs to join them in drawing up a peace plan. But intransigent

31 Curran, *Free State*, pp.170-71.

32 Davis, *Arthur Griffith*, p.40.

republicans would have none of it, among them Mellows. Mellows was a civilian politician and member of the Dáil; he was also a military commandant and a member of the Four Courts garrison who repudiated the authority of the Dáil. Two weeks of behind-the-scenes efforts produced no common ground, leaving Collins and de Valera to take up where the army officers had failed.

Griffith then moved in the Dáil on 19 May that dates be set for the election. He declared that he acknowledged no authority in the country higher than the people. If the people were against him, he would hold on to his own views, but he would not attempt by intimidation or violence or threats to prevent them from following the course they had decided on. If he could not persuade them by arguments he would not persuade them at all. There was nothing more insolent in the history of Ireland, or in the history of modern civilisation as it appeared to him, than the claim by a minority of men that the people had no right to decide on an issue which affected their whole future.

He had thought the issue of the Treaty was the greatest that could be placed before the people, but a greater one had now arisen - one that struck at every right they had struggled for and every conception they had. The issue before the people was that they had no right to decide their own future in their own country. All civilisation and all modern progress was dependent on men substituting the rule of the ballot for the bullet, the vote for armed force.

Regardless of the intimidation or methods used against them, they were going to have the expression of the people's opinion. They had gone through months of talk while the nation was being destroyed, while brigandage, robbery, murder, and the destruction of commercial life were going on. They had offered everything short of the indefeasible right of the people to pronounce on the issue - and if they gave that away, they would go down as the basest cowards in Irish history.[33]

On the following day, he moved an amendment of his own motion. This was seconded by de Valera and carried unanimously. It envisaged a different kind of election from that which Griffith had in mind the previous day. What had happened in the interim was that Collins and de Valera reached a 'pact'. Basically this envisaged the two sides in the Dáil contesting the election as a 'National Coalition Panel'. The government to be formed afterwards was to consist of the President, the Minister for Defence representing the army, and nine other ministers, five from the pro- and four from the anti-Treaty side. All other interests were to be free to contest the election as well.

When he was informed of the pact Griffith was shocked and told

33 *Official Report of 2nd Dáil*, pp.460-62.

Collins 'You've given them everything!' He was convinced it ignored the Treaty and the responsibility associated with it. Blythe gave a vivid account of Griffith's reaction:

> He was very dissatisfied with the 'pact' and he did his best to prevent it. I remember the cabinet meeting at which the 'pact' was agreed with, and when he was asked did he accept it he spent three minutes considering it nervously, pulling at his tie and wiping his glasses, and it was very clear that he found it extremely hard to accept it. We were all, for a period of time that seemed to me to be very long, silent, waiting for an answer from him.[34]

Collins signed his agreement with de Valera without consulting his colleagues. 'This action ended Collins's close alliance with Griffith which had been central to the achievement and acceptance of the Treaty', Hopkinson observed. Griffith never afterwards called Collins by his first name. MacNeill thought that the pact deprived the people of the right to vote. Blythe was against it.

The cabinet was faced with a *fait accompli*. They rationalised the pact on the grounds that it would enable order to be restored so that the election could be held. Mulcahy afterwards regretted going so far in the quest for political and military unity. Kevin O'Higgins described the 'toleration' and 'magnanimity' shown as the most 'despicable' in the whole history of Ireland. Although the anti-Treatyites seemed to have gained more, the pact really 'amounted to little more than a postponement of the issue', in Hopkinson's opinion.[35]

The British requested a meeting. There was a distinct possibility that they would denounce the pact and repudiate the Treaty. Because he was seen as the only one who could make an impression on the London cabinet, Griffith was asked to go. His first reaction was one of anger: what was he to say to the British? Then he calmed down and listened quietly while the case for the pact was made, and finally he named the ministers he wanted to accompany him (Collins, Cosgrave, O'Higgins and Duggan). They met with the British signatories of the Treaty. Whoever else they may have doubted, the British regarded Griffith as a man of integrity.

He dismissed with scorn the accusation that they were deviating from the Treaty. They had signed and meant to adhere faithfully to the document. He was amazed that anyone should suspect them of failing to honour their signatures. The pact was an internal Irish matter, did

34 Ó Lúing, *Ó Gríofa*, p.396. Translated by the writer.

35 Hopkinson, *Green against Green*, p.99.

not concern the British, and did not prevent the Treaty coming into effect. Cosgrave coined a memorable phrase to describe the meeting: 'Griffith spoke to them like a virgin who had been affronted by a rude remark'. The British were assured that there would be no question of the Treaty being repudiated. Cosgrave dealt with the difficulties of holding a normal election, given the situation. The British were reassured that the pact was legitimate and expedient.[36]

A committee to draft a constitution had been appointed by Griffith and Collins in January. Its members were not politicians but were pro-Treaty. Griffith and Collins genuinely believed that the de Valera camp could be satisfied if the new constitution were seen to assert all the powers conferred by the Treaty. They decided to exclude the monarchical symbolism, to which the anti-Treatyites objected so much. They presented the draft constitution to the British at the beginning of June.

The British were not happy. The draft so incensed them that they demanded an immediate and definite declaration that it would strictly conform to the terms of the Treaty. This was a clear ultimatum accompanied by contingent military plans in case of a Dublin rejection. The stark choice for Griffith and Collins once again was between the Treaty and war. Again they took the only realistic option. The Collins-de Valera pact had been an attempt to reconcile the irreconcilable. Collins accepted as much when he repudiated the pact in a speech in his native Cork on 14 June, two days before polling day.

Collins and O'Higgins later argued that a better deal could have been secured on the constitution had the opposition not been so active at home, thereby causing the British to dig in their heels. No doubt British suspicion of the Collins-de Valera pact led to such a searching British analysis of the constitution.

The constitution, which was amended in line with British demands, stressed Irish internal authority far more than the role of the Crown. To facilitate both Irish and British sentiment, contradictory intentions were set side by side in the same article. While Griffith hailed the new constitution, and republicans denounced it, the seeming British victory was more apparent than real. 'As with the Treaty, both Britain and Ireland paid a price for peace, and - once again - the British paid more', as Curran remarked.

The expert on constitutional history, Leo Kohn, characterised the document as being in spirit essentially republican, along continental lines. It made a mockery of monarchical forms. Percipient British observers of that time, such as A.B. Keith, saw that the Irish were the

36 Colum, *Griffith*, pp.347-55.

real victors in the struggle over the constitution. Over the next fifteen years, those who forced the Crown and Empire on Ireland were repaid in kind.[37]

The constitution was published on the morning of polling day, 16 June. Griffith and Collins were attacked by anti-Treatyites for making it public only at the last minute, but the time factor made earlier publication difficult if not impossible. It is unlikely that it would have affected the election results anyway. Most people were pro-Treaty and probably accepted the Crown as the price to be paid for peace and self-government. The republican minority would have voted for anti-Treaty candidates anyway, regardless of the form of the constitution.

Two days before the election, Collins repudiated the pact with de Valera. He had become convinced that it would not work. Griffith had no faith in it. The proposed coalition partners could not even agree on the name of the new assembly, let alone government composition and policy. Also there was little chance of the anti-Treaty IRA obeying the new parliament: talks aimed at army unity had collapsed in early June and a large anti-Treaty IRA faction wanted to attack the British immediately. The failure to get an overtly republican constitution was the ultimate blow.

Regardless of the contention of anti-Treaty authors like Macardle, there is no doubt whatever that the Treaty was the most important issue in the election, and those opposed to it were overwhelmingly defeated. 78% of the vote was pro-Treaty and 72 of the elected deputies (92 out of 128) were for the Treaty. Hopkinson's view is worth giving in full: 'The election result, and the fact that the election was held at all, represented a success for the politicians within the Irish government. Griffith had won the democratic authority he had so long demanded. Prospects for the Treaty settlement and for Anglo-Irish relations appeared enormously improved'.[38]

The prospects were to be immediately dashed. On 22 June, Sir Henry Wilson, former Commander of the Imperial General Staff and recent security adviser to the Northern Irish government, was assassinated outside his home in London by two IRA men. Griffith was unequivocal in his condemnation of the shooting: 'It is a fundamental principle of civilised government that the assassination of a political opponent cannot be justified or condoned'. The incident greatly heightened tensions both between Britain and Ireland and within Ireland itself.

37 Curran, *Free State*, pp.217-18.

38 Hopkinson, *Green against Green*, pp.111-12.

Events in Dublin moved rapidly towards a climax. Several incidents on 26 June were the immediate preliminaries to the outbreak of the Civil War. The anti-Treaty IRA demanded money from two firms to support the Belfast boycott. The government announced that it would order the arrest of anyone who pursued such tactics in the future. The IRA raided a garage and took cars which had been imported despite the boycott, and which they intended to use to launch an attack on the North. The leader of this raid was captured and in retaliation the IRA kidnapped the Free State deputy chief of staff, General J.J. ('Ginger') O'Connell, and held him at the Four Courts as a hostage for the release of their men.

On the afternoon of 26 June the cabinet met to discuss the garage raid and the IRA threat to attack the British. Although a decision was deferred until the following day, Griffith and Mulcahy later stated that the decision to attack the Four Courts was essentially made at that meeting. The taking of O'Connell by the IRA displayed utter contempt for the government and strengthened those who wanted immediate action. Churchill's statement in the House of Commons on the same day caused some resentment and hesitation among them,[39] but it was now inevitable that they would issue an ultimatum to the Four Courts' garrison.

Anti-Treatyites argued afterwards that their opponents bowed to British anger following Wilson's assassination. The other side retorted that it was O'Connell's kidnapping that spurred them into action. There was more to what happened than that. Griffith believed the countrywide unrest would go on as long as the Four Courts continued as its focal point. He had called for action from the outset, but had failed to convince Collins and other army leaders that they had no chance of reaching an accord with their old comrades-in-arms. There was also Mulcahy's advice that militarily they were not yet strong enough to take action.

Now that the constitution had been agreed with the British and the election won, Griffith wanted to govern the country. He argued that peace could be restored only if they made it clear that they had both the will to govern and the military force behind that will. Only thus could the new Ireland come into existence and cease making itself ridiculous in the eyes of the world.

How his country was perceived meant a great deal to him. It disturbed him to see the British worried that the agreement he had signed would be repudiated, that the Irish people were only capable of anarchy, that his people could still shoot at departing British soldiers and

39 He warned that if the occupation of the Four Courts was not ended, the British would regard the Treaty as formally violated.

send killers to the heart of England's capital city. There was no need to be grateful for British generosity, but they had not been unjust, and he had no quarrel with them as a result. Their reaction to Wilson's death served to make him more indignant and determined. It was not British anger, but the reason for it, which had an impact on him.

The taking of General O'Connell was all he needed to force the issue. Although the military leaders were convinced of the political reasons for implementing the Treaty they needed something more to overcome their hesitancy at attacking former comrades.

The Dedicated Democrat

Was the Civil War in Ireland inevitable? Could the differences over the Treaty not have been resolved constitutionally? Those who did not approve of the Treaty had only to win a Dáil majority to repudiate it. If the Dáil decided otherwise, then as true democrats they would have to accept that decision. When the Dáil accepted the Treaty, it reflected the attitude of the people in general. When the terms were first made public, the people were delighted that a final peace seemed at hand, and most thought it gave Ireland substantial freedom. When de Valera published his opposition, and the subsequent Dáil debates took effect, public opinion remained steadily in support of Griffith and Collins.

If the republican movement was genuinely democratic, differences over the Treaty could have been resolved peacefully and constitutionally. But what had been an outwardly democratic movement from 1917 to the end of 1918 had undergone an internal take-over by what Kee described as 'violent, undemocratic forces'. The protestations from both sides during the Treaty debate that members' only responsibility was to their constituents rang hollow as a result. As Kee remarked: 'Collins himself, of all people, actually proclaimed: "I would not be one of those to commit the Irish people to war without the Irish people committing themselves to war"'.

It was the Volunteers of course, who acted without considering the wishes of the people at all, who had brought about the situation in which the Treaty became possible. It was not surprising that many of them thought they should be no more responsive to public opinion now than they had been since 1919. They were now better armed than ever. Large numbers of eager young men had joined, wishing to imitate their elders. The veterans felt they had beaten the British; they enjoyed the hero-worship of the public. *They* would decide, regardless of the politicians.[40]

40 Kee, *Ourselves Alone*, p.158.

It is important to remember the poor example many of the politicians showed them. It was surely too much to expect the army to obey the majority decision of the Dáil when elected TDs did not do so. Brugha, who instigated army obedience to the Dáil, failed to abide by the Dáil's decision.

Contempt for the processes of parliamentary democracy, for the give-and-take of political discussion, was too deep-rooted in the Irish republican tradition for the Treaty to go unchallenged. Many republicans refused even to accept Document No.2 or any other compromise. They stood for what Pearse exalted as 'the strength and peace of mind of those who never compromise'. They saw the Treaty split in spiritual versus material terms. De Valera said that the Irish people would not want him to save them materially at the expense of their national honour.

The biblical images used by MacSwiney and Mellows were indicative of the quasi-religious fervour which so frequently informs revolutionary politics. The religious motif was detectable in many anti-Treaty speeches during the Dáil debate, and showed what Fanning described as 'the common reluctance of revolutionaries to see politics as the art of the possible'.

As in many revolutionary creeds, faith was all - opponents who had wavered in their faith were urged to recant and yield but *they* could not yield to their opponents, as MacSwiney said. The exposition of this kind of republican theology, positing a choice between absolutes, caused the pro-Treaty TD, Lorcan Robbins, to protest: 'Damn principles, but give us Irish freedom by any road we can get it....You would think we were a crowd of theologians instead of Irishmen'.

But the powerful attraction of such ideas for Irish revolutionaries is indisputable. Irish republicanism had a long history of political and military failure, and apparent indifference to defeat - it was imperative to fight whether one won or lost.

A notable characteristic of such an attitude is that it is anti-democratic. Pearse had again and again spelt out the lesson that a minority could be right and the majority wrong to the point where it was indelibly printed on republican minds, and it was constantly reiterated during the Treaty debate. The most celebrated expression of the anti-democratic sentiment of the revolution occurred in a well-known passage from one of de Valera's speeches (he had only to examine his own heart and it told him straight off what the Irish people wanted; he would go down in the creed of 1916 to the grave).

He immediately acted upon this doctrine that there was nothing sacred about majority rule when, following the Dáil vote in favour of the Treaty, he rejected Collins's proposal for a committee of public safety made up of both sides, and demanded a cabinet composed for the time being of those who stood definitely by the republic. The same spirit motivated his supporters when they proposed his re-election as President of the Dáil. That de Valera and his followers refused to accept those votes as a final verdict but clung fast to their concept of the republic, meant that the Treaty split proved permanent.[41]

The causes of the Civil War start with the Treaty. The split that led to armed conflict resulted from that document. But the disagreement over the Treaty revealed an even deeper division in Ireland over the principle of 'the right of the people to govern themselves', which Collins 'rightly' argued was more important than all others, according to Curran. (By choosing Collins as his spokesman for democratic right, Curran did not seem to be aware of the irony, noted by Kee, of Collins's lack of concern for the people's democratic rights in the 1917–21 period.)

The Treaty's enemies did not shirk this issue and were undeterred by their lack of popular support. Was not there a precedent there from 1916? The people were exhausted and afraid of renewed war and might be tempted to abandon the republic, but if its defenders kept faith through the difficult time, the people would soon rally again behind the republican cause.

Those of this school expressed its thought variously: the people's will (the expression of only one generation) was transcended by the people's sovereignty (which expressed the life of the race for all time), according to Childers's *Poblacht na hÉireann* (5 April 1922). 'The majority have no right to do wrong', was de Valera's simpler gloss on this. Childers, perhaps, gave it its best definition: a nation had not the right to surrender its declared and established independence and a minority had the right to resist such a tendency by force.

Curran rightly dismissed these expressions as 'an unqualified denial of the people's right to govern themselves'. But the idea of a self-appointed elect was deeply buried in Irish history, was present in all Irish national (including constitutional) movements, but was most prevalent among the 1916 leaders and some of those who followed in their footsteps. The real beginnings of the Civil War lay in the issue of democracy versus dictatorship, and the Free State versus Republic issue was a mere veneer.[42]

In Munster, in mid-March 1922, de Valera made a series of extraordinary speeches. He condemned the Treaty as an obstacle to

41 For a fuller discussion of this and related aspects, see Fanning, *Independent Irl.*, pp.2-7.

42 Curran, *Free State*, pp.230-31.

independence and declared that it was only by civil war that that independence could afterwards be achieved. He also said that in order to achieve full Irish freedom, they might have to march over the dead bodies of their fellow-countrymen and wade through the blood, not only of the soldiers of the new Irish government, but perhaps of members of that government as well. At Killarney, on 18 March, he told his audience 'the people had never a right to do wrong'. Griffith vowed that he would not share a room with de Valera again until he withdrew this incitement.

Despite the defence of de Valera by his authorised biographers, that he was warning against the danger of civil war, Curran rightly considered the speeches 'irresponsible and dangerous'. People needed no warnings about the threat of civil war, and excitable young armed men, who often formed the bulk of de Valera's listeners, certainly did not need them. 'For a leader of his stature to utter prophecies of bloody domestic conflict only increased its likelihood'. De Valera ignored his own counsel, given at the end of the debate on the Treaty, that no one should talk of fratricidal strife, and 'encouraged others to do the same thing with guns as well as words'.[43]

The anti-Treaty IRA repudiation of Dáil authority in late March put de Valera in a dilemma. He had often proclaimed his support of civil authority. He took no part in the banned army convention, privately disagreeing with its declaration of independence, but he did not want to split the anti-Treaty forces. Indeed, he probably believed this action on the part of the anti-Treaty IRA would strengthen his own position. It was a case of republicanism winning over constitutionalism when de Valera finally defended the convention. He was afterwards to regret this action, but by then it was too late, and he was unable to influence the course of the events which his defence of the IRA had helped to precipitate.

The Civil War, with its extremely serious results for the future of Ireland, was seen by Davis as the climactic working out of the full ramifications inherent in the seemingly theoretical divisions of the 1907 Sinn Féin constitution. Looked at from this point of view, Griffith's signing of the Treaty, and his determination that the militant anti-Treatyites should be removed from the heart of Dublin by force, was the consequence and not the cause of a basic national dichotomy which he had tried to minimise but which he could never eradicate. The presumption that both believers in passive resistance and physical force

43 Curran, *Free State*, pp.173-5.

could cooperate up to the point of compromise, and then diverge peacefully, had finally been demolished.[44] Griffith had striven to his utmost to achieve what turned out to be unachievable.

Finally, personal rivalry and ambition cannot be ruled out as another important element in the split. Of all the leaders, Griffith had the least personal ambition at the time because, as Glandon phrased it, 'he placed the cause of democracy above the retention of his prominent position in the government'. In the words of his old friend, Liam Ó Briain, he rested his case for the Treaty on the dictum 'Salus populi suprema lex est' ('The good of the people is the supreme law'), and defied those who tried to impose a republic.

It is generally agreed that Griffith was willing to give up public leadership. However, having signed the Treaty in the belief that it was in the public interest, he insisted on the right of the Irish people to express themselves on the issue. He agreed to abide by their decision, but until an election could be held, and the popular will ascertained, he continued as a leader to make sure that this was done.[45]

Griffith believed that representative government was the best form of government that mankind had evolved. During the Treaty debate he had argued that it was the duty of a public representative to voice the opinion of his constituents. Otherwise, he said, they would kill representative government in Ireland. The Treaty symbolised what he had hoped to achieve for his country - the substance of freedom with the door to unity open by means of the link with the Crown. He abhorred the use of force but he was prepared to resort to it in order to defend rights which he regarded as more precious than life itself.

44 Davis, *Arthur Griffith*, p.41.

45 Glandon, *Griffith and Advanced-Nationalist Press*, pp.203,210.

Part V

The Place of Literature in the National Struggle

'When the Irish National Theatre ceases
to be national it will also cease to be artistic,
for nationality is the breath of art.
The artist who, condemning his nation and his
age, has wrought for the world and for all time
- who was he and where is his grave?
The world and time have forgotten him,
as he forgot his share of the world
and his share of time....
If the Irish Theatre ceases to reflect Irish life
and embody Irish aspiration,
the world will wag its head away from it'.

United Irishman, 17 October 1903

Chapter I

Cooperation and Conflict

Griffith was not solely interested in the political scene of his time. Literature was among his passions and he became readily embroiled in the literary issues and controversies of his day. This has drawn the attention of literary historians.

He read avidly from an early age. He attended literary societies while still in his teens and the papers he presented indicate the diverse nature of his reading. On 22 November 1889, for example, he gave a paper to the Leinster Literary and Debating Society on Joseph Addison (1672-1719), English essayist and critic. On 26 September 1891, he read a paper entitled 'Irish writers of the 16th, 17th and 18th centuries', and on 5 February 1892, one on 'The Elizabethan poets'.[1]

P.S. O'Hegarty recalled that the talk was mainly of books during their very first meeting, and the amount Griffith knew about 18th-century literature was 'extraordinary'. James Stephens described him as 'profoundly versed in literature', especially English poetry. Seamus O'Sullivan said his knowledge of 18th-century literature, even of the minor poets of that era, was immense, and that he was quickly and correctly able to attribute to an author some 'chance line or fragment of prose which had been quoted by one of our company'.[2]

Some of the foremost writers of his time contributed to his papers. Despite his close professional cooperation with them initially, however, Griffith's relations with the leading figures of the Anglo-Irish literary movement were to become progressively complex and difficult.

Cooperation

Dublin was an exciting place at the turn of the century when Griffith began editing the *United Irishman*. The great interest in literary and political issues was reflected in the numerous articles and letters appearing in the newspapers. R.M. Kain wrote that their editors brought 'artistic and national aspirations to a wide public', and exercised

1 Ms. 19,935 NLI.

2 O'Hegarty, *Sunday Independent*, 12 August 1945; Stephens, *Journalist and Statesman*, p.15; O'Sullivan, *Essays*, p.106.

'a considerable influence in promoting and disseminating opinion'. T.P. Gill of the *Daily Express* and D.P. Moran of the *Leader* were given special mention by Kain, but Griffith was singled out as 'the most influential of them all'.[3]

Scanning through the various issues of Griffith's *United Irishman* one sees how intrinsic a part of this whole ferment he was. The paper was one of the best-written journals of its time. Its contributors included Yeats, Lady Gregory, Stephens, Colum, George Bermingham, George Moore, O'Sullivan, Gogarty and Katherine Tynan. As Colum observed, it seemed for a time that 'the journal would become the organ of a purely literary, purely critical movement'.[4]

Griffith got on well with Yeats in the early years of the *United Irishman*. Yeats's new play, *The Countess Cathleen*, generated controversy in 1899. It tells the story of a countess who sold her soul in order to save her starving tenants during a famine in Ireland. The play was condemned by the Catholic Primate, Cardinal Logue, but Griffith rejected the case he made against the production.[5]

The nationalist MP and historian, F.H. O'Donnell, attacked the play as an insult to faith and Christian doctrine. A group of students from the Catholic Royal University jeered during the performance. The Gaelic League paper, *An Claidheamh Soluis*, which had little time for the idea of a 'national' drama in English, also denounced the play. Griffith rebuked the jeering students for their 'narrow-mindedness and prejudice', and in his editorial came down emphatically on Yeats's side.[6]

Yeats's *Cathleen Ni Houlihan* had a profound impact on Griffith. The hero is a young man who is about to be married but who decides to give up everything to follow an old woman who represents Ireland. Seamus O'Sullivan was with Griffith at the first performance (early April 1902). He described him as being moved to the depths of his being by the play. Robert Brennan recorded the following anecdote from his time with Griffith in Gloucester Jail in 1918-19:

> AG told us a curious and interesting thing in connection with Yeats's play *Cathleen Ni Houlihan*. The poet read the manuscript of the play for AG and said he felt that the end was not rounded out as it should be, or sufficiently dramatic. As it stood then, the ending was

3 R.M. Kain, *Dublin in the Age of William Butler Yeats and James Joyce* (Norman, 1962), p.49.

4 O'Connor, *Terrible Beauty*, p.31; Padraic Colum, *The Road Round Ireland* (New York, 1926), p.301.

5 *United Irishman*, 13 May 1899.

6 *ibid.*

> bald. Michael, abandoning his bride-to-be, had gone out of the house to follow the Old Woman, and Brigid had taken into her arms the weeping Delia, the forsaken bride. Yeats said he knew there should be a last line, but he could not get it. Griffith said: 'Why not have the father ask the young boy something like this - did you see an old woman going down the road? - and have the boy reply - I did not, but I saw a young girl and she had the walk of a queen'. Yeats at once accepted the suggestion, only putting in the word 'path' instead of 'road'.... I have related this story to several poet friends of mine and they all doubted it, but I knew Griffith very well. He was the most unassuming and modest of men, and he would never have dreamed of making a claim of such a nature if it was unfounded.

Griffith in fact claimed, in a *Sinn Féin* article in February 1914, to have composed those lines. He explained that Yeats asked him and Frank Fay to assess the play, and he recommended the final lines to strengthen its propaganda value.[7]

James Flannery believed that Yeats became involved with the Irish National Theatre Society (INTS) because he realised that 'it placed him in direct touch with politics'. The particular form of politics Yeats had in mind was mainly concerned with 'a cultural kind of consciousness-raising' and was represented in his view by Griffith. Yeats helped with the drafting of a programme for Cumann na nGaedheal, and Griffith was initially one of the poet's most spirited supporters. The two also cooperated on the Transvaal Committee during the Boer War, and in opposition to Queen Victoria's visit in 1900.[8]

Griffith proposed Yeats as one of the directors of the *United Irishman* in January 1902. In July of the previous year Yeats asked him to review his *Land of Heart's Desire* so that people would take him more seriously as a playwright. The following eulogy of Yeats's work appeared in an early number of the *United Irishman* (apart from the comments on Yeats, Griffith's piece is interesting for its view on the importance of poetry in a civilised society):

> I walk on the stones and in the grass and I meet betimes men and women who have never read Yeats, and yet consider themselves intelligent Irish persons....Yeats is Irish literature, and Irish belief, and Irish faith, hope and aspiration. In every properly governed and

7 Seamus O'Sullivan, *The Rose and Bottle and Other Essays*, (Dublin, 1946), p.121; Brennan, *Allegiance*, pp.203-4; *Sinn Féin*, 14 February, 1914.

8 James Flannery, *W.B. Yeats and the Idea of a Theatre* (New Haven and London, 1976), pp.323-4; Ulick O'Connor, *Celtic Dawn: A Portrait of the Irish Literary Renaissance* (London,1985), pp.264-5.

> sensible community the people would spend half their time in making, reading and comprehending poetry....A poet comes who lifts the veil, gives them glimpses of the laws. Mr Yeats sings of what he knows and sings more beautifully than ever Irish poet sang before....Mr Yeats lets us into the reality of ourselves....[9]

Flannery and Ulick O'Connor are among a few literary historians who have emphasised the warm collaboration between Griffith and Yeats. Others have ignored it. Yeats avoided mention of it in his *Autobiographies.* Séan Ó Lúing remarked on Radio Éireann in May 1965 that not much had been written on the relationship between the two, but as evidence that they had been close enough at one time, he quoted from a letter he had received on the subject from Seamus MacManus, the Donegal novelist.

MacManus felt disappointed and surprised that Yeats had no reference to Griffith in his autobiography and he wrote to the poet to convey these sentiments. Yeats replied that he did not know Griffith very well. This perplexed MacManus and he reminded Yeats of an occasion on which he entered the *United Irishman* office to find the poet sitting on the floor, his back to the wall and his knees propping up his chin, engaged in earnest conversation with Griffith. This second MacManus letter was unanswered.[10]

Colum gave an insight in 1926 into the dramatic movement that led eventually to the Abbey Theatre. Its predecessor, the Irish Literary Theatre, which was ushered in by Yeats, Lady Gregory, George Moore and Edward Martyn, functioned simply by hiring halls and actors and was not a dramatic company properly understood. It was, in process of time, subsumed by the Irish National Dramatic Company, of which W.G. Fay was the guiding light, and to which his brother Frank, Dudley Digges, Frank Ryan, Mary Walker (Maire Ni Shiubhlaigh), and Colum himself belonged. It was formed from Inghinidhe na hÉireann and the Celtic Literary Society.

While the company was rehearsing AE's *Deirdre*, Yeats arrived and gave them *Cathleen Ni Houlihan.* Colum commented: 'The two plays, produced together by young men and women who were devoted to the idea of national resurgence, brought an enthusiasm into the theatre, an enthusiasm that the former experiment of the Irish Literary Theatre was

9 Davis, *Non-Violent Sinn Féin*, p.13; Colum, *Griffith*, p.47.

10 'Ioldanacht Airt Ui Ghríofa' ('The versatility of Arthur Griffith'), a talk given by Seán Ó Lúing on Radio Éireann, 7 May 1965. Most of it was published in the magazine, *Comhar* (Baile Atha Cliath, Samhain, 1972), pp.10-12. I would like to thank Mr Ó Lúing for sending me a copy of the lecture.

lacking in'.[11] Colum repeated this point half a century later in an interview. He pointed out that Yeats and Lady Gregory, contrary to the popular view, were not the initiators of the Irish theatre. It was created from the political societies, Cumann na nGaedheal and Inghinidhe na hÉireann, and from the Fay Comedy Group. He stressed that Yeats and Lady Gregory had joined the drama group by invitation, as had Griffith and Maud Gonne.[12]

Colum's account is borne out by evidence from elsewhere. On 13 September 1901, Griffith submitted a scheme to the Celtic Literary Society for Frank Fay to start a drama class. Fay contributed drama criticism to the *United Irishman*.[13] Griffith gave the dramatic movement generous space and support in his newspaper.

He and Maud Gonne became vice-presidents of the INTS, along with Yeats and Lady Gregory. Griffith had high hopes for the new dramatic movement. He proclaimed that the Irish national theatre had been established with the presentation of *Deirdre* and *Cathleen Ni Houlihan*; that the best writers in Ireland had written for it; that the Fays had trained the actors and deserved great praise for their patriotism and diligence, because they had done wonderful work to make the Irish national theatre independent and native.[14]

Maire Ni Shiubhlaigh, who was a member of Inghinidhe na hÉireann and of the INTS, confirmed in her memoirs Colum's version of the genesis of the theatrical movement. She referred to Griffith as one of their 'staunchest friends'.[15] But his involvement in the movement that eventually led to the Abbey Theatre came to an abrupt end with the arrival on the scene of J.M. Synge.

A Parting of the Ways

The unity of the INTS was shattered in late 1903. According to William Thompson, Griffith fell out with Yeats because of the poet's commitment to his theatre to the detriment of his nationalism. Thompson viewed Griffith as intolerant of anything that might divert public attention 'from its proper fixation on his campaign for Irish

11 Colum, *Road*, pp.274-5.

12 Des Smith and Gus Hickey, *A Paler Shade of Green* (London, 1972), p.15. Also, Colum, *Road*, pp.276-7.

13 Ms. 19,934 (i) NLI; Coxhead, *Daughters*, p.49.

14 *United Irishman*, 12 April 1902.

15 Maire Ni Shiubhlaigh, *The Splendid Years: Recollections of Maire Ni Shiubhlaigh as Told to Edward Kenny* (Dublin, 1955), pp.1-12;44.

independence'. Once Ireland was free the nation's literature could be allowed to develop in various directions, but until then, it must serve the cause of freeing the country.[16]

Flannery saw Griffith's views on the function of drama in society as signalling 'unfortunate consequences for the Irish dramatic movement'. He characterised Griffith as both commending the INTS as a national organisation, and at the same time warning Yeats and its members that art must serve nationalism. Yeats was quick to realise that Griffith's idea would ruin what he wanted the Irish dramatic movement to achieve, and he set out to prevent this taking place.

Firstly, he went to work on the structure and membership of the INTS. The Society was very democratic; the full membership voted whether to accept, amend or reject plays. This is evident from Colum and from Ni Shiubhlaigh's memoirs.[17] Many of the members considered the staging of plays as just one aspect of the wider political activity. This may be seen from what happened to two plays submitted to the Society. Lady Gregory's *Twenty Five* was initially rejected because it had an emigrant returning to Ireland with £100, a sum regarded as too large, because it might be seen as encouraging emigration; the amount had to be reduced to £20 before the play was accepted.

The Saxon Shillin' by Colum, a propaganda play against Irish recruitment to the British army, had won first prize in a contest sponsored by Cumann na nGaedheal. It ended with a deserter from the British army being shot by soldiers for defending his father from eviction. Flannery held that Willie Fay changed this ending to make it less melodramatic, but Colum suggested that it was because it had too overt a political message. According to Flannery, Griffith and Maud Gonne objected to the change and, when it was upheld, Maud Gonne resigned from the Society.

Yeats proposed the appointment of a reading committee to decide on plays, and in order to secure this he had to threaten to resign himself in February 1903. 'This gave him a measure of control over the repertoire', Flannery wrote, 'but until the establishment of a limited company in the fall of 1905, with the artistic control absolutely in the hands of Yeats, Synge and Lady Gregory, the "preposterous" [the word was Yeats's] democratic method of approving plays and even roles by a three-

16 W.I. Thompson, *The Imagination of an Insurrection: Dublin, Easter 1916* (New York, 1967), p.69.

17 Colum, *Road*, p.277; Ni Shiubhlaigh, *Splendid Years*, p.21.

quarters vote of the membership continued to allow politics to interfere with art'.[18]

This account is largely in agreement with Colum's recollection, except that Colum claimed that *both* Griffith and Maud Gonne resigned following the row over *The Saxon Shillin'*: 'With the departure of the two vice-presidents, the dramatic society became distinct from the political clubs'. That the dramatic movement mainly originated in these clubs is clear. Yeats had the ambition and strength of character to take it over.

According to Colum, Yeats was admired by the INTS members as 'a great poet, an influential literateur' and a dramatist more concerned with speech than with action, but what they did not suspect was that he was a skilled businessman and gifted organiser and administrator. They did not realise that his whole ambition was to direct the Irish dramatic movement. Colum went on to contend that Yeats

> ...needed a theatre to inaugurate his epoch. He was turning 40 at the time. At that age Shakespeare, Goethe and Ibsen had controlled, each of them, a theatre. He wanted to do more than write plays and have them produced. He wanted to inaugurate a dramatic era.[19]

Yeats presented to the general public his ideas on theatre in a series of lectures and articles. He was portraying himself mainly as a religious dramatist, according to Flannery, 'a product of, and in a sense the spokesman for, the religious sensibility of Ireland'. Flannery commented: 'For a Protestant - particularly a Protestant with his well-known mystical ideas - to make such claims would be dangerous enough in Ireland today. In 1902, it was reckless to the point of being foolhardy'.

Yeats's plea for freedom from religious or political censorship went unheeded, in Flannery's view, because it was being made to people 'whose intellectual development had been restricted by a narrow educational system and by exceptionally conservative forms of both Protestantism and Catholicism'. Even more significantly, he was presenting his case in the face of a political movement whose attitudes, already hardening, were leading to policies 'with a rigidly moralistic tone'.

Yeats's position hardened progressively against the extreme nationalists. Maud Gonne's marriage to John MacBride was one reason for this. 'Now that there was no longer hope of marriage, his raging

18 Flannery, *Yeats and the Idea of a Theatre*, pp.325-6.

19 Colum, *Road*, pp.277-9.

bitterness at the political "fanaticism and hate" that had stolen his love knew no bounds', was how Flannery described it. Another reason was the imminent financial support from a wealthy English admirer of Yeats, Anne Horniman. From the time that his interest in the dramatic movement began, Yeats believed that some form of subsidy would be needed if his ideals were to come to fruition. Flannery believed that Yeats regarded independent financial support as even more essential as a result of the increasing political interference. Horniman had to be given certain guarantees on the role - or more likely non-role - of politics in the INTS.

Flannery concluded that there was a third reason which encouraged Yeats to become tougher with the nationalists - the advent of Synge. Although he had Synge's plays for nearly a year, Yeats bided his time. He made the INTS members curious by dropping hints about a superb dramatist who was soon to join them, a genius whose plays would make them all famous. Looking back some 60 years later, Colum commented that Yeats and Lady Gregory decided that Synge was the only important dramatist they had in Ireland.[20]

20 Smith and Hickey, *Paler Shade*, p.15

Chapter II

The Shadow of Synge

It was over Synge's *The Shadow of the Glen* that the storm first broke. The play tells the story of the marriage between a young woman and an old man who decides to test his wife's fidelity by pretending that he is dead. A tramp comes to the house and the young wife decides to leave her home and join him on the roads. When Lady Gregory read the play to the assembled company of the INTS in her rooms in the Nassau Hotel in Dublin, it was decided to produce it, but not without a general murmur of complaint that it ran contrary to the spirit of the movement.

A prominent actor with the Society, Dudley Digges, and his wife-to-be, Maire Quinn, resigned at what they considered 'an insult to Irish womanhood'. In fact, the division of opinion within the Society over Synge's play led to the resignation of a number of its members.[1] By no means all the unfavourable reaction to Synge came from 'philistines' outside the dramatic movement. Griffith's critical reaction to *The Shadow of the Glen* was negative. It was not unique. Joseph Holloway, architect, inveterate playgoer and drama commentator, was not impressed, as his diary reveals: 'Now, the subject, no matter how literary clad, could never pass with an Irish audience as "a bit of real Irish life"'.[2]

On the day that Synge's work was to receive its first performance, a *United Irishman* article by John Butler Yeats praised the play for attacking 'an Irish institution' - the arranged, loveless marriage. That the play presented arranged, loveless marriages as typical of Ireland Colum regarded as explaining in large measure its hostile reception. He saw this reaction as growing from the burgeoning nationalist self-image, long accustomed to denigration at the hands of the unionist press. Yeats senior declared that the play would show a young woman leaving her house and husband to follow a tramp, and this would sound the death-knell of the type of marriage that was too widespread among the Irish peasantry and which was based on property rather than love.

Colum's comments on this are worth giving in full:

1 Flannery, *Yeats and Idea of a Theatre*, pp.326-32; Ni Shiubhlaigh, *Splendid Years*, p.42.

2 Joseph Holloway, 'Impressions of a Dublin Playgoer', NLI, Ms. 1801 (1903), pp.561,566.

> The article was read by the sort of men and women who were ready to fight for their ideal of Ireland and their ideal did not include a country in which such happenings were celebrated. The readers of John Butler Yeats's article got the notion that Synge was a propagandist for certain alien ideas. In the Ireland of the time, an Ireland that was still being defamed by the unionist press and by innumerable unionist institutions, there was a very ready defence mechanism. Who was John Synge? He was Anglo-Irish; that was certain. He was of the landowning class, the class that raked all that muck about Ireland into English journals and into religio-politico publications.

Looking back many years later, Colum reflected that every country, and especially a country in the position of Ireland in the early 20th century, wishes to project a particular image of itself onto the outer world. Synge was accused of destroying that image. It was unthinkable in those days that an Irish wife would go off with a tramp of the roads.[3]

Griffith was utterly against 'stage-Irishism'. His *United Irishman* regularly attacked the phenomenon. One example lampooned a play called *Muldoon's Picnic*, performed at the Queen's Theatre, Dublin:

> The thing is merely pantomimic, and as a representation of Irish character beneath contempt. Really it is time that the citizens of Dublin, who after all have these matters in their own hands, made a determined stand against this persistent caricaturing and libelling of their nation. If a solid opinion were brought to bear upon the matter, we should soon sweep, out of Ireland anyhow, these wretched freaks which Englishers and American imitators label Irishmen. Let us by all means welcome the healthy and high-toned drama; but we ought to value our self-respect sufficiently to make these manufacturers of brogue and balderdash understand that Irishmen are intelligent enough to discriminate between humour and horseplay.[4]

Ni Shiubhlaigh, the female lead in *The Shadow of the Glen*, said it provoked 'unfounded indignation'. She did not blame Griffith for this but many of the criticisms she cited were his - the play's unIrish nature, its insult to the rural people, its being based on Boccaccio's *Decameron* and on decadent Greek literature. She accounted for this reaction in a manner similar to Colum's: Ireland was on the verge of a renaissance and only the nobility of the Irish character was to be presented to the world. Griffith's condemnation of the play was 'the saddest aspect of

3 Colum, *Road*, pp.359-60; Smith and Hickey, *Paler Shade*, p.16.

4 *United Irishman*, 4 March 1899.

the whole unnecessary controversy', because he 'had hitherto been one of our staunchest friends'.[5]

Synge's biographers, D.H. Greene and E.M. Stephens, submitted Griffith's reaction to the play to detailed scrutiny. Their assessment seems fair and accurate. They thought that the stark realism of *The Shadow of the Glen* and Yeats's cold regard for what he considered philistinism were bound to be attacked in an atmosphere so charged with political feeling. They pointed out that the *Irish Independent* struck even before the play had a chance to be heard, while the *United Irishman* at least waited for it to be performed before attacking.

In his review, Griffith attacked Yeats for indulging the feelings of 'West Britons'. He upbraided him for publishing favourable reviews from the British press in his magazine, *Samhain*, and for taking his company to England. Griffith denounced the play as unIrish, as being based on the *Decameron* and on the decadent Greek story the *Widow of Ephesus*, as libelling Irish women, and as being unrealistic in that nobody like the tramp or the wife ever really existed in Ireland.

Yeats's response, printed in the *United Irishman* the following week, attacked the ignorance of the politician who would reject every idea not of immediate use to his cause, and proclaimed that his theatre would have no propaganda save that of good art. To this Griffith responded that a theatre which would produce good art but not propaganda had no right to call itself Irish or national. He implied that Synge, who lived mainly outside Ireland, had succumbed to foreign influence and represented, no doubt in good faith, adultery as a feature of Irish rural life and held up women's frailty to laughter.

Synge saw the weakness in Yeats's position: the word 'national' in his theatre implied that it was playing a part in the evolving destiny of Ireland itself. 'Yeats was willing to harness his theatre to the nationalists' bandwagon when he needed their help, but now that Miss Horniman was waiting with a purse full of English pounds, he could not be blamed for wanting to save himself and his theatre for what any artist would call a higher destiny than writing propaganda for revolutionaries', declared Greene and Stephens.

Griffith's inimical attitude to *The Shadow of the Glen* was eclipsed by the far more extensive opposition to *The Playboy of the Western World* in 1907. Although Griffith's paper was read by few 'outside the small circle of extreme nationalists', Yeats realised that his influence, however small,

5 Ni Shiubhlaigh, *Splendid Years*, pp.41-4.

was likely to do damage, 'if he were allowed to alienate nationalist sympathy from Synge's work'.[6]

Flannery, in his treatment of Griffith's reaction to *The Shadow of the Glen*, recounted how Maud Gonne and Dudley Digges staged a conspicuous walk-out on the play's opening night, and that Gonne and James Connolly[7] both supported Griffith in the pages of the *United Irishman*. In succeeding issues of that paper 'the controversy raged, with Griffith and Yeats exchanging blow for blow', Flannery wrote, the climax being reached when the two men put forward their definitions of a nationalist. Yeats declared that he regarded himself as a nationalist and defined that type of person as 'one who is prepared to give up a great deal that he may preserve to his country whatever part of her possessions he is best fitted to guard'. Griffith, to use Lyons's words, 'had no difficulty in disposing of this equivocal definition', when he replied: 'He who is prepared to give up a great deal for his country is no doubt a good man, but unless he is prepared to give up all, we do not deem him a nationalist'.

Although Griffith conceded that Yeats was sincere in his nationalism, he saw a basic flaw in his opponent's position:

> Mr Yeats does not give any reason why, if the Irish National Theatre now has no propaganda save that of good art, it should continue to call itself either Irish or national. If the theatre be solely an art theatre, then its plays can only be fairly criticised from the standpoint of art. But whilst it calls itself Irish National, its productions must be considered and criticised as Irish National productions.

The poet's counter-definition of 'national' literature as 'the work of writers who are moulded by influences that are moulding their country, and who write out of so deep a life that they are accepted there in the end', did not satisfy Yeats himself, so that it could hardly have been found adequate by Griffith.[8]

Flannery argued that Griffith's opposition could reasonably be justified from the political standpoint of what he was trying to achieve. Griffith believed that Ireland's shortcomings at the time, especially her economic ones, could in part be attributed to English domination, but

6 D.H. Greene and E.M. Stephens, *J.M. Synge 1871-1909* (New York, 1959), pp.145-53,175-8.

7 Confused with the Labour leader by Flannery, but correctly identified by Lyons as Griffith's friend, the literary critic Seamus O'Connolly. Lyons, *Famine*, p.242.

8 F.S.L. Lyons, *Culture and Anarchy in Ireland 1890-1939* (Oxford, 1978), pp.67-8.

Griffith and Collins in a jovial mood, January-June 1922

were also the result of the failure of the Irish people themselves to embrace a common feeling of responsibility, determination and dignity. Griffith could see this clearly, as could far-seeing unionists like Horace Plunkett and Lord Dunraven, as well as Yeats himself. 'All sought to create programmes based upon a proud spirit of nationalism that would motivate practical action for the good of Ireland as a whole', Flannery wrote.

Some accounts of the controversy would have us believe Griffith and his followers were the only opponents of Synge's play in 1903. Reference to the *Irish Independent* (middle-class Catholics) and the *Irish Times* (ascendancy and upper middle-class Protestants) of the period disprove this. They strongly objected to the 'unwholesome' and 'excessively distasteful' nature of *The Shadow of the Glen*. Flannery thought this understandable in that the work was one of the least satisfactory of Synge's dramas, 'a problem play with a solution to the problem that could not hope to be acceptable in either Catholic or Protestant Ireland'.[9]

For any kind of appreciation of Griffith's reaction to the play, the context of the battle against the 'stage Irishman' has to be taken into account. His condemnation of the *Shadow* as unIrish, unrealistic, an insult to rural dwellers, and a plagiarism from decadent Greek

9 Flannery, *Yeats and Idea of a Theatre*, pp.333-4.

literature was consistent with this approach. A corollary of this hostility to stage Irishness was the desire to see the higher virtues of the nation exalted on the Irish stage, and particularly on the stage of a theatre which called itself an 'Irish national' theatre. To Griffith, national drama meant moulding public sentiment against British rule. For him, *Cathleen ni Houlihan* represented the ideal, because it portrayed the image of heroic self-sacrifice. This can be seen clearly in his and Yeats's conflicting definitions of what constituted a nationalist.

Playboy Pandemonium

Synge's *Playboy of the Western World* provoked a much stormier reaction, both inside and outside the theatre. Some newspaper comments on the subject, on the 80th anniversary of its first production,[10] might incline one to believe that Griffith was the play's leading and harshest critic. According to Joseph Holloway, the *Playboy* broke up in confusion on the first night because of 'the coarseness of the dialogue'. He continued:

> I maintain that this play...is not a truthful or just picture of the Irish peasants, but simply the outpourings of a morbid, unhealthy mind ever seeking on the dunghill of life for the nastiness that lies concealed there....Synge is the evil genius of the Abbey and Yeats is his able lieutenant. Both dabble in the unhealthy.[11]

Greene and Stephens, who described Griffith as Synge's 'nemesis', recorded how he called the *Playboy* 'a vile and inhuman story told in the foulest language we have ever listened to from a public platform'. They suggested that the opposition to the play sprang from the fact that 'a resurgent Ireland would no longer passively accept the caricature known to generations of theatregoers as the stage Irishman, especially when it was offered to them on the stage of a theatre they wanted to think of as a national theatre'. But the Abbey was not a national theatre. Greene and Stephens preferred to see it as 'the personal property of an Englishwoman who was antipathetic to Irish nationalism and merely wanted to further the career of W.B. Yeats'. The Abbey's playwrights insisted on presenting the Irish peasant as they saw him and not as they were expected to see him, according to Greene and Stephens, who offered the following balanced assessment:

10 Tomas MacAnna, 'Synge and the first Abbey row', *Irish Times*, 26 January 1987; S.J.L. 'Window on the past', *Irish Press*, 2 February 1987; Michéal Ó hAodha, 'Poet and peasant?', *Irish Times*, 14 March 1987.

11 Holloway, 'Impressions', Ms.1805 (i), NLI, (1907), pp.63-4,72-4.

> Reduced to its essentials, the story of the riots is the story of a clash between two groups of dedicated people. Arthur Griffith and the other nationalist leaders were not philistines, even if they did bear the chief responsibility for the opposition to Synge and Yeats. No doubt they attempted quite clearly to absorb every movement and organisation in Ireland into their own orbit, because they believed that the effort to establish a free Ireland would be strengthened if every activity which touched the people could be drawn into the struggle. Like politicians everywhere, they were quite literal in demanding that if Irish writers could not be eulogistic of what was called the national character, they should at least not be critical.[12]

R.J. Loftus was less tolerant: Sinn Féin's 'vitriolic campaign against *The Playboy of the Western World* represented a low point in the national movement'. Loftus believed Yeats was justified in condemning those 'responsible for the narrow and cruel attacks upon Synge'. They were '"Paudeens" who, when confronted by an image of great passionate art, whether Don Juan in Hell or Christy Mahon in a village in Co. Mayo, could only "rail and sweat/ Staring upon his sinewy thigh"'.[13]

Similarly, Thompson had little sympathy for Griffith's attitude: he was 'one of the most vigorous and outspoken' opponents of the *Playboy*. Although thorough in his review of the play, and not modest in his claims as a literary critic, his programme was one of 'internal self-reliance', part of which was never to acknowledge or utilise 'the services or forces of the enemy'. By calling in the police to protect the play, Yeats had 'sinned most grievously'. Thompson quoted Griffith's reaction to this use of the occupying power: 'On Tuesday this story of unnatural murder and unnatural lust, told in foul language, was told under the protection of a body of police and concluded to the strains of "God Save the King"'.

Yeats's period as 'a popular Irish nationalist' came to an end, in Thompson's view, when he employed Trinity students to cheer the play, when he spoke about the people in the stalls as having superior taste to the ruffians in the pit, and when he 'lectured about the freedom of art while ordering in the police'. There was no doubt about Griffith's opinion, as evident from the following passage from *Sinn Féin*:

> As to his country, Mr Yeats claimed on Monday night that he had served it, and the claim is just. He served it unselfishly in the past. He

12 Greene and Stephens, *Synge*, pp.245,250-1.

13 R.J. Loftus, *Nationalism and Modern Anglo-Irish Poetry* (Madison and Milwaukee, 1964), p.14.

> has ceased to serve it now - to our regret. It is not the nation that has changed towards Mr Yeats - it is Mr Yeats who has changed towards the nation.

Thompson noted Griffith's satisfaction that the Gaelic League and other patriotic groups were establishing a theatre that would be genuinely national, and that 'the Abbey would be left to serve the same function for Ireland that the sewers do for Dublin'. This mode of attack was new, according to Thompson, and caused Yeats to think long about its 'shrillness'. This 'quality of a movement impelled by hatred' gave the poet food for thought; he lacked the ability 'to lock the will in a single-minded fixation upon one thing', in contrast to Griffith, who had 'enormous will-power in this respect'. Thompson regarded 'this single-mindedness, and its resultant petrification of the heart' as a flaw, although not one confined to Griffith alone.[14]

To characterise Griffith as motivated by shrill hatred is too convenient, and is identical to the censure levelled at him and his movement by Yeats himself. Griffith's motivations were more considered and complex than that. P.S. O'Hegarty said that once he admitted someone to his friendship, nothing could shake him except what he regarded as reneging the cause. 'He lived for Ireland, and he was merciless in his writings about those who were false to her or who, even honestly, injured her'. Sean-Ghall described this phenomenon cogently:

> He toiled terribly in poverty and in hunger, and had a profound contempt for any doctrines or ideals that did not find expression in hard work....Griffith believed, wrongly many of us thought and told him so, that art for art's sake was pure humbug, that all literature and science and history and art were but the handmaidens of nationality, and that if they were not teamed for forced labour in its cause, they were worthless....He parted from some of the greatest creative minds [of his time] on this and allied grounds.[15]

James Kilroy placed the reaction to the *Playboy* within the context of the campaign against the stage Irishman, the 'hypersensitivity' of the nationalists 'to any questioning of their nation's virtues', the differing conceptions of a national theatre, and the limits, or lack of them, on artistic licence. Kilroy wrote:

> Much of the discussion voiced in the editorials, letters and public

14 Thompson, *Imagination of an Insurrection*, pp.69-71.

15 O'Hegarty, *Sunday Independent*, 12 August 1945; Sean-Ghall, Ms.23,516 NLI.

statements stems from disagreement over just what a national theatre should be. To the nationalist, the issues were simple: a national theatre should serve as an instrument of propaganda; clearly this production was not flattering to Ireland; it must, then, be anti-Irish. Even to those less committed to political causes, it seemed irrational for the directors of what called itself a national theatre to persist in showing a play which the leading newspapers and most of the audience found repulsive. Those arguments that a playwright should serve his audience and not defy its opinions are all too familiar today. Finally, there occurs in these discussions the still unresolved question of the author's licence both in using realistic but shocking language and in frankly treating distasteful subjects. In other words, the issues raised are central questions of literary criticism and aesthetics.

Kilroy reviewed and gave detailed extracts from the main newspapers of the day. They convey the universal rejection, condemnation and outrage the play provoked. The *Independent* described Christy Mahon as 'a familiar and insulting stock character'. Such a portrayal was likely to evoke fury from the young nationalists because 'one of their campaigns had been directed against the offensive Paddys so common in popular English plays'.[16]

In a hurried interview with the *Evening Mail*, while the play was in progress, Synge was asked if he had thought beforehand about how the public would receive his play. He replied: 'I never thought about it. It does not matter a rap. I wrote the play because it pleased me, and it just happens that I know Irish life best, so I made my methods Irish'.

This inspired Griffith to write the satirical rejoinder 'The Fable of the Fiddler'; the story of a fiddler who set up a booth at a fair and proclaimed that his was 'the only genuine Irish music'. When a character called the 'Irish Public' paid to hear him play, he was subjected to a dreadful cacophony, but when he protested that this was not Irish music, he was told he was an 'ignoramus', who knew nothing about Ireland or art. When the Irish Public begged the Fiddler to play 'The Coulin' or 'The Fair Hills of Ireland', he was berated as an 'impudent, ignorant, interrupting illiterate imbecile', and asked did he not know that it was the fiddler who called the tune.

The Fiddler continued to play; when the Irish Public could stand it no longer and implored him to stop, the police were summoned, to whom the Irish Public was described as 'an organised interrupter'. The police joyfully stood guard, while the Fiddler's rasping tune caused his listener's teeth to chatter, whereupon his arrest was demanded. The

16 James Kilroy, *The 'Playboy' Riots* (Dublin, 1971) pp.5-6,7-9,11-13

Irish Public was dragged off and put in jail, while the Fiddler cried 'hurrah for freedom!', and the moral of the story was - 'This is Ireland'.[17]

Kilroy also provided extracts from a Yeats interview in the *Freeman's Journal*, where he saw the main issue as 'the freedom of the theatre', and contemptuously dismissed his opponents as people with 'no books in their houses'. Holloway was greatly angered at Yeats's use of the police and the diligence with which he pursued the prosecution of protesters.[18] This caused the *Freeman* to dub the play 'the police-protected drama', and it reported on Yeats's prosecution of Piaras Béaslaí.

Kilroy wrote that 'the accusation of the disturbances being organised was never proven'. Yeats insisted that it was an organised campaign, and even Flannery referred to Griffith 'leading an organised attempt' to drive the play from the stage.[19] In a *Sinn Féin* editorial, Griffith denied that the opposition was organised. He wrote that the Abbey invited the opinion of the public, and when that proved unfavourable, 'invited the aid of Dublin Castle to crush its expression'. He then asked what the directors meant by 'freedom'. As applied to the press, he argued that it did not mean 'licence to publish obscenity or licence to libel with impunity', but such seemed to be the understanding of the Abbey management.[20]

Kilroy pointed out that Sinn Féin's attack was mild when compared with the *Freeman's Journal* and the *Leader*. The latter saw the Abbey's 'freedom of judgement' as 'a misnomer for freedom of slander and for freedom for hurling obscene insults at the peasants of Mayo'. The play was a 'Triumph of the Grotesque', which selected for treatment 'filial affection, the sacredness of life, and the modesty of women'. Yeats and Synge 'claim that their works are unsuited for the common air; they are precious plants and need the neurotic atmosphere of the Abbey in which to thrive'.[21]

It is important to note that Griffith wrote so little on the *Playboy* in contrast to his large output on *The Shadow of the Glen*. His central purpose was to show that such plays were not appropriate performances for a theatre which called itself the Irish national theatre. He fought the battle over the first production, and, by the time of the *Playboy*, must have decided that the fight was a futile one.

17 *Sinn Féin*, 9 February 1907, reprinted in Kilroy, *'Playboy' Riots*, pp.94-6.

18 Holloway, 'Impressions' Ms. 1805 (i), NLI (1907) pp.79-80.

19 W.B. Yeats, *Explorations* (London, 1962), p.114; Flannery, *Yeats and Idea of a Theatre*, p.335; Kilroy, *op. cit.*, pp.32,35-6,51.

20 Kilroy, *op. cit.*, pp.65-7.

21 *ibid.*, pp.68-71.

Vale Synge

Colum thought Griffith 'persistently and consistently wrong' in his attitude to Synge.[22] Yet, when Griffith reviewed *Riders to the Sea* in *Sinn Féin*, he stated that 'its tragic beauty powerfully affected the audience'. (Greene and Stephens were unique among literary historians in referring to his praise for *Riders*.) Although he was less than enthusiastic about Synge's *Well of the Saints*, he did find passages of lyrical beauty in the play.[23] Synge was only in his late thirties when he died in 1909. In a valediction, Griffith described *Riders to the Sea* as his greatest play, the playwright himself as 'a potentially great dramatist', and the *Playboy* as concealing 'the sufferings of a man who was brave enough to bear them without seeking sympathy from the world, or even from his friends'.[24] But though he had some good things to say of Synge, they hardly redressed the balance of his sharp criticism of the great playwright. While his views may be understood in terms of what he wished to achieve, the blindness to Synge's art is hard to understand in one who possessed such literary skills and perception.

Criticism which dismissed Griffith's reaction to the *Shadow* and the *Playboy* as mere middle-class philistinism[25] should not be given too much weight. It is flawed in a number of ways. One is that it ignores the origin of the dramatic movement which led eventually to the Abbey Theatre and of which Griffith was an intrinsic part. A second is that it is simplistic and assertive, ignoring the complexity of the issues and arguments involved, and ascribing all opposition to shrill hatred.

A third is that it is polemical, labelling Yeats's and Synge's opponents as philistines, hacks, bigots and obscurantists. A fourth would be its vagueness, such as that Griffith was the main spokesman for the morals and mores of the early 20th-century Irish middle class; that he was an 'extremist'; that his newspapers spent their time attacking Yeats, Synge and the Abbey Theatre; that he preached 'a vague creed of sentimentality and puritanism', and so on.

Quite apart from how much more attention was given to other issues, *Sinn Féin* was unusual among newspapers of early 1907 in publishing a

22 Colum, *Road*, p.302.

23 *Sinn Féin*, 5 March 1904; Greene and Stephens, *Synge*, p.159; *Sinn Féin*, 11 February 1905.

24 *Sinn Féin*, 3 April 1909.

25 Loftus, *Nationalism in Anglo-Irish Poetry*, pp.9-11,14,42,44,199-200; Peter Costello, *The Heart Grown Brutal: The Irish Revolution in Literature, from Parnell to the Death of Yeats, 1891-1939* (Dublin, 1977), pp.40-41.

letter in defence of the *Playboy.* The paper contained many articles and letters lamenting Yeats's loss to the national cause, and in support and praise of him.[26]

Cast a Cold Eye

What of Griffith and Yeats following their differences over Synge's drama? It would seem that the poet was deeply wounded and never forgave Griffith. Many years afterwards, in his book *Dramatis Personae*, Yeats referred to Griffith as the 'slanderer of Lane and Synge'.[27] Sir Hugh Lane, nephew of Lady Gregory, was an art collector. For much of 1913, Dublin was agitated about a suitable site for a building to house his valuable collection of paintings which he had offered as a gift to the city.

Griffith supported Lane's efforts to house his collection in Dublin and was warm in his praise of him. He was, however, critical of the art collector's fastidiousness about a site and at one point accused him of publicity seeking. He also said that Lane acquired his knighthood on the foot of his 'gift' which he then withdrew. Such suggestions were certainly unworthy, but Griffith's role in the complex affair amounted to a lot more than mere 'slander'.[28]

Yeats found it difficult to say anything good about Griffith after their dispute. In one of his last poems, 'The Municipal Gallery Revisited', written some 30 years after the time of their clashes, he described the portrait which hung in the Gallery of his erstwhile opponent and one-time collaborator as 'Griffith staring in hysterical pride'.

On the other hand, the respect that Griffith had for Yeats as a poet never diminished. When he was in Gloucester Jail in 1918, he commemorated Yeats's birthday (13 June) with a dinner and oration, in which he praised him highly as the greatest Irish poet who ever lived. One of Yeats's biographers, J.M. Hone, stated that Griffith was willing to forget the things that had happened between them.[29]

That Griffith's esteem for Yeats remained high was evidenced from

26 See, for example, *Sinn Féin*, 9 February 1907; 26 September 1908; 22 December 1906; 6 November 1909.

27 W.B. Yeats, *Dramatis Personae* (London, 1936), p.39.

28 *United Irishman*, 17 December 1904; *Sinn Féin*, 25 January 1908; 3 August 1912; 9 November 1912; 30 November 1912; 25 January 1913; 8 February 1913; 22 March 1913; 19 April 1913; 28 July 1913; 9, 16, 30 August 1913; 13, 20, 27 September 1913; 4, 11, 25 October 1913.

29 Ó Lúing, *Ó Gríofa*, pp.148-9.

the suggestions for the first Dáil he managed to get smuggled out from Gloucester in January 1919. One of these was that the poets be mobilised in the cause, and he expressed the hope that Yeats 'would use his muse for Ireland now'.[30] Yeats was one of Griffith's nominees for the first Senate of the Irish Free State. In a speech in the Senate, in March 1923, Yeats showed that some, at least, of the anger had abated:

> I was on many points deeply opposed to Mr Arthur Griffith during his lifetime on matters connected with the arts, but time has justified him on the great issue that most concerns us all. He was a man with the most enduring courage and the most steadfast will. I have good reason for knowing how enduring his courage was. For many years, at least two or three years, before the end, it must have seemed to him that he was carrying on an almost hopeless struggle, and when the final crisis came, he showed himself a man of particular value to this country, if it were only in this, that when the final test came he gave his faith, not to an abstract theory, but to a conception of this historical nation - and we are all theory-mad. On that point he kept himself thoroughly sane, and we therefore owe to his memory great honour - honour that will always be paid by this country.[31]

30 'Important letter of 1919', *Capuchin Annual*, 1969, p.334.

31 Ms. 23,516 NLI.

Chapter III

Deserters, Humourists and Exiles

What was Arthur Griffith's relationship with some of the other literati of his day? Colum described Griffith as an exclusive person who judged men and women by their readiness to work impersonally for Irish freedom; 'as soon as one whom he thought had such a dedication faltered, [he] was no longer cordial to him or her'.[1]

One such was T.W. Rolleston, a graduate of Trinity College Dublin and a brilliant linguist. Rolleston, like Yeats, was an admirer of the old Fenian, John O'Leary. He was a member of the CLS for a time[2], but soon withdrew from the nationalist scene. When the Boer War broke out, he wrote a pamphlet defending Britain and recommending that the Irish support the Empire. Griffith thereafter generally referred to him as 'Mr Rollingstone'. He was eventually employed as a translator in the British Intelligence Service.

In a letter to Lily Williams from Reading Jail in November 1916, Griffith referred to him as a cultured person with a great knowledge of the Irish language and went on:

> He lives not far from here and is doing his best for the Empire he loves, at a low war-salary. He censors all the books relating to Ireland which are sent for or applied for by the rebel prisoners here, and advises what should be scored out, and furthermore he supplies the government with biographical notes from his personal and private knowledge of the senders and of those to whom they refer in their letters. This valuable labour far transcends in value the payment he receives for it, for many would object to do such work at any price and apply the ugliest of names to those who did it. But those who are aware that the cause of the British Empire is greater than mere conventions of honour, morality and gentlemanliness will appreciate the good work. I do not suppose you ever met Mr Rolleston. He banished himself from Ireland in the 1460th year after the miracle of St Patrick.[3]

1 Colum, *Griffith*, p.74.

2 Ms. 19,934 (i) NLI.

3 Ms. 5943 NLI.

Griffith greatly admired the mystic, poet and painter, George William Russell (AE). In a letter to AE (16 December 1905), thanking him for a subscription to the *United Irishman*, Griffith wrote: 'I am exceedingly glad of your letter, for you are one of the men whose good opinion I sincerely value'. During the strike and lockout in Dublin in 1913, AE became deeply involved on the side of the workers. He then committed a fatal error in Griffith's eyes. This was when he went to England to express thanks for the foodship which had been sent to Dublin by some of the English trade unions. In *Sinn Féin*, Griffith wrote:

> Mr George Russell is on the road to become one with Rolleston and Yeats. On Saturday night he appeared before the Great British Public and told it that the generosity of England to Ireland had obliterated the memory of many an ancient tale of wrong. When shall we hear of a Polish nationalist going to St Petersburg to denounce one section of his countrymen before the nation which oppresses all sections and to tell the tyrants that the amount of coal, biscuits and jam they have sent to Poland to keep civil strife alive there in Russia's interest has obliterated the memory of the treacherous destruction of Poland as an independent nation...? It was thus Rolleston began and Yeats ended in John Bull's bosom. Russell is and always was an infinitely better man and better Irishman than either and the road they travelled is no ground for his feet.

In an article in *Nationality*, in January 1916, entitled 'Down among the dead men', Griffith returned to the same theme:

> Rolleston and Yeats, Hannay and Lynd, these are the dead men. It was not in them in the ultimate to become other than they have become, but it was in the man Russell. For the souls of the others few Irishmen will ever breathe a prayer hereafter; but for the dead soul of Russell we can all pray a resurrection.[4]

Griffith's attitude to the poet and playwright Oscar Wilde certainly did not smack of the prudishness some claimed to detect in him. In a review of a play called *The Degenerates*, by a Mr Grundy, Griffith wrote:

> When will the hack-writers of the English stage cease to give us reminiscences of Mr Oscar Wilde? With all his faults, his plays were literature, and his paradoxes were winged shafts that pierced the joints in the armour of self-conceit, not lumps of platitude thrown, like mud, to stick.

When Wilde died in 1900, Griffith described him as 'one of the most

4 Ms. 10,872 NLI; *Sinn Féin*, 8 November 1913; *Nationality*, 29 January 1916.

brilliant Irishmen' of the previous century, and castigated the 'highly moral' Dublin newspapers for only printing of his death in their back-columns: 'It was not because Wilde was a sinner that our cowardly journals kept silence - it was because they feared to shock the fetid consciences of pharsaical England'.

About a year later, he attacked the hypocrisy of Hawkins St Theatre and the *Irish Independent* for failing to give the name of the author of *The Importance of Being Earnest*: 'Oscar Wilde is dead. He was the brilliant son of a great Irishwoman. Whatever his sin, it is not for the press or the public to judge him, and the suppression of his name from a theatrical playbill or in a newspaper notice of it is the meanest form of hypocrisy we can imagine'.[5]

James Stephens, poet and novelist, was a close friend of Griffith. Griffith 'discovered' him and published his early prose and poetry in *Sinn Féin*. The two became close associates. Stephens joined Sinn Féin and wrote a poem, 'Epithalamium', celebrating Griffith's marriage. When Griffith died, Stephens praised the Sinn Féin movement, along with the Gaelic League, as 'the two essential forces in the creation of modern Ireland'. Loftus professed bewilderment concerning the enduring friendship between Griffith and Stephens. In part, this incomprehension was due to the misconception that Griffith was humourless, and that therefore he should not have been friendly with an author who treated the old Irish legends so comically. Loftus purported to discern many similarities between Stephens's and Synge's work, and wondered why Griffith could not see the affinities. Because he had no real understanding of literature, attacked Synge to get at Yeats, and had no real moral scruples about Synge's treatment of Irish women or peasants, was how Loftus answered his own question.[6]

So hostile a speculation is almost too unbalanced to be believed. Griffith's understanding of literature is well documented. His criticism of Yeats was never personal; it arose from his perception that the poet's outstanding ability made him so irreplaceable a loss to the nationalist cause. Synge's *Shadow* was condemned by Griffith as 'a libel on Irish womanhood', and this was why he so tenaciously defended the parallel he saw between the play and the *Widow of Ephesus*. He did not idealise the west of Ireland rural dwellers in the way that some of the writers of the Irish literary renaissance did, but he thought that Synge's *Shadow* and *Playboy* treated them in a stock, stage-Irish fashion.

Griffith gave the novelist James Joyce one of the earliest press notices

5 *United Irishman*, 20 October 1900, 8 December 1900, 30 November 1901.

6 Loftus, *Nationalism in Anglo-Irish Poetry*, pp.200-201, 203-7, 212-13.

W.T. Cosgrave gives the graveside oration at Griffith's funeral, August 1922

he received. This concerned a privately published pamphlet by Joyce on the Irish Literary Theatre called 'The Day of the Rabblement'. Griffith disagreed with his criticism of that theatre but commended him for having the courage to express his views despite the censorship which would not allow them to appear in *St Stephen's*, the official publication of University College, Dublin.[7]

In 1902, Griffith published the collected poems and ballads of his recently deceased friend, William Rooney. Joyce reviewed the publication for the *Daily Express*. He attacked them for being derivative and 'full of tears and curses...And yet [Rooney] might have written well if he had not suffered from one of those big words which make us so unhappy'. In response Griffith quoted some of the review in an advertisement in the *United Irishman*, and after 'big words' he added 'Patriotism'. Richard Ellmann, Joyce's biographer, remarked that this was a stroke Joyce himself could admire, although he himself was the target.

From then on, according to Ellmann, Joyce followed Griffith's activities closely. A few years later, in a letter to his brother Stanislaus, he praised Griffith for being the only one to revive the separatist ideal in their generation. In her soliloquy in the final section of Joyce's novel *Ulysses*, Molly Bloom complains about her husband: 'he was going about with some of them Sinner Féin lately or whatever they call

7 *United Irishman*, 2 November 1901.

themselves talking his usual trash and nonsense he says that little man he showed me without the neck is very intelligent the coming man Griffith is he well he doesn't look it that's all I can say still it must have been him he knew there was a boycott...'

In a letter to his brother in 1906, Joyce asserted that a recent speech in Dublin by Griffith had justified the existence of his newspaper. One of the things advocated by Griffith in this speech was the boycott of English goods mentioned in Molly's speech above. When one thinks of politics in relation to Joyce one thinks of his regret for the loss of Parnell, but Ellmann has shown that he was a supporter of Griffith's programme.

He believed that the time for parliamentary agitation, of the type espoused by Parnell, was over and that an economic boycott was likely to prove more effective. He did not like the extremist wing of Sinn Féin, satirising it in *Ulysses* in the character of the Citizen whose battle-cry, 'Sinn Féin amháin' ('Ourselves alone'), was a stick used to beat anyone he did not like. But Griffith's moderate policy and approach appealed to Joyce.

There were other reasons for Joyce's admiration of Griffith. In September 1911, Griffith published a letter from him in Trieste complaining of the difficulty he had with two publishers, Grant Richards of London and Maunsel of Dublin. Both had given him written contracts that they would publish *Dubliners*, but both subsequently refused unless he altered passages referring to Edward VII in the story 'Ivy Day in the Committee Room'.[8] Joyce had sent copies of his letter to all the newspapers in Dublin. Only two published it, and only Griffith risked a libel action by publishing it in full.

The following year, when Joyce was in Dublin, he sought and received Griffith's help against the behind-the-scenes manoeuvrings of an Irish publisher, again in relation to *Dubliners*. On this trip also, he acquired two of Griffith's recent pamphlets on the third Home Rule Bill which was being debated in parliament at the time. Joyce repaid Griffith's support by mentioning him more times than any other politician in *Ulysses*. The 'hero' of the novel, Leopold Bloom, is Hungarian, a fact which caused Joyce to relate him to Griffith's programme. One of the characters, Martin Cunningham, says that Bloom gave Griffith the idea of the Hungarian system.

Some of the references to Griffith are humorous, especially in Molly Bloom's closing soliloquy. She is afraid that her husband might lose his job with the *Freeman's Journal*: 'we'll have him coming home with the sack soon out of the *Freeman* too like the rest on account of those Sinner Féin or the Freemasons then we'll see if the little man he

8 *Sinn Féin*, 2 September 1911.

showed me dribbling along in the wet all by himself round by Coady's Lane will give him much consolation that he says is so capable and sincerely Irish he is indeed judging by the sincerity of the trousers I saw on him...'

Joyce was completing *Ulysses* in early January 1922 at the time Griffith was elected President of the Dáil. Joyce could not and did not resist this coincidence, according to Ellmann. The references to Griffith in the final chapter of the novel are very deliberate as Joyce wished to honour his finally successful efforts. This was how Ellmann expressed the conjuncture:

> Ireland was achieving independence just as *Ulysses* was achieving publication. The political emancipation of Ireland had been accomplished by his old ally Griffith, and the emancipation of its conscience - Joyce's own lifetime's work - was also approaching culmination. Bloom's sometime socialism, and Joyce's sometime socialism and anarchism, are put behind in order to hail, in Joyce's own fashion, the new country and the political leader to whom he felt most closely allied.[9]

Costello dismissed the idea of Joyce admiring Griffith. This was only to be expected given Costello's hostile perception of Griffith's role in the literary controversies of the time but his evidence for driving a broad wedge between the two Dubliners was extremely dubious. Vituperation and rant were all Griffith was capable of according to Costello.[10] But if any Irish nationalist of that generation provides evidence of the 'hard thought' Costello found so lacking at the time, it is Griffith.His newspapers and pamphlets are full of detailed, well thought-out schemes, such as a solution to the Dublin slum problem, a conciliation system for labour disputes, industrial projects, afforestation plans, suggestions for arbitration courts, cooperative banks and so on.

R.M. Fox and Nicholas Mansergh referred to Griffith as a man who had no time for poets and who regarded them as somewhat mad.[11] Nothing could be further from the truth. At an early stage in his career as an editor, he declared that in all civilised societies people should spend half their time reading, understanding and writing poetry. And many

9 Richard Ellmann, *James Joyce* (New York, 1959; paperback edition, 1983, cited in notes), pp.237-9,334-5. Also, Richard Ellmann, *The Consciousness of Joyce* (London, 1977), pp.86-9.

10 Costello, *Heart Grown Brutal*, pp.56-8,67,186-7,188.

11 R.M. Fox, *Green Banners: The Story of the Irish Struggle* (London, 1938), p.68; Nicholas Mansergh, *The Irish Question 1840-1921* (London, 1940; revised edition, 1966, cited in notes), p.262.

years later, when he was making suggestions for activities by the first Dáil, he urged that the poets be mobilised in the cause.[12]

It was because he had such a deep respect for creative writers, and appreciated the enormous power they could wield, that he wished to harness them to the cause of freeing their country. It was because he realised Yeats's profound potential to the full that he clashed so vehemently with him. He felt his loss, and that of others like Lynd and Russell especially, in an acutely personal way. So devoted and single-minded was he in his commitment to his country that he could not understand or forgive what he perceived as a shirking of duty in others.

But ultimately he must be adjudged wrong, as one of his oldest and closest friends, Sean-Ghall, said he was, to have held that literature was but the handmaiden of nationality, and was worthless unless it served faithfully in that cause. Creative minds cannot be circumscribed in that way. Many writers remained his friends to the end, but the loss of the others he must have felt sorely.

12 'Important letter of 1919', *Capuchin Annual*, p.334.

Part VI

Constructive Friend or Destructive Foe: The Debate about Griffith's Relations with Irish Labour

'There is no greater existent danger to civilisation than the growth of capitalism, the accumulation of the world's wealth - or what men are pleased to consider wealth, and starve amidst plenty for lack of - in the hands of a few, and a cataclysm similar to that which overturned the Roman Empire awaits civilisation if the aggregation of wealth and power by the few... proceeds unchecked'.

United Irishman, 28 May 1904

Chapter I

The Cause of Ireland is the Cause of Labour

As a propagandist on behalf of Irish nationalism, Griffith paid close attention to the role of Labour in the struggle for independence. He was in contact with Labour activists throughout his public life.

Nowhere has Griffith been more harshly criticised than by some Labour historians. They have been more damaging to his reputation than his most hostile anti-Treaty critics. Many of them, though not all, have written from a Marxist viewpoint. What has been most controversial about their depiction of Griffith is their portrayal of him as a racist, an imperialist and an anti-Semite. Despite skimpy, contradictory and inconclusive evidence, they have had no hesitation in judging and damning him.

Contact, Joint Action, and Agreement to Differ

James Connolly arrived in Dublin in 1896, on the invitation of a small group of socialists in the city, and shortly afterwards formed the Irish Socialist Republican Party (ISRP). There is ample evidence of contact, interaction, cooperation - and disagreement - between Griffith and the Dublin socialists. Two prominent Dublin socialists, Fred Ryan and T.J. Lyng, were members of the CLS. At the end of November 1896, for example, Ryan spoke to the motion 'That socialism is consistent with Irish nationality', at a CLS meeting. Connolly attended a number of such gatherings. Griffith's *United Irishman* gave coverage to ISRP meetings. One such report, of September 1899, referred to 'an eloquent speech by Mr James Connolly'.[1] When the Boer War broke out, the Irish-Transvaal Committee was formed, with Griffith and Connolly as members. George A. Lyons, a member of the Committee, of the CLS and the IRB, recalled a vigorous demonstration against the visit of the Colonial Secretary, Joseph Chamberlain, to Dublin late in 1899. This involved Connolly and E.W. Stewart of the ISRP, Maud Gonne, Lyons and Griffith driving through parts of the city in an open carriage or

1 Ms.19,934 NLI; *United Irishman*, 2 September 1899.

brake, pursued by policemen and cheering crowds, and some hand-to-hand fighting with mounted policemen armed with swords.[2] The Committee also campaigned against recruitment to the British army and the visit of Queen Victoria to Dublin in March 1900. In his memoirs, the Labour leader William O'Brien, told of the cooperation on nationalist matters between the ISRP, of which he was a member, and the CLS.[3]

But all was not sweetness and light as far as Griffith and the socialists were concerned. Lyons recorded that socialists came to CLS meetings to scoff at the Society's expressed aims. For instance, they regarded as pointless the attempt to stimulate a living interest in dead history. Likewise, the effort to restore a dead language (Irish) they thought just as futile as trying to revive a dead tree. But, most of all, the promotion of national distinctions they saw as 'opposed to the progress of the world, which tended towards cosmopolitanism and "universal brotherhood"'. Lyons considered such socialism 'unsavoury', and declared that Griffith, Rooney and others 'were moved with great zest to protect the Society from being used as a platform for such propaganda'.[4]

In his autobiography, the playwright Sean O'Casey, who was closely involved with organised labour for a time, created the scene of a fictitious ISRP public meeting outside the old Parliament House in Dublin. Connolly addressed the gathering, and O'Casey had Griffith listening coldly to his words. (In fact, he had one of Connolly's followers, who was moving among the audience selling pamphlets, describe Griffith as a 'little bourgeois bastard!') According to O'Casey, Griffith regarded as 'cheek' the socialists claiming that the English were their brothers.[5]

Desmond Ryan drew a similar picture to O'Casey's. Again it was an ISRP meeting in the shade of the Bank of Ireland opposite Trinity College. But in marked contrast to O'Casey, who had Griffith listening in a cold, expressionless and impassive manner, Ryan described him as a 'wild-eyed Dublin working man', who 'gnashed his teeth and growled, impassioned' at the socialists: 'Listen to them! Telling me that an Englishman is my brother!' It was 'war to the knife' between some CLS members and the socialists, according to Ryan.

One of the socialists, 'Comrade Lyng', was described by Ryan as a

2 Lyons, *Some Recollections*, Chapter III; *United Irishman*, 23 December 1899.

3 Edward MacLysaght, *Forth the Banners Go: the Reminiscences of William O'Brien* (Dublin, 1969), p.24.

4 Lyons, *op. cit.*, pp.4-5.

5 Sean O'Casey, *Mirror in My House: The Autobiographies of Sean O'Casey, iii, Drums under the Windows* (New York, 1956), p.22.

'deadly antagonist' of Griffith. However, Lyng was a member of the CLS, and Griffith lamented his failure to be elected to the Dublin Corporation in 1903.[6] Ryan, like Lyons, pointed to the socialists' disdain for the Irish language and the ideal of a free Ireland, and saw something sterile in their aloofness from their surroundings and their learning by rote the works of their god, Marx. 'Griffith could write and talk them all under the table'.[7]

Some later biographers of Connolly treated his interaction with Griffith very differently from the earlier ones. The Marxist C.D. Greaves clearly followed O'Casey when he wrote that Griffith listened to Connolly's open-air meetings with a glum face. Greaves gave merely a passing mention to the Transvaal Committee cooperation between the two. Griffith's one passion was Irish nationality, which he 'pursued with miser-like singleness of purpose', but in an 'unphilosophic and ill-defined' way, according to Greaves. This enormous generalisation could be discussed at length but, because the subject here is Griffith's relations with Labour, and not his theory of nationality, one will pass on, giving Greaves's assertion simply to show the hostile case he set out to build against Griffith from the outset.

Greaves was the first author to charge Griffith with racism, imperialism and anti-Semitism (accusations which will be examined below). Suffice it here to reflect on the following pronouncement:

> The small trading class [Griffith] represented was jealous of the big, cross-Channel mercantile interests, but wanted to share the pickings, not abolish them....But fear of the working class arose from the feeling that the concessions trade-union action was wringing from big business, which could afford them, would ruin the small employer.[8]

What is exasperating about the Marxist author is a tendency to formularise and simplify so that everything fits neatly into a predetermined pattern. To what extent did Griffith represent 'the small trading class'? No socioeconomic analysis of his followers or organisations has been undertaken. Doubtless there were some small traders - Walter Cole, for instance - but there were also trade-union officials (P.T. Daly, Peadar Macken and others), as well as teachers, civil servants and so on.

In his introduction to a study of Connolly, published a decade after

6 *United Irishman*, 24 January 1903.

7 Ryan, *Sion*, pp.53-5,57-8.

8 C.D. Greaves, *The Life and Times of James Connolly* (London, 1961), pp.93-4,98.

Greaves's, Owen Dudley Edwards proclaimed himself a socialist, thus from the outset alerting his readers that he was writing from a particular viewpoint. There have been few more hostile commentators on Griffith. Although there is an impressive weight of evidence pointing to a fair degree of Griffith-Connolly cooperation, to Edwards's way of thinking Connolly had nothing in common with the 'racist and anti-socialist Griffith'.[9]

The first serious student of Irish Labour history was the American academic, J.D. Clarkson, whose book on Labour and nationalism was published just three years after Griffith's death. Clarkson was in no doubt that there was quite regular cooperation between Griffith and Dublin socialists: 'For Labour candidates who were also nationalists - even though they might be socialists - the *United Irishman* entertained feelings of the warmest friendship'. Clarkson went on to note Griffith's well-known recommendation of Connolly when the latter contested the Wood Quay ward in the Dublin municipal elections of January 1903.

Another who wrote extensively on Irish Labour, R.M. Fox, also pointed to this endorsement of Connolly's candidature. He presumed that such enthusiastic support from a 'conservative' like Griffith for 'a man who was regarded in conventional circles as a dangerous, if obscure, social revolutionary, was a sign of the respect which Connolly's qualities of character and intellect were gaining'. A biographer of Connolly in the Irish language, Proinsias Mac an Bheatha, in addition quoted Connolly's grateful acknowledgement of support from Griffith's paper, when, in 1908, he wrote that his ISRP suffered from a boycott of all the Dublin newspapers 'with the single honourable exception' of Griffith's.[10]

In his memoirs, William O'Brien also referred to Griffith's championing of Connolly, and added that Griffith did so despite the fact that Connolly's opponent in the election was 'J.J. McCall' (actually P.J. McCall), publican, patriotic poet, ballad writer and personal friend of Griffith. (In fact, he wrote regularly for Griffith's newspapers.) Arthur Mitchell also adverted to Griffith's call on the nationalists of Wood Quay to cast their votes for Connolly, and he agreed that his paper

9 Owen Dudley Edwards, *The Mind of an Activist: James Connolly* (Dublin, 1971), pp.x,130.

10 J.D. Clarkson, *Labour and Nationalism in Ireland* (New York, 1925), pp.256,259; R.M. Fox, *Green Banners*, p.72; R.M. Fox, *James Connolly: the Forerunner* (Tralee, 1946), p.47; Proinsias Mac an Bheatha, *Tart na Córa: Seamus Ó Conghaile, A Shaol agus A Shaothar* (Dublin, n.d.), p.47.

publicised ISRP activities when the other Dublin journals refused to do so.[11]

The evidence is there in the newspapers. Some historians acknowledged it, but others chose either to ignore it completely or to interpret it differently. Greaves, for example, offered the assurance that 'Griffith was very sparing of publicity for Connolly's activities', despite Connolly's own statement to the contrary in his *Harp* of March 1908 (the *Harp* was a journal which Connolly published in America). The municipal election endorsement was mentioned by Greaves, but with the reservation that Griffith must not have seen Connolly's 'avowedly socialist' manifesto, or he would not have seconded him.

But Griffith, who knew Connolly well for a number of years by 1903, must have been fully familiar with his professed socialism. More conclusive is the fact that while Griffith's commendation appeared in the 10 January issue of the *United Irishman*, two weeks later, in the same journal, he lamented the failure of Connolly and his ISRP colleague, Lyng, to get elected. Surely he was familiar with the manifesto by then? Yet, he retracted nothing. It was not because he was a socialist, but because he was an able and honest man who would fight corruption in the Corporation, that Griffith was recommending Connolly.[12] Edwards, in his study of Connolly, did not refer at all to either publicity from Griffith for the ISRP or his support for Connolly's candidacy.

The question of whether a friendship existed between Griffith and Connolly is very revealing of some authors' attitudes towards Griffith. Connolly's earliest biographer, Desmond Ryan, believed that there were 'many informal and friendly discussions' between the two in the CLS and that, although Griffith was one of Larkin's 'most hostile and outspoken critics', he 'preserved throughout a cordial admiration for Connolly'. Griffith described Connolly in 1913 as 'a man of his word', remembering 'their old unshaken friendship which dated from their common membership of the CLS'. Ryan saw Griffith as the best example that could be advanced in support of Connolly's claim that 'a conservative temperament is not necessarily allied to social abuses or industrial sweating, but may be, very often is, the most painstaking of

11 MacLysaght, *Banners*, p.34; Arthur Mitchell, *Labour in Irish Politics* 1890-1930 (Dublin, 1974), p.55.

12 Greaves, *Connolly*, pp.94,125; *United Irishman*, 10,24 January 1903.

all the elements making for the correction of such abuses within certain limits'.[13]

In her personal memoir of her father, Nora Connolly O'Brien did not mention Griffith, but many years later she disclosed that while her father was in America, one of her tasks was to send him every issue of the *United Irishman.* Robert Lynd, in his preface to her memoir, compared Connolly to Griffith: they both 'struggled on through dark years, indifferent to failure, indifferent to poverty, confident of the journey's end that [they] might not even live to see'.[14]

Fox's opinion was that Griffith and Connolly respected each other's 'dogged and honest qualities', being 'similar in temperament, though they differed widely in social opinions', and he saw both as 'completely honest and not at all self-seeking'. Mac an Bheatha agreed with both Ryan and Fox that the two men knew and respected each other of old.[15]

The view of Greaves and Edwards contrasts sharply with the above. 'The story of a long intimate connection between Connolly and Griffith is completely apocryphal', proclaimed Greaves. Edwards quoted Greaves's opinion with full approval.[16] Edwards ignored Griffith's endorsement of Connolly in the local elections, while Greaves offered the feeble excuse that Griffith must not have seen Connolly's election manifesto. Connolly wrote an article from America, discussing the possibility of a rapprochement between socialists and Sinn Féin, which was published in W.P. Ryan's *Irish Nation and Peasant* in January 1909. In the course of the article, Connolly referred to 'my old friend, Mr Griffith'. Greaves referred to the article but gave prominence only to Connolly's criticism of Griffith's economics, and completely ignored the 'friend' reference.

Similarly, in *Sinn Féin* in September 1913, Griffith described Connolly as 'the man in the leadership of the Transport Union with a head on his shoulders', and later in the same article stated: 'Mr Connolly is a man of whom in years past we had experience, which satisfied us that his word was his bond'.[17] Greaves and Edwards ignored this.

In fact, from its first issue the *United Irishman* championed the cause of

13 Desmond Ryan, *James Connolly: His Life, Work and Writings* (Dublin, 1924), pp.19,74-6.

14 Nora Connolly O'Brien, *Portrait of a Rebel Father* (Dublin, 1935), p.10; Nora Connolly O'Brien, 'The Pearse I knew', in *Hibernia*, 15 April 1977.

15 Fox, *Connolly*, p.48; Mac an Bheatha, *Tart na Córa*, p.95.

16 Greaves, *Connolly*, p.94; Edwards, *Connolly*, fn.16, p.130.

17 *Irish Nation and Peasant*, 23 January 1909; *Sinn Féin*, 27 September 1913.

labour. Griffith expressed pleasure that the first local elections, under the extended franchise that resulted from the 1898 Local Government Act, saw some good results for Labour. For the first time in Irish history 'the reins of representative government [had] fallen within the grasp of the toilers'. He urged the newly-elected Labour deputies not to align themselves with any existing political factions, but to try to carry out the work for which they were chiefly elected.

In the same article, Griffith had much to say about raising the social, moral and political status of the workers, and also about the urgent need to improve housing in Dublin city. He returned to the same topics over the following weeks and urged local government representatives to work for the provision of libraries and reading-rooms throughout the country, so that workers could improve themselves. He also urged them to ignore the question of a university for the sons of middle-class Catholics, as this would only be 'to the advantage of a class that has been generally opposed to the vindication of national rights'.[18]

Greaves asserted that 'Griffith conceived the ingenious notion of capturing a majority of the new local authorities [and] using their limited powers to the full in support of industrial expansion'.[19] It was symptomatic of Greaves's distorted treatment of Griffith that he made no mention of his welcome for increased Labour representation, and completely ignored his ideas on using the new local bodies to help workers.

The activities of Sinn Féin representatives on Dublin Corporation caused them to become identified in the public mind as Labour deputies. They attacked slum landlordism and demanded the investigation of tenements owned by members of the Corporation, so that they were regarded as standing for labour. P.T. Daly was an example of one who upheld labour and Sinn Féin interests.

The history of the Dublin Trades Council explored the Sinn Féin-trade union axis in some detail. It listed four active trade unionists who were also members of Sinn Féin - P.T. Daly, Michael O'Lehane, William P. Partridge and Peadar Macken. All four supported Griffith in his calls for a national rather than an international exhibition of goods in Dublin in 1904, but they were in a minority within the trade-union movement as a whole.

Sinn Féin ran 'an organised party ticket' for the Corporation election of 1905. A manifesto was issued by its six sitting members, three of whom were trade-union officials. Among other things, it called for the

18 *United Irishman*, 4,11,18 March 1899.

19 Greaves, *Mellows*, p.28.

abolition of slums; the provision of better housing; the furnishing of university and technical education and a network of public libraries; 'the municipalisation of undertakings such as would be under the control of all progressive municipalities'; the defence and application of the principles of trade unionism; the establishment of the Corporation as a model employer, and evening Corporation committee meetings to facilitate working-class members.

These were all ascribed by the historians of the Dublin Trades Council to the influence of the trade unionists on the Sinn Féin ticket. The manifesto was published in the *United Irishman.* It should be pointed out, however, that many aspects of this election declaration were discussed by Griffith in the same paper over the six preceding years. These trade-union historians remarked that the Sinn Féin Party was regarded as a type of Labour Party, that its agenda was definitely directed towards the working class, that the trade unionist, M.J. Lord, was elected first chairman of the Sinn Féin Corporation group, and that classifying trade-unionist Sinn Féin adherents as Labour men was encouraged by their own party.

In 1903, P.T. Daly was portrayed in the *United Irishman* as a Dublin Trades Council, Labour Electoral Association and National Council candidate, this general image being reflected in the national newspapers until 1907. So, for example, John Farren was described as a 'Sinn Féin/ Labour/Dublin Trades Council' candidate.[20] Yet, Greaves could declare that Griffith was 'strongly opposed to any association with Labour' in late 1908 and early 1909.[21] No evidence was provided to support this statement, which is surprising in view of the close Griffith/Labour cooperation over the previous eight years.

This interest in the potential of municipal politics induced MacDonagh and Ó Lúing to see a parallel between Griffith's Sinn Féin and the Fabian Society in Britain. MacDonagh believed that Griffith intended that Sinn Féin should perform in Ireland functions akin to those of the Fabian Society: 'policy formation through discussion, propaganda, the permeating of existing bodies and organisations, and political action at local level on terms of an agreed "non-party" programme'. Ó Lúing was struck by the similarity between Fabian pamphlets and many of the strategies advocated by Griffith, such as worker self-betterment through a network of libraries and reading-

20 Seamus Cody, John O'Dowd and Peter Rigney, *The Parliament of Labour: 100 Years of the Dublin Council of Trade Unions* (Dublin, 1986), pp.76-7.

21 Greaves, *Connolly*, p.189.

rooms, and participation in existing groups and structures, which could help to ameliorate their conditions.[22]

Griffith was disappointed with some Labour representatives on Dublin Corporation - those whom he saw as aligning themselves with pre-existing political cliques and 'whiskey rings', and who did nothing about slums, unemployment and high rates.[23] Labour members elected under the Local Government Act of 1898 accomplished little or nothing for the workers - becoming involved instead in jobbery and corruption, and often joining forces with long-time IPP members. This was especially bad in Dublin, where members who were supposed to reform the Corporation became its employees. Connolly in his *Workers' Republic* and Griffith in the *United Irishman* condemned them.[24]

Debating with the Socialists

Griffith's *United Irishman* was open to correspondents with radical views, among them Connolly and Lynd. Clarkson was probably right in describing Fred Ryan as 'the ablest and most energetic exponent of the views of thoughtful advocates of the rights of labour'. In one of his articles for the paper, 'Capitalism and Nationalism: a Socialist View', Ryan argued that socialism should be the goal of the political nationalist's philosophy. He frequently attacked the anti-socialist stance of D.P. Moran's *Leader*. In one particular article, 'Bigotry and Irish Nationality', he assailed the bigotry displayed in a *Leader* piece entitled 'Protestants and the Irish Nation'. He also contributed to the *United Irishman* on the university question. Basically, he was opposed to the idea of a sectarian Catholic university for the sons of the well-to-do and called for the reformation of Trinity College.[25] This was exactly Griffith's own position.

But, more often than not, Ryan and Griffith were at loggerheads. Ryan attacked Griffith's economics, his dual-monarchy policy, and most of all his attitude to socialism. He eventually emigrated to Egypt where he worked with the British anti-imperialist poet, W.S. Blunt, and edited an Egyptian nationalist newspaper. When he died in early April 1913, Griffith wrote a warm obituary of him in *Sinn Féin*. Concerning this, Desmond Ryan remarked: 'Once he wrote a very generous obituary

22 MacDonagh, *States*, p.61; Seán Ó Lúing, private communication with the writer, 2 October 1988.

23 *United Irishman*, 18 October 1902, 24,31 January 1903.

24 Mitchell, *Labour in Irish Politics*, pp.20,55.

25 *United Irishman*, 29 December 1900, 4 May, 6 July, 17 August 1901.

of a persistent critic of himself, Fred Ryan, and added that such as his late critic were the saviours of the world, even when their onslaughts blew off the hats of the just as well as the unjust'.[26]

Clarkson maintained that although the columns of the *United Irishman* were open to views like Ryan's, this in no way indicated acceptance of them by the editor. 'On the contrary, the *United Irishman* also ran a series of articles on "industrial possibilities", pleading for sacrifices in the interests of an Irish industrial revival'.[27] (The articles in question were not by Griffith.) His desire for an expansion of Irish industry is well known, and he certainly demanded sacrifices from his compatriots, but not just from one section of them. Fox ascribed to Griffith the belief that Irish workers ought to be willing to make all kinds of sacrifices to ensure the success of Irish industry. 'That this might mean increasing prosperity for the owners, while the workers remained poor, did not strike him as important'.[28] Unfortunately Fox did not give any evidence on which he based this view.

Mitchell was partially correct in his belief that 'Griffith accepted most of the conventional capitalist ideas of the time, seeking a revival of Irish industry by means of low wages for the workers and small profits for the investors'. Mitchell alluded to a passage from Larkin's *Irish Worker* where Sinn Féin was accused of offering 'cheap Irish labour' in an attempt to attract 'foreign capitalists' to Ireland. Connolly's declaration that 'an Irish industrial revival built upon the sacrifices of the workers would not be worth the effort', was also noted by Mitchell.[29] But, against this, in the *United Irishman* in February 1905 (on behalf of coopers in Guinness's brewery), and again in May of the same year (on behalf of employees of the Dublin Port and Docks Board), Griffith called for higher wages for the workers concerned.[30]

Socialists and radicals like Connolly, Fred Ryan and W.P. Ryan, lost few opportunities for attacking Griffith. Connolly, who claimed to know that 'the National Council has promised lots of Irish labour at low wages to any foreign capitalist who cares to establish in Ireland', was seen by Davis as expressing 'the irritation of men fighting the notoriously low Irish wages' system'. However, Griffith's *Sinn Féin*

26 *Sinn Féin*, 12 April 1913; Ryan, *Unique Dictator*, pp.63-4.

27 Clarkson, *Labour and Nationalism*, pp.261-2.

28 Fox, *Connolly*, p.48.

29 Mitchell, *Labour in Irish Politics*, pp.55,57.

30 *United Irishman*, 25 February, 27 May 1905.

Policy did not offer cheap labour, but extensive natural resources, as the lure for overseas capitalists.

Connolly insisted that socialists could have no sympathy with Sinn Féin's economic position because it appealed 'only to those who measure a nation's prosperity by the volume of wealth produced in a country, instead of by the distribution of that wealth among the inhabitants'.[31] This complaint was unfair. Its sharpest rebuttal is to be found in Griffith's address to the Sinn Féin central branch in October 1913. In 'Sinn Féin and the Labour Question', delivered when the 1913 lockout was at its height, Griffith promised that he would seek to have the powers of the proposed Home Rule parliament increased until they amounted to national independence, 'and with the increase of its powers, increase not only the wealth of the country, which is not prosperity, but the just distribution of that wealth, which is prosperity'.[32]

That Griffith opened his newspapers to correspondents with radical views received no mention from Greaves. On the contrary, he regarded the *United Irishman* as a poor successor to 'the spirited *Shan Van Vocht*', because its editor, whose 'outlook was that of the shopkeeper', was no intellectual and had no interest in ideas.[33]

Did Griffith have a Social Policy?

The building in which Griffith was born, 61 Upper Dominick St, was a four-storey house which his family shared with two other families. It was not a tenement by the standards of the time. A tradesman's wages were needed to live in as good a house as the Griffiths occupied. But sanitary arrangements were poor; there were no baths, lamps and candles provided the only light, and buckets of water had to be carried from pumps in the yard.

Because he was such a promising student, Griffith was transferred to St Mary's, Seville Place, from Strand St Christian Brothers School. The idea was to groom him for the Intermediate Certificate, the new secondary system then being operated by the Dublin Castle Education Board. Boys who did the Intermediate often stayed in school until they

31 *Irish Nation and Peasant*, 23 January 1909.

32 *Sinn Féin*, 25 October 1913.

33 Greaves, *Connolly*, p.94. The *Shan Van Vocht*, properly *An tSean Bhean Bhocht* (The Poor Old Woman), was a Belfast journal of the late 1890s, edited by poets Alice Milligan and Anna Johnston. When it closed down due to lack of support, the editors passed on their subscription list to the *United Irishman*.

were eighteen, but this was not to be Griffith's destiny. Like any other tradesman's son, he was sent to work at twelve.[34]

Clarkson wrote that Griffith 'realised keenly the sufferings of Dublin slum dwellers, and resented any peculiarly gross handling of the subject of poverty by smug and comfortable persons'. He cited Griffith reprimanding a leader writer in the *Freeman's Journal*, who suggested that Irish people were so innately bad that if they were paid higher wages, and thus enabled to live in comparative comfort, they would abandon both morality and religion. To this Griffith retorted:

> There are, of course, some exceptions. The leader writer of the *Freeman*, for instance, can enjoy a salary and a degree of comfort which would be sufficient to damn a whole village in Connemara, and still be saved, and the shareholders of the *Freeman* itself can pocket their annual eleven per cent, without any fear of a fiery hereafter.

Griffith went on to give an example of a friend, who lived in a tenement house in the Coombe in Dublin, and supported a wife and seven children on fifteen shillings a week, working twelve hours a day in a brewery. He doubted that this man's soul would be damned if he could earn twice his weekly wage working only two-thirds of the time.[35]

Griffith was a tradesman, as was his father; he was born and reared in a neighbourhood in which the kind of men who followed Jim Larkin were plentiful; he had as hard a life as any of them, and he was by no means blind to the injustice and oppression practised on Dublin's poor. He drew the attention of the public to the misery and sordid conditions of the houses in which the impoverished of the city lived, as evidenced by the following:

> The poor of Dublin are living miserably in slums that would shock a Kaffir. They pay rents that enable the owners to lead a leisurely life and to give generously to charities. The death rate is higher among them than in any city in England, Scotland, France or Germany....The kind of houses in which the poor of Dublin live is a source of shame to the civilised world.

He denounced the 1903 Wyndham Land Act because the favourable terms for landlords amounted to a robbery of the poor. As a journalist,

34 Ms.22,293 NLI.

35 Clarkson, *Labour and Nationalism*, pp.262-3.

he repeatedly expressed deep concern for the appalling living conditions of the Dublin working class.[36]

Despite revealing this concern, Griffith refused to commit himself to any comprehensive remedial social policy and insisted instead on 'a concentration of all forces in the struggle for national independence'. Clarkson supported this conclusion with a long excerpt from a Griffith article on socialism of November 1904. The gist of this was that there were few in Ireland who did not agree that the ownership of the soil of Ireland belonged to the people of Ireland; that it was a mistake to see socialism as synonymous with atheism, but that the time for deciding whether Irish national development should be along collectivist or individualist lines was when Ireland was politically free. However, Irishmen were discouraged from contact with English socialism, as it taught that Irish independence was unimportant and was therefore a denationalising influence.[37]

Sinn Féin's earliest historian, R.M. Henry, believed that there was no place for Labour in its framework. He considered that it had many plans to relieve Ireland from the evils of the English connection, but none to relieve the workers from the evils of which they complained.[38] Henry was wrong. Surely, bad housing and low wages were 'evils' from which the workers needed 'relief'? Both Sinn Féin members of Dublin Corporation and Griffith in his newspapers worked to alleviate such problems.

Griffith and Sinn Féin did not lack a social policy. It was part of Griffith's programme to use the Health Acts, the Dwellings Acts and other remedial acts to put an end to the slums. He campaigned vigorously against giving any increases in salary to Corporation officers 'while the poor are living on top of each other in one-room tenements. At present, when 27,000 out of 59,000 families are living in one-room tenements, the town clerk of this city is getting a salary higher than nine out of twenty ministers in the English cabinet, which is ruling the British Empire'. (*Sinn Féin*, 1 February 1908)

He also proposed opening playing fields for the children of the poor, and physical-education centres for the young of the city, to encourage healthy activities among them. The following from *Sinn Féin* of May 1908 shows how Griffith envisaged the beneficial effects of his scheme for building houses for the workers of the city:

36 *United Irishman*, 25 January 1902, cited in Ó Lúing, *Ó Gríofa*, p.227; Davis, *Griffith and Non-Violent Sinn Féin*, p.137; Glandon, *Griffith and Advanced-Nationalist Press*, p.52.

37 Clarkson, *Labour and Nationalism*, pp.263-4.

38 Henry, *Evolution*, p.92.

> An end will be put to the slums, and end will be put to the congested neighbourhoods in the old part of the city, and thousands of men, women and children, who live in them now, will be taken out into the clean sea and mountain air.

The 1905 municipal election manifesto of the National Council, with its points on slums, better housing, education, libraries, public control and so on, showed that Griffith and Sinn Féin were not devoid of a social policy.[39]

The Sinn Féin scheme to improve the dwellings of the Dublin working class, which Alderman Tom Kelly and his colleagues tried but failed to get the Corporation to adopt in 1908, was a progressive and practical way of tackling a very major problem. Griffith frequently expressed his opposition to the policy of buying up slums, because it only made their owners richer to the cost of the taxpayer. It encouraged some of the owners to neglect their property so that they could sell it at a higher price to the Corporation. The latter owned acres of land at Baldoyle and Blanchardstown on which decent and comfortable houses could be built and let at rents which were being paid in the city for tenements of one or two rooms. Baldoyle was already on the tram-line which could be extended to Blanchardstown so that the new dwellings would only be twenty minutes from the city centre. Thousands of cottages with front and back gardens could be built on land already owned by the Corporation.

Glandon wrote that Griffith's interest in improving the homes of working-class Dubliners was threefold: it was humanitarian; it could act as an antidote to social turmoil, and, most importantly, 'it was something the Irish could do for themselves - under existing laws - which would help to rebuild the nation and to strengthen the fabric of Irish society'.[40] The latter aspect was, of course, an example of Sinn Féin or self-reliance in practice.

That Griffith was opposed to the amalgamation of Irish and British trade unions was recorded by a number of historians. Clarkson saw it as evidence of Griffith's anxiety 'to break every bond between the two islands', and quoted from a mid-1906 article on the subject in *Sinn Féin.*

Griffith began by proclaiming his sympathy with the Irish artisan, praising his honesty and willingness to work hard, and declaring he was in no way to blame for Irish industrial backwardness. But he lamented the recent declaration of the Irish Trade Union Congress (ITUC) for a federation of Irish trade unions with those of England.

39 Cody et al., *Parliament of Labour,* pp.61,66-7; Ó Lúing, *Ó Gríofa,* pp.227-8.

40 Glandon, *Griffith and Advanced-Nationalist Press,* pp.52-3,57.

This, in Griffith's words, was to call for 'the government of the Irish artisans from England, the exportation of the Irish workingman's money to London, [and] the subservience of the Irish workingman's interests to those of England'.[41]

The history of the Dublin Trades Council revealed that a section of Dublin Labour (those who were in Sinn Féin) tried unsuccessfully to have an Irish trade-union federation formed. In fact, a rebuke was administered to Cumann na nGaedheal by the parliamentary committee of the ITUC for urging trade unionists to form such a federation.[42]

Mitchell also stressed Griffith's opposition to the merging of Irish with British trade unions, his call for arbitration courts in 1908 being seen as a device to keep out 'English intervention' in Irish industrial disputes. Griffith's resistance to integration was based on its denationalising effects on Irish workers, Mitchell observed.[43]

This attitude of Griffith's to what he perceived as the interference of British trade unions in Irish industrial affairs is crucial when one comes to consider his reaction to the arrival of Larkin on the Irish trade-union scene.

41 Clarkson, *Labour and Nationalism*, pp.264-6.

42 Cody et al., *Parliament of Labour*, p.78, and chapter entitled 'The Sinn Féiners', *passim*; Clarkson, *op. cit.*, p.205.

43 Mitchell, *Labour in Irish Politics*, p.56.

Chapter II

Enter Prometheus

Big Jim versus Little Arthur

Even before Larkin's arrival in Dublin, Griffith's aversion to the presence of British trade unions in Ireland was well established. When Larkin called the Dublin carters out on strike in 1908, he did so in his capacity as organiser for the British-based National Union of Dock Labourers (NUDL). Griffith has been castigated unfairly by some historians for his reaction. Clarkson wrote that he did not see the dispute on its merits, but simply in terms that 'England must not be allowed to participate in the washing of Ireland's dirty linen'.

It was not correct that Griffith ignored the 'merits' of the disagreement. Clarkson himself revealed as much in a quotation from Griffith's second article on the Dublin strike, where he accepted that the carters did indeed have grievances. The truth was that Griffith did recognise that the quarrel had some merits of its own, but these he considered less important than what he saw as a mischievous meddling by English trade unionists in Irish industrial affairs. In fact, the article from which Clarkson quoted was mainly a warning to the Dublin strikers that they would be abandoned by Larkin's English union, as the Belfast workers had been shortly before.

Clarkson neglected to note that in this article, also, Griffith was very much concerned with finding a settlement to the dispute. He recommended the Lord Mayor and the two Archbishops of Dublin as mediators, a suggestion taken up by W.P. Partridge, described by Greaves as 'at that time an engineering worker of considerable influence in labour circles'.[1] (Partridge was a member of Sinn Féin.) Clarkson was wrong in giving the impression of a mere tirade against English influence on Irish trade unions. In his third article on the strike, Griffith expressed satisfaction that his suggestion had been so promptly taken up by the workers. He hoped for a speedy settlement, and stated that he was therefore refraining from comment on the merits of the

1 C.D. Greaves, *The Irish Transport and General Workers' Union: the Formative Years* (Dublin, 1982), p.24.

dispute. Clarkson's only reference to this article was a quotation about the National Council bringing into final form a scheme for industrial arbitration courts, which would settle differences without English intervention. Again, this solitary example gave the false impression that this was Griffith's sole concern. Actually, to put it in context, he thought arbitration necessary because of what he saw as the failure of the Dublin Trades Council to defend the interests of its affiliated societies.

Nor did his interest in the strike end there, although Clarkson alluded no further to his role. In subsequent weeks, during December 1908 and early January 1909, Griffith expressed his regret at the failure of mediation, blamed the employers for this, and called yet again on the Dublin Trades Council to work for reinstatement of the workers and a fair settlement of their grievances. He believed the employers would treat with the Council as it bore no responsibility for the dispute. He was particularly concerned for the men around Christmastime, when their families would feel their poverty acutely.

When the Lord Lieutenant, Lord Aberdeen, intervened and restored harmony on the lines *Sinn Féin* had been advocating all along, Griffith deplored the needless misery the strikers had had to endure. He also called for the release of those arrested and sentenced during the strike, considering their violence mild compared with the fury of Larkin's language, and describing them as unfortunate Irishmen misled by his incitements. When they were released almost immediately, he expressed his pleasure.[2]

Fox dealt briefly and negatively with Griffith's part in this dispute. He declared that 'early in 1908' (actually, Griffith first wrote about Larkin in late November of that year), the editor of *Sinn Féin* penned a series of attacks on Larkin, dubbing him the 'Strike Organiser', the Dublin carters' strike being 'the immediate cause of Griffith's wrath'. Emmet Larkin stated that Griffith was 'bitterly critical' of Larkin and condemned him during the carters' dispute as the representative of 'English trade unionism in Ireland'. This historian referred to the first two of Griffith's six articles on the strike, as if these were all he wrote about it, and as if, in the two mentioned, the only concern was with denouncing the trade-union leader.[3]

In his history of the early years of the Irish Transport and General Workers' Union (ITGWU), Greaves, when discussing this dispute, referred to the suggestion of W.P. Partridge, on 6 December 1908, of

2 Clarkson, *Labour and Nationalism*, pp.267-8. See *Sinn Féin*, 28 November; 5,12,19 December 1908; 2 January 1909.

3 Fox, *Green Banners*, p.71; Emmet Larkin, *James Larkin: Irish Labour Leader 1876-1947* (London, 1965), p.63.

inviting the mediation of the Lord Mayor and the two Archbishops of Dublin. Greaves neglected to mention that Griffith had put forward this very proposition in the *Sinn Féin* issue of the previous day. His sole allusion to Griffith's part was that he 'denounced the evils brought on Ireland' by English trade unionism.

Not only did he ignore Griffith's prior call for intercession, but also anything that was constructive uttered by him on behalf of the workers - his acknowledgement of their having taken up his proposal; his hope for a speedy settlement and refusal, therefore, to discuss the merits of the dispute (*Sinn Féin*, 12 December 1908); his subsequent regret that the mediation failed and his belief that 'in this instance the masters acted wrongly'; his concern for the strikers' families in the winter conditions and the loss of trade to Dublin port, which could lead to docker unemployment; his urging the Dublin Trades Council to treat with the masters to have the men reinstated and their grievances allayed (*Sinn Féin*, 19 December 1908); his call for the release of the men imprisoned during the strike (*Sinn Féin*, 26 December 1908) - these are all disregarded in Greaves's one-sided narrative.[4]

The historians of the Dublin Trades Council had Partridge making the call for mediation at a meeting on Thursday, December 3. Greaves stated that he put forward the suggestion on December 6. Griffith's identical proposal appeared in *Sinn Féin* on December 5. Griffith's weekly came out on Thursdays. (Although it appeared on Thursdays, it carried the following Saturday's date. So, the issue dated December 5 actually came out on December 3.) Partridge, a member of Sinn Féin, most likely got his idea of mediation from Griffith.

The employers proved intransigent in this dispute but it soon became clear that they had erred. A report issued by the mediators was sympathetic to the men. The Lord Mayor made a donation to the strike fund and the employers were attacked by most Dublin newspapers. 'Even Griffith had to admit that the masters acted wrongly', wrote the historians of the Dublin Trades Council. These authors obviously considered Griffith the implacable enemy of the men although it was he who suggested the intermediaries in the first place. There is no reason, other than his criticism of Larkin, to conclude that he acknowledged the employers' wrong grudgingly.

These Labour historians refused to discern any positive contribution by Griffith. They believed that Sinn Féin influence on and support from the working class in Dublin was on the increase until 1908. Then, Griffith denounced Larkin and the striking workers (there is evidence for only the first part of this assertion), 'and a long and bitter exchange

4 Greaves, *ITGWU*, pp.24-5.

of insults was traded between the *Sinn Féin* newspaper and the strike leaders'. But this view cannot be substantiated. On 28 November 1908, Griffith described Larkin as 'a strike organiser from England'; on 19 December he was seen as 'devoid of a policy', and the only method his 'shallow brain' could devise was violence; on 26 December he was accused of using violent language. These references were all to Larkin, not to any other 'strike leaders'.

The historians of the Dublin Trades Council stated that Griffith urged 'the respectable members' of the Council to settle the dispute, and they believed he defined 'the respectable members' as 'the conservative, anti-Larkin members'. Griffith did not use the term 'respectable' at all. In *Sinn Féin*, on 19 December, he wrote: 'Our proposal, therefore, is that the prominent members of the Trades Council, who have not taken sides in the present dispute, and the master carters, should meet and devise an arrangement by which the strikers will be reinstated in their situations and their grievances fairly dealt with'. Not the 'respectable' but the 'prominent' trades councillors were called on to act urgently, and further those 'who have not taken sides' in the dispute. What Griffith wrote was given an unwarranted slant by these Labour historians.[5]

Larkin was suspended by the NUDL and turned to setting up the ITGWU. This did not placate 'Griffith's violent antipathy', Clarkson maintained. He even considered him to be in sympathy with the Liverpool executive of Larkin's former union!:

> ...it was a 'monstrous state of affairs' that Irishmen should enter on a strike 'without the sanction of the executive of the union to which the men were affiliated', though such action was the obvious corollary of Sinn Féin's own axiom that Irishmen should not strike at the behest of an English executive.[6]

The inconsistency was not so stark as Clarkson suggested. The *Sinn Féin* article from which the above quotations were taken was Griffith's last on the carters' strike. He saw one of the consequences of the dispute as that the suspended Larkin was seeking to organise an Irish transport union. Griffith urged any prospective Irish union to have nothing to do with suspended or dismissed officials of English unions, and he published a letter from James Sexton, general secretary of the NUDL, to show that Larkin acted at his own behest in organising the strikes in Ireland during 1908. The 'monstrous state of affairs' was the individual

5 Cody et al., *Parliament of Labour*, pp.60-61,77,80-81.

6 Clarkson, *Labour and Nationalism*, pp.268-9.

acting in his own capacity, without reference either to trades councils or union executives in either country.

One must allow some inconsistency in Griffith resorting to any appeal whatsoever to British trade unions, given his constant criticism of their interference. But it was hardly a case of sympathy with an English executive, as Clarkson contended. His argument that it was putting Sinn Féin theory into practice must also be regarded as unsound, because while Griffith would indeed advise Irishmen not to strike 'at the behest of an English executive', he would most assuredly not recommend them to stop work at the bidding of an English organiser acting entirely on his own. This latter, and the chaos that resulted, was surely what Griffith saw as 'a monstrous state of affairs'.

Later students of Irish labour made much of this apparent contradiction on his part. Fox thought it surprising that Griffith should have launched attacks on Larkin given 'the militant national colouring' that the ITGWU had taken on from the start, often invoking the names of Wolfe Tone and Fintan Lalor. However, Griffith erroneously persevered in condemning its actions as 'English trade unionism', Fox lamented. Describing the men striking without the permission of their Liverpool executive as 'a monstrous state of affairs', reached 'the climax of absurdity'.[7]

Davis saw the contradictory Griffith flay Larkin as 'the paid servant of an English trade union, while at the same time calling strikes without sanction from his Liverpool employers'. Likewise, Mitchell judged Griffith's attitude to Larkin incompatible because, on the one hand he assailed him as an English union representative, and on the other continued to criticise him after he 'established an Irish-based union'. The *Sinn Féin* article, from which Mitchell quoted, contained the explanation.

Griffith was aware that moves were afoot to found an Irish transport union. It was wished well and promised his assistance provided it was a 'genuine Irish organisation', and to prove such the 'first essential' was held to be that 'those connected with it were not suspended or dismissed officials of the English union which they formerly lauded as the one and only union to which Irishmen should belong'. Griffith went on to publish Sexton's letter confirming Larkin's suspension from the NUDL, and any union with which he was involved could not be authentically Irish, in Griffith's eyes.[8]

7 Fox, *Green Banners*, pp.71-2; *Fox, Larkin*, p.77.

8 Davis, *Non-Violent Sinn Féin*, p.138; Mitchel, *Labour in Irish Politics*, p.56. See *Sinn Féin*, 23 January 1909.

William O'Brien, who was closely associated with the ITGWU, referred briefly to the Griffith-Larkin conflict in his memoirs. When Larkin first mooted the idea of a specifically Irish union, he was censured by those who knew of his hostility to Irish trade unionism before that time. O'Brien referred to Griffith's writing to Sexton, whose reply confirmed Larkin's suspension from the NUDL. O'Brien remarked that the date given by Sexton for Larkin's dismissal was very close to the time he first hinted about a purely Irish trade union. O'Brien made no comment about Griffith being inconsistent and seemed in agreement with him that Larkin never thought about setting up an Irish union until his suspension from the British one.

O'Brien and Larkin parted company acrimoniously, so one should be alert to his unsympathetic attitude to his erstwhile adversary. In his memoirs he classified Larkin as one who was difficult to get on with, who brooked no argument, and who 'seemed to go out of his way to make personal enemies by attacking anybody who was opposed to him in a bitter fashion'. O'Brien acknowledged that Larkin's *Irish Worker* was important in organising the ITGWU, but considered the paper 'strange', there being 'a good deal of personal attacks'.[9]

There was an extraordinary difference between Griffith's relationship with Connolly and his attitude to Larkin. Desmond Ryan summarised it as 'his fair conflict with Connolly, his by no means fair conflict with Larkin', and also referred to 'acrid personalities'.[10] That Griffith was not fair to Larkin cannot be disputed, in that he could see no good in the man or his methods at all, but it must be added that the opposite was equally the case. 'Acrid personalities' may refer to a clash of temperaments, of which there must have been an element, but an appraisement of the blows exchanged in the course of the tussle will confirm that when it came to personal abuse, Larkin outdid his opponent with flying colours.

A cursory survey of Larkin's *Irish Worker* revealed such descriptions as 'little Arthur' (sometimes 'Li'l Arthur'), who was 'loud-mouthed'. Such statements as the following were also in evidence: 'His principal work has been planting waste minds with thistles'; 'Not being able to do anything himself, he is now acting the dog-in-the-manger policy of trying to thwart others'; 'Arthur, you are a little man with a little mind'; 'But enough of Arthur. Now to talk of men...'; 'When the pot boils, the scum comes to the top'; 'Arthur is spitting out his weekly dose of venom, well I have not time to spare on a paper or editor of a paper that has

9 MacLysaght, *Forth the Banners Go*, pp.56,60,62.

10 Ryan, *Connolly*, p.74.

neither (*sic*) circulation, morals, nor influence, thanks to Arthur'; 'Lying little Arthur is at it again'; 'There is nothing more dishonest than a disappointed politician, and Arthur Griffiths (*sic*), misleader of the late Sinn Féin party, seeing no hope of ever advancing to the position of ruler in the Irish republic, spends all his time and whatever little brains he possesses in vilefying (*sic*) and abusing those...' Griffith was also sneered at as 'would-be-dictator-of-Ireland, under the constitution of '82'.[11]

An equivalent scanning of *Sinn Féin*, between 1908 and 1913, showed Larkin depicted as 'the Strike Organiser from England'; 'the Dictator of the Irish Transport Union'; 'a demagogue' with a 'shallow brain...devoid of a policy'. The 'violence of his language' and his 'journalism of personal abuse' were both condemned. Griffith's antipathy to Larkin must have had a personal as well as a political element, in that he preserved good relations with other Labour leaders such as Connolly, O'Brien and Thomas Johnson, while often disagreeing with their ideas.

Three Strikes

Griffith viewed the strike as a weapon of last resort in industrial relations. The alacrity with which the fiery Larkin utilised it was certainly one of the reasons for Griffith's antagonism towards him. Irish manufacturing industry was regarded by Griffith as a fragile and delicate plant which needed careful nurturing, and he feared that the frequent occurrence of strikes would damage it irreparably.

When considering Griffith's comments on the Cork strike in mid-1909, Clarkson put forward the conflicting view that he was 'filled with commiseration' for the strikers 'while bitterly denouncing' them. In the *Sinn Féin* article from which Clarkson quoted, he curiously omitted a sentence immediately preceding his citation, which would substantiate the first part of his contention, because in it Griffith expressed sympathy for the workers. He described them as 'unfortunate men who are foolish enough to strike without being satisfied that they have both the material resources to sustain their action and the moral support which a good cause ensures them in any community'.

The extract Clarkson gave questioned the efficacy of the strike as an instrument for settling disputes, condemned a leader who habitually resorted to strikes, and found the Trades Council negligently inactive. It was not correct to construe these comments as 'bitterly denouncing' the Cork strikers. Clarkson was certainly accurate in ascribing bitterness to Griffith, when he wrote about this strike, but it was

11 *Irish Worker*, 2,9,16,23,30 September 1911; 7 October 1911; 10 February 1912.

directed at the lack of sympathetic or reciprocal action by trade unionists in British ports and not at the striking workers.[12]

Clarkson's look at Griffith's writing on the 1911 rail dispute was introduced by his belief that 'in Irish strikes and lockouts, Griffith ever saw the sinister hand of the "damned Englishman"'. The evidence was similar to that cited in the case of the 1909 stoppage because it showed once again Griffith's conviction that British trade-union labour never reciprocated and never would.[13]

Griffith's remedy for the bad conditions of the railways and other public transport methods at the time was to put them under public control: '...the control and management of transit by rail, road and water... for the national benefit by a national authority approved by the people of Ireland'. This would have greatly improved the lot of workers, but it was a solution that was not listened to at that time.[14]

Glandon gave a misleading impression about Griffith and the 1911 rail dispute. She wrote that when the delivery of food to Dublin was blocked by the strikers in September 1911, 'the Sinn Féin press called upon the government to guarantee its transportation by using the services of soldiers'. As a result, according to Glandon, 'Larkin scoffed at Griffith's patriotism, and remarked in his usual style: "When the pot boils, the scum comes to the top"'. It was not 'the Sinn Féin press' that made the call for British soldiers to be used to guarantee food delivery. It was actually made in a letter to *Sinn Féin* by an anonymous correspondent, using the pen-name 'Boyesen of Kollund'. W.T. Cosgrave wrote to the *Irish Worker* immediately to dissociate Sinn Féin from such advocacy. Glandon's statement is in error by implying that Griffith in an editorial wanted such action.[15]

The dispute in Pierce's Ironworks in Wexford in 1911, where the employees wished to join Larkin's ITGWU, and their employers refused to allow them to do so, drew much from Griffith's pen. A number of historians considered what he wrote. The following from his first article: 'Whatever causes the area of manufacturing to contract in Ireland dangerously affects the future as well as the present prosperity of the country', was seen by Clarkson as 'the constant refrain of *Sinn Féin's* charming song'. The stoppage 'summoned forth all the denunciatory power of which *Sinn Féin* was capable'. Griffith 'hurled

12 Clarkson, *Labour and Nationalism*, p.270. See *Sinn Féin*, 3,24 July 1909.

13 *ibid.*, p.274; *Sinn Féin*, 23 September 1911.

14 *Sinn Féin*, 7 October 1911.

15 Glandon, *Griffith and Advanced-Nationalist Press*, p.100. See *Irish Worker*, 30 September 1911, for W.T. Cosgrave's letter.

his invective at the heads of those who permitted themselves to be driven from their employment rather than abandon the trade union of their choice'. In support of this view Clarkson cited the following: 'If...they desire to merge themselves in a union of unskilled labourers directed from Dublin and subservient to a majority unconnected with their trade, we think the employers have legitimate grounds for objecting'.[16]

Griffith could not see the issue as simply the right of workers to join whichever union they wished. His first article on the dispute had a worried reference to a recent census which revealed manufacturing industry as directly supporting two-thirds of the population of Britain, but less than one-third in Ireland. The twin consequences of this were (a) the country was not sufficiently industrially developed to provide an outlet for the surplus agricultural population, and (b) that any cause of a decrease in the Irish manufacturing sector dangerously affected the present and future well-being of the country ('*Sinn Féin's* charming song', according to Clarkson).

Griffith regarded the Wexford iron industry as succeeding under very unfavourable conditions - far from sources of coal and iron, and markets, and with an industrially inexperienced workforce - and yet holding its own against much bigger surrounding competitors. Its survival was a feat to be proud of and showed the inherent capacity of the Irish as an industrial and commercial people. He painted a glowingly optimistic picture of a future manufacturing country, with Wexford as the 'nucleus of a vast industry, which will create in Ireland an industrial population of millions, sustained and fed by a doubled agricultural population'.

But such a future depended on the people themselves. It was thus vital to preserve the Wexford ironworks, and the dispute was seen as threatening its ruin, with its trade then going to Britain and America. Griffith's concern was not solely with the employers, because he concluded that it would not be they who would be pauperised but the 700 workers and their families who would be thrown onto an already overcrowded labour market.[17] Henry suggested that Griffith preached something amounting to 'abject surrender' on the workers' part on this and other occasions in 1911.[18] The opposite was the case. Griffith's overriding interest was with saving the iron industry, because he saw it as the seed from which a great, countrywide concern could grow.

A correspondent to a Wexford paper accused him of proposing that

16 Clarkson, *Labour and Nationalism*, pp.271-2.

17 *Sinn Féin*, 9 September 1911.

18 Henry, *Evolution*, p.96.

the workers should sell their labour for less than a living wage. He denied the charge, pointing out that the dispute was not about wages but about the men's right to join Larkin's union. His compromise suggestion was that they form their own foundry-workers' union, and this was actually the basis on which Connolly settled the dispute early in 1912. Griffith opposed Larkin's union because of his horror at the possible effects of sympathetic strikes on the fragile Irish economy.

To Griffith, iron was a country's wealth. He saw the Wexford ironworks in danger, and he spoke out on behalf of the directors, but it should not be assumed from that that he was blind to the rights of the workers, Ó Lúing rightly observed.[19]

Greaves commented ironically that the Wexford strike gave Griffith the opportunity 'to express sympathy with his countrymen fighting tyranny, and *Sinn Féin* published a blistering attack on Larkin'.[20] Greaves did not refer to any particular article but the above summary of his first article was certainly not a devastating assault on Larkin. As for compassion with employers battling dictatorship, the large amount Griffith wrote on the dispute, between September 1911 and February 1912, showed as much concern for the fate of the employees (especially in *Sinn Féin*, 3 February 1912), but his primary thought was for the welfare of the country's industry, rather than for the good of either worker or director.

As has already been noted, the survival of the iron industry Griffith saw as absolutely vital, because from it could grow a successful nationwide concern. He considered the Wexford employers' offer to the men of their own foundry-workers' union, or membership of unions in allied trades, a fair one. His anxiety for the industry's survival blinded him to the fundamental right of the workers to join any union they wished.

Capitalism and Trade Unionism

Clarkson regarded Griffith as inconsistent because he denounced '"the English economics" of *laissez-faire*', while accepting 'the *fait accompli* of capitalism'. The Marxist historian, Strauss, wrote that Griffith longed for an 'ideal Gaelic Manchester', and labelled him 'the evangelist of Irish capitalism'.[21]

19 Ó Lúing, *Ó Gríofa* , pp.225-7.

20 Greaves, *Connolly*, p.221.

21 Clarkson, *Labour and Nationalism*, p.267; Strauss, *Irish Nationalism and British Democracy*, p.219.

Griffith put all the blame for the bad state of Ireland on English misrule, and argued that this was the cause of worker poverty and city slums. He did not often fault the industrialists for bad working conditions or poor pay. He was reluctant to do so because he saw the entrepreneur as having a vital role to play in the industrial revolution he thought was so necessary for Ireland.

He wished for Irish industrial development along individualist lines, but to set him up as preaching capitalism at all costs is not to do justice to the facts. For example, in his article, 'Capital and Labour', while it is true that he charged 'demagogy' with partly causing the series of strikes that Ireland had just gone through, he immediately added, 'if there had been no oppression and grinding of the face of the poor, there would have been no means for demagogy to usurp the roles of democracy'.

He saw relations between employer and employed as solely a 'cash nexus' in England, and detected a hardening of hearts *on both sides* in Ireland in recent years, owing to the twin influences of English businessmen and English labour unions. During the 1913 Dublin lockout, he again viewed *both parts* of the industrial equation as 'suffering from an inflammation of the brain', and insisted on the worker's right to 'a fair share of the joint produce of labour and capital'. It was the duty of the nation or the state to enforce that entitlement.

The tragedy of the confrontation in 1913 provoked Griffith into a remarkable address ('Sinn Féin and the Labour Question') to the central branch of his organisation in October of that year. Capitalism, as it had developed in England, he saw as denying 'its obligation to the moral law', and he attacked this 'savage doctrine of the irresponsibility of capital to aught but itself', because 'it had begotten a misery on the social system', which had driven people to place their faith in the socialist panacea. This he defined as 'a revival of feudalism with the state instead of the noble as the all-provider - wherein the subject is relieved by a benevolent despotism from the exercise of his personal initiative and the discipline of personal responsibility'.

It was not capitalism, but its abuse, which oppressed labour, and it had to be made subject to the law of the state, 'interpreting the conscience and interest of the nation'. His wide-ranging address also included the following statement: 'That country, no matter howsoever wealthy it be, is not prosperous where abundant wealth exists and yet poverty and unemployment are the lot of a considerable proportion of its people'. These examples from Griffith's writing sit uneasily among the beliefs of an evangelical capitalist.[22]

Glandon believed, contrary to Clarkson and Strauss, that the address

22 *Sinn Féin*, 8 March, 13 September, 25 October 1912.

just cited showed Griffith was no defender of *laissez-faire* capitalism. Quite the opposite, in fact, as he judged it 'a false doctrine which promoted pauperism'. He saw the nation as having a mediating role between the two sides of commerce, ensuring that there was no exploitation The duty of both sides was to serve the community as a whole; the state had to protect the community's interests, and should be free to intervene when the loss of profit to either workers or employers was threatened by a dispute.[23]

What was Griffith's attitude to trade unionism? His father was a member of the Dublin Typographical Provident Society (DTPS) all his working life. He often represented the union in negotiations with the employers. Like many in his trade, he suffered unemployment, and had to emigrate to England for a time. Griffith's brother, William (Billy) was a barber and was the registrar of the Irish Union of Hairdressers and Allied Workers. Griffith himself was a card-carrying member of the DTPS.[24]

Clarkson called pre-Larkin organised labour in Ireland 'old trade unionism', and what succeeded it 'new trade unionism'. He believed Griffith was unprepared to tolerate the latter because it 'might interfere with the infinitely-to-be-desiderated Irish industrial revival'. The 'new trade unionism' was for Griffith merely 'English trade unionism in Ireland'.[25] This was to simplify Griffith's reaction to Larkin's aims and methods. While it is true that he saw the weapon of the sympathetic strike as potentially disastrous for Irish economic prosperity, he saw a greater threat in Larkin as a latent wrecker of his beloved Irish nation, where employer and employed would coexist peacefully.

In a long editorial at the end of September 1911, Griffith attacked what Larkin stood for as ' the syndicalism of the French revolutionary socialists'. Concerning this editorial, Clarkson wrote that '*Sinn Féin* stripped off the gloves and hurled defiance'. But there was much more to the piece than that. Griffith denied that syndicalism, with its technique of the sympathetic strike, was genuine trade unionism, which he defined as 'the perfectly legitimate and laudable combination of men of particular trades to advance their interests'. Calling upon all advocates of the latter to speak out against what he saw as this new syndicalism, he warned that tyranny - whether of the capitalist or 'the

23 Glandon, *Griffith and Advanced-Nationalist Press*, pp.55-6.

24 Ms.22,293 NLI; Ms.22,288 NLI.

25 In a footnote, Clarkson, *Labour and Nationalism*, p.267, described this as '*Sinn Féin*'s usual heading for articles on Larkinite strikes', but of a total of 22 on strikes and lockouts, in which Larkin had a part between 1908 and 1912, this heading is to be found only once, and the word 'English' occurs in only two other headings.

demagogic terrorist' - would find no place under the flag of the Irish nation which he wished to see unfurled.[26]

Two later historians supported Clarkson. Davis agreed that to Griffith 'the Irish "new unionism" was simply English trade unionism in Ireland'. Mitchell wrote that Griffith was totally against 'new unionism' in Ireland as represented by Larkin and the ITGWU, that during the industrial unrest in Ireland between Larkin's arrival and his departure for America, Griffith's twin preoccupations were the damage inflicted on the Irish economy and the influence of English unions and socialists. Glandon agreed that one of Griffith's basic objections to Larkinism was its links with British unions, but another was that it 'distracted Irishmen from their duty to their country, and directed them towards a narrow class interest'.[27]

Brennan rejected the charge that Griffith was unfriendly to the Labour movement. He described him as 'a staunch trade unionist', and a member of the DTPS, which union Brennan described as 'one of the most rigid trade unions existing in Ireland'. Griffith often praised the DTPS to Brennan, and advocated that 'all sections of Irish labour should be organised on similar lines'. Mitchell later cited Brennan's memoirs on this point, and added his own view that Griffith was not opposed to 'craft unionism' as long as it was strictly Irish based. Stating that he was not inimical to 'craft unionism' suggests that he was opposed to unskilled labour organising, which was not the case.[28]

Brennan held that Griffith was 'bitterly hostile to the Larkin type of Labour leader, whose aim was not trade unionism at all, but a sort of proletarian dictatorship through the instrumentality of one big union dominated and directed by one man'. Griffith did indeed, at least once, describe Larkin as 'the Dictator of the Transport Union'. He saw the potential of Larkin's ambitions as the establishment of a tyranny of the worst kind. With the Russian soviet system in mind, Brennan told of Griffith remarking to him: 'A dictatorship is bad enough, but a proletarian dictatorship is infinitely worse. If there is to be a dictatorship, let it be of the cultured classes'. He made it explicitly clear to Brennan that by the 'cultured' he did not mean the 'propertied' classes.[29]

Part of an article, written by Griffith at the end of September 1911,

26 Clarkson, *Labour and Nationalism*, pp.267,273-4. See *Sinn Féin*, 30 September 1911.

27 Davis, *Griffith and Non-Violent Sinn Féin*, p.138; Mitchell, *Labour in Irish Politics*, p.56; Glandon, *Griffith and Advanced-Nationalist Press*, p.101.

28 Brennan, *Allegiance*, p.218; Mitchell, *op. cit.*, p.56.

29 Brennan, *op. cit.*, pp.218-19.

supports Brennan's judgement. In it the ITGWU was described as threatening that if a disagreement arose between an employer and his workers in one town in Ireland, it had the right to call out men in every town and in every type of industry in the country, and thus to choke the whole commercial life of the island.[30] That, to Griffith was not trade unionism.

Henry's early history of the Sinn Féin movement declared that 'its official organ was against strikes'. This is generally true, but from a pragmatic rather than a principled point of view, as Griffith never denied the right to strike. He took this attitude because he regarded industrial stoppages as retarding the country's trade and manufacturing output. They were damaging gestures that weakened the country, did widespread harm to the nation, and benefited neither weak nor strong:

> The slash of a knife can destroy the noblest picture that human hand painted, the blow of a hammer can destroy the finest engine that mental ingenuity and manual skill created. But neither knife nor hammer can restore them. An Irish industry can be destroyed by strikes and lockouts. But, until the end of time, a destructive weapon of that kind will never establish an Irish industry.[31]

30 *Sinn Féin*, 30 September 1911.

31 Henry, *Evolution*, p.92; *Sinn Féin*, 23 September 1911.

Chapter III

The Poor Left to Fester in Slums

What Griffith Wrote: Truth and Myth

The great 1913 strike and lockout in Dublin was caused by the Connolly-Larkin demand for recognition of the ITGWU by William Martin Murphy and his Employers' Federation. During the five months that the dispute dragged on, Griffith wrote about it weekly in his newspaper. What he wrote has been variously interpreted.

To Clarkson, 'the epic struggle of 1913' could not 'budge the stalwart champion of Ireland's nationhood from his hostility to the leaders of social revolt'. The word 'leaders' could be amended to 'leader', because nowhere in *Sinn Féin* can criticism of Connolly be found. Clarkson quoted from Griffith's opening editorial: 'the poor were left to fester in the slums', and those who could have acted but did nothing about it were now 'horrified and amazed' that 'out of their misery some of them have fallen victims to the socialistic spellbinders'.

Clarkson gave Griffith the credit of opening his columns, 'as usual', to correspondents whose views varied greatly from his own. One correspondent wrote that unless support was given to the workers, they would be 'flung into the ranks of the enemy'. To this letter, Clarkson stated, Griffith 'appended the ever-ready reply that "so long as any section of Irishmen can be led to think that earthquake pills are the cure for all ills, and that there is no colourable difference between the green flag of Irish nationalism and the red banner of English socialism, so long will such a section of Irishmen be catspaws of England"'.

But to be fair to Griffith, his response to this correspondent was not so ready-made as Clarkson suggested. He did not see Irish labour problems being solved by what he termed 'quack remedies' which came to Ireland via England. Urging a study of conditions in countries nearer akin to Ireland, such as Norway and Denmark, instead of England and the United States, whose problems were very different, Griffith concluded: 'It is the right of every Irishman willing to work to be secured a fair living in his own country'.

But he maintained that that entitlement could never be realised as long as Ireland was subject to English exploitation. His reply was not as snappy or dismissive as Clarkson implied. Although his contention was, first get the British out and then we can tackle Irish social ills, his attitude was not to do nothing in the meantime. He called for a study of countries more similar to Ireland, where more useful lessons could be learnt.

In the same issue of *Sinn Féin* Griffith attacked Dublin Corporation for its negligence in prosecuting owners of tenement houses which were allowed fall into decay, and which often collapsed, killing and injuring their inhabitants. There had just been such an occurrence in Church St, and he recalled a previous incident in Townsend St (he actually discussed it in the *United Irishman* at the time).[1] He then turned his attention to the general housing conditions of Dublin's poor; this was to be a constant theme throughout his weekly writing on the tragedy in Dublin between September 1913 and February 1914.

While the dispute dragged on, Griffith devoted most of his writing space to a consideration of Irish, and mainly Dublin, social conditions. Clarkson gave little attention to this output. For example, from an article entitled 'Labour, Capital and the Nation', the following only was extracted: 'To elaborate a national policy at a time when employer and employed are suffering from inflammation of the brain would be a waste of energy'.

The gist of the article in question was that the nation stood as the protector of labour from abuse by capital, and that in any naked confrontation between the two, without this intermediary, capital must always win. He saw the two basic causes of the labour unrest of the time as (a) the increase in the cost of living accompanied by the failure of wages to keep pace, and (b) the dreadful housing conditions. Clarkson ignored this, as well as Griffith's repeated recommendation of arbitration courts and/or conciliation boards to prevent or settle industrial disputes.

Griffith noted that Connolly, in a letter to the *Freeman's Journal*, stated that the ITGWU had always desired such machinery, and remarked that this was news to him, because when it was put forward by Sinn Féin four years before, he could not recall it receiving any support from that union or, he was careful to add, from employers either. In this article, Griffith suggested that the IPP should be the guarantor for any decision reached by arbitration.

Totally omitted also by Clarkson was a very extensive leader, presenting a detailed housing scheme, with a comprehensive costing, and ideas on how the finance could be raised (for details of which, see below). Why was so much that was constructive on Griffith's part wholly ignored by this historian, who gave the impression that the editor of

1 *United Irishman*, 18 October 1902.

Sinn Féin performed only the role of an assailant of the Labour movement in 1913? The omission was unfortunate because Clarkson's work had a major impact on many subsequent authors of Irish Labour history.[2]

The views of those who wrote about Griffith in relation to 1913, after Clarkson, ranged from balanced to extremely censorious. Ryan declared that *Sinn Féin* 'regarded strikes as the unpardonable sin', and that its editor was among 'the most hostile and outspoken critics of Larkin and the workers'. Yet, a survey of both the *United Irishman* and *Sinn Féin* shows that Griffith devoted more space during the 1913 upheaval to the causes of, and solutions for, labour unrest than was devoted to labour matters generally in the life of those journals combined.

Never, in the course of the vast amount that he wrote, did he criticise the workers without faulting the employers as well[3], but, far from devoting his energies to censure, most of his attention was given to what he discerned as the twin causes of the trouble, and very genuine worker grievances: dreadful dwelling conditions and low wages. Ryan also stressed Griffith's many calls for a conciliation board and, indeed, judged him as becoming 'more mellow and open-minded in his views on these questions towards the end of his life'.[4]

Interestingly, Fox asserted the very opposite, believing that Griffith's 'anti-Labour views became more bitter as time went on'. It was Fox's opinion that Griffith reserved 'his full bitterness...for the unskilled workers in Dublin who had sufficient regard for their manhood and independence to refuse to sign a pledge binding themselves not to join an Irish trade union'. It is true that Griffith never referred directly to the employers' demand that their employees should sign a promise not to join Larkin's union. Some indirect references might be his regret that there had been a hardening of hearts, and his description of both sides as suffering from an inflammation of the brain.

Because he disliked the 'one big union' idea, he probably did not regard the refusal of the men's right to membership of the Transport Union as a real hardship. But, nowhere in what he wrote can he be seen to have reserved his 'full bitterness' for the locked-out and striking workers. Indeed, Fox's extracts from national newspapers during the Dublin dispute showed, as he stated himself, 'how the mass of the

2 Clarkson, *Labour and Nationalism*, pp.276-8. See *Sinn Féin*, 6,13,20,27 September 1913; 11,18 October 1913; 1,8 November 1913; 17 January 1914.

3 See, for example, *Sinn Féin*, 13,27 September 1913.

4 Ryan, *Connolly*, p.75.

people were regarded'.[5] Nothing that Griffith ever wrote came even remotely close to the general media condemnation. In fact, in an article entitled 'Jack Yeats's Pictures', he paid fulsome tribute to the painter for inspiring Irish people with his scenes from the west of Ireland at a time when Dublin city dwellers were being portrayed in the media as little better than beasts.[6]

Greaves dubbed *Sinn Féin* 'the only paper which saw no harm in the employers'. He could not have read the newspapers of the time too carefully, if he did not detect their distinct partiality for the employers, and he either ignored or was unaware of the fact that Griffith's paper, while it referred directly to the warring sides only twice in the course of a massive output on social matters, devoted almost all its attention to solving what it regarded as the fundamental problem of bad housing.[7]

Davis devoted some attention to Griffith's interest in conciliation boards and arbitration courts. Griffith referred to such machinery existing in New Zealand. Davis pointed out that 'the chief feature of the New Zealand system was the power of the arbitration court to make compulsory awards binding on both parties'. By 1913, militant trade unionists in that country - admirers and, in some cases, friends of Larkin - were rebelling against it. Surprisingly, Davis made no reference to Griffith's much stronger recommendation of the French 'prudhomme' system, in which there was an appeal structure and only ultimate compulsion.[8]

This particular feature in Griffith's programme still had some appeal for moderate Labour leaders, and Davis cited Griffith's praise of Connolly, in September 1913, for accepting the conciliation idea. As Ireland, unlike New Zealand, had no national structure to enforce any agreement reached through arbitration, Griffith suggested that the IPP, which still retained the country's confidence, should take on this role. Davis wrote that the proposal was guaranteed to estrange socialists, 'who had reason to doubt the sympathy of many bourgeois parliamentarians'.[9]

The labour discontent in Dublin, which reached its peak in 1913, finally focused public attention on the awful housing conditions in the city's working-class areas. Griffith once again drew attention to the 1908

5 Fox, *Connolly*, p.48; Fox, *Green Banners*, p.72; Fox, *Larkin*, p.97.

6 *Sinn Féin*, 28 February 1914.

7 Greaves, *Connolly*, p.257; Greaves, *Mellows*, p.52; Greaves, *ITGWU*, p.110.

8 Griffith, in *Sinn Féin*, 6 July 1912 and 27 September 1913, outlined and discussed in detail this scheme.

9 Davis, *Non-Violent Sinn Féin*, pp.138,142.

Sinn Féin scheme for removing the evil by means of a housing development away from the city centre. The proposed location was an estate owned by the Corporation twenty minutes by tram from the centre. One of Griffith's suggested methods of meeting the cost of the new development was somewhat idealistic.

This was his call on the wealthy of Dublin to advance one-and-three-quarter million pounds to the Corporation, interest-free for three years. He believed that 10,000 dwellings could be built with this and, even with the expense of transport, that the workers would be much better off than living in the decaying city-centre slums. Griffith saw it as a way of preserving social harmony, from which the whole city of Dublin would benefit. He was convinced that there were men rich enough in the urban area to take on the financial burden. But, as happened in 1908, Sinn Féin's remedy for the chronic Dublin housing problem was again ignored in 1913.[10]

Strauss was wrong when he wrote that not even Daniel O'Connell's vitriolic condemnations of trade unionism were more 'bitter and determined' than Griffith's attacks on Larkin and the strikers during the lockout.[11]. Peter Beresford Ellis was worse. He asserted that Griffith 'attacked the workers, commenting that he would like to see every last one of them bayoneted'.[12] No source was given for this alleged outburst, and one will certainly not find it in the pages of *Sinn Féin*.

Importing Food and Exporting Children

One episode Griffith wrote about concerned the shiploads of food sent to help its Irish counterpart by British Labour. This gesture, Clarkson contended, 'fanned to fever-heat the passions of the great-souled patriot', so that 'furiously did he bellow forth his honourable rage at this insult offered to Irishmen in their hour of trial'. Using an extract from a *Sinn Féin* editorial Clarkson added as an afterthought: 'Nor did Griffith neglect to point out that the English brethren spent the money at home, thus getting some benefit themselves'.

In fact, Griffith's three articles, far from howling out wrath, were a cooly-argued analysis of the object-lesson in economics, vis-a-vis the Irish. Indeed, two of the articles had the title, 'The Economics of the Foodship', and Clarkson's afterthought was actually the thrust of Griffith's whole point.

10 Glandon, *Griffith and Advanced-Nationalist Press*, p.54.

11 Strauss, *Irish Nationalism and British Democracy*, p.219.

12 Peter Beresford Ellis, *A History of the Irish Working Class* (London, 1972), p.97.

He argued that *English* subscribers had the good economic sense to spend their money at home, to the benefit of *English* production and employment, and to send *food* to Dublin instead of *cash*, which could have provided some stimulation for the *Irish* economy. He also revealed that the food came from an English cooperative firm, whose directors and shareholders were prominent English Labour leaders, who would thus profit *directly* from the transaction. *Sinn Féin* also considered it important to warn that the same firm was seeking to make inroads into the Irish market at the expense of Irish industry and loss of Irish employment.

To a correspondent who asked: 'Can we blame the Saxon for showing us in a dramatic way our want of common humanity?', Clarkson wrote that Griffith 'retorted malevolently': 'Can we blame the Saxon for showing us in a dramatic way our want of elementary economic sense?' But there was more to the reply than mere malevolence. The same correspondent, in a second letter, urged Griffith to put aside any personal dislike he felt for Labour leaders or organisations, and warned that the fruit of the employers' 'right-to-starve-the-women-and-the-children policy' would be just that class war that Griffith pleaded Ireland could not afford. But Griffith 'could only return to the topic of England's sinister machinations'.[13]

In the foodship, Griffith saw, according to Greaves, 'not solidarity taking the only course left open to it, but a nefarious plot to advance British exports over the ruins of Irish trade'.[14] But there was at least one other course 'solidarity' could have taken, which would have been the most effective from Dublin Labour's point of view, and that was sympathetic strike action. Nevertheless, Griffith was wrong in his attitude to the foodships and should have acknowledged the humanity of the gesture.

The attempt to send unemployed workers' children to English homes, while the dispute in Dublin endured, gained considerable notoriety during the lockout. Two historians, writing almost half-a-century apart, referred to Griffith's link with it, and their comments are strikingly similar. Clarkson believed that 'fervent hatred of England threw Griffith into the arms of Archbishop Walsh in opposition to the proposal'. He had Griffith 'boasting' that

> the number of Dublin parents, who would consent to send their children to be nurtured in the homes of the enemies of their race and nation, do not form five per cent of the parents affected by the strike.

13 Clarkson, *Labour and Nationalism*, pp.278-80. See *Sinn Féin*, 4,11,18 October 1913.

14 Greaves, *Connolly*, p.257.

> The English Labour leaders, Scotch professors and citizenesses of the world, who are panting to take over charge of our affairs in the event of any form of self-government being obtained in the near future in this country, burned their fingers badly when they thought that the Dublin workingman on strike would permit his children to be used for an advertisement.

These two sentences amounted to Griffith's only comment on the entire affair. They were written *after* the event, and arose from a letter submitted by a Sheffield correspondent, who stated that the children of the poor lived in appalling conditions in some English cities, and warned that transplanting would be a threat to the Irish children's nationality and religion. As can be seen, Griffith said nothing about religion at all, so Clarkson's avowal that he was thrown into the arms of the Catholic Archbishop of Dublin was groundless and erroneous. Griffith simply expressed his belief - wrong though it may have been - that it would go against their natural temper for Irishmen to entrust their children to English care.

Similarly, Davis adjudged that 'like the clerical authorities, Griffith was particularly incensed by the proposal for transporting the children of locked-out workers to English homes'. The evidence Davis cited in support was from an article, in reply to a correspondent, in which Griffith asked him had he heard that 'Irish children have been deported to England'.[15] To include 'the clerical authorities' on the basis of this sole passing reference was not justified.

Groundless Anglophobia? Republican Solidarity?

In an overview of the Larkinite Labour movement, Clarkson placed great emphasis of Griffith's anglophobia, while not allowing it any foundation whatever. The lack of reciprocity of British railworkers during the 1911 Irish dispute has already been noted, and, indeed, there was no sympathetic strike action in Britain during any of the Irish stoppages. Clarkson's comments, in the summary of his study, on the attitude of British to Irish Labour, are interesting:

> British Labour, guided by an unerring instinct of self-preservation, has long interested itself in the affairs of the Irish working class. By the attraction of its superior wealth and power, it drew Irish workers into its own organisation. But support of Irish trade unionists engaged in industrial disputes has ever been

15 Clarkson, *Labour and Nationalism*, p.281; Davis, *Griffith and Non-Violent Sinn Féin*, p.138.

> conditioned by certain considerations, viz., that British interests be at stake in the disputes....With the peculiar aspirations of revolutionary Irish workers British Labour has never betrayed the slightest sympathy.

In the light of the above, how he could not bring himself to an understanding of Griffith's position is even more interesting.

Griffith attacked Ben Tillet, leader of the British dock labourers, for telling Dublin workers that Irish nationalism was irrelevant, but still failing to sanction sympathetic strikes in Britain in support of those same workers. This was not mentioned by Clarkson. Griffith must have experienced a certain crusty pleasure when he read the 'stinging criticisms' Connolly made of some former British Labour allies, who turned into 'ultra jingoes' at the outbreak of war in 1914. The men Connolly had in mind were Tillet and Tom Mann, described by Ryan as 'former targets of Mr Griffith's most acid approaches'.

This was what Connolly had to say about them:

> These two men were, before the war, the greatest of internationalists, and rather despised our Irish love of our own nationality, as being mere sentimental slop, and entirely out of date. Now they are raving jingoes, howling for the blood of every rival of the British capitalist class.[16]

A number of historians compared the attitudes of *Irish Freedom* (organ of the republican wing of Sinn Féin) on labour questions with those of Griffith's newspaper. According to Henry, *Irish Freedom* 'attempted to do what the old Sinn Féin had not as yet done, that is, get into direct touch with labour questions and the labour movement, though not very successfully'. This latter qualification contrasted with the opinions of such later historians as Greaves and Edwards, who tended to make enthusiastic pronouncements only to discover that they were difficult to sustain.

A survey of the *United Irishman* and *Sinn Féin* does not bear out Henry's view that pre-1910 Sinn Féin ignored both working-class issues and organisations. The link between Labour and the republican wing of Griffith's movement was seen by Henry as a shared wish for a 'free and independent nation, enjoying a true republican freedom', but he believed they disagreed on almost everything else, and gave as an example the young republicans objecting to English trade unions sending 'English money' to finance Irish strikes.[17]

16 Clarkson, *Labour and Nationalism*, p.477; Ryan, *Connolly*, pp.74,76.

17 Henry, *Evolution*, pp.95-6,100.

Clarkson regarded *Irish Freedom*'s 'tone' as very different from Griffith's, but his brief survey of the journal revealed few differences of substance. One learns that *Irish Freedom* attacked *Sinn Féin* during the 1911 rail strike, accusing it of taking the 'surest way to rivet the chains of English dictation more tightly round the necks of Irish railway workers' by advocating 'unconditional surrender'. Griffith's journal never called for surrender.

However, Clarkson made it clear that not all readers of, and contributors to, the republican paper supported tying the national and social struggles together, and there was a quarrel between the two schools of thought. For example, the following appeared in an editorial of April 1913: 'The independence of this country is the first practical step towards the building up of a decent civilisation'. This was a position akin to Griffith's. Clarkson also pointed out that in 'From a Hermitage' (1913) 'Pearse wrote to denounce the horrible conditions existing in Dublin, though blaming them on foreign domination', and this, again, is undiluted Griffith. *Irish Freedom* regarded both socialism and capitalism as foreign imports, and this, too, was true of Griffith.[18]

Greaves declared that Larkin's 'series of spectacular strikes' clearly showed 'the revolutionary potential of the working class'. Those associated with *Irish Freedom* were interested in 'the new militancy of the proletariat', but other separatists, and especially Griffith, Greaves considered as denying working-class claims.

Edwards went further, putting Tom Clarke forward as 'a most eloquent commentator on the social evils of the day'. Unfortunately, he produced no evidence for this odd assertion apart from Clarke's letter condemning police brutality during the lockout. The constabulary were, of course, the constant targets of nationalist hostility, and Griffith denounced them every other week in his newspapers. Clarke's letter is hardly sufficient evidence on which to build a case for his social conscience. Edwards omitted to mention that Griffith published this letter in *Sinn Féin*, adding his own voice firmly to that of the IRB man. This surely gives the lie to Edwards's statement that in Griffith's view policemen beating up strikers was 'wholly irrelevant'.

In any event, Edwards insisted Clarke was 'a totally different proposition' to Griffith for two reasons - his commitment to revolution, albeit of a purely political nature, and his lack of devotion to conservative economic thought. But Clarke was hardly an economic theorist and a far stronger case for a social conscience can be made for Griffith, given the vast amount he wrote on social issues. Indeed, in his

18 Clarkson, *Labour and Nationalism*, pp.281-7.

stimulating look at Irish nationalism, Edwards bracketed Griffith and Clarke together on the same 'wing'.[19]

Davis correctly maintained that *Irish Freedom* treated Larkin in a 'more balanced' manner than Griffith's *Sinn Féin.* There was a great debate in *Irish Freedom* about the social subsuming the political struggle, and in *Sinn Féin,* too, many argued that the social did not and should not have to await the success of the political battle. Davis stated that the republican monthly 'did not condemn the workers' but stressed the damage that was being done to Ireland.[20] This was Griffith's approach exactly.

It would be harder to find a fairer, more accurate summary of Griffith's position as regards the 1913 crisis than the following from Marie O'Neill's biography of Jennie Wyse Power:

> Griffith refused to take sides in the dispute. He did not want to split Sinn Féin on what he saw as a side-issue. His policy was national, not sectional. He favoured justice and fair conditions for the workers, but did not oppose the system of capitalism.[21]

19 Greaves, *Mellows*, pp.46-7; Edwards, *Mind of an Activist*, pp.74-5; Owen Dudley Edwards, Gwynfor Evans, Ioan Rhys and Hugh MacDiarmaid, *Celtic Nationalism* (London, 1968), pp.131,180.

20 Davis, *Non-Violent Sinn Féin*, p.138.

21 O'Neill, *Wyse Power*, pp.70-71.

Chapter IV

From World War to Civil War

Exit Larkin: Farewell Connolly: Sinn Féin Expands

The turbulence of the initial Larkin era in Irish Labour history was not to be repeated. Dublin Labour was exhausted after the titanic struggle of 1913 and the next few years were spent recovering and regrouping. With the outbreak of war in Europe and Larkin's departure to America, Griffith's relations with Irish Labour recovered something of the even tenor of the pre-1908 period.

William O'Brien recalled a conference arranged by Eamon Ceannt in the library of the Gaelic League at 25 Parnell Square on 9 September 1914, and listed as among those present Clarke, MacDermott, Plunkett, Pearse, Ceannt, Connolly, MacDonagh (all subsequent signatories of the 1916 Proclamation), Sean T. O'Kelly, John MacBride, as well as Griffith and O'Brien himself. Out of this grew the Irish Neutrality League, with Connolly as president, Thomas Farren (of the ITGWU) as treasurer, Sean T. O'Kelly as secretary, and Countess Markievicz, Seán Milroy, J.J. Scollan, Francis Sheehy-Skeffington, Griffith and O'Brien as committee members. Its inaugural meeting in the Antient Concert Rooms on 12 October was well attended, according to O'Brien who, along with Connolly, O'Kelly, Milroy, Scollan, MacBride and Griffith, addressed the gathering.

O'Brien also recollected that some time before the Easter Rising, Connolly told him a civil provisional government was envisaged, and he was authorised to request O'Brien to act in it. The latter agreed to do so. Its other members were to be Griffith, Alderman Tom Kelly, Seán T. O'Kelly and Hannah Sheehy Skeffington.[1] With Labour/Sinn Féin cooperation against partition and recruiting on the outbreak of the First World War, Connolly and Griffith again combined, as in the Boer War. It was pointed out by Greaves that Larkin had no part in the Irish Neutrality League, divulging nine years later his doubt about the organisation. Greaves speculated that Griffith was 'the stumbling block' to Larkin's membership.

1 MacLysaght, *Forth the Banners Go*, pp.270-71,278.

Connolly's 'What is Our Programme?' (*Workers' Republic*, late January 1916) Greaves believed to be aimed at Griffith and his colleagues. The belief was based on Connolly's phrase 'our fervent advanced patriots' whom he rebuked for attacking, betraying, being anxious to destroy, and even applauding British government harassment of, the trade-union movement, instead of supporting it, and developing its organisation all over Ireland, so that it would then have had the power 'to crumple up and demoralise every offensive move by the enemy against the champions of Irish freedom'.

Concerning this, Greaves stated:

> In the literature of the Irish revolution, this passage is little quoted; when Irish Labour capitulated, first to Sinn Féin, and then to the Free State, the myth of Connolly's friendship with Griffith was extremely useful, and it was overlooked.[2]

This was a curious contention, because Connolly's criticism was aimed at the military men, the Volunteer leadership, of whom he was suspicious at this time. He knew perfectly well Griffith's stance on violent action.

The 1916 Rising claimed the lives of Connolly and of a number of other Labour activists who had also been in Sinn Féin, such as Peadar Macken and William Partridge. The event also greatly extended the appeal of Sinn Féin. O'Brien (at the time general treasurer of the ITGWU) told of Griffith, who had been recently released from Reading Jail, calling to his home in January 1917, and proposing a federation of Volunteers, Sinn Féin, the INL and Labour. O'Brien believed that the Volunteers would not work with Griffith, but he did not tell him this. Instead, he informed him of his belief that the Labour Party would not be willing to merge in Griffith's proposed catch-all grouping.

Later, in a second reference to this same visit, O'Brien revealed that the reason he thought the Volunteers would not cooperate with Griffith was because of his association with MacNeill, but he did not put this to him as he 'thought it would be offensive'. In any event, Griffith informed O'Brien of the plan to run Count Plunkett in the North Roscommon by-election and, as it turned out, O'Brien took a very full part in this campaign, with Griffith and others.

After his success Count Plunkett set up a by-elections' committee, on which O'Brien and Thomas Farren of Labour served, along with Griffith, Alderman Tom Kelly, Fr O'Flanagan, Collins, Figgis, Rory O'Connor and others. This functioned in both the South Longford and

2 Greaves, *Connolly*, pp.290-91,306-7.

East Clare by-elections of 1917, O'Brien and Farren having no difficulty working with Griffith. Quite the opposite, as can be seen from O'Brien's account of the Mansion House conference, which Plunkett called in April 1917, and which the Labour activist attended as part of a delegation sent to voice support.

At this gathering, according to O'Brien, Fr O'Flanagan proposed a committee of seven to draft a constitution. Griffith, seconding the proposal, 'said he thought that Labour should be represented on it, and he would submit the name of Mr William O'Brien, whom he felt was friendly to the whole movement'. At the subsequent first meeting of this committee, O'Brien was nominated chairman by Griffith's followers, and he accepted the post.[3]

Greaves's discussion of the background to the first by-election of 1917 did not mention O'Brien's record of Griffith's visit to him in January of that year to try to get a coalition formed of the various groups. In fact, as has been noted, the ITGWU man mentioned it twice. The visit must indicate that Griffith envisaged a role for Labour along with the various anti-Redmondite factions. Similarly, Greaves's account of the Mansion House conference ignored Griffith's nomination of O'Brien.[4] Mitchell was the only Labour historian who referred to Griffith's approach to O'Brien. He mentioned briefly the various by-elections in which O'Brien and Farren were active throughout 1917, from which Sinn Féin was 'the ultimate beneficiary'.[5]

Clarkson discussed post-1916 Sinn Féin's interaction with Labour, but seldom referred to Griffith. However, he did indicate his conviction that the latter 'had changed not a whit since those eventful years when, through the pages of *Sinn Féin*, he bade Labour repudiate socialism and resume its rightful place as the humble servant of the nation - occasionally to be petted, perhaps, but never to speak until it was spoken to'.

Clarkson believed that de Valera, the new President of Sinn Féin, 'long steeped in the abstractions of mathematics...was an easy prey to the social abstractions of his colleague', Griffith. So, in his inaugural presidential speech, in October 1917, he espoused Griffith's entreaty that 'in a free Ireland, with the social conditions that obtained in Ireland, Labour had a far better chance than it would have in capitalist England'. On this Clarkson commented: 'Apparently, 1913 had meant nothing to

3 MacLysaght, *Forth the Banners Go*, pp.134-5,140,143-7,149-50.

4 Greaves, *Mellows*, pp.113,115.

5 Mitchell, *Labour in Irish Politics*, pp.81-2.

him'.[6] Henry discerned no special role for Griffith in post-1916 Sinn Féin's relations with Labour, in marked contrast to Greaves, who singled out Griffith as the *eminence grise* (or perhaps *bête noire*), formulating a consistent anti-Labour policy.

Greaves looked in some detail at the October 1917 Sinn Féin convention. He remarked on the absence of any social dimension from the programme worked out there, the workers and small farmers being ignored. He also noted that the constituent assembly it was proposed to form after the postwar elections 'was not even pledged to perform the function inherent in its name - that of enacting a new constitution'. Greaves detected a possible link between these two phenomena, and explained it as Griffith and his supporters feeling that some connection with England, whether a common head of state or the perpetuation of some constitutional arrangements, would protect against the danger of social revolution.[7]

This conclusion is almost too much of a *non sequitur* to bear analysis. True, the convention in question concerned itself purely with the political question of achieving independence. Griffith's reluctance as regards the goal of a republic was grounded in two considerations - that the aim of the movement be a feasible one and that it retain some hope of maintaining the unity of the country. The question of 'a social revolution' did not exercise his mind in any way.

Mitchell diverged somewhat from Greaves in his interpretation, because he wrote that the reorganised Sinn Féin, which emerged from its October 1917 convention, 'from the beginning proclaimed its sympathy with Labour'. But, as if to contradict this alleged affinity, Mitchell gave the belief of the socialist republican, Peadar O'Donnell, that 'the place Connolly purchased for the organised Labour movement in the leadership of the independence struggle was being denied or reneged'.

O'Donnell believed that Labour's refusal of a share in the forefront of the struggle for political autonomy made it easy for 'de Valera to call Griffith in and shut Labour out'.[8] Griffith hardly needed to be called in to an organised grouping which he had initiated, and of which he had been the leading light for a decade more than most of the other prominent members. But it is clear from O'Donnell's statement that he believed Griffith stood for the very antithesis of Labour's aspirations.

Griffith took no part in the pre-1918 general election negotiations

6 Clarkson, *Labour and Nationalism*, pp.336-7.

7 Henry, *Evolution*, p.276; Greaves, *Mellows*, pp.138-40.

8 Mitchell, *Labour in Irish Politics*, p.83.

between Sinn Féin and Labour, as he was in prison. A standing committee ran Sinn Féin during his and de Valera's absence. Robert Brennan, Fr O'Flanagan, Alderman Tom Kelly and Harry Boland met with Labour representatives and persuaded them not to participate in the political contest.

As he viewed matters from exile in America, Larkin was not happy. As Mitchell expressed it: 'He was suspicious of a republic that had Arthur Griffith, his old adversary, as its vice-President (and, for almost a year, its acting-President)'. Actually, Griffith filled the second role for a year-and-a-half. (He was not, of course, vice-President or acting-President of a republic, but of the Dáil.)

Larkin expressed his concern in a letter to Thomas Foran, president of the ITGWU. He returned to New York early in 1918 to find changes in the Irish and socialist movements there, many of which he disliked. He was very disturbed by the success of Sinn Féin among the American-Irish, to the loss of the socialist and Labour movements. He wrote to Foran that the Sinn Féin movement in America was 'anti-Labour' and regarded socialists as 'anti-Christs', having tried to persuade the American public that a Catholic revolution had occurred in Ireland. Larkin accused the members of being 'the most violent American jingoes'. They nauseated him with their pomposity and showiness. He described them all as political 'tricksters'. The Irish who had recently arrived to raise money and stimulate an interest in Ireland were also attacked by Larkin. The most prominent were Hannah Sheehy-Skeffington (who was 'just an apologist for the Sinn Féin crowd', never spoke of the Labour movement or socialist party, and who gave the impression that she and her late husband were members of the organisation in Ireland); Nora Connolly (who 'follows the same lines'), and Dr Patrick MacCartan (categorised as 'a rank reactionary [who] struts about like a stage hero').

Even more infuriatingly, 'They make out Arthur Griffith is a God-given saint and statesman, nobody in Ireland done (*sic*) anything but Sinn Féin. Connolly and the other boys recanted socialism and labour, and were good Sinn Féiners. My God, it is sickening'. He told Foran he would do his best to get to Ireland, as he was worried that the initiative was being snatched from Labour by Sinn Féin, and he wanted to know what O'Brien and his associates were doing permitting 'the Griffith gang to monopolise all the credit for the effort'.[9]

9 Mitchell, *Labour in Irish Politics*, pp.95-101,106-7; Larkin, *Larkin*, pp.220-22.

Setting Bounds to the March of the Revolution?

Dáil Éireann's performance on social issues between 1919 and 1921 was examined by a number of historians. The 'democratic programme', one of the documents read on the opening day of the first Dáil, was the twin product of the Labour Party leader, Thomas Johnson, and Seán T. O'Kelly. Collins and the IRB strongly objected to the original draft and would not have agreed to the document being put forward at all, unless O'Kelly amended it, which he did.

It was Strauss's view that the programme was passed only because of the absence due to imprisonment of the moderate Sinn Féin leaders, especially Griffith. Mitchell also held that the latter would not have approved 'the programme's philosophy', and offered as evidence to support this contention the fact that 'he never publicly referred to it'.[10]

These views must be open to serious doubt. The 'democratic programme' was so vague in its aspirations that most politicians of the time could have given their allegiance to it. Strauss and Mitchell were obviously not familiar with Griffith's letter of January 1919, from Gloucester Jail, tendering some hurried suggestions for the consideration of the first Dáil. Many of the subjects dealt with in that letter appeared in the 'democratic programme': the abolition of the poor-law system and its replacement; the development of the country's natural resources; industrial development, including along cooperative lines; the creation of a consular service; the national control of transport.

Indeed, all of these had been planks in the Sinn Féin programme as far back as its foundation in 1905. There was nothing in the document read before the first Dáil that would have been anathema to Griffith. He was hardly unusual in never having referred to it afterwards, a point on which Mitchell laid emphasis. Few others - and most of them lived much longer than Griffith - ever did so either except, perhaps, in embarrassment.[11]

Griffith, from the time he was appointed to replace de Valera as head of the Dáil, was seen by Greaves as directing affairs 'with the advantage of a man who knew his own mind'. His proposal to establish a fund to provide land for landless men was judged to have contributed to partition: 'The northern industrialists might just conceivably have stomached the revolutionary expropriation of southern landlords, but

10 Strauss, *Irish Nationalism and British Democracy*, p.263; Mitchell, *Labour in Irish Politics*, p.110.

11 See *Minutes of Proceedings of First Dáil*, pp.22-3; also, 'Important letter of 1919', in *Capuchin Annual*, 1969, pp.330-35.

compensating them out of their own profits was another matter'. This is a bewildering observation. Griffith's motion in the Dáil made no stipulation about compensation, but simply proposed establishing a land fund to purchase land for the landless.[12]

When the British government abolished war-time price controls on agricultural products, in the late spring of 1920, there was great activity in the west of Ireland - cattle drives, uprooting of fences, attacks on landlords, the seizure, breaking up and cultivation of ranches and demesnes. The big landowners, according to Greaves, 'flocked' to the Dáil seeking help.

The activity of the smallholders and landless men was seen, 'not as a means of fulfilling the democratic programme of Dáil Éireann, but as a "threat to the stability" of the national movement to which the landlords did not belong', Greaves wrote. The Dáil intervened to stop this spontaneous upsurge, instituting land arbitration courts, and a land bank. Griffith was referred to by Greaves as stating in a secret session of the Dáil, on 29 June, that the land bank had effected a settlement of the crisis in the west, and that the land courts had prevented the land question from being used 'to divert the energies of the people from the national issue'. To Greaves this agrarian policy had crucial results for the whole Irish revolution:

> For the first time the power of Dáil Éireann had been directed against the masses. That Griffith had long hankered after the landlord alliance is, of course, well known. The new relation with the landlords who flocked to Dublin to save their estates implied a new relation with the southern unionists. Griffith had started the process which was later to produce partition and the Free State.

This ranks as an extraordinary verdict by any standards. Griffith's 'hankering after the landlord alliance' is not as well known as Greaves presumed, and one is no wiser on the topic from this non-treatment of it. As to the 'new relation with the southern unionists', Griffith did indeed envisage some role for them in the independent Ireland he foresaw. That he was the chief architect of partition was a highly dubious assertion.

It must be pointed out that the decree on land seizures was introduced into the Dáil by Austin Stack, as Minister for Home Affairs. Cathal Brugha made it clear that the ministry as a whole agreed on this

12 See *Minutes of Proceedings*, p.121.

approach. Only one member of the Dáil, P.J. Ward of Donegal South, objected to it.[13]

Other material from this session of the first Dáil was used by Greaves to get in another swipe at Griffith. Collins was credited as 'the spokesman of the left' (albeit with the qualification 'in this session at any rate') willing to implement 'a socialist programme'. The subject was the development of the country's natural resources, which Collins said should be in the hands of the county councils and other public bodies, to prevent their exploitation by private syndicates. Another deputy, David Kent, agreed with Collins and named a promising coal-mine in his own constituency.

Greaves's narrative continued:

> But Griffith would have none of this....He replied that 'if the coal and other deposits, of which Mr Kent spoke, existed, it was the business of the people to endeavour to attract capital to work them'. Capitalist dogmatism completely befogged him. The democratic programme of Dáil Éireann was a scrap of paper, and Labour, alone able to defend it, was not present. The leader of Sinn Féin declared that the revolution had gone far enough.

Now, Kent had said, 'while they [i.e., the Dáil] had money, they should use it to the best advantage'. Greaves omitted this, and the quotation he gave was *part* of Griffith's reply to Kent. Griffith pointed out that the Dáil 'could not undertake the working of mineral deposits with the resources *at present* at its disposal. The whole loan of £250,000 would not be sufficient to work two coal-mines'.[14] (Writer's italics.) From this it is clear that he was not ruling out public development of the country's natural wealth, and was not so 'completely befogged' by 'capitalist dogmatism' as Greaves liked to believe.

The idea of the people of the area attempting to attract capital to develop their mine was simply Griffith's old chestnut of self-help or Sinn Féinism, in the absence of the Dáil's ability to come to their aid. The development of the country's mineral resources was, of course, an old pet topic of Griffith's, to which he devoted much attention long before Dáil Éireann came into being, and if Greaves had contented himself with even a token examination of Griffith's writings, he would have seen many calls for county council and General Council of County Councils' action on the matter.

Indeed, the same Dáil *Minutes*, from which Greaves selectively

13 *Minutes of Proceedings*, pp.178-9.

14 *ibid.*, pp.174-5.

quoted, show that one of Griffith's first actions on becoming acting-President, was to establish a commission of enquiry into the country's natural resources.[15] Flimsier evidence could not have been chosen by Greaves on which to base his sweeping assertion that 'the leader [actually, ex-leader] of Sinn Féin declared that the revolution had gone far enough'.

The interview which Griffith and MacNeill gave to the *Financial Times* in mid-September 1920, when they reassured businessmen as to the safety of their potential investments in Ireland, was treated very differently by Greaves and Mitchell. To the former it made 'the equal rights and equal opportunities', pledged by the 'declaration of independence' to all Irish citizens, 'subject to the interests of foreign financiers'. Thus, Griffith was declared to have been 'setting the course for compromise', while the ordinary people of the country, who 'judge their leaders by themselves', were risking their all carrying on the struggle for freedom, totally unaware of what he was planning. Griffith was thereby depicted in the sinister role of betrayer of a fighting and trusting people.

By contrast, Mitchell interpreted the interview simply as evidence of the 'conservative tendencies' of the Dáil government, to which 'the Labour leadership was sensitive'. So, the Labour newspaper, *Irish Opinion*, 'reacted sharply', discerning in the interview 'the replacement of French [the Lord Lieutenant] and Greenwood [the Secretary of State for Ireland] by Messrs Griffith and MacNeill - and nothing more'. Nevertheless, Mitchell regarded the Dáil under Griffith as having a praiseworthy performance on social issues - a separate Labour ministry, a national conciliation board, a 'labour arbitration tribunal', a conciliation board for local government bodies and their employees, and a number of attempts to mitigate the increasing unemployment.[16]

Strauss put forward the view that 'social tension within Irish society' following the First World War was to be found in the lower classes in the towns, the landless labourers of the south, and the land-hungry tenants and small farmers of the west. The guerilla fighters of the Anglo-Irish War belonged mainly to 'the underprivileged sections of the town population'.

They had no chance of outright military victory and their best option would have been a broadening of the fight to the social arena, by combining 'armed guerilla warfare with the spontaneous rebellion of

15 *Minutes of Proceedings*, pp.122-3.

16 Greaves, *Mellows*, pp.169-70,172-4,179,188-92,195-6; Greaves, *ITGWU*, pp.275-6; Mitchell, *Labour in Irish Politics*, pp.115-17.

all dissatisfied elements in Irish society'. In Strauss's estimate, the political nub of those years of upheaval was how the moderate wing of the Sinn Féin leadership prevented such a development taking place. He believed that Griffith 'strained every nerve' to ensure that Sinn Féin did not become involved in the social conflict, and that he used 'his great prestige' to counteract social turmoil.

The only evidence offered to support the latter contention was extremely skimpy. It was an extract from Griffith's address to the 1919 Sinn Féin ard-fheis, in which he described the movement as 'a composite party', and continued: 'No part of that composition may claim its own individual programme until the national ideal of freedom has first been attained. Then we may press forward our separate ideals. Until then, we must sink ourselves that the nation may gain from our unity'.

Such sentiments from Griffith may be found in the *United Irishman* as far back as 1904,[17] and it is questionable to single him out as the central figure in keeping down social unrest in the 1917-22 period. Indeed, a few short lines later, Strauss confirmed as much. He stated that land seizures made in the west, in the spring of 1918, led to 'the central leadership of the Volunteers' ordering members not to participate in such activity. Griffith was not part of the Volunteer leadership.

Greaves concurred wholeheartedly with Strauss's views. He regretted that nobody in the first Dáil 'contemplated the type of mass revolutionary struggle of which the working class must be the centre'. Instead, such forces as industrial unrest and land agitation were rejected as a means of complete political power. 'The conception of a democratic revolution of workers and small farmers, attracting to themselves the middle strata, and neutralising the capitalists' had no place in Griffith's thinking, Greaves declared.[18] Nor in the thinking of anyone else in Dáil Éireann, one might add.

Thomas Johnson wrote a manifesto entitled 'The Country in Danger' for the ILPTUC, which was issued at Easter 1921. In his memoirs, O'Brien narrated that Johnson, on asking him if he thought Griffith would agree with it, was surprised to be informed that he almost certainly would not. O'Brien stated that he, in his turn, was 'greatly surprised' when Griffith received it favourably and told them they should discuss it with Robert Barton, Minister for Agriculture in the

17 See *United Irishman*, 19 November 1904.

18 Strauss, *Irish Nationalism and British Democracy*, pp.264-5; Greaves, *Mellows*, pp.179-80.

Dáil cabinet. Despite this evidence, Greaves could declare blithely that Johnson's document was 'utterly repugnant' to Griffith.

According to Johnson's biographer, J.A. Gaughan, the Labour leader and the other members of the ILPTUC executive were grateful when Griffith, on behalf of Sinn Féin, welcomed the manifesto. But Gaughan added that the Dáil ministry, worried that the document would create rather than solve problems, decided that the Ministers for Labour, Trade and Commerce and Agriculture would confer to take whatever steps were needed to prevent a class war occurring, and would try to arrange a conference between farmer and labour representatives.[19]

Hostility From Abroad: Support from at Home

The signing of the Treaty provoked Larkin to display what Fox called his 'forceful powers of vituperation and rhetoric'. From Comstock Jail in the United States, he issued a statement on the Treaty, four days after it was signed. The statement was printed in the *Voice of Labour* in Dublin, in the first week of January 1922, the editors dissociating both the ITGWU and the journal from its sentiments. Larkin referred to the signatories as 'unscrupulous, ambitious creatures that have climbed to power over the dead bodies of our comrades'. The fate wished for them was proclaimed with venom:

> We demand that the creatures who discussed and agreed to such an unholy bargain be dismissed from the ranks, that they be execrated publicly, that in our opinion they are foresworn traitors, that the land of Ireland is too small to accommodate their treacherous bodies, that the fate that was meted out to the mean-spirited traitors, spies and informers during the past struggle, is too holy a death for these six [?] helots; that the fate of Judas is the only fate they merit; that a sufficient length of rope should be provided them, and they be invited to go out of the land of Ireland and utilise their length of rope in the kingdom of their adoption - on London bridge, within sight of the spot whereon they tried to sell the people of Ireland.

With this statement in mind, Emmet Larkin believed that 'in justice...Larkin must be asked to bear some measure of the responsibility for the Civil War in Ireland', because 'he cast serious doubts on the integrity of those who signed the Treaty'. The Labour leader's hostility to the Treaty was 'seconded only by his intense dislike

19 Mac Lysaght, *Forth the Banners Go*, p.209; Greaves, *Mellows*, p.241; J.A. Gaughan, *Thomas Johnson 1872-1963* (Dublin, 1980), p.185.

of the chief supporter and architect of the document, Arthur Griffith'. In the *Workers' Republic* of June 1922, Larkin submitted Griffith to further 'vicious criticism'.[20]

Labour representatives tried to reach a compromise between the pro- and anti-Treaty sides during the Christmas 1921 recess of the Dáil, before the Treaty was voted on. The Labour proposals have been summarised earlier. Both Gaughan and Mitchell pointed out that Griffith and the pro-Treaty group 'gave the proposals a friendly reception'. This led the Labour executive to hope that a basis for agreement had been discovered, but, as the 1922 report of the ILPTUC put it, 'this hope was shattered at the interview with Mr de Valera'.[21]

Three days after a majority of the Dáil voted support for the Treaty, a Labour delegation addressed the assembly on the urgency of dealing with the pressing problem of unemployment. Clarkson's opinion was that Griffith 'curtly but benignly' assured the Labour representatives that he understood the question of unemployment and, with his offer of a committee to deal with the issue, 'dismissed them from the room and apparently dismissed all thought of the matter from his head'. Clarkson was convinced that the Treaty split absorbed all the leaders' attention (he was surely largely correct in this), so that 'labour must wait' was their 'monotonic response'.

Gaughan also referred to Griffith's proposal of a committee to meet the Labour representatives to try to deal with unemployment. He added that the leader of the Dáil and his colleagues were impressed by the Labour delegation, because the cabinet minutes of the following day, which recorded a discussion of names for the Provisional Government, contained a promise from the Minister for Labour, Joseph McGrath, 'to ascertain the feelings of Labour leaders regarding representation thereon'. It was also noted by Gaughan that a fortnight later Griffith, Collins and a number of other ministers met the ILPTUC executive 'to receive their detailed proposals for reducing unemployment'.

Like Gaughan, but unlike Clarkson, Mitchell was of the opinion that the Labour group was not 'completely dismissed' by Griffith and his colleagues. Again, he was similar to Gaughan in alluding to the meeting between Griffith's cabinet and the Labour executive. The lack of action was due to political concerns being uppermost in the new government's mind, Mitchell argued in common with Clarkson.[22]

20 Fox, *Larkin*, pp.161-2; Larkin, *Larkin*, pp.255-6.

21 Gaughan, *Johnson*, pp.194-5; Mitchell, *Labour in Irish Politics*, pp.147-8.

22 Clarkson, *Labour and Nationalism*, pp.439-41; Gaughan, *Johnson*, pp.195-6; Mitchell, *Labour in Irish Politics*, pp.149-51.

At the conference held to choose its candidates in late February 1922, the Labour Party voted overwhelmingly to call for a plebiscite on the Treaty before the general election to the new independent parliament. Johnson corresponded with Griffith on Labour's desire for a referendum, either before or on the same day as the election. The Dáil cabinet rejected the first as impracticable, because of the existing circumstances in the country, and the second as likely to be confusing for the voters.

However, at the Mansion House conference, called by Archbishop Byrne to try to bring the opposing sides on the Treaty together, and which Johnson and O'Brien of Labour attended, Griffith and Collins agreed to hold such a plebiscite before the elections, but de Valera did not.[23] Labour's best endeavours failed to prevent the fratricidal strife which finally erupted in earnest in late June 1922.

It was unfortunate for Griffith's historical reputation that he proved such an inveterate enemy of Larkin. This aspect of his career, from 1908 to 1914, may have predisposed even fairly moderate Labour historians to look only for evidence of criticism of working-class organisations on his part during those years, and caused them not only to ignore his Labour views *before* that time, but also his more constructive contributions during the many social upheavals of that particular period. His anti-Larkin renown may also account for the comparative lack of attention paid by Labour historians to the 1914-22 span of his life. The net result of this focusing on the 1908-14 years has been the neglect of the two longer sections of his public career when his interaction with Labour was much more congenial.

Fox found a passage from *The Resurrection of Hungary* of 'special interest' because it showed how 'Griffith could detect, *outside Ireland*, the imposture of condemning all progressive ideas as "foreign" and so raising prejudice against them'. (The italics were Fox's.) The gist of this passage was that at a meeting of the independent Hungarian parliament the 'Intransigeant' party wished to amend the constitution so that there would be liberty and equality and the serfs would be set free. The nobles denounced these as 'French ideas' and the serfs actually accepted their argument that providence ordained the nobles as their natural leaders. So, while the Intransigeants, 'an insignificant minority in the Diet, fought to free the peasant, the peasant reviled them for their pains'.

Fox commented on the excerpt: 'Such an incisive commentary on the methods of reaction reads strangely from Griffith, who could see how

23 Gaughan, *Johnson*, p.198; Mitchell, *Labour in Irish Politics*, pp.155,157.

Hungarian nobles shrieked "French ideas" to defend their privileges, while he himself scolded Irish workers for their "English trade unionism"'.[24]

Whatever about 'scolding', Griffith's warnings against the influence of English on Irish trade unionism were three-fold: (a) its denationalising tendency (given some substance by Connolly's condemnation of Tillet and Mann); (b) its self-interest (no reciprocity or sympathetic strike action - Clarkson's summary confirmed this aspect of Griffith's opposition); (c) its potential for destroying Irish trade and industry while leaving those of its own country intact. (It was ascribing too sinister a motive to English trade unions to argue that they provoked strikes in their Irish branches to win increased trade for their own English employers.)

But it must be stressed that Griffith defended trade unionism, was a member of a trade union himself, and that there was a history of very active trade unionism in his family. What he understood by 'English trade unionism' (as represented by Larkin) was syndicalism, with its ideas of the one big union and the general strike. The thought that because one group of workers was in dispute with an employer, workers in all other unrelated areas would come out in sympathetic strike horrified Griffith. To him this spelt disaster for the fragile, under-developed Irish manufacturing and industrial economy.

It must be remembered that the passage given by Fox described a post-independence situation. Political freedom was always an absolute priority with Griffith. Would he have been among the 'Intransigeants' had not death untimely struck him down? It is by no means impossible.

24 Fox, *Green Banners*, pp.73-4.

Chapter V

The Frankenstein Image

Griffith a Racist?

The suggestion that Griffith was a racist has a relatively recent pedigree. Edwards was the first to strongly assert this. He contended that John Mitchel's racism was restored by Griffith from 'the subconscious to the conscious Irish nationalist mind'. Further, Griffith carried the Young Irelander's 'hatred of English, Negroes and Jews to the point of a fairly general xenophobia'. It was not just a case of Griffith faithfully presenting every aspect of Mitchel's thought but 'the racial aspects of Mitchel's writing were integral to Griffith's view of nationalism'.

Griffith advocated 'a self-centred nationalism, whose racist features were intended to buttress the Irishman's estimate of himself'. An example of Griffith's racism in practice was that 'an effective socialist speaker could be silenced at his public meetings by refusing to grant the right of vocal expression to anyone who was not an Irishman'.[1]

The 'effective socialist speaker' just referred to was Edwards's own grandfather[2], and this incident may well have affected the grandson's attitude as a whole to Griffith. As Mitchel was mentioned by him, Edwards obviously had in mind the preface by Griffith to Mitchel's *Jail Journal*. In this, Griffith refused to apologise for Mitchel's defence of slavery in the southern United States during his time in America, holding that no excuse was needed 'for an Irish nationalist declining to hold the Negro his peer in right'.

Griffith went on to declare:

> The right of the Irish to political independence never was, is not, and never can be dependent upon the admission of equal rights in all other peoples. It is based on no theory of, and dependent in nowise for its existence or justification on, the 'Rights of Man'. It is

1 Edwards et al., *Celtic Nationalism*, pp.126-8.

2 See *Irish Nation and Peasant*, 2 January 1909.

independent of theories of government and doctrines of philanthropy and universalism.[3]

But, as will be seen below, a later historian believed that Griffith changed his mind about this and, certainly, evidence can be adduced from his writings which contradict the stance he seemed to be adopting here.

Greaves asserted that Griffith expressly denied African and Asian equality with Europeans, and that he was not above referring to 'niggers' in his paper. He then proceeded to link this attitude in Griffith with his complete failure to distinguish between capitalist and worker in Britain. The obvious inference Greaves wished drawn was that to Griffith the workers were a lesser breed, to be exploited at the whim of unscrupulous employers.[4]

It is true that the primary influence on Griffith's nationalism came from the Young Irelanders. But, Thomas Davis exerted a greater sway over him than Mitchel. As Richard Davis perceptively remarked, 'the actual content of Mitchel's writings, as opposed to his spirit and style, influenced Griffith hardly at all'.[5] These mid-19th century Irish nationalists, like their European counterparts, romantically exalted the concepts of race and nation. But does it follow from this that Griffith's nationalist philosophy was seriously contaminated with racist attitudes? There is a substantial body of evidence, mainly from his own writings, which suggests that it was not.

In August and November 1899, and May 1900, he wrote about and condemned Cecil Rhodes's conquest and appropriation of the Matabele and Mashona and their territories in southern Africa. In one of his articles he referred to 'the slaughter of the Matabele and the peaceful, industrious, inoffensive Mashona'. In another, he declared: 'To quote the late, lamented Bishop Moriarty: "Hell is not hot enough, nor eternity long enough" to punish the white devils led by Rhodes....Murder and rape were frequent....The Matabele were no match for maxim guns....I cannot describe the horrors of that war in the columns of a paper'.

The British treatment of the native Africans infuriated him. He referred with bitter irony to Bibles being given to them, but slavery being established in tandem.

The Kaffir chief, Luke Jantjes, was disinterred and decapitated and the head kept as a trophy of victory by one British army captain. In the

3 Arthur Griffith (ed.), *Jail Journal* (Dublin, 1913), pp.xii-xiv.

4 Greaves, *Connolly*, p.94.

5 Davis, *Griffith and Non-Violent Sinn Féin*, p.151.

conquest of Rhodesia, the troopers were under orders to rob, rape, pillage, and torture prisoners to death: 'No newspaper in the world could possibly publish anything like a true account of how the English "pacified" Rhodesia - murder of the wounded on the battlefield, mutilation of the bodies of the dead, torturing of prisoners before execution - these are simple and pious things to other deeds of the standard-bearers of civilisation'.

He gave the following account of an experience of his own in South Africa:

> I knew a virtuous Briton to burn a couple of hundred wretched Kaffirs alive. [The term 'Kaffir' was not pejorative at that time.] Of course, he did it for a good purpose. The mine was afire and the Kaffirs were below and the virtuous Briton battened down the hatches to save his property. When some of the gentiles remonstrated ['gentiles' suggests the Briton was a Jew], my old acquaintance remarked that the saving of some £50,000 was of more importance than the lives of a few hundred damn niggers.

Writing in 1901, he declared that 70 years before that the British 'knocked the shackles off the slave', and yet the slave-trade still flourished in British Rhodesia. Continuing, he wrote: 'Three years [ago] I stood in the Zanzibar slave-market, and watched the poor iron-collared, wrist-and-ankle-chained wretches being bought and sold...' This passage sits uneasily with his failure to question Mitchel's defence of slavery.

In September 1900, there were two very interesting articles by him on the African peoples. The Zulus, in particular, fascinated him, a fascination that was to continue right through his life, as will be seen from the following.

A banquet was given by some of the Irish in London for the Treaty delegates. Griffith said little during the meal but, after a few coffees with brandy in them, he opened up. Among the subjects he talked of were the Zulus - their magnificent physique and fine morals (he said, for example, that they were never known to steal). In fact, he praised them so much that one of those present at his table remarked: 'Sir, they must be angels, not men'.[6]

After his death an anonymous author, who disagreed with him over the Treaty, penned the following about him in the course of a tribute: 'He had a keen regard for the Boers, but was not satisfied with the treatment the Blacks got from either Boers or English, and on one

6 Ms.22,293 NLI.

occasion he told me that the future of South Africa belonged to the Zulus, who were rapidly advancing in civilisation'.[7]

Griffith's attitude to what constituted 'Irishness' was certainly free from any racist taint. One of the issues discussed in the early *United Irishman* was who was and was not Irish, some taking the view that only the Gaelic Irish were the true Irish, while others held with Thomas Davis that one did not have to be Gaelic to be Irish.

Basically, Griffith defined an Irishman as one who regarded Ireland as his country and was prepared to work for it: 'Be he Gael or Cromwellian, French Hugenot or Spanish-Irish, the man who swears to an Irish nation - and he only - is an Irishman'.[8] As Robert Kee further observed, Griffith was 'free of a racial view of Irish nationality even in his attitude to the language'.[9]

It will be recalled that in the extract from his preface to the *Jail Journal* cited above, Griffith declared that Ireland's right to independence was unrelated to any doctrines of universalism. H.V. Brasted argued that the theory of 'universalism' gained some recruits in Ireland, where its main achievement was to hold in check the 'self-centred' and 'chauvinistic' interpretations which 'Mitchel, and to a lesser extent, Griffith attempted to impose on Irish nationalism'.

Griffith was seen by Brasted as originally having no time for 'sentimental ideals of national brotherhood', and the *Jail Journal* preface extract given above, where he asserted that the Irish right to independence was totally unrelated to the right of peoples elsewhere to freedom, was quoted by Brasted. However, Brasted regarded Griffith as later acknowledging that 'Ireland was not alone and did not have to go it alone'.[10]

Glandon agreed with Kee that Griffith's understanding of Irish nationality did not depend upon race or creed but upon 'the indissoluble unity of the whole people of Ireland in one community'. She believed that his ideas on nationality were similar in some ways to the German romantics, especially Herder, because Griffith saw Irish nationalism as 'an indigenous historical and cultural phenomenon which, in its uniqueness was not transferable to any other nationalistic

7 *Southern Cross*, 18 August 1922.

8 *United Irishman*, 23 March 1901.

9 Kee, *Bold Fenian Men*, p.152.

10 H.V. Brasted, 'Irish nationalism and the British Empire in the late 19th century', in Oliver MacDonagh, W.F. Mandle and Pauric Travers (eds.), *Irish Culture and Nationalism 1750-1950* (London, 1983), pp.97-8.

cause'.[11] But his attitudes to imperialism (which are examined below) do not reveal this exclusiveness in his nationalism.

Griffith an Imperialist?

The charge that Griffith harboured imperialist longings emanated from the far left. Greaves asserted that, far from being an anti-imperialist, Griffith lusted after an 'Anglo-Irish empire in which Britain and Ireland would jointly exploit the lesser breeds'. Beresford Ellis was in complete agreement with Greaves.[12]

Nowhere in what he wrote did Griffith ever refer to an 'Anglo-Irish empire'. The imputation to him of imperial designs, and a desire to exploit non-white races, may well be based on a misreading of a series of articles in *Sinn Féin*, between January and May 1911, under the collective title 'Pitt's Policy'. Whatever about 'desiring' anything, Griffith argued that an 'Anglo Hibernian Dual Monarchy' (very different from an 'Anglo-Irish empire') *could have been* established by Pitt (English Prime Minister at the time of the Act of Union), and this would have maintained Britain's power in Europe (not exploited other peoples anywhere), where Germany was then displacing her.[13]

In the very first issue of the *United Irishman*, Griffith made his position on empire crystal clear. He referred to a *Daily Express* article on the British Sudan campaign, which asked why Irishmen refused to take part in the extension of the British Empire. To this question he replied: 'Ireland and the Empire are incompatible. One cannot be an African "civiliser" and an Irish nationalist; one cannot trample on the rights of other people and consistently demand his own'.[14]

The Young Irelander Griffith admired most was Thomas Davis. In one of many references to him, he wrote: 'The truth is that Davis hated England because of her Empire. He was too able a man not to see that, within her own borders England had done great things in literature, law and statesmanship. Beyond her borders she failed. Since 1845, we have had the Irish famine, the Indian Mutiny, the massacre of the Maoris, the seizure of Egypt', and the Boer War then raging. 'Alone among the

11 Glandon, *Griffith and Advanced-Nationalist Press*, pp.42-3.

12 Greaves, *Connolly*, p.94; Beresford Ellis, *History of Irish Working Class*, p.176.

13 For 'Pitt's Policy', see *Sinn Féin*, January-May 1911.

14 *United Irishman*, 4 March 1899.

Great Powers, this beneficent Empire has human blood marking its track every year without exception'.[15]

The following passage, about the Boxer uprising in China in 1900, certainly does not reveal the mind of an imperialist:

> I admire Boxers. I trust every right-minded man and woman will not be shocked at the statement. I am a man of comparative truth and I deem it passive lying to withhold an expression of esteem for Pat Murphy because the people who do not know anything about Pat, except what his enemies tell them, consider him a monster of iniquity, and are liable to be shocked and angry if one maintains Pat is really a good fellow.
>
> I have read about the general devilishness of the Boxers in the English press. I believe there must be something good in any individual, body or nation which the English press reviles. I have sufficient knowledge of who and what the Boxers are to be aware that they are not robbers and murderers with a penchant for harpooning pious Christians....No Boxer would waste his time searching for a Christian when there are plenty of white devils to be happily despatched. Of course, there is a popular delusion that 'white man' and 'Christian' are nearly synonymous terms. This delusion is utilised by the English press.
>
> Old Jim Jams many years ago went to China where he swore more horribly than ever the English army did in Flanders, and drank more deeply than the same army does at present in Egypt. By tickling the feet of his servants and licking the feet of his masters, he waxed fat and made his pile. His morals gave the Orientals jumping fits and the only god he served dwelt in his belly. But he was rough on the heathen. He made himself an image of Confucius, and spent half-an-hour each day playing Aunt Sally with it in his back garden. In the evening time he called out the benighted heathen and spent a pleasant 40 minutes sipping gin-and-water and telling him how much he despised the memory of the heathen's ancestors. This made the heathen tired, so he rose up and smote Jim Jams on the head, whereupon Jim cursed God and died.
>
> This horrible atrocity stirred Christian England to its depths. The British fleet blew a few thousand Celestial men, Celestial women and Celestial children into immortality from the nearest Chinese coastal town worth looting. A memorial table was erected to the Christian martyr in St Paul's, and the Archbishop of Canterbury delivered a panegyric on the blessed Jim Jams which affected the Stock

15 *United Irishman*, 19 May 1900.

> Exchange to tears. But my sympathies are with the heathen who smote Jim on the head....
>
> ...Yet, though the Boxer fails, why should I not admire him? Ignorant, as we reckon ignorance, conservative, fanatical, he is still an Oriental Nationalist. He wants China for the Chinese, and he would get it too if he gripped the solemn truth the Japanese has grasped, that the Art of Destruction must be learned from the Christian nations.[16]

Edwards's assertion that Griffith advocated a self-centred, racist nationalism is surely refuted by this example of his support for Oriental nationalism. It will be seen below that he was also enthusiastic about Jewish nationalism, or Zionism. And in April 1907, he told a journalist from the *Daily Express* that Sinn Féin was encouraging the similar national movement in Egypt: 'We are giving all the support we can to the attempt out there to throw off British rule'. A number of years later, he again referred to the Egyptian nationalist movement, and urged the Irish people to give sympathy and support to its leaders in pursuit of their goals.[17]

He condemned Cecil Rhodes as a buccaneer whose only interests were self-enrichment and self-aggrandisement. When he died, in May 1902, Griffith wrote: 'England failed and Rhodes is dead, leaving South Africa a thousand fold worse than he found it, leaving it with the native question - its great and burning question - unsolved and pressing, and the dream of it as a White Man's country passing away in a stream of white man's blood. In a free community, this man would have been hanged after he shot down the miners of Kimberly; but he lived to help on the destruction of the Empire which has coined its gold out of the blood of peoples and is now finding its nemesis'.[18] How could one who could write thus ever be conceived of as wanting an 'Anglo-Irish empire'?

Griffith an Anti-Semite?

Once again, anti-Semitism, like racism and imperialism, was first ascribed to Griffith by left- or extreme left-wing historians like Greaves and Edwards. (Interestingly, although Labour journals of the period, such as Larkin's *Irish Worker*, contain articles where fun is poked at Jews, or they are attacked or ridiculed, no anti-Semitic charge was laid

16 Ms.22,293 NLI.

17 *Daily Express*, 5 April 1907; *Éire-Ireland*, 26 October 1914.

18 Ms.22,293 NLI.

by the historians mentioned at the door of these publications.)[19] Stringent modern analysts of Irish nationalism, often referred to as 'revisionist' historians, took up the charge. So, Conor Cruise O'Brien described Griffith as 'virulently anti-Semitic', and Roy Foster thought that 'the anti-Semitic ravings of Arthur Griffith's *United Irishman* in the early 1900s make chilling reading'.[20]

There is no doubt that prejudice against Jews was widespread in Europe in the late 19th century when Arthur Griffith was growing up. One has only to think of Shakespeare's Shylock or Dickens's Fagin to get some idea of the popular image. Griffith was a product of his time and his environment, which would have meant exposure to anti-Semitism from a young age. He served his apprenticeship in the *Nation*, a newspaper with a Catholic slant. It denounced, from time to time, Jewish Liberalism in Vienna.[21]

Griffith encountered some unsavoury examples of individual Jews during his time in South Africa. He blamed a Jewish element in Johannesburg, in alliance with English capitalists, for bringing about the Boer War.[22] This view was shared by the English novelist, poet and journalist, G.K. Chesterton, whose anti-Semitism stemmed from his opposition to the Boer War, because he was so opposed to the imperialistic buccaneers in South Africa, some of whom had Jewish names.[23]

In 1899, Griffith wrote the following:

> There is, perhaps, no more heartless set of scoundrels in any part of the world than the rich men of the Rand [the Witwatersrand goldbearing ridge in the Transvaal]. Less than two years ago, when Uitlanders [literally, 'outlanders' or foreigners, usually British] were dying of hunger in the back streets of Johannesburg, and every day when some poor fellow was shooting or hanging himself in Fordsburg, a movement was started to provide at least food for the hungry. The workingman responded generously, but the capitalists kept their pockets closed. I have seen in these days homeless and starving men watching, from the corners where they crouched, drunken millionaires reeling through the streets of driving out with abandoned women in their carriages.

19 See *Irish Worker*, 17 July, 5 August, 26 August, 16 September 1911.

20 *Sunday Times*, 14 February 1988; *Irish Times*, 7 March 1989.

21 Ms. 22,293 NLI.

22 *ibid.*

23 See 'The mystery man of Notting Hill', in *Irish Times*, 11 March 1989.

There are references in Griffith's *Courant* articles to Solly Joel and Barney Barnato, both of whom were Jews who had made fortunes in South Africa. In August 1900, he wrote about the De Kaap valley, 150 miles east of Pretoria, where gold was discovered in 1879: 'The news spread abroad and the Jew, the Englishman, the digger and the desperado came spying out the land....The town of Barberton sprang up like Jonah's gourd....On the whole Barberton was not too bad a place in those early days, though Jewish and English cut-throats were fairly common'.

He also wrote about Lydenburg, also 150 miles from Pretoria, and which he visited:

> The Irish were the pioneers of the Lydenburg gold diggings, and they spread themselves over the face of the land, washing and fossicking for the yellow metal. Wherever he goes, Africa or Australia, Asia or America, the Irishman is always the pioneer. By and by when he has pioneered worth something, the Englishman and the Jew - arcades ambo - come along, and a while later you meet the Irishman plodding across the desert, with his blanket and his billycan and his pipe, seeking new lands to pioneer, and striving to figure out how the Saxon and the Hebrew have scooped him.

The diggers and the Boers fraternised, and nobody ever starved, according to Griffith. It was only when some English and Jews got their hands on the country that people began to starve. Lydenburg became half deserted when the enriched English and Jews moved to Johannesburg. Griffith held that Paul Kruger, leader of the Boers, was a consistent friend of the workingman, for which he was hated by the English and Jewish mine owners.[24] (The story of how one Jewish mine owner saved his burning mine, at the cost of hundreds of his native workers' lives, was given above in the first part of this chapter.)

The 'Dreyfus Affair', when the Jewish captain, Alfred Dreyfus, was found guilty of passing secret French military information to Germany, deeply divided French society in the 1890s. According to the historian of the Irish pro-Boers, D.P. McCracken, it was commonly believed in Ireland, as it was among the Boers themselves, that the Jews of Johannesburg had caused the war, and extreme Irish nationalists were strongly anti-Dreyfus.[25] The accusation of anti-Semitism against

24 Ms. 22,293 NLI.

25 D.P. McCracken, *The Irish Pro-Boers 1877-1902* (Johannesburg and Cape Town, 1989), p.156.

Griffith is in part based on what appeared in his paper in 1899 about the Dreyfus case.

The first article on Dreyfus by Griffith (15 April 1899) was a model of fairness and balance. It simply rehearsed the details of the by then four-and-a-half-year-old *cause celebre* in France in a dispassionate manner. The conclusion of the article reflected this even-handed approach:

> It is hard to tell whether Dreyfus is guilty or not, whether there has been a conspiracy to ruin him, of which Esterhazy* has been the real tool, or whether the ex-artillery captain, the lonely exile of the Ile de Diable, is really the author of the treason for which, if so, he is but receiving his deserved fate. Other interests have come to be so linked with the original case that the channels of justice have become vitiated. Passions have been aroused, prejudices awakened, that conceal the true issue in a tumultuous clamour.

(*Major Esterhazy was the real culprit in the whole affair.)

The second article (3 June 1899), which was also by Griffith, was similar to the first. It declared that 'the truth is not yet manifest, and until the whole structure is complete with the mosaics of all the facts, one must suspend judgement'. Griffith's third article (17 June 1899) referred to Dreyfus being *en route* to France where a court-martial at Rennes was to retry his case. The prediction in the article was that it was 'very probable' that Dreyfus would be acquitted and would retire from 'the army in which he has suffered the most melancholy fate of modern times'. It was also predicted that Esterhazy would be blamed for forging the original memorandum on which Dreyfus was convicted and that, for the rest, the court would return a verdict of 'not proven'.

There followed three articles in the *United Irishman* on the Dreyfus case (29 July, 16 September, 30 September 1899), which were all written by 'The Foreign Secretary'. A comprehensive list of the various pseudonyms used by Griffith in his papers was provided for his first biographer, Seán Ó Lúing, by Seán Milroy, who was a close collaborator of the Sinn Féin founder and compiled a large amount of material for a biography of Griffith. 'The Foreign Secretary' was not one of those pseudonyms.[26] The writer has been unable to establish the identity of this contributor to the *United Irishman.*

These articles pointed out that Jews were not promoted to high rank in the Austrian, German or Russian armies, not because of their religious beliefs, but because of their doubtful patriotism: 'The Jew has at heart no

26 For this list, see Ó Lúing Papers, NLI.

country but the Promised Land. He forms a nation apart wherever he goes'. The author of these articles argued that the Jews would do everything in their power to discredit the French army for not exonerating Dreyfus. (The Rennes court-martial granted him a pardon on grounds of clemency, but did not exculpate him.)

The campaign to undermine the French military establishment would be orchestrated by the Jewish-financed press, according to 'The Foreign Secretary', who wrote about these newspapers in strong language: 'As a matter of fact, the newspapers in question are almost all Jew rags which, outside of England and the United States, represent nothing but the impotent ravings of a disreputable minority, which is universally regarded as a community of thieves and traitors from Madrid to St Petersburg'.

The only other contribution of Griffith to the Dreyfus debate was to comment on the attacks on France in some sections of the Irish press. Having reported on those in the *Evening Herald* and *Evening Telegraph*, he wrote (5 August 1899):

> What's Hecuba to us? What have the Irish people to do with Captain Dreyfus's guilt or innocence - what right have we to interfere in the domestic affairs of France? Will Irish nationalists continue to tolerate the mud-slinging at Ireland's most faithful and most powerful friend by the corrupt and ignorant Home Rule press of Dublin?

Nearly a month later (2 September 1899), he considered the attacks on the French army by certain sections of the English press and by the *Irish Times* and *Irish Independent*. Some English scandals, which the press in that country had suppressed, were then referred to, and the conclusion reached was:

> We can recognise in all this the cloven hoof. England hates and fears France; that much is certain. She will do all in her power, by fair means or foul, to injure the Republic; that also is certain. And the deduction, true and unfailing, is that England and her press see in the Dreyfus case a powerful engine to work disorder and demoralisation in France.

However, in late September 1899, when Dreyfus accepted the pardon the Rennes court-martial granted him, this seemed to convince Griffith of his guilt, because he wrote that an innocent man would not have accepted such a pardon, but would have fought on to prove his innocence.[27]

The balanced tone of Griffith's articles was in marked contrast to that displayed by 'The Foreign Secretary'. On 9 September 1899, Griffith published a letter from a correspondent condemning the 'anti-Semitic ravings' of 'The Foreign Secretary'. Nowhere did he take sides in the dispute. Indeed, some of his references to Dreyfus revealed a certain sympathy for what had happened to him ('the lonely exile of the Ile de Diable'; '...the army in which he has suffered the most melancholy fate of modern times'). But Dreyfus's acceptance of a pardon based on clemency persuaded Griffith of his guilt, because he wrote that Dreyfus 'has just accepted a pardon that sends him forth with the brand of traitor on his brow - a pardon an innocent man would have scorned to accept'.

From the end of September 1899 until January 1904, Griffith wrote no more about the Jews. In July 1900, he published a letter from a Limerick man complaining about a Jewish colonisation of that city, and maintaining that they had raised rents and taken a great share of the city's trade. In November 1903, an article by the painter John B. Yeats, father of W.B. and Jack, referred to the English upper classes as 'Jew-ridden'.[28]

In January 1904, when the Limerick Redemptorist, Fr Creagh, gave a sermon virulently attacking the Jews of the city, and was assailed from various quarters as a result, Griffith defended him. From the outset he made it clear that Jews' religious beliefs were not in question, but that it was their business methods Fr Creagh was attacking. However, Griffith did make the wild assertion that three-quarters of Irish Jews were engaged in usury (lending money at exorbitant rates of interest), and dishonest business practices.

He went on to say that he had no objection to a Jew seeking an honest livelihood in Ireland, but that he did object to his seeking a dishonest one, 'and howling out that he is being martyred for his faith when people object to him putting his hand in their pockets'. He declared that he was proud that Ireland had no tradition of persecuting Jews, but that that was all the more reason why Jews should not persecute Ireland.

Griffith expressed his unease at the rates of emigration of the native Irish (this was a regular theme in his newspapers and he devoted a series of editorials in 1910 in particular to the problem) and immigration of foreign Jews. Following the promulgation of the May Laws in Russia in 1882, many Jews fled that country and some settled in Britain and

27 *United Irishman*, 15 April, 3,7 June 1899; 29 July, 16,30 September 1899; 5 August, 2,23 September 1899.

28 *ibid.*, 7 July 1900; 14 November 1903.

Ireland. Over the next twenty years, the Jewish population of Ireland rose tenfold, but it was still less than 4,000 by the time of the Limerick incident. Griffith saw these immigrants as contributing to the exodus of the indigenous population because of their business methods.

'We are told the Jews are industrious people and deserve to prosper. We do not object to their prospering by industry. We object to their prospering by usury and fraud', he remarked. He also expressed resentment at the ease with which the settlers acquired finance from Irish banks, when native workers and tradesmen found it so difficult to do so. This special, privileged treatment was another reason why Jews were resented, he contended.

Now there is absolutely no doubt that Griffith had a wildly exaggerated notion of the extent of Jewish involvement in money-lending and devious business practices. As Louis Hyman, the historian of the Jews of Ireland, pointed out, the Jews of Limerick were mainly small traders - milk vendors and travelling drapers. Nevertheless, Griffith made it very clear that it was usury he was condemning:

> When Catholics - as Catholics - are boycotted, it constitutes undoubtedly an outrageous injustice, and similarly if Jews - as Jews - were boycotted, it would be outrageously unjust. But the Jew in Limerick has not been boycotted because he is a Jew, but because he is a usurer. And we deny that we offend against ethics by most heartily advocating the boycott of usurers, whether they be Jew, Pagan or Christian.

On the other hand, his language must be judged intemperate and his assertions unmeasured. This is evident where he described the majority of Irish Jews as 'usurers and parasites of industry', and as an economic evil because they produced no wealth themselves but drew it from others. He criticised them as the most successful sellers of foreign goods, and as being in unfair competition with the rate-paying Irish shopkeeper. They always remained aliens, he further declared, and did not integrate themselves into Irish society.

As against this he had the height of admiration for Jewish nationalists or Zionists - 'those honest and patriotic Jews who desire the re-establishment of the Hebrew nation in Palestine'. He held that although these were a minority of Jews as a whole, they felt bitterly 'the humiliation of their race through the sordid pursuit of gold by the majority'. For them he had the same esteem he had for 'all patriotic and lofty-minded men'.

Fred Ryan wrote to the *United Irishman* to disagree with Griffith and argue that the Jews in Limerick were being boycotted because they were

Jews, and not because they were usurers. In support of this, Ryan cited a passage from Fr Creagh about the martyrdom and persecution of Christians by Jews in ancient times. Concerning this, Griffith replied that he believed Fr Creagh would have been better to have 'let the dead past bury its dead, for if Jews under the Roman Emperors proved themselves relentless persecutors of Christians, Christians in later times showed as little of the spirit of true religion'.

Ryan also took exception to Griffith's statement, 'Attack a Jew - other than a Zionist Jew - and all Jewry comes to his assistance'. In this context, Ryan declared that the Dreyfus case was an example of pure anti-Semitism, and that Jews subscribed money to defend him, not to ruin France. To this, Griffith responded that Dreyfus was convicted of selling France's secrets to France's enemies, and imprisoned, and that Jews everywhere came to his aid.

'A retrial before a tribunal favourable to him resulted in the affirmation of his conviction, and the man wrote himself down guilty with his own hand by accepting a conditional pardon', Griffith continued. It is hard to understand how he could have considered a court consisting of army officers 'favourable' to Dreyfus. It should, however, be pointed out in his defence that Dreyfus was not finally exonerated until 1906, so that in 1904 Griffith still felt as he had about Dreyfus at the end of September 1899.[29]

For the rest of his life, in the vast extent of his journalism, one finds very few references to Jews from Griffith. In January 1909, in the course of discussing the Dublin municipal elections, he wrote: 'The latest element of the population publicly appealed to to vote against the Sinn Féin candidates is the Jewish element, to whom an appeal is made in the correspondence columns of the *Evening Telegraph*. As this is done openly by a Jew, we have nothing to say on the matter, except to regret that the Jews in Dublin should cast their votes as Jews instead of as citizens'.[30]

In September 1912, he referred to a recent congress which considered Ireland as a country suitable for the permanent settlement of Jewish people. He explained that an ancient Irish source, quoted by Gaelic annalists, showed that the Gaelic Irish could trace some Hebrew ancestry.[31] This must show that whatever earlier antipathy he had felt to the idea of Jews making Ireland their home had by this time completely disappeared.

Griffith counted a number of friends among the Irish Jewish

29 *United Irishman*, 23 January, 23 April, 14,28 May 1904.

30 *Sinn Féin*, 16 January 1909.

31 *ibid.*, 14 September 1912.

community. One of these was Dr Edward Lipman, who himself told of returning to Dublin on leave during the First World War, and visiting Griffith's favourite haunt, the Bailey. As he was wearing his British army uniform, he sensed the occupants of the bar were hostile towards him, and he left. He had gone just a short distance when he was overtaken by a panting Griffith who explained that he had not seen him when he came in and was anxious to assure him that the uniform did not interfere with their friendship in any way. Another Jewish friend of Griffith was Jacob Elyan.[32] And, of course, Joyce's Leopold Bloom, who was supposed to have inspired Griffith's Hungarian policy, was a fictitious acquaintance.

But there is no doubt that Griffith's closest Jewish friend was the solicitor Michael Noyk. Béaslaí described Noyk as one of Griffith's 'favourite companions' and also as his 'intimate friend'. Noyk himself gave an account of his activities on behalf of Irish nationalism to the Bureau of Miliary History around 1950. In this he stated that he met Griffith for the first time in late 1909 or early 1910, that he became a close friend, spent many evenings at his home, and acquired an intimate knowledge of his character.[33]

Griffith's daughter, Ita, vouched for the closeness that existed between the Noyk and Griffith families. She recalled being a flower girl at Noyk's wedding and playing with the Noyk children at both her own and their home. She also remembered Philip Sayers as another Jewish friend of her father's. The world-renowned gynaecologist and master of Dublin's Rotunda Hospital, Bethel Solomons, who was also a member of the Irish Jewish community, contributed to the purchase of a house for Griffith on his marriage in 1910.[34]

Glandon, who subjected the nationalist and Labour journals of the 1900-1922 period in Ireland to a comprehensive scrutiny, found some evidence of anti-Semitism in them. She referred to Moran of the *Leader* advising his readership how to avoid allowing Jews take control of Irish commerce. Of the *Catholic Bulletin*, edited by J.J. O'Kelly (who used the Irish pen-name 'Sceilg'), she remarked that it 'seldom bothered to rationalise its anti-Semitic bias and was the most vituperative of the Irish journals which expressed anti-Semitism'. Her overall conclusion was that the anti-Semitism found in these papers stemmed from the

32 Louis Hyman, *The Jews of Ireland: from Earliest Times to the Year 1910* (Shannon, 1972), pp.136,333,202.

33 Béaslaí, *Collins*, i, pp.155,351; Ms. 18,975 NLI.

34 Interview with Mrs Ita Gray, Dublin, 22 August 1995; list of subscribers in library of late Nevin Griffith, Dublin.

suspicion and fear of foreigners which is an inevitable aspect of 'the narrow creed of nationalism' itself.[35]

It is significant that Louis Hyman, the historian of Ireland's Jews, believed that Griffith's anti-Jewish comments in 1904 had their origin in the xenophobia Glandon was referring to, and were not the result of any deep-seated hatred of, or obsessive preoccupation with Jews as such.[36]

The question of Griffith's attitude to Jews is a difficult one. It is difficult because of what happened in Europe nearly two decades after his death, because of the sickeningly named 'Final Solution', because of the history of the Third Reich and the appalling slaughter of six million innocents. If what Griffith wrote can be construed as contributing in any way to that unrelenting nightmare in human history then, indeed, he must stand indicted. But should not what he wrote on the subject of Jews be examined in the context of his time and in relation to the issues he was considering? Is not any other approach anachronistic and ahistorical?

He edited newspapers for more than twenty years. If hatred of Jews was an obsession with him, why was there so little output from him on the subject? The articles that he wrote in 1899 on the Dreyfus case could not be interpreted as anti-Semitic. In relation to the 1904 Limerick incident, he defended the right to condemn usury and dishonesty in business, but displayed the common prejudice of the time that Jews were involved to a much greater extent than any other group in such reprehensible practices.

It should be pointed out that on a number of occasions he attacked the existence of Catholic associations which were attempting to give Catholics an unfair advantage in commerce. He thought it completely wrong that someone's chances for a job, or doing business, should be supported on the basis of professed religious beliefs, rather than suitability for the post, or competence in getting the work done.[37] The idea of discriminating against people because of religious beliefs was utterly repugnant to him. Yet, he was never indicted as anti-Catholic.

From 1904 until his death in 1922 one finds virtually nothing from him about Jews. Perhaps a growing acquaintance with members of Ireland's Jewish community, and an especially close friendship with one of that community, purged him of the prejudice acquired in his youth.

35 Glandon, *Griffith and Advanced-Nationalist Press*, pp.9,43,67,162.

36 Hyman, *Jews of Ireland*, pp.212-14,217.

37 See, for example, *United Irishman*, 23,30 January; 5 March 1904; *Sinn Féin*, 3 August 1912.

Griffith may be compared with G.K. Chesterton in that the opposition of both to the Boer War stemmed in part from their distaste for the activities of piratical imperialists in South Africa, some of whom were Jews.

One of Chesterton's biographers, commenting on his anti-Semitism, felt that he expected too thick a skin from the Jews. The same could be said of some of the things Griffith wrote about them in his 1904 articles on the Limerick incident. Chesterton reviled what Hitler stood for, and declared that 'I am quite ready to believe now that...I will die defending the last Jew in Europe'.[38] There is no reason to believe that Griffith would have responded any differently.

In the final analysis it is difficult to be categorical on this question. If the view that policies and persons should be judged in relation to the times and circumstances of *their* time, and not of *ours*, is accepted, then Griffith can hardly be judged an anti-Semite. But when the horror of what centuries of anti-Semitism led to is considered, it must be deeply regretted that Griffith, at one stage in his life, believed some of the things that he seemed to about the Jews.

38 *Irish Times*, 11 March 1989.

EPILOGUE

GRIFFITH'S LEGACY

Dual monarchy

During the Treaty negotiations Griffith took the view that if the British were to adopt a neutral stance, an internal Irish settlement could be reached which would safeguard the special interests of Northern unionists. He forewarned that the Northern State could never function with a dissenting minority of 400,000. He knew as well that a million Protestants could not be coerced into a united Ireland, and that an Irish state with so large a dissenting minority would find it very difficult to function. From this came his conviction that the dual monarchy was a concept broad enough to encompass Irish people of all political persuasions.

When the 1925 Boundary Commission failed to provide a way to end partition, Kevin O'Higgins, Vice-President of the Executive Council (deputy-Prime Minister), Minister for Justice and External Affairs, resurrected the dual-monarchy proposal in 1926/27 as an avenue towards Irish unity. He first discussed the idea with Edward Carson, who proved receptive, and who encouraged O'Higgins to broach the matter with the Prime Minister of Northern Ireland. O'Higgins then raised the subject with L.S. Amery, Secretary of State for the Dominions, with whom he had two meetings. Amery, who was sympathetic to the proposal, prepared a substantial memorandum for the British cabinet.

Amery wrote to Craig, who was totally opposed to the idea. The Secretary of State for Foreign Affairs, Austen Chamberlain, also prepared a cabinet paper in which he expressed doubts about the dual-monarchy arrangement. When the full British cabinet considered O'Higgins's proposal at a meeting in late January 1927, the Prime Minister, Stanley Baldwin, was rather dismissive of it. Undeterred, O'Higgins pushed ahead, meeting Amery again the following June.

There were rumours that summer that Lord Londonderry (first Minister for Education in Northern Ireland, who had resigned in 1925 in disillusionment at the sectarian obstacles he encountered) had come to

Dublin for secret discussions. In private, O'Higgins, on the day before his tragic assassination (10 July 1927), predicted that within five years the dual-monarchy arrangement would have achieved effective Irish unity.[1]

Griffith's revolutionary proposal for achieving Irish independence while maintaining Irish unity died with its second principal sponsor in July 1927. Since then it has never been resurrected. Following the eruption of bloody strife in Northern Ireland in the late 1960s, references to the dual monarchy as a possible solution may be seen from time to time in the letter pages of Irish newspapers. The son of Griffith's friend, The O'Rahilly, Aodogán, who took arms against the Treaty in 1922/23, has been one of the most interesting and persistent latter-day advocates of the dual monarchy as a possible answer to the Northern Irish conflict. Another notable convert has been the Fianna Fail TD, Eamon O Cuiv, grandson of de Valera, who recently called for Ireland's re-entry into the Commonwealth.[2]

Non-Violence

For long the accepted 'official' version of Irish history taught in schools was that Irish freedom was won by force, that the heroic gesture of the men of 1916 was completed by the defeat of the Black and Tans, which forced the British to negotiate. As a result, the role that the passive resistance advocated by Griffith played in the achievement of independence was either obscured or ignored. Whether the same freedom could have been secured without resort to force was a question not posed in Irish history teaching.

The issue of non-violence remained relevant in relation to the continued existence of partition and whether it was legitimate to use force to try to reunite the country. The 1937 Constitution allowed for ambiguity on the question. Because it applied in theory to the whole country, was it justifiable to use force to try to implement its claims, or were only non-violent methods and moral persuasion to be used? The IRA's answer was to wage a number of futile and bloody campaigns in the late thirties and the fifties.

The problem arose again in Northern Ireland in the late 1960s and is still current. At first the non-violent Civil Rights Association was

1 *Irish Times*, 18 April 1990.

2 ibid., 29 September 1994; 12 May 1995; 20 August 1994.

supported by IRA men who had become temporarily disillusioned with physical force. But as the struggle became more intense, it became more difficult, and then impossible, to maintain a purely peaceful, passive-resistance approach. There are definite parallels between Northern Ireland in the late sixties and the independence struggle in the rest of Ireland in the 1919-21 period.

For the past three decades, a section of Northern Irish nationalism has once again turned to violence to try to achieve its goals. In the second half of the 1990s, that section seems to be lending an ear once more to what Griffith advocated from almost the beginning of the century.

Dáil Éireann/Democracy

Perhaps Griffith's greatest monument is Dáil Éireann, the Irish parliament whose establishment he advocated almost from the outset of his nationalist propaganda work. He had always argued that the elected representatives of Ireland should not attend Westminster but should remain in Dublin and set up their own constituent assembly. When that finally came to pass in 1919, the programme it attempted to implement was based on what he had worked out in 1905 in *The Sinn Féin Policy*. So, the basic design of Dáil Éireann grew out of the many years of thought Griffith had devoted to national planning. The Dáil formed the moral and democratic foundation for the final years of the Irish independence struggle.

The extent to which Griffith emerged as the champion of democracy, during and after the Treaty divide has been explored earlier. He was determined to make sure that the will of the people would be supreme and that no authoritarian regime would be established. Ireland has been one of the few states, which have won their freedom in the 20th century, where there has not been even a temporary suspension of constitutional government.

Through the upheaval caused by the Treaty split and Civil War, the Dáil remained in being, and it was through it that the first independent Irish government established the institutions of the independent Irish State, which have remained secure ever since. For the first five years of the State, the main opposition remained outside the Dáil, and therefore posed an anti-democratic, extra-constitutional threat. But that opposition was forced to take its place in the Dáil in 1927 and, five years later, there was a peaceful transition of power from the victors to the vanquished of the Civil War.

This was an extraordinary achievement, and its significance should not be underestimated, because it has never been easy to create successfully a democratic order in a country, particularly in a country with a low level of economic development as Ireland had at the time. There was therefore something of a cruel irony when, on the centenary of Griffith's birth in 1971, in response to a request to have a commemorative stamp struck in his honour, the Taoiseach of the day, Jack Lynch, rejected the appeal in the Dáil on the basis that Griffith was a 'Civil War figure'.[3]

Professor Michael Hayes, who had been a member of the first Dáil, Speaker of the House for the first ten years of the State, and who was the prime mover behind the writing of the first biography of Griffith in English, was provoked into a thoughtful response by Lynch's comment:

> It surely ill becomes the head of our Irish government to dismiss Arthur Griffith as unfit to be honoured as an Irish leader on the centenary of his birth. Griffith's work for Ireland goes back many a long year before 1922. He was a young man when Parnell died in 1891. From then on Griffith never ceased to work for Ireland. He died in August1922, head of an Irish government, with one half-penny in his pocket. If he left nothing to his family, his ideas and his leadership left to Ireland the sovereign Irish parliament in which Mr Lynch now occupies first place. To Griffith, more than to any other man, the Taoiseach owes his honours and his emoluments.[4]

Protestants/Anglo-Irish

Griffith was an early advocate of Proportional Representation, the most democratic way of ensuring the expression of minority opinion. This electoral system was retained by the express will of the Irish people in two referendums (1959 and 1968).

The very day the Treaty was signed, Griffith met with three representatives of the Southern unionist population and assured them that PR would be the electoral system in the new State, and that they would have fair representation in the new Senate. A few weeks before his death, he met with them again and concluded an agreement about the composition and powers of the Senate. His main concession was

3 *Irish Times*, 21 April 1971.

4 ibid., 23 April 1971.

that half the 60 members of the new House were to be elected by the Dáil, and the other half to be nominated by the President of the Executive Council 'in a manner calculated to represent minorities or interests not adequately represented in the Dáil'.[5]

The Southern unionist representatives realised that a genuine effort was being made to integrate them into the new State. Griffith fulfilled his promise because, of the 30 Senators nominated, sixteen were from the Southern unionist tradition (seventeen, if Yeats is included). Among them were Sir Horace Plunkett, the Earl of Dunraven, the Earl of Mayo, Lord Glenavy, and the Dowager Countess of Desart.

One of the most effective of their number, J.G. Douglas, had the following to say of Griffith in the Senate in March 1923:

> There is one thing that I think ought to be emphasised in any reference to the memory of the late Arthur Griffith, and that is that he set his face sternly against any distinctions or differences being made in Ireland between any class or creed. He hated these differences; he never believed in them nor never felt them. In this matter he was particularly anxious, not only that the people here who knew what he felt, but the world at large should see that the representation provided in the first Seanad of the Irish Free State would be a proof that there was no feeling of intolerance and no feeling of bitterness, and that the calumny as to the tyranny because of class or creed which had been spread abroad would be given the lie to, and that from now on we should forget such things ever existed. I make this reference as one who may regard himself as belonging to the minority, and as one who for many years knew how keenly Arthur Griffith felt with regard to the rights of minorities.[6]

To what extent has this particular legacy of Griffith been honoured? To a very large extent, it can be said. True, successive governments tended to enshrine and uphold Catholic social teaching. True, Article 44 of de Valera's 1937 Constitution allocated to the Catholic Church a special position (which was removed in 1972 following a referendum). Such developments were probably inevitable in a country with a population which was overwhelmingly Catholic. But instances of discrimination, on the grounds of religious belief, were by and large negligible.

5 Donal O'Sullivan, *The Irish Free State and Its Senate* (London, 1940), pp.75-82.

6 Ms. 23,516 NLI.

Economics

The essence of Griffith's economic doctrine was industrial development behind a wall of protective tariffs. But by 1900 the British and Irish economies had become closely interwoven. A complete restructuring of the banks and stock exchange to aid an Irish industrial revival was contemplated by Griffith, but the long-established links between the two economies could not be broken painlessly.

Sinn Féin tried to reconcile industrial protection and a more intensive agriculture. Griffith proposed industrial development together with a contraction of grazing and a major increase in tillage, all to be carried out under protection. His case was that both agriculture and industry had identical interests and both were necessary for a healthy state to exist.

Griffith's death removed, according to AE, 'the only political leader whose name was associated in the Irish mind with a definite economic policy'.[7] His successors had little economic expertise and the civil service was dominated by those who had run the country under Britain. The methods and approaches they took with them into the new administration were characterised by strict control over public spending, Department of Finance control over government expenditure, and government non-intervention in the economy. The economy of the new State remained closely integrated with Britain.

Economic policy was determined, not by the government, but by commissions of experts: the Commission on Agriculture, the Fiscal Inquiry Committee, the Banking Commission. These favoured making no changes. Parity and the financial links with sterling were to be maintained, food was to be produced for Britain, and free trade was to be retained in the industrial sector. The main concentration was on agriculture. As the Agriculture Minister, Patrick Hogan, expressed it in January 1924: 'national development in Ireland, for our generation at least, is practically synonymous with agricultural development'.[8]

The report of the Fiscal Inquiry Committee (1923) came down heavily on the side of free trade. This led to increased pressure for protection, many of those who lobbied for it having been members of local Industrial Development Associations and of Sinn Féin. They were

7 *Irish Statesman*, 19 August 1922.

8 M.E. Daly, *Industrial Development and Irish National Identity, 1922-1939* (Dublin, 1992), pp.7-9,14-16.

very angry with the FIC's report, one of them asking 'is advocating Arthur Griffith's policy treason in the Free State?'

J.J.Walsh, Minister for Posts and Telegraphs, resigned from Cumann na nGaedheal (the name taken by the pro-Treaty party in 1923) before the September 1927 general election. In his letter of resignation he accused the party of going over to 'the most reactionary elements of the State who will henceforth control its policies. Followers of Arthur Griffith's economic teaching will now be forced to subordinate their lifelong conviction to the dictates of people whose only concern appears to be the welfare of England'.

Richard Mulcahy, Minister for Defence, and Joseph McGrath, Minister for Industry and Commerce, had resigned from the cabinet in 1924 as a result of the army crisis, and O'Higgins was assassinated in 1927. Years later, Mulcahy asserted that the departure of McGrath, O'Higgins, Walsh and himself left 'the directing force in the parliamentary party and in the government completely denuded of those people and names who stood for the Griffith approach and policy in relation to industrial development'. But Griffith's policies had not been put into practice systematically by Cumann na nGaedheal, and O'Higgins had not supported them. This was partly the result of the influence of existing interests, and arose in part because no holder of an important economic ministry, with the possible exception of McGrath, advocated them.[9]

It remains one of the curiosities of Cumann na nGaedheal's history that Griffith's political heirs did not follow his economic testament. Some tariffs were applied and Ernest Blythe, Minister for Finance between 1923 and 1932, declared that the government was not committed rigidly to either free trade or protection. A Tariff Commission was set up in 1926 but proceeded very slowly. The large and well-established industries, brewing and distilling, did not want protection, and agricultural products were exempt completely from tariffs.

In typically uncompromising fashion, O'Higgins declared, countering the charge that the government was betraying a vital aspect of Griffith's legacy: 'The propagandist writings of any one man cannot be accepted simply as revealed truth, requiring no further investigations, something that must be accepted forever as beyond question, beyond doubt, beyond the need of examination'.

To J.J. Lee, this declaration of O'Higgins's was 'as illusory as it was

9 Daly, *Industrial Development and Irish National Identity*, pp.22,35-6.

courageous' because no detailed analysis was carried out by the government. While Griffith's set of unproven assumptions made at least some attempt to wrestle with the evidence of economic history, the new government substituted for them another set of unproven assumptions based on no historical evidence at all, in Lee's view. The Fiscal Inquiry Committee of 1923 seemed to be a major investigation of industrial policy, but Lee maintained it was arranged in such a way as to secure a safe majority for dogmatic free traders, and provided little of the additional investigation O'Higgins proclaimed necessary.[10]

The end of the 1920s saw a movement towards greater protection, the result of changing external circumstances (a world economic recession) and increasing internal pressure. The major external change was the establishment of a protectionist government in Britain. Fianna Fáil, a new political party set up in 1926 by anti-Treaty politicians led by de Valera, strongly favoured protection, and this gave protectionists a new focus lacking in the early years of the State. Ironically, Griffith's economic doctrine was to prove a winning electoral formula for de Valera.

When Fianna Fáil entered government in 1932 it pursued a policy based on the old Griffithite programme of protection and economic self-sufficiency. De Valera proved most adept at stealing Griffith's clothes in all sorts of ways. Even in his famous St Patrick's Day address to the nation in 1943, there was a lineament of Griffith's economics.

Although Griffith was an enthusiast for industrial development, he condemned the evils of the factory system, and predicted that electricity would revive domestic industry. The result of this would be small rural industries as against big factories in unhealthy, overcrowded cities. This thinking was echoed in de Valera's 1943 speech where he referred to 'a land whose countryside would be bright with cosy homesteads, whose fields and villages would be joyous with the sounds of industry'.[11]

The Fianna Fáil governments experienced undoubted economic success in the thirties and forties with the growth of native industries and the employment these generated. However, as the economic historian Mary Daly has pointed out, while the message of protection

10 For O'Higgins's attitude to this question, and the partial implementation of tariffs, see Brian Maye, *Fine Gael 1923-1987* (Dublin, 1993), pp.9-12.

11 Maurice Moynihan (ed.), *Speeches and Statements of Eamon de Valera 1917-73* (Dublin and New York, 1980), p.466.

and economic control was communicated very effectively, efficiency and productivity were ignored.[12] Although Griffith was a strong advocate of protection for native industries, he was alert to the dangers of exploitation and profiteering inherent in such a policy. These drawbacks were indeed in evidence when Fianna Fáil pursued its protectionist programme between 1932 and 1958.

Concerning the dangers, Griffith wrote: 'We must offer our producers protection where...necessary....Protection does not mean the exclusion of foreign competition. It does not mean that we shall pay a higher profit to any Irish manufacturer, but that we shall not stand by and see him crushed by mere weight of foreign capital...because his foreign competitor has larger resources at his disposal'.[13] As economist Moore McDowell remarked, 'Griffith clearly wanted the minimum necessary protection, with minimum attendant costs, in contrast to the policy pursued from 1932 onwards'.[14]

By the late 1950s, the economic nationalism inspired by Griffith and implemented by Fianna Fáil was deemed to have failed. The system of tariffs was gradually dismantled and foreign firms were encouraged to set up in Ireland by means of various inducements. By the eighties this approach was again seen to be yielding a doubtful harvest, and many were arguing for a return to self-sufficiency by means of native control of industry. Perhaps Griffith had the right idea after all, if only the pitfalls he had warned against had been given more attention.

12 Daly, *Industrial Development and Irish National Identity*, pp.55-6,132.

13 *Resurrection of Hungary*, 1918, p.146.

14 *Cork Examiner*, 17 August 1972.

Select Bibliography

Papers in National Library of Ireland

Robert Barton Papers
Arthur Griffith Papers
Joseph Holloway Diary
M.J. Lennon Papers
Joseph McGarrity Papers
Michael Noyk Statement
Seán T. O'Kelly Papers
Seán Ó Lúing Papers

Irish Government Documents

Dáil Éireann: Minutes of Proceedings of First Parliament of Republic of Ireland, 1919-1921
Dáil Éireann: Official Correspondence relating to the Peace Negotiations, June-September 1921
Dáil Éireann Official Report: Debate on the Treaty between Great Britain and Ireland, 14 December 1921-10 January 1922
Dáil Éireann Official Report: 16 August 1921-8 June 1922
Dáil Éireann: Private Sessions of Second Dáil: Minutes of Proceedings and Report of Debates, 18 August 1921-6 January 1922
Dáil Éireann: Treaty Negotiation Documents, 1921. DE 2/304 series National Archives of Ireland
Dáil Cabinet and Provisional Government Minutes 1922. National Archives of Ireland.

Unpublished Sources

Labour Pamphlet Collection, Ir 941p, NLI.
Letter from A.T. Davies, MP, to Arthur Griffith, 28 July 1920, in library of late Nevin Griffith, Dublin.
Letter from Bishop Michael Fogarty of Killaloe to Mrs Griffith, 29 November 1920, *loc. cit.*
Letter from Arthur Griffith to Mrs Griffith, undated but probably 10 October 1921, *loc. cit.*
Letter from Arthur Griffith to Mrs Griffith, 24 November 1921, *loc. cit.*

Letter from Sylvia Lynd to Arthur Griffith, 30 March 1922, *loc. cit.*
Letter from D. Carolan Rushe to H.E. Kenny, 3 September 1922, *loc. cit.*
Liam O Briain statement, 6 September 1973, *loc. cit.*
Minute Book of Young Ireland League, *loc. cit.*

Newspapers

An Claidheamh Soluis, Comhar, Cork Examiner, Daily Express, Dublin Trade and Labour Journal, Éire-Ireland, Evening Herald, Evening Press, Free State, Gaelic American, Harp, Hibernia, Irish Bulletin, Irish Freedom, Irish Homestead, Irish Independent, Irish Labour Journal, Irish Nation and Peasant, Irish Press, Irish Statesman, Irish Times, Irish Weekly Independent, Irish Worker, Irish Worker and People's Advocate, Leader, Liberator and Irish Trade Union, Nationality, New Statesman and Nation, Observer, Poblacht na hÉireann, Reynold's News, Scissors and Paste, Sinn Féin (weekly and daily), *Southern Cross, Spark, Sunday Independent, Sunday Press, Sunday Times, Sunday Tribune, United Irishman, Voice of Labour, Watchword of Labour, Workers' Republic, Young Ireland-Éire Óg.*

Periodicals

S.J. Brown, 'The Dublin newspaper press: a bird's eye view, 1658-1916', in *Studies* XXV (March, 1936), pp.109-22.
Nora Connolly O'Brien, 'The Pearse I knew', in *Hibernia*, 15 April 1977.
W.T. Cosgrave, 'Arthur Griffith', in J.R.H. Weaver (ed.), *Dictionary of National Biography 1922-30* (London, 1937), pp.364-8.
C.P. Curran, 'Griffith, MacNeill and Pearse', in *Studies* LV (Spring, 1966), pp.21-8.
R.P. Davis, 'Griffith and Gandhi: a study in non-violent resistance', in *Threshold*, Vol. III, No. 2, Summer 1959, pp.29-44.
R.P. Davis, 'The advocacy of passive resistance in Ireland, 1916-22', in *Anglo-Irish Studies*, III, 1977, pp.35-55.
R.P. Davis, 'Arthur Griffith, 1872 (sic)-1922: Architect of Modern Ireland', in *History Today*, 1979, 29 (3), pp.139-46.
R.P. Davis, 'Arthur Griffith, 1872 (sic)-1922: Architect of Modern Ireland', in *History Today*, 1979, 29 (4), pp.248-56.
R.P. Davis, 'Ulster Protestants and the Sinn Féin press', in *Éire-Ireland*, 1980, XV, 4, pp.60-85.
Alexis Fitzgerald, 'Erskine Childers', in *Hibernia*, 15 April 1977.
A.S. Green et al, 'Arthur Griffith', in *Studies* II (September, 1922), pp.337-55.
Arthur Griffith, 'Important letter of 1919', reprinted in *Capuchin Annual*, 1969, pp.330-35.

Michael Hayes, 'The importance of Dáil Éireann', in *Capuchin Annual*, 1969, pp.336-9.
Michael Laffan, 'The Sinn Féin Party 1916-21', in *Capuchin Annual*, 1970, pp.227-35.
Michael Laffan, 'The unification of Sinn Féin in 1917', in *Irish Historical Studies*, XVII (March, 1971), pp.353-79.
Robert Lynd, 'The ethics of Sinn Féin', in *The Irish Year-Book/Leabhar na hÉireann* (Dublin, 1909), pp.356-68.
F.S.L. Lyons, 'James Joyce's Dublin', in *Twentieth Century Studies* (November, 1970), pp.14-24.
Donal McCartney, 'The political use of history in the work of Arthur Griffith', in *Journal of Contemporary History*, VIII (January, 1973), pp.3-19.
R.M. McEvatt, 'Arthur Griffith and his early Sinn Féin policies', in *Capuchin Annual*, 1971, pp.232-8.
K.N. McKenna, 'In London with the Treaty delegates', in *Capuchin Annual*, 1971, pp.313-32.
Brian Maye, 'Why it is time for a new biography of Arthur Griffith', in *Études Irlandaises*, XVIII, December 1993, pp.123-9.
Arthur Mitchell, 'Labour and the national struggle', in *Capuchin Annual*, 1971, pp.261-88.
Arthur Mitchell, 'The Irish Labour movement and the foundation of the State', in *Capuchin Annual*, 1972, pp.362-74.
Peter Neary, 'The failure of economic nationalism', in *The Crane Bag*, VIII (Dublin, 1984), pp.68-77.
Seán T. O'Kelly, 'Arthur Griffith', in *Capuchin Annual*, 1966, pp.132-50.
Seán Ó Lúing, 'Arthur Griffith 1871-1922: thoughts on a centenary', in *Studies* LX (Summer, 1971), pp.127-38.
Seán Ó Lúing, 'Ioldanacht Airt Ui Ghriofa', i g*Comhar* (Baile Átha Cliath, Samhain 1972), ll.10-12.
Pilib Ó Mordha, 'The Griffiths of Laurelhill, Co. Monaghan, and associated families', in *The Clogher Record*, XIV, 4, 1993, pp.111-24.
Seán Ó Riain, 'Dáil Éireann, 1919', in *Capuchin Annual*, 1969, pp.323-9.

Other Published Sources

D.H. Akenson, *The United States and Ireland* (Harvard, 1973).
Arthur Griffith, Michael Collins: Commemorative Booklet (Dublin, n.d.).
Piaras Béaslaí, *Michael Collins and the Making of a New Ireland* (Dublin, 1926).
Piaras Béaslaí, *Songs, Ballads and Recitations of Arthur Griffith* (Dublin, n.d.).
J.C. Beckett, *The Making of Modern Ireland 1603-1923* (London, 1966).
George A. Bermingham, *Pleasant Places* (London, 1940).
Marcus Bourke, *John O'Leary: a Study in Irish Separatism* (Tralee, 1967).
Marcus Bourke, *The O'Rahilly* (Tralee, 1967).

John Bowman, *De Valera and the Ulster Question 1917-73* (Oxford, 1982).
H.V. Brasted, 'Irish nationalism and the British Empire in the late 19th century', in Oliver MacDonagh, W.F. Mandle and Pauric Travers (eds.), *Irish Culture and Nationalism 1750-1950* (London, 1983).
Andrew Boyle, *The Riddle of Erskine Childers* (London, 1977).
D.G. Boyce, *Englishmen and Irish Troubles* (London, 1972).
Robert Brennan, *Allegiance* (Dublin, 1950).
F.M. Carroll, *American Opinion and the Irish Question 1910-23* (Dublin, 1978).
Mairéad Ni Chinnéide, *Máire de Buitléir: Bean Athbheochana* (Baile Átha Cliath, 1993).
J.D. Clarkson, *Labour and Nationalism in Ireland* (New York, 1925).
Seamus Cody, John O'Dowd and Peter Rigney, *The Parliament of Labour: 100 Years of the Dublin Council of Trade Unions* (Dublin, 1986).
Padraic Colum, *The Road Round Ireland* (New York, 1926).
Padraic Colum, *Arthur Griffith* (Dublin, 1959).
Nora Connolly O'Brien, *Portrait of a Rebel Father* (Dublin, 1935).
T.P. Coogan, *Michael Collins* (London, 1990).
T.P. Coogan, *De Valera: Long Fellow, Long Shadow* (London, 1993).
Lewis Copeland and Lawrence Lamb (eds.), *The World's Great Speeches* (New York, 1968).
Art Cosgrave and Donal McCartney (eds.), *Studies in Irish History presented to Robin Dudley Edwards* (Dublin, 1979).
Peter Costello, *The Heart Grown Brutal: The Irish Revolution in Literature from Parnell to the Death of Yeats 1891-1939* (Dublin, 1977).
Tom Cox, *Damned Englishman: a Study of Erskine Childers 1870-1922* (New York, 1975).
Elizabeth Coxhead, *Lady Gregory: a Literary Portrait* (London, 1961).
Elizabeth Coxhead, *Daughters of Erin* (London, 1965).
J.M. Curran, *The Birth of the Irish Free State 1921-23* (Alabama, 1980).
Sydney Czira ('John Brennan'), *The Years Flew By* (Dublin, 1974).
M.E. Daly, *Industrial Development and Irish National Identity 1922-1939* (Dublin, 1992).
M.E. Daly, 'Local government and the first Dáil', in Brian Farrell (ed.), *The Creation of Dáil Éireann* (Dublin, 1994).
George Dangerfield, *The Damnable Question: a Study in Anglo-Irish Relations* (London, 1976).
Richard Davis, *Arthur Griffith and Non-Violent Sinn Féin* (Dublin, 1974).
Richard Davis, *Arthur Griffith* (Dundalk, 1976).
Terence de Vere White, *Kevin O'Higgins* (London, 1948).
Terence Ryle Dwyer, *Michael Collins and the Treaty: His Differences with de Valera* (Dublin/Cork, 1981).
Terence Ryle Dwyer, *De Valera's Darkest Hour: in Search of National Independence 1919-32* (Dublin/Cork, 1982).
Owen Dudley Edwards, *The Mind of an Activist: James Connolly* (Dublin, 1971).

Select Bibliography

Owen Dudley Edwards, Gwynfor Evans, Ioan Rhys and Hugh MacDiarmaid, *Celtic Nationalism* (London, 1968).

Ruth Dudley Edwards, *Patrick Pearse: the Triumph of Failure* (London, 1977).

Richard Ellmann, *James Joyce* (New York, 1959).

Richard Ellmann, *The Consciousness of Joyce* (London, 1977).

Peter Beresford Ellis, *A History of the Irish Working Class* (London, 1972).

Richard Fallis, *The Irish Renaissance: an Introduction to Anglo-Irish Literature* (London, 1978).

Ronan Fanning, *Independent Ireland* (Dublin,1983).

Brian Farrell, *The Founding of Dáil Éireann: Parliament and Nation-Building* (Dublin, 1971).

Brian Farrell (ed.), *The Creation of Dáil Éireann* (Dublin,1994).

Darrell Figgis, *Recollections of the Irish War 1914-21* (London, 1927).

Desmond FitgGerald, *The Memoirs of Desmond FitzGerald 1913-16* (London, 1968).

J.W. Flannery, *W.B. Yeats and the Idea of a Theatre* (New Haven and London, 1976).

Margery Forester, *Michael Collins: the Lost Leader* (London, 1971).

R.F. Foster, 'Anglo-Irish literature, Gaelic nationalism and Irish politics in the 1890s', in J.M.W. Bean (ed.), *The Political Culture of Modern Britain* (London, 1987).

R.F. Foster, *Modern Ireland 1600-1972* (London, 1988).

R.M. Fox, *Green Banners: the Story of the Irish Struggle* (London, 1938).

R.M. Fox, *James Connolly: the Forerunner* (Tralee, 1946).

R.M. Fox, *Jim Larkin: the Rise of the Underman* (London, 1957).

Tom Garvin, *The Evolution of Irish Nationalist Politics* (Dublin, 1981).

J.A. Gaughan, *Austin Stack: Portrait of a Separatist* (Dublin, 1977).

J.A. Gaughan, *Thomas Johnson 1872-1963* (Dublin, 1980).

Virginia Glandon, *Arthur Griffith and the Advanced-Nationalist Press: Ireland 1900-1922* (Kansas, 1985).

Oliver St John Gogarty, *As I Was Going Down Sackville Street* (New York, 1937).

C.D. Greaves, *The Life and Times of James Connolly* (London, 1961).

C.D. Greaves, *Liam Mellows and the Irish Revolution* (London, 1971).

C.D. Greaves, *The Irish Transport and General Workers Union: the Formative Years* (Dublin, 1982).

D.H. Greene and E.M. Stephens, *J.M. Synge 1871-1909* (New York, 1959).

Arthur Grffith (ed.) *The Poems and Ballads of William Rooney* (Dublin, 1901).

Arthur Griffith, *The Resurrection of Hungary* (Dublin, 1904).

Arthur Griffith, *The Sinn Féin Policy* (Dublin, 1905).

Arthur Griffith, *How Ireland is Taxed* (Dublin, 1907).

Arthur Griffith (ed.), *The Irish Year Book/Leabhar na hÉireann* (Dublin, 1908,1909,1910,1911).

Arthur Griffith, *The Home Rule Bill Examined* (Dublin, 1913).

Arthur Griffith (ed.), *Jail Journal*, by John Mitchel (Dublin, 1913).

Arthur Griffith (ed.), *Meagher of the Sword* (Dublin, 1914).

Arthur Griffith (ed.), *The Felon's Track*, by Michael Doheny (Dublin, 1914).
Arthur Griffith (ed.), *Thomas Davis: the Thinker and Teacher* (Dublin, 1914).
Kenneth Griffith and Timothy O'Grady, *Curious Journey: an Oral History of Ireland's Unfinished Revolution* (London, 1982).
Stephen Gwynn, *A Student's History of Ireland* (Dublin, 1925).
W.K. Hancock, *A Survey of British Commonwealth Affairs: i, Problems of Nationality 1918-36* (London, 1937).
R.M. Henry, *The Evolution of Sinn Féin* (Dublin, 1920).
Bulmer Hobson, *Ireland Yesterday and Tomorrow* (Tralee, 1967).
Edgar Holt, *Protest in Arms: the Irish Troubles 1916-23* (London, 1960).
J.M. Hone, *W.B. Yeats 1865-1939* (London, 1942).
Michael Hopkinson, *Green against Green: the Irish Civil War* (Dublin, 1988).
Louis Hyman, *The Jews of Ireland: from Earliest Times to the Year 1910* (Shannon, 1972).
T.A. Jackson, *Ireland, Her Own* (London, 1946).
Norman Jeffares, *W.B. Yeats: Man and Poet* (London, 1949)
D.S. Johnson, 'Partition and cross-border trade in the 1920s', in Peter Roebuck (ed.), *Plantation to Partition: Essays in Ulster History in honour of J.L. McCracken* (Belfast, 1981).
Thomas Kabdebo, *The Hungarian-Irish 'Parallel' and Arthur Griffith's Use of His Sources* (Maynooth, 1988).
R.M. Kain, *Dublin in the Age of W.B. Yeats and James Joyce* (Norman, 1962).
H.A. Kenny, *Literary Dublin: a History (New York, 1974).*
Richard Kearney, *The Irish Mind: Exploring Intellectual Traditions* (Dublin, 1984).
Robert Kee, *The Bold Fenian Men* and *Ourselves Alone*, volumes II and III of *The Green Flag* (London, 1972; published in 3 volumes in 1976).
James Kilroy, *The 'Playboy' Riots* (Dublin, 1971).
Mary Kotsonouris, 'The courts of Dáil Éireann', in Brian Farrell (ed.), *The Creation of Dáil Éireann* (Dublin, 1994).
Michael Laffan, *The Partition of Ireland 1911-25* (Dublin, 1983).
Emmet Larkin, *James Larkin: Irish Labour Leader 1876-1947* (London, 1965).
Sheila Lawlor, *Britain and Ireland 1914-23* (Dublin, 1983).
Joseph Lee, 'Some aspects of modern Irish historiography', in Ernst Schulin (ed.), *Gedenkschrift Martin Gohring* (Wiesbaden, 1968).
J.J. Lee (ed.), *Irish Historiography 1970-79* (Cork, 1981).
J.J. Lee, *Ireland 1912-85: Politics and Society* (Cambridge, 1989).
J.J. Lee, 'The significance of the first Dáil', in Brian Farrell (ed.), *The Creation of Dáil Éireann* (Dublin, 1994).
Leah Levenson, *With Wooden Sword: a Portrait of Francis Sheehy-Skeffington* (Boston and Dublin, 1983).
Samuel Levenson, *James Connolly* (London, 1973).
R.J. Loftus, *Nationalism in Modern Anglo-Irish Poetry* (Madison and Milwaukee, 1964).

Earl of Longford, 'The Treaty negotiations', in T.D. Williams (ed.), *The Irish Struggle 1916-26* (London, 1966).
Earl of Longford and T.P. O'Neill, *Eamon de Valera* (London, 1970).
Patrick Lynch, 'Ireland since the Treaty', in T.W. Moody and F.X. Martin (eds.), *The Course of Irish History* (Dublin, 1967).
Robert Lynd, *Galway of the Races* (Dublin, 1990).
G.A. Lyons, *Some Recollections of Arthur Griffith and His Times* (Dublin, 1923).
F.S.L. Lyons, *Ireland since the Famine* (London, 1971).
F.S.L. Lyons, *Culture and Anarchy in Ireland 1890-1939* (Oxford, 1978).
J.B. Lyons, *Oliver St John Gogarty: the Man of Many Talents* (Dublin, 1980).
J.B. Lyons, *The Enigma of Tom Kettle* (Dublin, 1983).
Dorothy Macardle, *The Irish Republic* (London, 1937).
Proinsias Mac an Bheatha, *Tart na Córa: Seamus Ó Conghaile, A Shaol agus A Shaothar* (Baile Átha Cliath, dáta ar bith).
Maud Gonne MacBride, *A Servant of the Queen* (London, 1938).
L.J. McCaffrey, *The Irish Question 1800-1922* (Kentucky, 1968).
D.P. McCracken, *The Irish Pro-Boers 1877-1902* (Johannesburg and Cape Town, 1989).
Oliver MacDonagh, *Ireland: the Union and its Aftermath* (London, 1977).
Oliver MacDonagh, *States of Mind: a Study of Anglo-Irish Conflict 1780-1980* (London, 1983).
Edward MacLysaght, *Forth the Banners Go: the Reminiscences of William O'Brien* (Dublin, 1969).
Edward MacLysaght, *Changing Times: Ireland since 1898* (London, 1978).
N.S. Mansergh, *The Irish Question 1840-1921* (London, 1940).
Brian Maye, *Fine Gael 1923-1987* (Dublin, 1993).
Arthur Mitchell, *Labour in Irish Politics 1890-1930* (Dublin, 1974).
Keith Middlemas (ed.), *Tom Jones: Whitehall Diary, iii, Ireland 1918-25* (London, 1971).
Maurice Moynihan (ed.), *Speeches and Statements of Eamon de Valera 1917-73* (Dublin and New York, 1980).
H.F. Mulvey, '20th century Ireland', in T.W. Moody (ed.), *Irish Historiography 1936-70* (Dublin, 1970).
J.A. Murphy, *Ireland in the 20th Century* (Dublin, 1975).
Eoin Neeson, *The Civil War in Ireland 1922-23* (Cork, 1966).
Edward Norman, *A History of Modern Ireland* (London, 1971).
J.V. O'Brien, *William O'Brien and the Course of Irish Politics 1881-1918* (University of California, 1976).
Leon Ó Bróin, *The Chief Secretary: Augustine Birrell in Ireland* (Connecticut, 1970).
Leon Ó Bróin, *Revolutionary Underground: the Story of the Irish Republican Brotherhood 1858-1924* (Dublin, 1976).
Sean O'Casey, *Mirror in My House: the Autobiographies of Sean O'Casey* (New York, 1956).

Frank O'Connor, *The Big Fellow: Michael Collins and the Irish Revolution* (Dublin, 1937).
Ulick O'Connor, *Oliver St John Gogarty* (London, 1964).
Ulick O'Connor, *A Terrible Beauty Is Born* (London, 1975).
Ulick O'Connor, *Celtic Dawn: a Portrait of the Irish Literary Renaissance* (London, 1985).
Florence O'Donoghue, *No Other Law* (Dublin, 1954).
P.S. O'Hegarty, *The Victory of Sinn Féin* (Dublin, 1924).
P.S. O'Hegarty, *A History of Ireland under the Union* (London, 1951).
Seán Ó Lúing, *Art Ó Gríofa* (Baile Átha Cliath, 1953).
Seán Ó Lúing, *I Die in a Good Cause: a Study of Thomas Ashe* (Dublin, 1970).
Ernie O'Malley, *The Singing Flame* (Dublin, 1978).
Marie O'Neill, *From Parnell to De Valera: a Biography of Jenny Wyse Power* (Dublin, 1992).
T.P. Ó Néill agus Padraig Ó Fíannachta, *De Valera* (Baile Átha Cliath, 1968 agus 1970).
Donal O'Sullivan, *The Irish Free State and Its Senate* (London, 1940).
Seamus O'Sullivan, *Essays and Recollections* (Dublin, 1944).
Seamus O'Sullivan, *The Rose and Bottle and Other Essays* (Dublin, 1946).
M.A.G. Ó Tuathaigh, 'Ireland 1800-1921', in Joseph Lee (ed.), *Irish Historiography 1970-79* (Cork, 1981).
Frank Pakenham (Earl of Longford), *Peace by Ordeal* (London, 1935).
Desmond Ryan, *James Connolly: His Life, Work and Writings* (Dublin, 1924).
Desmond Ryan, *Remembering Sion* (London, 1934).
Desmond Ryan, *Unique Dictator: a Study of Eamon de Valera* (Dublin, 1936).
Máire Nic Shiubhlaigh, *The Splendid Years: the Recollections of Maire Nic Shiubhlaigh as told to Edward Kenny* (Dublin, 1955).
M.Q. Sibley (ed.), *The Quiet Battle: Writings on the Theory and Practice of Non-Violent Resistance* (New York, 1963).
Des Smith and Gus Hickey, *A Paler Shade of Green* (London, 1972).
Robin Skelton, *The Writings of J.M. Synge* (London, 1974).
James Stephens, *Arthur Griffith: Journalist and Statesman* (Dublin, n.d.).
Emil Strauss, *Irish Nationalism and British Democracy* (Connecticut, 1951).
Rex Taylor, *Michael Collins* (London, 1958).
W.I. Thompson, *The Imagination of an Insurrection: Dublin, Easter 1916* (New York, 1967).
Michael Tierney, *Eoin MacNeill: Scholar and Man of Action 1867-1945* (Oxford, 1980).
Charles Townshend, *The British Campaign in Ireland 1919-21: the Development of Political and Military Policies* (Oxford, 1975).
Charles Townshend, *Political Violence in Ireland: Government and Resistance since 1848* (Oxford, 1983).
M.G. Valiulis, *Portrait of a Revolutionary: General Richard Mulcahy and the Founding of the Irish Free State* (Cork, 1992).

Select Bibliography

A.J. Ward, *Ireland and Anglo-American Relations 1899-1921* (Toronto, 1969).
Margaret Ward, *Unmanageable Revolutionaries* (London, 1983).
Margaret Ward, *Maud Gonne: Ireland's Joan of Arc* (London, 1991).
Burke Wilkinson, *The Zeal of the Convert: the Life of Erskine Childers* (New York, 1976).
W.B. Yeats, *Dramatis Personae* (London, 1936).
W.B. Yeats, *Explorations* (London, 1962).
Calton Younger, *Ireland's Civil War* (London, 1968).
Calton Younger, *A State of Disunion* (London, 1972).
Calton Younger, *Arthur Griffith* (Dublin, 1981).

Index

Index

Index

Index

Index